PENGUIN POETS

THE PENGUIN BOOK OF LIGHT VERSE

Gavin Ewart was born in 1916. He has worked in advertising and for the British Council, and is now a freelance writer. His books of verse include *Poems and Songs*, *Londoners*, *Pleasures of the Flesh*, *The Deceptive Grin of the Gravel Porters*, *The Gavin Ewart Show*, *Be My Guest!*, *No Fool Like an Old Fool*, *Or Where a Young Penguin Lies Screaming* and *All My Little Ones*. He has edited the *Batsford Book of Verse for Children* and *The Batsford Book of Light Verse for Children*. His latest books are *The Collected Ewart 1933–1980*, *The New Ewart*, *More Little Ones* and *The Ewart Quarto*.

The Penguin Book of Light Verse

Edited with an Introduction by Gavin Ewart

Penguin Books

Penguin Books Ltd, Harmondsworth, Middlesex, England
Viking Penguin Inc., 40 West 23rd Street, New York, New York 10010, U.S.A.
Penguin Books Australia Ltd, Ringwood, Victoria, Australia
Penguin Books Canada Limited, 2801 John Street, Markham, Ontario, Canada L3R 1B4
Penguin Books (N.Z.) Ltd, 182–190 Wairau Road, Auckland 10, New Zealand

First published 1980
Published simultaneously by Allen Lane
Reprinted 1981, 1984, 1986

Title-page illustration by Brian Grimwood

Printed and bound in Great Britain by
Cox & Wyman Ltd, Reading

Set in Monotype Fournier

Contents

Introduction

It's a long time now since a poet was called a laughter-smith and had his audience rolling about in stitches at the mead-bench. Yet this may have been one of the beginnings of light verse. Riddles are as old as Ancient Greece and Egypt but the medieval verse-riddles in Anglo-Saxon (of the eighth century, as in *The Exeter Book*) are genuine poems, extended metaphors that involve the imagination and have the playful quality that the best light verse often has. For these reasons, my anthology begins with them.

Light verse, which has suffered some conflicting definitions, should never deal in strong emotion (love – but not tragic love); or matters of life and death. It should never be solemn or sad. It should not have distressing content (unless this is humorously intended, as in the verse of Harry Graham and modern ballads like 'Frankie and Johnny'). This rules out almost all of the old ballads – as well as Kipling's 'Danny Deever' – which Auden included in his famous *Oxford Book of Light Verse*.

It may be humorous, or partly humorous. It can be bitter (Swift) or at least bitter-sweet ('Robin and Makyne'). It can be purely lyrical. Songs are obvious candidates, and the difficulty is to select from the hundreds available. It may be nonsense (and the playful intention is the criterion here – the verse of McGonagall, though it seems funny to us, was not intended to be). It may also, of course, be obscene. The Exeter riddles given here were put into this category by generations of scholars; and I have included one outspoken Rugger Song as an exemplar, the unblushing representative of so many others. The Earl of Rochester, too, was a writer who didn't mince his words. On the principle that the prudery of the few should not be allowed to limit the enjoyment of the many, I have included verse by him which would have frightened puritans of earlier generations. If anybody suggests that such poems are unsuitable for children (somebody usually does) let him or her direct their kids' attention to *The Batsford Book of Light Verse for Children* (also edited by me), where decorum is strictly preserved.

Briefly, I agree with Auden that ballads are admissible – Mr Kingsley Amis in his *New Oxford Book of Light Verse* takes the opposite view – but not on the grounds that they are dialect poetry or the 'verse of the people'. I include Pope, Dryden, Prior, Burns (all untouched by Amis, included by Auden). I have not funked Chaucer or Dunbar (easier for Scots than for others) or the old Scots verse where 'quhilk' does duty for 'which', and 'quhair' for 'where'. I have included poems by Donne, though the Elegie which begins 'Natures lay Ideot, I taught thee to love', with its sophisticated scorn, is perhaps a borderline case; on the other hand, it is certainly not tragic. The famous cricket poem by Francis Thompson, an exercise in nostalgia, is likewise not entirely 'light'; but I have included it on the grounds that cricket, after all, is only a game. I know that a good many cricketers won't agree with me.

Limericks, like Rugger Songs, pose special problems. There should be some, I felt, but not too many. If you have dozens of them together, they become counter-productive.

I have tried to help as much as possible with footnotes – though nobody ever wants to swamp the text with them. I have also marked accented syllables and the places where the 'e' at the end of the word is sounded, in the early poetry. Read the Chaucer aloud, remembering that each line is a perfect line and scans exactly. Any 'general reader' who misses out the Middle English poetry is missing a lot.

Acknowledgements

We are indebted to the copyright holders for permission to reprint certain poems:

KINGSLEY AMIS: from *Collected Poems 1944–79* (Hutchinson & Co. Ltd). W. H. AUDEN: reprinted by permission of Faber & Faber Ltd and Random House Inc. from *Collected Shorter Poems 1927–57*. GEORGE BARKER: reprinted by permission of Faber & Faber Ltd from *Villa Stellar*. PATRICK BARRINGTON: from *Punch* magazine. JAMES BAXTER: 'Obsequy For Dylan Thomas' from *The Bone Chanter*, 'From *Cressida:* In the Lecture Room, Bar Room Conversation', 'The Private Conference of Harry Fat', 'Harry Fat and Uncle Sam', 'Spring Song of a Civil Servant' from *The Holy Life and Death of Concrete Grady* (Oxford University Press, Wellington). SIR MAX BEERBOHM: 'Police Station Ditty' from *A Christmas Garland*, 'A Luncheon' from *Max in Verse: Rhymes and Parodies*, ed. J. Riewald (Rupert Hart-Davis, Ltd, Heinemann Ltd and the Stephen Green Press). MARTIN BELL: from *Collected Poems 1937–1966* (Macmillan & Co. Ltd). HILAIRE BELLOC: from *Cautionary Verses* (Gerald Duckworth & Co. Ltd and Alfred A. Knopf Inc.). E. C. BENTLEY: from *Clerihews Complete* (T. Werner Laurie Ltd). SIR JOHN BETJEMAN: from *Continual Dew* (John Murray (Publishers) Ltd). EARLE BIRNEY: from *The Collected Poems of Earle Birney* and *Ghosts in the Wheels* (McClelland & Stewart Ltd). MORRIS BISHOP: from *A Bowl of Bishop* (The Dial Press, New York). ANTHONY BRODE: from *Punch* magazine. ALAN BROWNJOHN: from *A Song of Good Life* (Secker & Warburg Ltd). ROY CAMPBELL: from *Adamastor* (Curtis Brown, on behalf of the estate of Roy Campbell). CHARLES CAUSLEY: from *Union Street* (David Higham Associates and Faber & Faber Ltd). G. K. CHESTERTON: from *Collected Poems of G. K. Chesterton* (A. P. Watt Ltd on behalf of the estate of the late G. K. Chesterton and Methuen & Co. Ltd). GREGORY CORSO: from *Selected Poems* (Laurence Pollinger Ltd). SIR NOEL COWARD: from *The Lyrics of Noel Coward* (Curtis Brown Ltd on behalf of the estate of Sir Noel Coward and Heinemann Ltd and Doubleday & Co. Inc.). E. E. CUMMINGS: from *Complete Poems 1913–1962* (Granada Publishers Ltd and Harcourt Brace Jovanovich Inc.). KEVIN CROSSLEY-HOLLAND: from *The Exeter Book Riddles* (published by

The Folio Society for its members). SIMON CURTIS: from *On the Abthorpe Road and Other Poems* (Davis-Poynter Ltd). ANTHONY C. DEANE: from *A Parody Anthology* (Dover Publications Inc.). WALTER DE LA MARE: from *A Choice of Walter de la Mare's Verse* (by permission of the Literary Trustees of Walter de le Mare and The Society of Authors). LAWRENCE DURRELL: reprinted by permission of Curtis Brown Ltd and Faber & Faber Ltd from *Selected Poems 1935–1963*. T. S. ELIOT: reprinted by permission of Faber & Faber Ltd and Harcourt Brace Jovanovich Inc. – 'Two Five Finger Exercises' from *Collected Poems 1909–1935* and 'Macavity the Mystery Cat', 'Cat Morgan Introduces Himself' from *Pold Possum's Book of Practical Cats*. SIR WILLIAM EMPSON: from *Collected Poems* (Chatto & Windus Ltd and Harcourt Brace Jovanovich Inc.). D. J. ENRIGHT: from *Daughters of the Earth* (Chatto & Windus Ltd). GAVIN EWART: 'Poets' from *No Fool Like an Old Fool* (Gollancz Ltd), 'Office Friendships', 'The World-Bird' from *Pleasures of the Flesh* (Alan Ross), 'Fiction: The House Party' from *The Gavin Ewart Show* (Trigram Press). JAMES FENTON: 'South Parks Road', 'Lollipops of the Pomeranian Baroque' from *Terminal Moraine* (Secker & Warburg Ltd), 'From Wild Life Studies' from the *New Review*. ROY FISHER: from *The Thing About Joe Sullivan* (Carcanet New Press Ltd). DUNCAN FORBES: from *Encounter* magazine. ROBERT FROST: from *The Poetry of Robert Frost*, ed. Edward Connery Lathen (reprinted by permission of the Estate of Robert Frost, Jonathan Cape Ltd and Holt, Rinehart and Winston). JOHN FULLER: Two songs from *Fox Trot* (Chatto & Windus Ltd), others by permission of the author. ROY FULLER: from *Collected Poems* (André Deutsch Ltd). DAVID GASCOYNE: from *A Vagrant* (John Lehmann Ltd). EDWARD GOREY: from *The Listing Attic* (Abelard Schuman). HARRY GRAHAM: from *Ruthless Rhymes* and *More Ruthless Rhymes* (Edward Arnold Ltd). ROBERT GRAVES: from *The Collected Poems of Robert Graves* (reprinted by permission of A. P. Watt Ltd and Robert Graves). ROBERT GREACEN: prize winner in an *Irish Times* Competition, reprinted by kind permission of the author. ANTHONY HECHT: from *The Hard Hours* (reprinted by kind permission of the author, Oxford University Press and Atheneum Publishers Inc.). ADRIAN HENRI: Reprinted by permission of the author and Deborah Rogers Ltd. OLIVER HERFORD: from *Excuse It, Please* (Jo. B. Lippincott & Co Ltd). A. E. HOUSMAN: from *Collected Poems* (Jonathan Cape Ltd: reprinted by permission of the Society of Authors as the literary representatives of the Estate of A. E. Housman). JAMES JOYCE: from *Finnegans Wake* (reprinted by permission of the Society of Authors and Faber & Faber Ltd). SIR OSBERT LANCASTER: from *Facades and Faces* (John Murray Ltd). PHILIP LARKIN: reprinted by permission of Faber & Faber Ltd and Farrar, Straus and Giroux Inc. – 'Naturally the Foundation Will Bear Your Expense' and 'Self's The Man' from *The Whitsun Weddings*, 'Vers de Société' from *High Windows*. D. H. LAWRENCE: from *The Complete Poems* (reprinted by permission of Laurance Pollinger Ltd on behalf of the Estate of the late Mrs Frieda Lawrence, and The Viking Press). LAURENCE LERNER: from *A.R.T.H.U.R.* (Harvester Press Ltd and the University of Massachusetts Press). NEWMAN LEVY: from *Opera Guyed* (Alfred A. Knopf Inc.). GEORGE MACBETH: from *The Orlando Poems* (Macmillan & Co. Ltd). PHYLLIS MCGINLEY: from the *New Yorker*. ROGER MCGOUGH: Reprinted by permission of the author and Hope Leresche & Steele. LOUIS MACNIECE: from *The Collected Poems of Louis MacNeice* (Faber & Faber Ltd and Oxford University Press Inc.). GERDA MEYER: Reprinted by permission of the author. CHRISTOPHER MIDDLETON: from *Pataxanadu* (Carcanet New Press Ltd). ADRIAN MITCHELL: from *Ride the Nightmare* (Jonathan Cape Ltd). EGBERT MOORE: ('Lord Beginner'): 'Victory Calypso, Lord's' printed by permission of the author. EDWIN MORGAN: from *Glasgow to Saturn* (Carcanet Press Ltd). VLADIMIR NABOKOV: from *Poems and Problems* (Weidenfeld & Nicolson and McGraw Hill Inc.). OGDEN NASH: from *Collected Verse from 1929 on* (A. P. Watt Ltd on behalf of the estate of the late Ogden Nash). TED PAUKER: first printed in *The Times Educational Supplement* and reprinted by kind permission of the author. MERVYN PEAKE: from *Titus Groan* (Methuen & Co. Ltd). WILLIAM PLOMER: from *Collected Poems* (Jonathan Cape Ltd). COLE PORTER: Reprinted with permission of Chappell Music Ltd and Warner Bros. Music Inc. PETER PORTER: 'The World of Simon Raven' and 'From *Nine Points of the Law*' from *Poems Ancient and Modern* (Scorpion Press). EZRA POUND: reprinted by permission of Faber & Faber Ltd, and New Directions Publishing Corp: from *The Selected Poems of Ezra Pound*. SIR ARTHUR QUILLER COUCH: from *Green Bays* (Oxford University Press Ltd). PETER READING: 'Correspondence', 'Ballad' from *The Prison Cell & Barrel Mystery* and 'From Travelogue (Camping Provençal)' from *Nothing for Anyone* (Secker & Warburg Ltd). HENRY REED: from *A Map of Verona* (Jonathan Cape Ltd). ALAN ROSS: from *A Cricketer's Companion* (Eyre & Spottiswoode Ltd). SIEGFRIED SASSOON: Reprinted by permission of G. T. Sassoon and The Viking Press Inc.

SIR OWEN SEAMAN: from *Owen Seaman. A Selection* (Constable (Publishers) Ltd). STANLEY SHARPLESS: 'In Praise of Cocoa, Cupid's Nightcap' reprinted by permission of the *New Statesman*; all others by permission of the author. L. A. G. STRONG: from *The Body's Imperfection* (Methuen Ltd and Associated Book Publishers Ltd). JULIAN SYMONS: Reprinted by kind permission of the author. E. J. THRIBB: from *So, Farewell Then ... and Other Poems* (Elm Tree Books Ltd.) ANTHONY THWAITE: from *A Portion for Foxes* (Oxford University Press Ltd). JOHN UPDIKE: from *Telephone Poles* (André Deutsch Ltd). ROGER WODDIS: Reprinted by permission of the author and the New Statesman Ltd; KIT WRIGHT: from *The Bear Looked Over the Mountain* (Salamander Imprint); D. B. WYNDHAM LEWIS: Reprinted by permission of A. D. Peters & Co.

Every effort has been made to trace the copyright holders. The publishers would be interested to hear from any copyright holders not here acknowledged.

ANONYMOUS

Three Riddles from *The Exeter Book*

No. 25

I'm a strange creature, for I satisfy women,
a service to the neighbours! No one suffers
at my hands except for my slayer.
I grow very tall, erect in a bed,
I'm hairy underneath. From time to time
a beautiful girl, the brave daughter
of some churl dares to hold me,
grips my russet skin, robs me of my head
and puts me in the pantry. At once that girl
with plaited hair who has confined me
remembers our meeting. Her eye moistens.

Answer: Onion (*or Penis*)

No. 44

A strange thing hangs by man's hip,
hidden by a garment. It has a hole
in its head. It is stiff and strong
and its firm bearing reaps a reward.
When the retainer hitches his clothing
high above his knee, he wants the head
of that hanging thing to find the old hole
that it, outstretched, has often filled before.

Answer: Key (*or Penis*)

No. 54

A young man made for the corner
where he knew she was standing; this strapping churl
had walked some way – with his own hands
he whipped up her dress, and under her girdle

(as she stood there) thrust something stiff,
worked his will; they both shook.
This fellow quickened: one moment he was forceful,
a first-rate servant, so strenuous
that the next he was knocked up, quite
blown by his exertion. Beneath the girdle
a thing began to grow that upstanding men
often think of, tenderly, and acquire.

Answer: Churning (or Lovemaking)

versions by *Kevin Crossley-Hollan*

ANONYMOUS

Cuckoo Song

Summer is y-comen in,
   Loudë sing, cuckoo!
Groweth seed and bloweth meed
   And spring'th the woodë now –
            Sing cuckoo!

Ewë bleateth after lamb,
   Low'th after calfë cow;
Bullock starteth, buckë farteth.
   Merry sing, cuckoo!

   Cuckoo, Cuckoo!
Well sing'st thou, cuckoo:
   Ne swike[1] thou never now!

Sing cuckoo, now! Sing, cuckoo!
Sing cuckoo! Sing, cuckoo, now!

[1] cease

ANONYMOUS

Alison

Bytuenë Mershë ant Averil
    When spray biginneth to spring,
The lutel foul hath hirë wyl
    On hyrë lud[1] to synge:
Ich libbë[2] in love-longïnge
For semlokest[3] of allë thynge,
He[4] may me blissë bringe,
    Icham in hire bandoun[5].
An hendy[6] hap ichabbe y-hent[7],
Ichot[8] from hevene it is me sent,
From allë wymmen my love is lent
    Ant lyht[9] on Alisoun.

On heu hire[10] her is fayr ynoh,
    Hire browë broune, hire eyë blake;
With lossum[11] chere he on me loh;[12]
    With middel smal ant wel y-make;
Bote he[13] wollë to hire take
For to buen[14] hire owen make,[15]
Long to lyven ichulle forsake
    Ant feyë[16] fallen adoun.
An hendy hap, etc.

Nihtës[17] when I wende[18] and wake,
    For-thi[19] myn wongës waxeth won;[20]

[1]in her language [2]I live [3]seemliest [4]she [5]thraldom
[6]gracious [7]seized, enjoyed [8]I wot [9]alighted [10]her hair
[11]lovesome [12]laughed [13]unless she [14]be [15]mate
[16]like to die [17]at night [18]turn [19]on that account
[20]cheeks grow wan

Levedi,[21] al for thinë sake
  Longinge is y-lent me on.[22]
In world his non so wyter mon[23]
That al hire bountë tellë con;
Hire swyre[24] is whittorẹ than the swon,
  Ant feyrest may[25] in toune.
An hendy hap, etc.

Icham for wowyng al for-wake,[26]
  Wery so watèr in wore;[27]
Lest eny revë[28] me my make
  Ichabbe y-yernëd yore.[29]
Betere is tholien[30] whylë sore
Then mournen evermore.
  Geynest under gore,[31]
  Herknë to my roun[32] –
An hendy hap, etc.

GEOFFREY CHAUCER

The Milleres Tale

Whylom ther was dwellinge at Oxenford
A richë gnof,[1] that gestës heeld to bord,
And of his craft he was a Carpentèr.
With him ther was dwellinge a povre scolèr,
Had lernëd art, but al his fantasỳe
Was turnëd for to lerne astrologỳe,
And coude a certeyn of conclusioùns[2]
To demen by interrogacioùns,

[21] lady [22] arrived to me [23] so wise a man [24] neck [25] maid
[26] worn out with vigils [27] as water in a weir [28] rob
[29] long been distressed [30] to endure
[31] comeliest under women's apparel [32] tale, lay
[1] churl [2] knew a certain number of operations

If that men axëd him in certein houres,
Whan that men sholde have droghte or ellës shoures,
Or if men axëd him what sholde bifalle
Of every thing, I may nat rekene hem alle.
This clerk was clepëd hendë[3] Nicholàs;
Of dernë[4] love he coude[5] and of solàs;[6]
And ther-to he was sleigh and ful privèe,
And lyk a mayden mekë for to see.
A chambre hadde he in that hostelrỳe
Allone, with-outen any companỳe,
Ful fetisly[7] y-dight with herbës swote;[8]
And he him-self as swete as is the rote[9]
Of licorys, or any cetëwale.[10]
His Almageste[11] and bokës grete and smale,
His astrelabie,[12] longinge for his art,[13]
His augrim-stonës[14] layen faire a-part
On shelvës couchëd at his beddës heed:
His presse y-covered with a falding reed.[15]
And al above ther lay a gay sautrỳe,[16]
On which he made, a nightës, melodỳe
So swetëly, that al the chambre rong;
And *Angelus ad virginem* he song;
And after that hė song the kingës note;
Ful often blessëd was his mery throte.
And thus this swetë clerk his tymë spente
After his freendës finding[17] and his rente.[18]
This Carpenter had wedded newe a wyf
Which that he lovëde morë than his lyf;
Of eightetene yeer she was of age.
Jalous he was, and heeld hir narwe in cage,

[3] clever, courteous [4] secret [5] knew, had experience of
[6] pleasure [7] pleasantly [8] sweet [9] root
[10] a plant resembling ginger [11] treatise by Ptolemy [12] astrolabe
[13] belonging to [14] counters [15] red cloth [16] psaltery
[17] so far as his friends provided for him [18] income

For she was wilde and yong, and he was old,
And demed him-self ben lyk a cokëwold.[19]
He knew nat Catoun, for his wit was rude,
That bad[20] man sholde wedde his similitude.
Men sholdë wedden after hir estaat,
For youthe and elde is often at debaat.
But sith that he was fallen in the snare,
He moste endure, as other folk, his care.
  Fair was this yongë wyf, and ther-with-al
As any wesele hir body gent and smal.
A ceynt[21] she werede barrëd al of silk,
A barmclooth[22] eek as whyt as mornë milk
Up-on hir lendës,[23] ful of many a gore.
Whyt was hir smok and brouded al bifore
And eek bihinde, on hir coler aboute,
Of col-blak silk, with-inne and eek with-oute.
The tapës of hir whytë voluper[24]
Were of the same suyte[25] of hir coler;
Hir filet[26] brood[27] of silk, and set ful hyë:
And sikerly she hadde a likerous[28] yë.
Ful smale y-pullëd were hir browës two,
And tho were bent, and blake as any sloo.
She was ful more blisful on to see
Than is the newë pere-jonettë tree;[29]
And softer than the wolle is of a wether.
And by hir girdel heeng a purs of lether
Tasseld with silk, and perlëd with latoun.[30]
In al this world, to seken up and doun,
There nis no man so wys, that coudë thenche[31]
So gay a popelote,[32] or swich a wenche.
Ful brighter was the shyning of hir hewe

[19] cuckold [20] said [21] girdle [22] apron [23] loins [24] cap [25] kind
[26] headband [27] broad [28] wanton [29] pear tree in spring
[30] studded with brass [31] imagine [32] darling

Than in the tour[33] the noble y-forgëd newe.
But of hir song, it was as loude and yerne[34]
As any swalwe sittinge on a berne.[35]
Ther-to she coudë skippe and makë game,
As any kide or calf folwinge his dame.
Hir mouth was swete as bragot[36] or the meeth,[37]
Or hord of apples leyd in hey or heeth.[38]
Winsinge she was, as is a joly colt,
Long as a mast, and upright as a bolt.[39]
A brooch she baar up-on hir lowe colèr,
As brood as is the bos of a boclèr.
Hir shoes were laced on hir leggës hye;
She was a prymerole,[40] a piggës-nye[41]
For any lord to leggen in his bedde,
Or yet for any good yèman to wedde.
  Now sire, and eft sire, so bifel the cas,
That on a day this hendë Nicholàs
Fil with this yongë wyf to rage[42] and pleye,
Whyl that hir housbond was at Oseneye,
As clerkes ben ful subtile and ful queynte;[43]
And prively he caughte hir by the queynte,[44]
And seyde, 'y-wis, but if ich have my wille,
For dernë love of thee, lemman, I spille.'[45]
And heeld hir hardë by the haunchë-bones,
And seydë, 'lemman, love me al at-ones,
Or I wol dyën, alsò god me save!'
And she sprong as a colt doth in the trave,[46]
And with hir heed she wryëd faste awey,
And seyde, 'I wol nat kisse thee, by my fey,
Why, lat be,' quod she, 'lat be, Nicholàs,

[33] the royal mint in the Tower [34] eager [35] barn
[36] a drink of honey and ale [37] mead [38] heather
[39] bolt of a cross-bow [40] primrose [41] name of a flower used as term of endearment [42] sport [43] artful [44] pudendum [45] perish
[46] frame for unruly horses

Or I wol crye out "harrow" and "allàs".
Do wey your handës for your curteisye!'
  This Nicholas gan mercy for to crye,
And spak so faire, and profrëd hir so faste,
That she hir love him grauntëd attë laste,
And swoor hir ooth, by seint Thomàs of Kent,
That she wol been at his comandëment,
Whan that she may hir leyser wel espye.
'Myn housbond is so ful of jalousye,
That but ye waytë wel and been privee,
I woot right wel I nam but deed,' quod she.
'Ye mostë been ful derne, as in this cas.'
  'Nay ther-of care thee noght,' quod Nicholàs,
'A clerk had litherly biset his whyle,[47]
But-if he coude a carpenter bigyle.'
And thus they been acorded and y-sworn
To wayte a tyme, as I have told biforn.
Whan Nicholas had doon thus everydeel,
And thakkëd[48] hir aboute the lendës weel,
He kist hir swete, and taketh his sautrye,
And pleyeth faste, and maketh melodye.
  Than fil it thus, that to the parish-chirche,
Cristes ownë werkës for to wirche,
This godë wyf wente on an haliday;
Hir forheed shoon as bright as any day,
So was it wasshen whan she leet[49] hir werk.
  Now was ther of that churche a parish-clerk,
The which that was y-clepëd Absolon.
Crul[50] was his heer, and as the gold it shoon,
And strouted[51] as a fannë large and brode;
Ful streight and even lay his joly shode.[52]
His rode[53] was reed, his eyen greye as goos;

[47] employed his time ill [48] stroked [49] left [50] curled
[51] spread out [52] parting [53] complexion

With Powlës window corven on his shoos,[54]
In hoses rede he wentë fetisly.
Y-clad he was ful smal and proprely,
Al in a kirtel of a light wachet;[55]
Ful faire and thikkë been the poyntës set.
And ther-up-on he hadde a gay surplys
As whyt as is the blosme up-on the rys.[56]
A mery child[57] he was, so god me save,
Wel coude he laten blood and clippe and shave,
And make a chartre of lond or acquitaunce.
In twenty manere coude he trippe and daunce
After the scole of Oxenfordë tho,
And with his leggës casten to and fro,
And pleyen songes on a small rubible;[58]
Ther-to he song som-tyme a loud quinible;[59]
And as wel coude he pleye on his giterne.
In al the toun nas brewhous ne taverne
That he ne visited with his solàs,
Ther any gaylard tappesterë[60] was.
But sooth to seyn, he was somdel squaymous[61]
Of farting, and of spechë daungerous.[62]
This Absolon, that jolif was and gay,
Gooth with a sencer on the haliday,
Sensinge the wyvës of the parish faste;
And many a lovely look on hem he caste,
And namely[63] on this carpenterës wyf.
To loke on hir him thoughte a mery lyf,
She was so propre and swete and likerous.
I dar wel seyn, if she had been a mous,
And he a cat, he wolde hir hente[64] anon.

[54] with the window of St Paul's carved on his shoes
[55] light blue cloth [56] branch [57] young man [58] fiddle [59] falsetto
[60] merry barmaid [61] squeamish [62] sparing
[63] especially [64] have caught

This parish-clerk, this joly Absolon,
Hath in his hertë swich a love-longinge,
That of no wyf ne took he noon offringe;
For curteisye, he seyde, he woldë noon.
The mone, whan it was night, ful brightë shoon,
And Absolon his giterne hath y-take,
For paramours he thoghtë for to wake.
And forth he gooth, jolif and amorous,
Til he cam to the carpenterës hous
A litel after cokkës hadde y-crowe;
And dressed him up by a shot-windòwe[65]
That was up-on the carpenterës wal.
He singeth in his vois gentil and smal,
'Now, dere lady, if thy willë be,
I preye yow that ye wol rewe on me,'
Ful wel acordaunt to his giternìnge.
This carpenter awook, and herde him singe,
And spak un-to his wyf, and seyde anon,
'What! Alison! herestow nat Absolon
That chaunteth thus under our boures wal?'
And she answerde hir housbond ther-with-al,
'Yis, god wot, John, I here it every-del.'
This passeth forth; what wol ye bet than wel?
Fro day to day this joly Absolon
So woweth hir, that him is wo bigon.
He waketh al the night and al the day;
He kempte hise lokkës brode, and made him gay;
He woweth hir by menës[66] and brocage,[67]
And swoor he woldë been hir ownë page;
He singeth, brokkinge[68] as a nightingale;
He sente hir piment,[69] meeth, and spycëd ale,
And wafres, pyping hote out of the glede;[70]

[65] casement [66] go-betweens [67] traffic in match-making
[68] quavering [69] sweetened wine [70] glowing coal

And for she was of toune, he profred mede.
For som folk wol ben wonnen for richesse,
And som for strokes, and som for gentillesse.
Somtyme, to shewe his lightnesse and maistrỳe,[71]
He pleyeth Herodes on a scaffold hye.
But what availleth him as in this cas?
She loveth so this hendë Nicholàs,
That Absolon may blowe the bukkës horn;
He ne hadde for his labour but a scorn:
And thus she maketh Absolon hir ape,
And al his ernest turneth til a jape.
Ful sooth is this proverbe, it is no lye,
Men seyn right thus, 'alwey the nyë slye[72]
Maketh the ferrë levë[73] to be looth.'
For though that Absolon be wood or wrooth,
By-causë that he fer was from hir sighte,
This nyë Nicholas stood in his lighte.
Now bere thee wel, thou hendë Nicholàs!
For Absolon may waille and singe 'allas.'
And so bifel it on a Saterday,
This carpenter was goon til Osenay;
And hendë Nicholas and Alisoun
Acorded been to this conclusioun,
That Nicholas shal shapen him a wyle
This sely[74] jalous housbond to bigyle;
And if so be the gamë wente aright,
She sholde slepen in his arm al night,
For this was his desyr and hir also.
And right anon, with-outen wordës mo,
This Nicholas no lenger woldë tarie,
But doth ful softe un-to his chambre carie
Bothe mete and drinkë for a day or tweye,
And to hir housbonde bad hir for to seye,

[71] skill [72] the cunning one near at hand [73] distant love [74] simple

If that he axëd after Nicholàs,
She sholdë seye she nistë where he was,
Of al that day she saugh him nat with yë;
She trowëd that he was in maladỳe,
For, for no cry, hir maydë coude him calle;
He nolde answere, for no-thing that mighte falle.
  This passeth forth al thilkë Saterday,
That Nicholas stille in his chambre lay,
And eet and sleep, or didë what him leste,
Til Sonday, that the sonnë gooth to reste.
  This sely carpenter hath greet merveyle
Of Nicholas, or what thing mighte him eyle,
And seyde, 'I am adrad, by seint Tomàs,
It stondeth nat aright with Nicholàs.
God shildë[75] that he deydë[76] sodeynly!
This world is now ful tikel,[77] sikerly;
I saugh to-day a cors y-born to chirche
That now, on Monday last, I saugh him wirche.
  'Go up,' quod he un-to his knave anoon,
'Clepe at his dore, or knokkë with a stoon,
Loke how it is, and tel me boldëly.'
  This knave gooth him up ful sturdily,
And at the chambre-dore, whyl that he stood,
He cryde and knokkëd as that he were wood:[78] –
'What! how! what do ye, maister Nicholay?
How may ye slepen al the longë day?'
  But al for noght, he herdë nat a word;
An hole he fond, ful lowe up-on a bord,
Ther as the cat was wont in for to crepe;
And at that hole he lookëd in ful depe,
And at the laste he hadde of him a sighte.
This Nicholas sat gaping ever up-righte,
As he had kykëd[79] on the newë mone.

[75] forbid [76] should die [77] unstable [78] mad [79] gazed

Adoun he gooth, and tolde his maister sone
In what array he saugh this ilkë man.
   This carpenter to blessen[80] him bigan,
And seydë, 'help us, seintë Fridëswyde!'
A man woot litel what him shal bityde.
This man is fallë, with his astromỳe,
In som woodnesse or in some agonỳe;
I thoghte ay wel how that it sholdë be!
Men sholde nat knowe of goddës privetee.
Ye, blessëd be alwey a lewëd[81] man,
That noght but only his bilevë can![82]
So ferde another clerk with astromỳe;
He walkëd in the feeldës for to prye
Up-on the sterrës, what ther sholde bifalle,
Til he was in a marlë-pit y-falle;
He saugh nat that. But yet, by seint Thomàs,
Me reweth sore of hendë Nicholàs.
He shal be rated[83] of his studying,
If that I may, by Jesus, hevene king!
   'Get me a staf, that I may underspore,[84]
Whyl that thou, Robin, hevest up the dore.
He shal out of his studying, as I gesse' –
And to the chambre-dore he gan him dresse.
His knave was a strong carl for the nonës,[85]
And by the haspe[86] he haf it up atones;
In-to the floor the dorë fil anon.
This Nicholas sat ay as stille as stoon,
And ever gaped upwàrd in-to the eir.
This carpenter wende he were in despeir,
And hente him by the sholdres mightily,
And shook him harde, and cryde spitously,
'What! Nicholay! what, how! what! loke adoun!

[80] cross himself   [81] ordinary   [82] knows his creed   [83] scolded
[84] thrust under   [85] as it happened   [86] hinge or fastening

Awake, and thenk on Cristës passioùn;
I crouchë[87] thee from elvës and fro wightes!'
Ther-with the night-spel[88] seyde he anon-rightes[89]
On fourë halvës of the hous aboute,
And on the threshfold of the dore with-oute:—
'Jesu Crist, and sëynt Benedight,
Blessë this hous from every wikkëd wight,
For nightës verye,[90] the white *pater-noster* —
Where wentestow, seynt Petres soster?'[91]
And attë lastë this hende Nicholàs
Gan for to sykë[92] sore, and seyde, 'allas!
Shal al the world be lost eftsonës now?'
This carpenter answerde, 'what seystow?
What! thenk on god, as we don, men that swinke.'[93]
This Nicholas answerde, 'fecche me drinke;
And after wol I speke in privetee
Of certeyn thing that toucheth me and thee;
I wol telle it non other man, certeyn.'
This carpenter goth doun, and comth ageyn,
And broghte of mighty ale a largë quart;
And whan that ech of hem had dronke his part,
This Nicholas his dorë fastë shette,
And doun the carpenter by him he sette.
He seydë, 'John, myn hostë lief and dere,
Thou shalt up-on thy trouthë swere me here,
That to no wight thou shalt this conseil wreye;[94]
For it is Cristës conseil that I seye,
And if thou telle it man, thou are forlore;
For this vengaunce thou shalt han ther-fore,
That if thou wreyë me, thou shalt be wood!'
'Nay, Crist forbede it, for his holy blood!'
Quod tho this sely man, 'I nam no labbe,[95]

[87] mark with the cross [88] night-charm [89] straightaway
[90] evil spirits [91] sister [92] sigh [93] labour [94] betray [95] blabber

Ne, though I seye, I nam nat lief to gabbe.
Sey what thou wolt, I shal it never telle
To child ne wyf, by him that harwed[96] helle!'
  'Now John,' quod Nicholas, 'I wol nat lye;
I have y-founde in myn astrologŷe,
As I have lokëd in the monë bright,
That now, a Monday next, at quarter-night,
Shal falle a reyn and that so wilde and wood,
That half so greet was never Noës flood.
This world,' he seyde, 'in lasse than in an hour
Shal al be dreynt,[97] so hidous is the shour;
Thus shal mankyndë drenche and lese hir lyf.'
  This carpenter answerde, 'allas, my wyf!
And shal she drenche? allas! myn Alisoun!'
For sorwe of this he fil almost adoun,
And seyde, 'is ther no remedie in this cas?'
  'Why, yis, for gode,' quod hendë Nicholàs,
'If thou wolt werken after lore and reed;
Thou mayst nat werken after thyn owene heed.
For thus seith Salomon, that was ful trewe,
"Werk al by conseil, and thou shalt nat rewe."
And if thou werken wolt by good conseil,
I undertake, with-outen mast and seyl,
Yet shal I saven hir and thee and me.
Hastow nat herd how savëd was Noë,
Whan that our lord had warnëd him biforn
That al the world with water sholde be lorn?'
  'Yis,' quod this carpenter, 'ful yore ago.'
  'Hastow nat herd,' quod Nicholas, 'also
The sorwe of Noë with his felawshipe,
Er that he mightë gete his wyf to shipe?
Him had be lever,[98] I dar wel undertake,
At thilkë tyme, than alle hise wetheres blake,

[96] harrowed [97] drowned [98] he would have preferred

That she hadde had a ship hir-self allone.
And ther-fore, wostou what is best to done?
This asketh haste, and of an hastif thing
Men may nat preche or maken tarying.
  Anon go gete us faste in-to this in[99]
A kneding-trogh, or elles a kimelin,[100]
For ech of us, but loke that they be large,
In whiche we mowë[101] swimme as in a barge,
And han ther-innë vitaille suffisànt
But for a day; fy on the remënànt!
The water shal aslake and goon away
Aboutë pryme up-on the nextë day.
But Robin may nat wite of this, thy knave,
Ne eek thy maydë Gille I may nat save;
Axë nat why, for though thou askë me,
I wol nat tellen goddës privetee.
Suffiseth thee, but if thy wittës madde,[102]
To han as greet a grace as Noë hadde.
Thy wyf shal I wel saven, out of doute,
Go now thy wey, and speed thee heer-aboute.
  But whan thou hast, for hir and thee and me,
Y-geten us thise kneding-tubbës three,
Than shaltow hange hem in the roof ful hye,
That no man of our purveyauncë spye.
And whan thou thus hast doon as I have seyd,
And hast our vitaille faire in hem y-leyd,
And eek an ax, to smyte the corde atwo
When that the water comth, that we may go,
And broke an hole an heigh, up-on the gable,
Unto the gardin-ward, over the stable,
That we may frely passen forth our way
Whan that the gretë shour is goon away –
Than shaltow swimme as myrie, I undertake,

[99] this house [100] brewing tub [101] may [102] go astray

As doth the whyte doke after hir drake.
Than wol I clepe, "how! Alison! how! John!
Be myrie, for the flood wol passe anon."
And thou wolt seyn, "hayl, maister Nicholay!
Good morwe, I se thee wel, for it is day."
And than shul we be lordës al our lyf
Of al the world, as Noë and his wyf.
　But of o thyng I warnë thee ful right,
Be wel avysëd, on that ilke night
That we ben entred in-to shippës bord,
That noon of us ne spekë nat a word,
Ne clepe, ne crye, but been in his preyerè;
For it is goddës ownë hestë[103] dere.
　Thy wyf and thou mote hangë fer a-twinne,[104]
For that bitwixë yow shal be no sinne
No more in looking than ther shal in dede;
This ordinance is seyd, go, god thee spede!
Tomorwe at night, whan men ben alle aslepe,
In-to our kneding-tubbës wol we crepe,
And sitten ther, abyding goddës grace.
Go now thy wey, I have no lenger space
To make of this no lenger sermoning.
Men seyn thus, "send the wyse, and sey no-thing"
Thou art so wys, it nedeth thee nat teche;
Go, save our lyf, and that I thee biseche.'
　This sely carpenter goth forth his wey.
Ful ofte he seith 'allas' and 'weylawey,'
And to his wyf he tolde his priveteè;
And she was war, and knew it bet than he,
What al this queyntë cast[105] was for to seye.
But nathëless she ferde as she wolde deye,
And seyde, 'allas! go forth thy wey anon,
Help us to scape, or we ben lost echon;

[103] behest　[104] apart　[105] strange contrivance

I am thy trewë verray wedded wyf;
Go, derë spouse, and help to save our lyf.'
  Lo! which a greet thyng is affeccioun!
Men may dye of imaginacioun,
So depë may impressioun be take.
This sely carpenter biginneth quake;
Him thinketh verraily that he may see
Noës flood come walwing as the see
To drenchen Alisoun, his hony dere.
He wepeth, weyleth, maketh sory chere,
He syketh with ful many a sory swogh.[106]
He gooth and geteth him a kneding-trogh,
And after that a tubbe and a kimelin,
And prively he sente hem to his in,
And heng hem in the roof in privetee.
His ownë hand he madë laddres three,
To climben by the rongës and the stalkes
Un-to the tubbës hanginge in the balkes,[107]
And hem vitaillëd, bothë trogh and tubbe,
With breed and chese, and good ale in a jubbe,[108]
Suffysinge right y-nogh as for a day.
But er that he had maad al this array,
He sente his knave, and eek his wenche also,
Up-on his nede to London for to go.
And on the Monday, whan it drow to night,
He shette his dore with-outë candel-light,
And dressëd al thing as it sholdë be.
And shortly, up they clomben allë three;
They sitten stillë wel a furlong-way.[109]
  'Now, *Pater-noster*, clom[110]!' seyde Nicholay,
And 'clom,' quod John, and 'clom,' seyde Alisoun.
This carpenter seyde his devocioun,
And stille he sit, and biddeth his preyere,
Awaytinge on the reyn, if he it here.

[106] groan [107] beams [108] pitcher [109] a little time [110] mum

The dedë sleep, for wery bisinesse,
Fil on this carpenter right, as I gesse,
Aboutë corfew-tyme, or litel more;
For travail of his goost he groneth sore,
And eft he routeth,[111] for his heed mislay.[112]
Doun of the laddrë stalketh Nicholay,
And Alisoun, ful softe adoun she spedde;
With-outen wordës mo, they goon to bedde
Ther-as the carpenter is wont to lye.
Ther was the revel and the melodye;
And thus lyth Alison and Nicholàs,
In bisinesse of mirthe and of solas,
Til that the belle of laudës gan to ringe,
And frerës in the chauncel gonnë singe.
This parish-clerk, this amorous Absolon,
That is for love alwey so wo bigon,
Up-on the Monday was at Oseneye
With companye, him to disporte and pleye,
And axëd up-on cas[113] a cloisterer
Ful privëly after John the carpenter;
And he drough him a-part out of the chirche,
And seyde, 'I noot, I saugh him here nat wirche
Sin Saterday; I trow that he be went
For timber, ther our abbot hath him sent;
For he is wont for timber for to go,
And dwellen at the grange[114] a day or two;
Or ellës he is at his hous, certeyn;
Wher that he be, I can nat sothly seyn.'
This Absolon ful joly was and light,
And thoghtë, 'now is tymë wake al night;
For sikirly I saugh him nat stirìnge
Aboute his dore sin day bigan to springe.

[111] snores [112] his head was uncomfortable [113] by chance
[114] abbey farm

So moot I thryve, I shal, at cokkës crowe,
Ful privëly knokken at his windòwe
That stant ful lowe up-on his bourës wal.
To Alison now wol I tellen al
My love-longing, for yet I shal nat misse
That at the lestë wey I shal hir kisse.
Som maner confort shal I have, parfay,
My mouth hath icchëd al this longë day;
That is a signe of kissing attë leste.
Al night me mette[115] eek, I was at a feste.
Therfor I wol gon slepe an houre or tweye,
And al the night than wol I wake and pleye.'
Whan that the firstë cok hath crowe, anon
Up rist this joly lover Absolon,
And him arrayeth gay, at point-devys.
But first he cheweth greyn[116] and lycorys,
To smellen swete, er he had kembd his heer.
Under his tonge a trewë love[117] he beer,
For ther-by wende he to ben gracious.
He rometh to the carpenterës hous,
And stille he stant under the shot-windowe;
Un-to his brest it raughte, it was so lowe;
And softe he cogheth with a semi-soun[118] –
'What do ye, hony-comb, swete Alisoun?
My fairë brid, my swetë cinamomë,
Awaketh, lemman myn, and speketh to me!
Wel litel thenken ye up-on my wo,
That for your love I swetë ther I go.
No wonder is thogh that I swelte[119] and swete;
I moorne as doth a lamb after the tete.
Y-wis, lemman, I have swich love-longìnge,
That lyk a turtel[120] trewe is my moornìnge;
I may nat ete na morë than a mayde.'

[115] I dreamt [116] ?grain [117] scented lozenge leaf of herb-paris
[118] a low noise [119] faint [120] turtle-dove

'Go fro the window, Jakkë fool,' she sayde,
'As help me god, it wol nat be "com ba[121] me."
I love another, and elles I were to blamë,
Wel bet than thee, by Jesu, Absolon!
Go forth thy wey, or I wol caste a ston,
And lat me slepe, a twenty devel wey!'
'Allas,' quod Absolon, 'and weylawey!
That trewe love was ever so yvel biset!
Than kissë me, sin it may be no bet,
For Jesus love and for the love of me.'
'Wiltow than go thy wey ther-with?' quod she.
'Ye, certës, lemman,' quod this Absolon.
'Thanne make thee redy,' quod she, 'I come anon;'
And un-to Nicholas she seydë stille,
'Now hust,[122] and thou shalt laughen al thy fille.'
This Absolon doun sette him on his knees,
And seyde, 'I am a lord at alle degrees;
For after this I hope ther cometh more!
Lemman, thy grace, and swetë brid,[123] thyn ore!'[124]
The window she undoth, and that in haste,
'Have do,' quod she, 'com of, and speed thee faste,
Lest that our neighëborës thee espye.'
This Absolon gan wype his mouth ful drye;
Derk was the night as pich, or as the cole,
And at the window out she putte hir hole,
And Absolon, him fil[125] no bet ne wers,
But with his mouth he kiste hir naked ers
Ful savourly, er he was war of this.
Abak he sterte, and thoghte it was amis,
For wel he wiste a womman hath no berd;
He felte a thing al rough and long y-herd,
And seyde, 'fy! allas! what have I do?'
'Tehee!' quod she, and clapte the window to;
And Absolon goth forth a sory pas.

[121]kiss [122]hush [123]bird [124]mercy [125]befell

'A berd, a berd!' quod hendë Nicholas,
'By goddës *corpus*, this goth faire and weel!'
This sely Absolon herde every deel,
And on his lippe he gan for anger byte;
And to him-self he seyde, 'I shal thee quyte!'
Who rubbeth now, who froteth now his lippes
With dust, with sond, with straw, with clooth, with chippes,
But Absolon, that seith ful ofte, 'allas!
My soule bitake I un-to Sathanas,
But me wer lever than al this toun,' quod he,
'Of this despyt awroken[126] for to be!
Allas!' quod he, 'allas! I ne hadde y-bleynt!'[127]
His hotë love was cold and al y-queynt;
For fro that tyme that he had kiste hir ers,
Of paramours he sette nat a kers,[128]
For he was helëd of his maladye;
Ful oftë paramours he gan deffye,
And weep as dooth a child that is y-bete.
A softë paas he wente over the strete
Un-til a smith men clepëd daun Gerveys,
That in his forgë smithëd plough-harneys;
He sharpeth shaar and culter bisily.
This Absolon knokketh al esily,
And seyde, 'undo, Gerveys, and that anon.'
'What, who artow?' 'It am I, Absolon.'
'What, Absolon! for Cristës swetë tree,
Why rysë ye so rathe,[129] ey, *ben'cite*
What eyleth yow? som gay gerl, god it woot,
Hath broght yow thus up-on the viritoot;[130]
By sëynt Note, ye woot wel what I mene.'
This Absolon ne roghtë[131] nat a bene

[126] avenged [127] started aside [128] cress [129] early [130] quick trot
[131] cared

Of al his pley, no word agayn he yaf;
He haddë more tow on his distaf
Than Gerveys knew, and seydë, 'freend so dere,
That hotë culter[132] in the chimenee here,
As lene it me,[133] I have ther-with to done,
And I wol bringe it thee agayn ful sone.'
  Gerveys answerde, 'certës, were it gold,
Or in a pokë nobles alle untold,
Thou sholdest have, as I am trewë smith;
Ey, Cristës foo! what wol ye do ther-with?'
  'Ther-of,' quod Absolon, 'be as be may;
I shal wel telle it thee to-morwe day' –
And caughte the culter by the coldë stele.[134]
Ful softe out at the dore he gan to stele,
And wente un-to the carpenterës wal.
He cogheth first, and knokketh ther-with-al
Upon the windowe, right as he dide er.[135]
  This Alison answerde, 'Who is ther
That knokketh so? I warante it a theef.'
  'Why, nay,' quod he, 'god woot, my swetë leef,
I am thyn Absolon, my derëling!
Of gold,' quod he, 'I have thee broght a ring;
My moder yaf it me, so god me save,
Ful fyn it is, and ther-to wel y-grave;
This wol I yevë thee, if thou me kisse!'
  This Nicholas was risen for to pisse,
And thoghte he wolde amenden al the jape,
He sholdë kisse his ers er that he scape.
And up the windowe dide he hastily,
And out his ers he putteth prively
Over the buttok, to the haunchë-bon;
And ther-with spak this clerk, this Absolon,
'Spek, swetë brid, I noot nat wher thou art.'

[132]ploughshare [133]lend it me [134]handle [135]before

This Nicholas anon leet flee a fart,
As greet as it had been a thonder-dent,
That with the strook he was almost y-blent;[136]
And he was redy with his iron hoot,
And Nicholas amidde the ers he smoot.
Of gooth the skin an hande-brede aboute,
The hote culter brendë so his toute,[137]
And for the smert he wendë for to dye.
As he were wood, for wo he gan to crye –
'Help! water! water! help, for goddës herte!'
This carpenter out of his slomber sterte,
And herde oon cryen 'water' as he were wood,
And thoghte, 'Allas! now comth Nowélis flood!'
He sit him up with-outen wordës mo,
And with his ax he smoot the corde a-two,
And doun goth al; he fond neither to selle,[138]
Ne breed ne ale, til he came to the selle
Up-on the floor; and ther aswowne he lay.
Up sterte hir Alison, and Nicholay,
And cryden 'out' and 'harrow' in the strete.
The neighebores, bothë smale and grete,
In ronnen, for to gauren[139] on this man,
That yet aswowne he lay, bothe pale and wan;
For with the fal he brosten hadde his arm;
But stonde he moste un-to his ownë harm.
For whan he spak, he was anon bore doun
With hendë Nicholas and Alisoun.
They tolden every man that he was wood,
He was agast so of 'Nowélis flood'
Thurgh fantasye, that of his vanitee
He hadde y-boght him kneding-tubbës three,
And hadde hem hangëd in the roof above;
And that he preyëd hem, for goddës love,
To sitten in the roof, *par companye.*

[136]blinded [137]buttocks [138]flooring [139]stare

The folk gan laughen at his fantasye;
In-to the roof they kyken and they gape,
And turnëd al his harm un-to a jape.
For what so that this carpenter answerde,
It was for noght, no man his reson herde;
With othes grete he was so sworn adoun,
That he was holden wood in al the toun;
For every clerk anon-right heeld with other.
They seyde, 'the man is wood, my levë brother;'
And every wight gan laughen of this stryf.
Thus swyvëd[140] was the carpenterës wyf,
For al his keping and his jalousye;
And Absolon hath kist hir nether yë;
And Nicholas is scalded in the toute.
This tale is doon, and god save al the route!

The Wife of Bath's Prologue

'Experience, though noon auctoritee
Were in this world, were right y-nough to me
To speke of wo that is in marïage;
For, lordinges, sith I twelf yeer was of age,
Thonkëd be god that is eterne on lyve,
Housbondes at chirchë-dore I have had fyve;
For I so oftë have y-wedded be;
And alle were worthy men in hir degree.
But me was told certeyn, nat longe agon is,
That sith that Crist ne wente never but onis
To wedding in the Cane of Galilee,
That by the same ensample taughte he me
That I ne sholdë wedded be but ones.
Herke eek, lo! which a sharp word for the nones
Besyde a wellë Jesus, god and man,

[140] lain with

Spak in repreve of the Samaritan:
"Thou hast y-had fyve housbondës," quod he,
"And thilkë man, the which that hath now thee,
Is noght thyn housbond;" thus seyde he certèyn;
What that he mente ther-by, I can nat seyn;
But that I axe, why that the fifthë man
Was noon housbond to the Samaritan?
How manye mighte she have in marïage?
Yet herde I never tellen in myn age
Upon this nombre diffinicioun;
Men may devyne and glosen[1] up and doun.
But wel I woot expres, with-outë lye,
God bad us for to wexe[2] and multiplye;
That gentil[3] text can I wel understonde.
Eek wel I woot he seydë, myn housbonde
Sholde lete[4] fader and moder, and take me;
But of no nombre mencioùn made he,
Of bigamye or of octogamye;
Why sholdë men speke of it vileinye?
Lo, here the wysë king, dan Salomòn;
I trowe he haddë wyvës mo than oon;
As, woldë god, it leveful[5] were to me
To be refresshëd half so ofte as he!
Which yifte of god hadde he for alle his wyvis!
No man hath swich, that in this world alyve is.
God woot, this noble king, as to my wit,
The firstë night had many a mery fit
With ech of hem, so wel was him on lyve!
Blessèd be god that I have wedded fyve!
Welcome the sixtë, whan that ever he shal.
For sothe, I wol nat kepe me chast in al;
Whan myn housbond is fro the world y-gon,
Som Cristen man shal weddë me anon;

[1] comment [2] increase [3] excellent [4] leave [5] allowable

For thanne th'apostle seith, that I am free
To wedde, a godd's half, wher it lyketh me.
He seith that to be wedded is no sinne;
Bet is to be wedded than to brinne.[6]
What rekketh me, thogh folk seye vileinye
Of shrewëd[7] Lameth and his bigamye?
I woot wel Abraham was an holy man,
And Jacob eek, as ferforth as I can;
And ech of hem hadde wyvës mo than two;
And many another holy man also.
Whan saugh ye ever, in any maner age,
That hyë god defended[8] marïage
By expres word? I pray you, telleth me;
Or wher commanded he virginitee?
I woot as wel as ye, it is no drede,
Th'apostel, whan he speketh of maydenhede;
He seyde, that precept ther-of hadde he noon.
Men may conseille a womman to been oon,
But conseilling is no comandëment;
He putte it in our owene jugëment
For haddë god comanded maydenhede,
Thanne hadde he dampned wedding with the dede;
And certës, if ther were no seed y-sowe,
Virginitee, wher-of than sholde it growe?
Poul[9] dorstë nat comanden attë leste
A thing of which his maister yaf noon heste.
The dart[10] is set up for virginitee;
Cacche who so may, who renneth best lat see.
  But this word is nat take of every wight,
But there as god list give it of his might.
I woot wel, that th'apostel was a mayde;[11]
But natheless, thogh that he wroot and sayde,
He wolde that every wight were swich as he,
Al nis but conseil to virginitee;

[6]burn [7]wicked [8]forbad [9]St Paul [10]prize [11]unmarried

And for to been a wyf, he yaf me leve
Of indulgènce; so it is no repreve[12]
To wedde me, if that my makë dye,
With-oute excepcioùn of bigamye.
Al were it good no womman for to touche,
He mente as in his bed or in his couche;
For peril is bothe fyr and tow t'assemble;
Ye knowe what this ensample may resemble.
This is al and som, he heeld virginitee
More parfit than wedding in freletee.[13]
Freeltee clepe I, but-if that he and she
Wolde leden al hir lyf in chastitee.
  I graunte it wel, I have noon envỳe,
Thogh maydenhede preferrë[14] bigamye;
Hem lyketh to be clene, body and goost,
Of myn estaat I nil nat make no boost.
For wel ye knowe, a lord in his housheòld,
He hath nat every vessel al of gold;
Somme been of tree,[15] and doon hir lord servyse.
God clepeth folk to him in sondry wyse,
And everich hath of god a propre yifte,[16]
Som this, som that, – as him lyketh shifte.[17]
  Virginitee is greet perfeccioùn,
And continence eek with devocioùn.
But Crist, that of perfeccioùn is welle,
Bad nat every wight he sholde go selle
All that he hadde, and give it to the pore,
And in swich wyse folwe him and his fore.[18]
He spak to hem that wolde live parfitly;
And lordinges, by your leve, that am nat I.
I wol bistowe the flour of al myn age
In th' actës and in fruit of marïage.

[12]reproach [13]frailty [14]surpass [15]wood [16]gift [17]ordained
[18]path

Telle me also, to what conclusioùn
Were membres maad of generacioùn,
And for what profit was a wight y-wroght?
Trusteth right wel, they were nat maad for noght.
Glose who-so wole, and seye bothe up and doun,
That they were makèd for purgacioùn
Of urine, and our bothe thingës smale
Were eek to knowe a femele from a male,
And for noon other causë: sey ye no?
The experience woot wel it is noght so;
So that the clerkës be nat with me wrothe,
I sey this, that they makëd been for bothe,
This is to seye, for office, and for ese
Of engendrure, ther we nat god displese.
Why sholdë men elles in his bokës sette,
That man shal yeldë to his wyf hir dette?
Now wher-with sholde he make his payëment,
If he ne used his sely[19] instrument?
Than were they maad up-on a creatùre,
To purge uryne, and eek for engendrùre.
But I saye noght that every wight is holde,
That hath swich harneys as I to yow tolde,
To goon and usen hem in engendrùre;
Than sholdë men take of chastitee no cùre.
Crist was a mayde, and shapen as a man,
And many a seint, sith that the world bigan,
Yet lived they ever in parfit chastitee.
I nil envye no virginitee;
Lat hem be breed of purëd whetë-seed,
And lat us wyvës hoten[20] barly-breed;
And yet with barly-breed, Mark tellë can,
Our lord Jesu refresshèd many a man.
In swich estaat as god hath clepèd us

[19] good [20] be called

I wol persevere, I nam nat precious.[21]
In wyfhode I wol use myn instrument
As frely as my maker hath it sent.
If I be daungerous[22] god yeve me sorwe!
Myn housbond shal it have bothe eve and morwe,
Whan that him list com forth and paye his dette.
An housbonde I wol have, I nil nat lette,
Which shal be bothe my dettour and my thral,
And have his tribulacioun with-al
Up-on his flessh, whyl that I am his wyf.
I have the power duringe al my lyf
Up-on his proprë body, and noght he.
Right thus th'apostel tolde it un-to me;
And bad our housbondes for to love us weel.
All this sentence me lyketh every-deel –

. . . .

I shal seye sooth, tho housbondes that I hadde,
As three of hem were gode and two were badde
The three men werë gode, and riche, and olde;
Unnethe[23] mighte they the statut holde
In which that they were bounden un-to me.
Ye woot wel what I mene of this, pardee!
As help me god, I laughë whan I thinke
How pitously a-night I made hem swinke;
And by my fey, I tolde of it no stoor.[24]
They had me yeven hir gold and hir tresoor;
Me nedëd nat do lenger diligence
To winne hir love, or doon hem reverence.
They lovëd me so wel, by god above,
That I ne tolde no deyntee[25] of hir love!
A wys womman wol sette hir ever in oon
To gete hir love, ther as she hath noon.

[21] scrupulous [22] grudging [23] scarcely [24] took no account of it
[25] value

But sith I hadde hem hoolly in myn hond,
And sith they hadde me yeven all hir lond,
What sholde I taken hede hem for to plese,
But it were for my profit and myn ese?
I sette hem so a-werkë, by my fey,
That many a night they songen "weilawey!"
The bacoun was nat fet for hem, I trowe,
That som men han in Essex at Dunmowe.[26]
I governed hem so wel, after my lawe,
That ech of hem ful blisful was and fawe[27]
To bringe me gayë thingës fro the fayre.
They were ful glad whan I spak to hem fayre;
For god it woot, I chidde hem spitously.

. . . .

Lordinges, right thus, as ye have understonde,
Bar I stifly myne olde housbondes on honde,
That thus they seyden in hir dronkenesse;
And al was fals, but that I took witnesse
On Janëkin and on my nece also.
O lord, the peyne I dide hem and the wo,
Ful giltelees, by goddes swetë pyne![28]
For as an hors I coudë byte and whyne.
I coudë pleyne, thogh I were in the gilt,[29]
Or ellës often tyme hadde I ben spilt.
Who-so that first to millë comth, first grint;
I pleynëd first, so was our werre y-stint.
They were ful glad t'excusen hem ful blyve
Of thing of which they never agilte hir lyve.
Of wenches wolde I beren him on honde,
Whan that for syk unnethes[30] mighte he stonde.
Yet tikled it his hertë, for that he
Wende that I hadde of him so greet chiertee.[31]

[26] the 'Dunmow flitch' was given to happily married couples
[27] glad [28] passion [29] wrong [30] scarcely [31] fondness

I swoor that al my walkinge out by nighte
Was for t'espye wenches that he dighte;[32]
Under that colour hadde I many a mirthe.
For al swich wit is yeven us in our birthe;
Deceite, weping, spinning god hath yive
To wommen kindëly,[33] whyl they may live.
And thus of o thing I avauntë me,
Atte ende I hadde the bettre in ech degree,
By sleighte, or force, or by som maner thing,
As by continuel murmur or grucching;
Namely[34] a-beddë hadden they meschaunce,
Ther wolde I chyde and do hem no plesaunce;
I wolde no lenger in the bed abyde,
If that I felte his arm over my syde,
Til he had maad his raunson un-to me;
Than wolde I suffre him do his nycetee.
And ther-fore every man this tale I telle,
Winne[35] who-so may, for al is for to selle.
With empty hand men may none haukës lure;
For winning wolde I al his lust endure,
And makë me a feynëd appetyt;
And yet in bacon hadde I never delyt;
That made me that ever I wolde hem chyde.
For thogh the pope had seten hem bisyde,.
I wolde nat spare hem at hir owene bord.
For by my trouthe, I quitte hem word for word.
As help me verray god omnipotent,
Thogh I right now sholde make my testament,
I ne owe hem nat a word that it nis quit.
I broghte it so aboutë by my wit,
That they moste yeve it up, as for the beste;
Or ellës hadde we never been in reste.
For thogh he lokëd as a wood leoùn,[36]

[32] lay with [33] naturally [34] especially [35] profit [36] mad lion

Yet sholde he faille of his conclusioùn.
  Thanne wolde I seye, 'gode lief, tak keep
How mekely loketh Wilkin ourë sheep;
Com neer, my spouse, lat me ba[37] thy cheke!
Ye sholdë been al paciènt and meke,
And han a swetë spycèd[38] consciènce,
Sith ye so preche of Jobës paciènce.
Suffreth alwey, sin ye so wel can preche;
And but ye do, certein we shal yow teche
That it is fair to have a wyf in pees.
Oon of us two moste bowen, doutelees;
And sith a man is morë resonàble
Than womman is, ye mostë been suffràble.
What eyleth yow to grucchë thus and grone?
Is it for ye wolde have my queynt[39] allone?
Why taak it al, lo, have it every-deel;
Peter! I shrewe yow but ye love it weel!
For if I woldë selle my *belë chose*,
I coudë walke as fresh as is a rose;
But I wol kepe it for your owene tooth.
Ye be to blame, by god, I sey yow sooth.'
  Swiche maner wordës haddë we on honde.
Now wol I speken of my fourthe housbonde.
  My fourthe housbonde was a reveloùr,
This is to seyn, he hadde a paramoùr;
And I was yong and ful of ragerye,[40]
Stiborn and strong, and joly as a pye.
Wel coude I dauncë to an harpë smale,
And singe, y-wis, as any nightingale,
Whan I had dronke a draughte of swetë wyn.
Metellius, the foule cherl, the swyn,
That with a staf birafte his wyf hir lyf,
For she drank wyn, thogh I hadde been his wyf,

[37] kiss [38] scrupulous [39] pudendum [40] wantonness

He sholde nat han daunted me fro drinke;
And, after wyn, on Venus moste I thinke:
For al so siker[41] as cold engendreth hayl,
A likerous[42] mouth moste han a likerous tayl.
In womman vinolent[43] is no defence,
This knowen lechours by experience.
  But, lord Crist! whan that it remembreth me
Up-on my yowthe, and on my joliteè,
It tikleth me aboute myn hertë rote.
Unto this day it dooth myn hertë bote
That I have had my world as in my tyme.
But age, allas! that al wol envenỳme,
Hath me biraft my beautee and my pith;
Lat go, fare-wel, the devel go therwith!
The flour is goon, ther is na-more to telle,
The bren,[44] as I best can, now moste I selle;
But yet to be right mery wol I fonde.[45]
Now wol I tellen of my fourthe housbonde.
  I seye, I hadde in hertë greet despyt
That he of any other had delyt.
But he was quit, by god and by seint Joce!
I made him of the samë wode a croce;
Nat of my body in no foul manere,
But certeinly, I madë folk swich chere,
That in his owene grece I made him frye
For angre, and for verray jalousye.
By god, in erthe I was his purgatorie,
For which I hope his soulë be in glorie.
For god it woot, he sat ful ofte and song
Whan that his shoo ful bitterly him wrong.
Ther was no wight, save god and he, that wiste,
In many wyse, how sorë I him twiste.
He deyde whan I cam fro Jerusalem,

[41] sure [42] greedy [43] full of wine [44] bran [45] try

And lyth y-grave under the rodë-beem,
Al is his tombe noght so curious
As was the sepulcre of him, Darius,
Which that Appelles wroghtë subtill,
It nis but wast to burie him preciously.
Lat him fare-wel, god yeve his soulë reste,
He is now in the grave and in his cheste.
  My fifthe housbonde, god his soulë blesse!
Which that I took for love and no richesse,
He som-tyme was a clerk of Oxenford,
And had left scole, and wente at hoom to bord
With my gossib, dwellinge in oure toun,
God have hir soule! hir name was Alisoun.
She knew myn herte and eek my privetee
Bet than our parisshe-preest, so moot[46] I thee!
To hir biwreyëd I my conseil al.
For had myn housbonde pissëd on a wal,
Or doon a thing that sholde han cost his lyf,
To hir, and to another worthy wyf,
And to my nece, which that I lovëd weel,
I wolde han told his conseil every-deel.
And so I dide ful often, god it woot,
That made his face ful often reed and hoot
For verray shame, and blamed him-self for he
Had told to me so greet a privetee.
  But now sir, lat me see, what I shal seyn?
A! ha! by god, I have my tale ageyn.
  Whan that my fourthe housbond was on bere,
I weep algate,[47] and made sory chere,
As wyvës moten,[48] for it is usage,
And with my coverchief covered my visàge;
But for that I was purveyed[49] of a make,
I weep but smal, and that I undertake.

[46] tell [47] everywhere [48] must [49] deprived

To chirchë was myn housbond born a-morwe
With neighebores, that for him maden sorwe;
And Jankin ourë clerk was oon of tho.
As help me god, whan that I saugh him go
After the bere, me thoughte he hadde a paire
Of legges and of feet so clene and faire,
That al myn herte I yaf un-to his hold.
He was, I trowe, a twenty winter old,
And I was fourty, if I shal seye sooth;
But yet I hadde alwey a coltës tooth.
Gat-tothed[50] I was, and that bicam me weel;
I hadde the prente of sëynt Venus seel.
As help me god, I was a lusty oon,
And faire and riche, and yong, and wel bigoon;[51]
And trewely, as myne housbondës tolde me,
I had the bestë *quoniam* mightë be.
For certes, I am al Venerien
In felinge, and myn herte is Marcien.
Venus me yaf my lust, my likerousnesse,
And Mars yaf me my sturdy hardinesse.
Myn ascendent was Taur, and Mars ther-inne.
Allas! allas! that ever love was sinne!
I folwed ay myn inclinacioùn
By vertu of my constellacioùn;
That made me I coude noght withdrawe
My chambre of Venus from a good felawe.
Yet have I Martës mark up-on my face,
And also in another privee place.
For, god so wis be my savacioùn,
I ne loved never by no discrecioùn,
But ever folwedë myn appetyt,
Al were he short or long, or blak or whyt;
I took no kepe, so that he lykëd me,
How pore he was, ne eek of what degree.

[50] gap-toothed [51] happy

What sholde I seye, but, at the monthës ende,
This joly clerk Jankin, that was so hende,[52]
Hath wedded me with great solempnitee,
And to him yaf I al the lond and fee
That ever was me yeven ther-bifore;
But afterward repented me ful sore.
He noldë suffre nothing of my list.[53]
By god, he smoot me onës on the list,[54]
For that I rente out of his book a leef,
That of the strook myn erë wex al deef.

. . . .

And with his fist he smoot me on the heed,
That in the floor I lay as I were deed.
And when he saugh how stillë that I lay,
He was agast, and wolde han fled his way,
Til attë laste out of my swogh I breyde:[55]
'O! hastow slayn me, falsë theef?' I seyde,
'And for my land thus hastow mordred me?
Er I be deed, yet wol I kissë thee.'
And neer he cam, and kneled faire adoun,
And seyde, 'dere suster Alisoun,
As help me god, I shal thee never smyte;
That I have doon, it is thy-self to wyte.[56]
Foryeve it me, and that I thee biseke'[57] –
And yet eft-sones I hitte him on the cheke,
And seyde, 'theef, thus muchel am I wreke;
Now wol I dye, I may no lenger speke.'
But attë laste, with muchel care and wo,
We fille acorded, by us selven two.
He yaf me al the brydel in myn hond
To han the governance of hous and lond,
And of his tonge and of his hond also,
And made him brenne his book anon right tho.

[52] courteous [53] desire [54] ear [55] started [56] blame [57] beseech

And whan that I hadde geten un-to me,
By maistrie, al the soveraynetee,
And that he seyde, 'myn owene trewë wyf,
Do as thee lust the terme of al thy lyf,
Keep thyn honòur, and keep eek myn estaat' –
After that day we hadden never debaat.

ANONYMOUS

Adam Lay Y-Bounden

Adam lay y-bounden
  Bounden in a bond;
Four thousand winter
  Thought he not too long;
And all was for an apple
  An apple that he took,
As clerkës[1] finden written
  In theirë book.

Ne had the apple taken been,
  The apple taken been,
Ne haddë never our Lady
  A been heaven's queen.
Blessed be the time
  That apple taken was!
Therefore we may singen
  '*Deo Gratias!*'

[1] learned men

I Have a Gentle Cock

I have a gentle cock
  Croweth me day;
He doth[1] me risen early
  My matins for to say.

I have a gentle cock
  Comen he is of great;[2]
His comb is of red coral
  His tail is of jet.

I have a gentle cock
  Comen he is of kind[3]
His comb is of red coral
  His tail is of inde.[4]

His leggës been of azure
  So gentle and so small;
His spurrës are of silver white
  Into the wortëwale.[5]

His eyen are of crystal
  Locken[6] all in amber;
And every night he percheth him
  In my lady's chamber.

A Henpecked Husband

How, hey! It is non les[1]:
  I dare not seyn[2] when she seith 'Pes!'[3]

[1]makes [2]of great family [3]of noble stock [4]indigo [5]root [6]set
[1]lie [2]speak [3]Quiet!

Ying[4] men, I warne you everichon,
Eldë[5] wivis tak ye non;
For I myself have on at hom –
  I dare not seyn when she seith 'Pes!'

When I cum fro the plow at noon,
In a reven dish myn mete is doon;[6]
I dare not askin our dame a spoon –
  I dare not seyn when she seith 'Pes!'

If I ask our damë bred,
She takith a staf and brekith myn hed,
And doth me rennin under the led[7] –
  I dare not seyn when she seith 'Pes!'

If I ask our damë flesh,[8]
She brekith myn hed with a dish:
'Boy, thou art not worth a rish!'[9] –
  I dare not seyn when she seith 'Pes!'

If I ask our damë chese,
'Boy', she seith, al at ese,[10]
'Thou art not worth half a pese!'[11] –
  I dare not seyn when she seith 'Pes!'

Jolly Jankin

'*Kyrië*',[1] so '*Kyrië*',
  Jankin singeth merry,
With '*elëison*'.[2]

[4]young [5]old [6]my food is put in a cracked dish
[7]and makes me run under the cauldron [8]meat [9]rush [10]coolly
[11]pea

[1]*Kyrie eleison* (Lord have mercy!) is the only piece of Greek in the Latin Mass [2]some versions have 'aleyson' (Alison, the girl's name)

As I went on Yulë day
  In our procession,
Knew I jolly Jankin
  By his merry tone –
  Kyrië elëison.

Jankin began the office
  On the Yulë day,
And yet me think'th it does me good
  So merry gan he say
'*Kyrië elëison*'.

Jankin read the pistle[3]
  Full fair and full well,
And yet me think'th it does me good,
  As ever have I sel.[4]
  Kyrië elëison.

Jankin at the *Sanctus*
  Crack'th a merry note,[5]
And yet me think'th it does me good –
  I payëd for his coat.
  Kyrië elëison.

Jankin cracketh notes
  An hundred on a knot[6]
And yet he hack'th them smaller
  Than wortës[7] to the pot.
  Kyrië elëison.

Jankin at the *Agnus*
  Beareth the pax-bread;

[3]epistle [4]as I hope always to be happy
[5]divides a note into short ones [6]cluster [7]herbs

He twinkëlëd[8] but said nought,
   And on my foot he tread.
   Kyrië elëison.

Benedicamus Domino,
   Christ from shame me shield!
Deo Gratias thereto –
   Alas! I go with child!
   Kyrië elëison.

Love Without Longing

I have a yong suster
   fer beyondyn the se;
Many be the drowryis[1]
   that sche sentë me.

Sche sentë me the cherye,
   withoutyn ony ston,
And so sche dede the dowë,[2]
   withoutyn ony bon.[3]

Sche sent me the brerë,[4]
   withoutyn ony rynde,[5]
Sche bad me love my lemman
   withoutë longỳng.[6]

How schulde ony cherye
   be withoutë ston?
And how schulde ony dowë
   ben withoutë bon?

How schulde any brerë
   ben withoutë rynde?

[8] winked   [1] presents   [2] dove   [3] bone   [4] briar   [5] bark   [6] desire

How schulde I love my lemman
  without longỳng?

Quan the cherye was a flour,
  than haddë it non ston;
Quan the dowë was an ey,[7]
  than haddë it non bon.

Quan the brerë was onbred,[8]
  than haddë it non rynd;
Quan the mayden hayt that sche lovit,
  sche is without longỳng.

WILLIAM DUNBAR

The Ballad of Kynd Kittok

My Gudame wes a gay wif, bot scho wes rycht gend,[1]
  Scho duelt furth fer in to France, apon Falkland fellis;
Thay callit her Kynd Kittok, quhasa[2] hir weill kend:
  Scho wes like a caldrone cruke cler under kellis[3]
They threpit[4] that scho deit of thrist,[5] and maid a gud end.
  Efter hir dede, scho dredit nought in hevin for to duell;
And sa to hevin the hieway driedless[6] scho wend,
  Yit scho wanderit, and yeid by to[7] ane elriche[8] well.
    Scho met thar, as I wene,
      Ane ask[9] rydand on a snaill,
      And cryit, 'Ourtane[10] fallow, haill!'
      And raid ane inche behind the taill,
    Till it wes neir evin.

[7] egg [8] not fully grown
[1] simple [2] those who [3] fair under her head-dress [4] maintained
[5] thirst [6] fearless *or* without doubt [7] reached [8] supernatural
[9] newt [10] overtaken

Sa scho had hap to be horsit to hir herbry,[11]
  Att ane ailhous neir hevin, it nyghttit thaim thare;
Scho deit of thrist in this warld, that gert[12] hir be so dry,
  Scho neuer eit, bot drank our mesur and mair.
Scho slepit quhill the morne at none, and rais airly;
  And to the yettis[13] of hevin fast can the wif fair,
And by Sanct Petir, in at the yet, scho stall prevely:
  God lukit and saw hir lattin in, and lewch[14] his hert sair.
    And than, yeris sevin
      Scho lewit a gud life,
      And wes our Ladyis hen wif:
      And held Sanct Petir at stryfe,
    Ay quhill scho wes in hevin.

Scho lukit out on a day, and thoght ryght lang
  To se the ailhous beside, in til an euill hour;
And out of hevin the hie gait[15] cowth[16] the wif gang
  For to get hir ane fresche drink, ye aill of hevin wes sour.
Scho come againe to hevinnis yet, quhen the bell rang,
  Sanct Petir hat hir with a club, quhill a gret clour[17]
Rais in hir heid, becaus the wif yeid[18] wrang.
  Whan to the ailhous agane scho ran, the pycharis[19] to pour,
    And for to brew, and baik.
      Frendis, I pray you hertfully,
      Gif ye be thristy or dry,
      Drink with my Guddame, as ye ga by,
    Anys[20] for my saik.

[11] harbour [12] caused to be [13] gates [14] laughed [15] way
[16] knew how to [17] bump [18] went [19] pitchers [20] once

To a Lady

Sweet rois[1] of vertew and of gentilness,
Delytsum lily of every lustyness,
    Richest in bontie and in bewtie clear,
    And everie vertew that is wenit[2] dear,
Except onlie that ye are mercyless.

Into your garth[3] this day I did persew;
There saw I flowris that fresche were of hew;
    Baith quhyte and reid most lusty were to seyne,[4]
    And halesome herbis upon stalkis greene;
Yet leaf nor flowr find could I nane of rew.[5]

I doubt that Merche, with his cauld blastis keyne,
Has slain this gentil herb, that I of mene;[6]
    Quhois piteous death dois to my heart sic paine
    That I would make to plant his root againe, –
So confortand his levis unto me bene.

JOHN SKELTON

Philip Sparrow

P l a ce bo!
Who is there, who?
Di le xi!
Dame Margery,
Fa, re, my, my.
Wherefore and why, why?
For the soul of Philip Sparrow
That was late slain at Carrow,

[1] rose [2] weened, esteemed [3] garden-close [4] to see [5] rue
[6] that I complain of

Among the Nunnës Black.
For that sweet soulës sake,
And for all sparrows' souls,
Set in our bead-rolls,
Pater noster qui,
With an *Ave Mari*,
And with the corner of a Creed,
The more shall be your meed.

When I remember again
How my Philip was slain,
Never half the pain
Was between you twain,
Pyramus and Thisbe,
As then befell to me.
I wept and I wailed,
The tearës down hailed,
But nothing it availed
To call Philip again
Whom Gib, our cat, hath slain.

Gib, I say, our cat,
Worried her on that
Which I lovëd best.
It cannot be exprest
My sorrowful heaviness,
But all without redress!
For within that stound,[1]
Half slumbering, in a sound[2]
I fell down to the ground.

Unneth[3] I cast mine eyes
Toward the cloudy skies.

[1] moment [2] swoon [3] hardly

But when I did behold
My sparrow dead and cold,
No creature but that would
Have ruëd upon me,
To behold and see
What heaviness did me pang:
Wherewith my hands I wrang,
That my sinews cracked,
As though I had been racked,
So pained and so strained
That no life wellnigh remained.

I sighed and I sobbed,
For that I was robbed
Of my sparrow's life.
O maiden, widow, and wife,
Of what estate ye be,
Of high or low degree,
Great sorrow then ye might see,
And learn to weep at me!
Such pains did me fret
That mine heart did beat,
My visage pale and dead,
Wan, and blue as lead:
The pangs of hateful death
Wellnigh had stopped my breath.

*

Like Andromach, Hector's wife,
Was weary of her life,
When she had lost her joy,
Noble Hector of Troy;
In like manner alsò
Increaseth my deadly woe,
For my sparrow is go.[4]

[4] gone

It was so pretty a fool,
It would sit on a stool,
And learned after my school
For to keep his cut,[5]
With 'Philip, keep your cut!'

It had a velvet cap,
And would sit upon my lap
And seek after small worms,
And sometime white bread-crumbs;
And many times and oft
Between my breastës soft
It would lie and rest;
It was proper and prest.[6]

Sometime he would gasp
When he saw a wasp;
A fly or a gnat,
He would fly at that;
And prettily he would pant
When he saw an ant.
Lord, how he would pry
After the butterfly!
Lord, how he would hop
After the gressop[7]
And when I said, 'Phip, Phip!'
Then he would leap and skip,
And take me by the lip.
Alas, it will me slo[8]
That Philip is gone me fro!

Si in i qui ta tes
Alas, I was evil at ease!

[5] behave himself [6] alert [7] grasshopper [8] slay

De pro fun dis cla ma vi,
When I saw my sparrow die!

*

The Requiem Mass

Lauda, anima mea, Dominum!
To weep with me look that ye come
All manner of birdës in your kind;
See none be left behind
To mourning look that ye fall
With dolorous songs funeral,
Some to sing, and some to say,
Some to weep, and some to pray,
Every bird in his lay.
The goldfinch, the wagtail;
The jangling jay to rail,
The fleckèd pie to chatter
Of this dolorous matter;
And robin redbreast,
He shall be the priest
The requiem mass to sing,
Softly warbeling,
With help of the red-sparrow,[9]
And the chattering swallow,
This hearse for to hallow;
The lark with his long toe;
The spink,[10] and the martinet alsò;
The shoveller[11] with his broad beak;
The dotterel, that foolish peke,
And also the mad coot,
With a bald face to toot;
The fieldfare and the snite;[12]
The crow and the kite;

[9] sedge-warbler [10] chaffinch [11] spoonbill [12] snipe

The raven, called Rolfë,
His plain-song to sol-fa;
The partridge, the quail;
The plover with us to wail;
The woodhack,[13] that singeth 'chur'
Hoarsely, as he had the mur;[14]
The lusty chanting nightingale;
The popinjay[15] to tell her tale,
That toteth[16] oft in a glass,
Shall read the Gospel at mass;
The mavis with her whistle
Shall read there the Pistle.
But with a large and a long
To keep just plain-song,
Our chanters shall be the cuckoo,
The culver,[17] the stockdowe,
With 'peewit' the lapwing,
The Versicles shall sing.

The bittern with his bumpe,
The crane with his trumpe,
The swan of Maeander,
The goose and the gander,
The duck and the drake,
Shall watch at this wake;
The peacock so proud,
Because his voice is loud,
And hath a glorious tail,
He shall sing the Grail;[18]
The owl, that is so foul,
Must help us to howl;
The heron so gaunt,
And the cormorant,

[13] woodpecker [14] catarrh [15] parrot [16] peeps [17] dove [18] Gradual

With the pheasant,
And the gaggling gant,[19]
And the churlish chough;
The knot[20] and the ruff;
The barnacle, the buzzard,
With the wild mallard;
The divendop[21] to sleep;
The water-hen to weep;
The puffin and the teal
Money they shall deal
To poorë folk at large,
That shall be their charge;
The seamew and the titmouse;
The woodcock with the longë nose;
The throstle with her warbling;
The starling with her brabling;
The rook, with the osprey
That putteth fishes to a fray;
And the dainty curlew,
With the turtle most true.

At this *Placebo*
We may not well forgo
The countering of the coe;[22]
The stork also,
That maketh his nest
In chimneys to rest;
Within those walls
No broken galls[23]
May there abide
Of cuckoldry side,
Or else philosophy
Maketh a great lie.

[19] gannet [20] red-breasted sandpiper [21] dabchick [22] jackdaw
[23] bitterness

The ostrich, that will eat
An horseshoe so great,
In the stead of meat,
Such fervent heat
His stomach doth fret;
He cannot well fly,
Nor sing tunably,
Yet at a braýd[24]
He hath well assayed
To sol-fa above E-la.
Fa, lorell, *fa*, *fa!*
Ne quando
Male cantando,
The best that we can,
To make him our bell-man,
And let him ring the bells.
He can do nothing else.

Chanticleer, our cock,
Must tell what is of the clock
By the astrology
That he hath naturally
Conceivëd and caught,
And was never taught
By Albumazer
The astronomer,
Nor by Ptolomy
Prince of astronomy,
Nor yet by Haly;
And yet he croweth daily
And nightly the tides
That no man abides,
With Partlot his hen,
Whom now and then

[24]at a push

He plucketh by the head
When he doth her tread.

The bird of Araby,
That potentially
May never die,
And yet there is none
But one alone;
A phoenix it is
This hearse that must bless
With aromatic gums
That cost great sums,
The way of thurification
To make a fumigation,
Sweet of reflare,[25]
And redolent of air,
This corse for to cense
With great reverence,
As Patriarch or Pope
In a black cope.
While he censeth the hearse,
He shall sing the verse,
Liber a me,
In *de*, *la*, *sol*, *re*,
Softly B molle
For my sparrow's soul.
Pliny sheweth all
In his *Story Natural*
What he doth find
Of this phoenix kind;
Of whose incineration
There riseth a new creation
Of the same fashion
Without alteration,

[25] perfume

Saving that old age
Is turned into corage
Of fresh youth again;
This matter true and plain,
Plain matter indeed,
Who so list to read.

But for the eagle doth fly
Highest in the sky,
He shall be the sub-dean,
The choir to demean,[26]
As provost principal,
To teach them their Ordinal;
Also the noble falcon,
With the ger-falcon,
The tarsel[27] gentil,
They shall mourn soft and still
In their amice[28] of gray;
The saker[29] with them shall say
Dirige for Philip's soul;
The goshawk shall have a roll
The choristers to control;
The lanners[30] and the merlins
Shall stand in their mourning-gowns;
The hobby[31] and the musket[32]
The censers and the cross shall fet;
The kestrel in all this wark
Shall be holy-water clerk.

And now the dark cloudy night
Chaseth away Phoebus bright,
Taking his course toward the west,
God send my sparrow's soul good rest!
Requiem aeternam dona eis, Domine! . . .

[26] conduct [27] hawk [28] loose ecclesiastical dress [29] hawk
[30] falcons [31] small falcon [32] sparrow-hawk

To Mistress Margaret Hussey

Merry Margaret,
As midsummer flower,
Gentle as falcon
Or hawk of the tower;
With solace and gladness,
Much mirth and no madness,
All good and no badness;
So joyously,
So maidenly,
So womanly
Her demeaning
In everything,
Far, far passing
That I can indite,
Or suffice to write
Of Merry Margaret
As midsummer flower,
Gentle as falcon
Or hawk of the tower.
As patient and as still
And as full of good will
As fair Isaphill,[1]
Coriander,
Sweet pomander,
Good Cassander,[2]
Steadfast of thought,
Well made, well wrought,
Far may be sought
Ere that ye can find
So courteous, so kind,

[1] Hypsipyle [2] Cassandra

As Merry Margaret,
  This midsummer flower,
Gentle as falcon
Or hawk of the tower.

ROBERT HENRYSON

Robin and Makyne

Robin sat on gude green hill,
  Kepand[1] a flock of fe:[2]
Mirry Makyne said him till[3]
  'Robin, thou rew[4] on me:
I haif thee luvit, loud and still,
  Thir yeiris twa or thre;
My dule in dern[5] bot gif thou dill,[6]
  Doutless but dreid[7] I de.'

Robin answerit 'By the Rude
  Na thing of luve I knaw,
But keipis my scheip undir yon wud:
  Lo, quhair they raik on raw.[8]
Quhat has marrit thee in thy mude,[9]
  Makyne, to me thou shaw;[10]
Or quhat is luve, or to be lude?[11]
  Fain wad I leir[12] that law.'

'At luvis lair gif thou will leir
  Tak thair ane A B C;
Be heynd,[13] courtass,[14] and fair of feir,[15]
  Wyse, hardy, and free:

[1]keeping [2]sheep [3]to him [4]pity [5]secret sorrow [6]soothe [7]without doubt [8]range in rows [9]upset you [10]show [11]loved [12]learn [13]gentle [14]courteous [15]demeanour

So that no danger do thee deir[16]
 Quhat dule in dern thou dre;
Preiss[17] thee with pain at all poweìr
 Be patient and prevìe.'[18]

Robin answerit hir againe,
 'I wat nocht quhat is lufe;
But I haif mervel in certaìne
 Quhat makis thee this wanrùfe:[19]
The weddir is fair, and I am fain;[20]
 My scheip gois haill[21] aboif;[22]
And[23] we wald pley us[24] in this plane,
 They wald us baith reproif.'

'Robin, tak tent[25] unto my tale,
 And wirk all as I reid,[26]
And thou sall haif my heart all haill,
 Eik and my maiden-heid:
Sen God sendis bute for baill,[27]
 And for murnyng remeìd,
In dern with thee bot gif I daill[28]
 Dowtles I am bot deid.'

'Makyne, to-morn this ilka tyde
 And ye will meit me heir,
Peradventure my scheip may gang besyde,
 Quhyle we haif liggit[29] full neir;
But mawgrë haif I,[30] and[31] I byde,
 Fra they begin to steir;[32]
Quhat lyis on heart I will nocht hyd;
 Makyn, then mak gude cheir.'

[16]daunt [17]endeavour [18]secret [19]unrest [20]lusty [21]healthy
[22]up above [23]if [24]complain [25]heed [26]advise
[27]remedy for hurt [28]deal [29]are lying [30]I am uneasy [31]if
[32]stray

'Robin, thou reivis[33] me roiff[34] and rest;
I luve bot thee allane.'
'Makyne, adieu! the sone gois west,
The day is neir-hand gane.'
'Robin, in dule I am so drest[35]
That luve will be my bane.'
'Ga luve, Makyne, quhair-evir thow list
For lemman[36] I luve nane.'

'Robin, I stand in sic a styll.
I sicht[37] and that full sair.'
'Makyne, I haif been here this quhyle;
At hame God gif[38] I wair.'
'My huny, Robin, talk ane quhyll,
Gif thow will do na mair.'
'Makyn, sum uthir man begyle,
For hamewart I will fair.'

Robin on his wayis went
As light as leif of tre;
Makyne murnit in hir intent,[39]
And trowd him nevir to se.
Robin brayd[40] attour the bent:[41]
Then Makyne cryit on hie,
'Now may thow sing, for I am schent![42]
Quhat alis[43] lufe at me?'

Makyne went hame withowttin fail,
Full wery eftir cowth weip;[44]
Then Robin in a ful fair daill
Assemblit all his scheip.

[33] robbest [34] quiet [35] beset [36] lover [37] sigh [38] I would to God
[39] inward thoughts [40] strode [41] coarse grass [42] destroyed
[43] ails (Why is love so angry with me?) [44] much weeping

Be that sum part of Makynis aill
   Out-throw his hairt cowd creip;[45]
He fallowit hir fast thair till[46] assaill,
   And till her tuke gude keip.[47]

'Abyd, abyd, thow fair Makŷne,
   A word for ony thing;
For all my luve, it sall be thyne,
   Withowttin departing.
All haill thy hairt for till haif myne[48]
   Is all my cuvating;[49]
My scheip to-morn, quhyle houris nyne,
   Will neid of no keping.'

'Robin, thow hes hard[50] soung and say,
   In gestis[51] and storeis auld,
The man that will nocht quhen he may
   Sall haif nocht quhen he wald.
I pray to Jesu every day,
   Mot eik[52] thair cairis cauld
That first preissis with thee to play
   Be[53] firth, forrest, or fauld.'

'Makyne, the nicht is soft and dry,
   The weddir is warme and fair,
And the grene woid rycht neir us by
   To walk attour all quhair:[54]
Thair ma na janglour[55] us espy,
   That is to lufe contrair;
Thairin, Makyne, baith ye and I,
   Unsene we may repair.'

[45] had crept [46] to [47] paid great attention
[48] May thy heart be whole till it has mine [49] coveting [50] heard
[51] romances [52] may he add to [53] by [54] everywhere [55] talebearer

'Robin, that warld is all away,
  And quyt brocht till ane end:
And nevir agane thereto, perfày,
  Sall it be as thow wend;[56]
For of my pane thow maid it play;
  And all in vane I spend:
As thow hes done, sa sall I say,
  "Murne on, I think to mend."'

'Makyne, the howp[57] of all my heill,
  My hairt on thee is sett;
And evirmair to thee be leill[58]
  Quhill I may leif but lett;[59]
Never to faill as utheris feill,
  Quhat grace that evir I gett.'
'Robin, with thee I will nocht deill;
  Adieu! for thus we mett.'

Makyne went hame blythe anneuche[60]
  Attour the holttis hair;[61]
Robin murnit, and Makyne leuche;[62]
  Scho sang, he sichit sair:
And so left him baith wo and wreuch,[63]
  In dolour and in cair,
Kepand his hird under a huche[64]
  Amangis the holttis hair.

[56] weened [57] hope [58] loyal [59] without hindrance [60] enough
[61] grey woodlands [62] laughed [63] peevish [64] cliff

WILLIAM SHAKESPEARE

A Sea Song

The master, the swabber, the boatswain and I,
  The gunner and his mate,
Loved Mall, Meg, and Marian and Margery,
  But none of us cared for Kate;
  For she had a tongue with a tang,
  Would cry to a sailor, 'Go hang!'
She loved not the savour of tar nor of pitch,
Yet a tailor might scratch her where'er she did itch:
  Then to sea, boys, and let her go hang.

from *The Tempest*

The Pedlar's Song

When daffodils begin to peer,
  With heigh! the doxy, over the dale,
Why, then comes in the sweet o' the year;
  For the red blood reigns in the winter's pale.

The white sheet bleaching on the hedge,
  With heigh! the sweet birds, O, how they sing!
Doth set my pugging[1] tooth on edge;
  For a quart of ale is a dish for a king.

The lark, that tirra-lirra chants,
  With, heigh! with, heigh! the thrush and the jay,

[1]In Old English *pug* means to pull or tug; but *pug* also once meant a darling or dear, applied to women or animals. He favoured the idea of pulling the sheet off the hedge and selling it for drink.

Are summer songs for me and my aunts,
  While we lie tumbling in the hay.

from *The Winter's Tale*

O Mistress Mine

O mistress mine, where are you roaming?
O, stay and hear! your true love's coming,
  That can sing both high and low:
Trip no further, pretty sweeting;
Journeys end in lovers meeting,
  Every wise man's son doth know.

What is love? 'tis not hereafter;
Present mirth hath present laughter;
  What's to come is still unsure:
In delay there lies no plenty;
Then come kiss me, sweet-and-twenty!
  Youth's a stuff will not endure.

from *Twelfth Night*

ANONYMOUS

Hye Nonny Nonny Noe

Down lay the shepherd swain
  so sober and demure
Wishing for his wench again
  so bonny and so pure
With his head on hillock low
  and his arms akimbò,
And all was for the loss of his
  hye nonny nonny noe.

His tears fell as thin
as water from the still,
His hair upon his chin
grew like thyme upon a hill,
His cherry cheeks pale as snow
did testify his mickle woe
And all was for the loss of his
hye nonny nonny noe.

Sweet she was, as kind a love
as ever fettered swain;
Never such a dainty one
shall man enjoy again.
Set a thousand on a row
I forbid that any show
Ever the like of her
hye nonny nonny noe.

Face she had of filbert hue
and bosomed like a swan
Back she had of bended ewe,
and waisted by a span.
Hair she had as black as crow
from the head unto the toe
Down down all over her
hye nonny nonny noe.

With her mantle tucked up high
she foddered her flock
So buxom and alluringly
her knee upheld her smock
So nimbly did she use to go
so smooth she danced on tip-tòe,
That all the men were fond of her
hye nonny nonny noe.

She smiled like a holy-day,
  she simpered like the spring
She pranked it like a popinjay,
  and like a swallow sing:
She tripped it like a barren doe,
  she strutted like a gorcrow,
Which made the men so fond of her
  hye nonny nonny noe.

To sport it on the merry down
  to dance the lively hay;
To wrestle for a green gown
  in heat of all the day
Never would she say me no
  yet me thought I had though[1]
Never enough of her
  hye nonny nonny noe.

But gone she is the prettiest lass
  that ever trod on plain.
Whatever hath betide of her
  blame not the shepherd swain
For why she was her own foe,
  and gave herself the overthrow
By being so frank of her
  hye nonny nonny noe.

BEN JONSON

Inviting a Friend to Supper

Tonight, grave sir, both my poor house and I,
  Do equally desire your company:
Not that we think us worthy such a guest,

[1]for all that

But that your worth will dignify our feast,
With those that come; whose grace may make that seem
Something, which, else, could hope for no esteem.
It is the fair acceptance, Sir, creates
The entertainment perfect: not the cates.
Yet shall you have, to rectify your palate,
An olive, capers, or some better salad
Ushering the mutton; with a short-legged hen,
If we can get her, full of eggs, and then,
Lemons, and wine for sauce: to these, a coney
Is not to be despaired of, for our money;
And, though fowl, now, be scarce, yet there are clerks,
The sky not falling, think we may have larks.
I'll tell you of more, and lie, so you will come:
Of partridge, pheasant, wood-cock, of which some
May yet be there; and godwit,[1] if we can:
Knat,[1] rail,[1] and ruff[1] too. How so e'er, my man
Shall read a piece of VIRGIL, TACITUS;
LIVY, or of some better book to us,
Of which we'll speak our minds, amidst our meat;
And I'll profess no verses to repeat:
To this, if ought appear, which I know not of,
That will the pastry, not my paper, show of.
Digestive cheese, and fruit there sure will be;
But that, which most doth take my *Muse*, and me,
Is a pure cup of rich *Canary*-wine,
Which is the *Mermaid's*, now, but shall be mine:
Of which had HORACE, or ANACREON tasted,
Their lives, as do their lines, till now had lasted.
Tobacco, *Nectar*, or the *Thespian* spring,
Are all but LUTHER's beer, to this I sing.
Of this we will sup free, but moderately,
And we will have no *Pooly*,[2] or *Parrot*[2] by;

[1]birds [2]Two well-known informers

Nor shall our cups make any guilty men:
  But, at our parting, we will be, as when
We innocently met. No simple word,
  That shall be uttered at our mirthful board,
Shall make us sad next morning: or affright
  The liberty, that we'll enjoy to-night.

THOMAS WEELKES

Madrigal

Ha ha! ha ha! This world doth pass
  Most merrily I'll be sworn,
For many an honest Indian ass
  Goes for a unicorn.
        Fara diddle dyno,
        This is idle fyno.

Tie hie! tie hie! O sweet delight!
  He tickles this age that can
Call Tullia's ape a marmasyte
  And Leda's goose a swan.
        Fara diddle dyno,
        This is idle fyno.

So so! so so! Fine English days!
  For the false play's no reproach,
For he that doth the coachman praise
  May safely use the coach.
        Fara diddle dyno,
        This is idle fyno.

JOHN DONNE

Epigrams

A Lame Begger

I am unable, yonder begger cries,
To stand, or move; if he say true, hee *lies.*

A Selfe Accuser

Your mistris, that you follow whores, still taxeth you:
'Tis strange that she should thus confesse it, though it be
true.

A Licentious Person

Thy sinnes and haires may no man equall call,
For, as thy sinnes increase, thy haires doe fall.

Klockius

Klockius so deeply hath sworne, ne'er more to come
In bawdie house, that hee dares not goe home.

Raderus

Why this man gelded *Martiall* I muse,
Except himselfe alone his tricks would use,
As *Katherine*, for the Court's sake, put downe Stewes.

Elegie VII

Natures lay Ideot, I taught thee to love,
And in that sophistrie, Oh, thou dost prove
Too subtile: Foole, thou didst not understand
The mystique language of the eye nor hand:

Nor couldst thou judge the difference of the aire
Of sighes, and say, this lies, this sounds despaire:
Nor by the'eye's water call a maladie
Desperately hot, or changing feaverously.
I had not taught thee then, the Alphabet
Of flowers, how they devisedly being set
And bound up, might with speechlesse secrecie
Deliver arrands[1] mutely, and mutually.
Remember since all thy words us'd to bee
To every suitor; *I*,[2] *if my friends agree*;
Since, household charmes, thy husbands name to teach,
Were all the love trickes, that thy wit could reach;
And since, an houres discourse could scarce have made
One answer in thee, and that ill arraid
In broken proverbs, and torne sentences.
Thou art not by so many duties his,
That from the worlds Common having sever'd thee,
Inlaid thee, neither to be seene, nor see,
As mine: who have with amorous delicacies
Refin'd thee' into a blis-full Paradise.
Thy graces and good words my creatures bee;
I planted knowledge and lifes tree in thee,
Which, Oh, shall strangers taste? Must I alas
Frame and enamell Plate, and drinke in Glasse?
Chafe waxe for others seales? breake a colts force
And leave him then, beeing made a ready horse?

Elegie VIII: The Comparison

As the sweet sweat of Roses in a Still,
As that which from chaf'd muskats[1] pores doth trill,
As the Almighty Balme of th'early East,
Such are the sweat drops of my Mistris breast,

[1] errands [2] aye, yes [1] musk-cat (musk-deer)

And on her brow her skin such lustre sets,
They seeme no sweat drops, but pearle coronets.
Ranke sweaty froth thy Mistresse's brow defiles,
Like spermatique issue of ripe menstruous boiles,
Or like the skumme, which, by needs lawlesse law
Enforc'd, Sanserra's[2] starved men did draw
From parboild shooes, and bootes, and all the rest
Which were with any soveraigne fatnes blest,
And like vile lying stones in saffrond tinne,[3]
Or warts, or wheales, they hang upon her skinne.
Round as the world's her head, on every side,
Like to the fatall Ball which fell on Ide,[4]
Or that whereof God had such jealousie,[5]
As, for the ravishing thereof we die.
Thy head is like a rough-hewne statue of jeat,[6]
Where marks for eyes, nose, mouth, are yet scarce set;
Like the first Chaos, or flat seeming face
Of Cynthia, when th'earths shadowes her embrace.
Like Proserpines white beauty-keeping chest,
Or Joves best fortunes urne, is her faire brest.
Thine's like worme eaten trunkes, cloth'd in seals skin,
Or grave, that's dust without, and stinke within.
And like that slender stalke, at whose end stands
The wood-bine quivering, are her armes and hands.
Like rough bark'd elmboughes, or the russet skin
Of men late scourg'd for madnes, or for sinne,
Like Sun-parch'd quarters on the citie gate,
Such is thy tann'd skins lamentable state.
And like a bunche of ragged carrets stand
The short swolne fingers of thy gouty hand.

[2] Sancerra, a Protestant town in France, besieged by Catholics in 1573 [3] false jewels set in tin made to look like gold
[4] ?Jove's thunderbolt, when he seized Ganymede on Mount Ida
[5] Eve's apple [6] jet

Then like the Chymicks masculine equall fire,
Which in the Lymbecks warme wombe doth inspire
Into th'earths worthlesse durt a soule of gold,
Such cherishing heat her best lov'd part doth hold.
Thine's like the dread mouth of a firëd gunne,
Or like hot liquid metalls newly runne
Into clay moulds, or like to that Aetnà
Where round about the grasse is burnt away.
Are not your kisses then as filthy, and more,
As a worme sucking an invenom'd sore?
Doth not thy fearefull hand in feeling quake,
As one which gath'ring flowers, still feares a snake?
Is not your last act harsh, and violent,
As when a Plough a stony ground doth rent?
So kisse good Turtles, so devoutly nice
Are Priests in handling reverent sacrifice,
And such in searching wounds the Surgeon is
As wee, when wee embrace, or touch, or kisse.
Leave her, and I will leave comparing thus,
She, and comparisons are odious.

RICHARD, BISHOP CORBET

A Proper New Ballad, Intituled The Fairies' Farewell; or, God-a-Mercy Will

Farewell rewards and Fairies,
    Good housewives now may say,
For now foul sluts in Dairies
    Do fare as well as they.
And though they sweep their hearths no less
    Than maids were wont to do,
Yet who of late for cleanliness,
    Finds Sixpence in her shoe?

Lament, lament, old Abbeys,
The Fairies lost command;
They did but change Priest's babies,
But some have chang'd your land:
And all your children stol'n from thence
Are now grown puritans;
Who live as changelings ever since
For love of your demains.

At morning and at evening both
You merry were and glad,
So little care of sleep and sloth
These pretty Ladies had;
When Tom came home from labour,
Or Ciss to milking rose,
Then merrily merrily went their Tabor,
And nimbly went their Toes.

Witness those rings and roundelayes
Of theirs, which yet remain,
Were footed in Queen Mary's days
On many a grassy plain;
But since of late, Elizabeth,
And later James came in,
They never danced on any heath
As when the time hath been.

By which we note the Fairies
Were of the old profession;
Their songs were Ave Maries,
Their dances were procession:
But now, alas! they all are dead
Or gone beyond the Seas,
Or further for Religion fled,
Or else they take their ease.

A tell-tale in their company
  They never could endure,
And whoso kept not secretly
  Their mirth was punished sure;
It was a just and Christian deed
  To pinch such black and blue:
O how the Common-wealth doth need
  Such Justices as you!

Now they have left our Quarters
  A Register they have,
Who looketh to their Charters,
  A Man both wise and grave;
A hundred of their merry pranks
  By one that I could name
Are kept in store, con twenty thanks
  To William for the same.

To William Churne of Staffordshire,
  Give laud and praises due;
Who every meal can mend your cheer,
  With tales both old and true;
To William all give audience,
  And pray you for his noddle;
For all the Fairies' evidence
  Were lost, if it were addle.

WILLIAM DRUMMOND

Madrigal

  Like the Idalian queen,
  Her hair about her eyne,
With neck and breast's ripe apples to be seen,

At first glance of the morn
In Cyprus' gardens gathering those fair flow'rs
Which of her blood were born,
I saw, but fainting saw, my paramours.
The Graces naked danced about the place,
The winds and trees amazed
With silence on her gazed,
The flowers did smile, like those upon her face;
And as their aspen stalks those fingers band,
That she might read my case,
A hyacinth I wish'd me in her hand.

ROBERT HERRICK

A Ring Presented to Julia

Julia, I bring
To thee this ring,
Made for thy finger fit;
To show by this,
That our love is
(Or should be) like to it.

Close though it be,
The joint is free:
So when Love's yoke is on,
It must not gall,
Or fret at all
With hard oppression.

But it must play
Still either way;
And be, too, such a yoke,
As not too wide,
To over-slide;
Or be so strait to choke.

So we, who bear,
  This beam, must rear
Ourselves to such a height
  As that the stay
  Of either may
Create the burden light.

  And as this round
  Is nowhere found
To flaw, or else to sever:
  So let our love
  As endless prove;
And pure as gold for ever.

Anacreontic Verse

Brisk methinks I am, and fine,
When I drink my capering wine;
Then to love I do incline,
When I do drink my wanton wine;
And I wish all maidens mine,
When I drink my sprightly wine;
Well I sup, and well I dine,
When I drink my frolic wine;
But I languish, lower, and pine,
When I want my fragrant wine.

His Prayer to Ben Jonson

When I a verse shall make,
  Know I have prayed thee,
For old religion's sake,
  Saint Ben, to aid me.

Make the way smooth for me,
  When I, thy Herrick,
Honouring thee, on my knee
  Offer my lyric.

Candles I'll give to thee,
  And a new altar;
And thou, Saint Ben, shalt be
  Writ in my psalter.

Cherry-ripe

Cherry-ripe, ripe, ripe, I cry,
Full and fair ones; come and buy.
If so be you ask me where
They do grow, I answer: There
Where my Julia's lips do smile;
There's the land, or cherry-isle,
Whose plantations fully show
All the year where cherries grow.

Delight in Disorder

A sweet disorder in the dress
Kindles in clothes a wantonness:
A lawn about the shoulders thrown
Into a fine distractiòn
An erring lace, which here and there
Enthrals the crimson stomacher:
A cuff neglectful, and thereby
Ribbands to flow confusedly:
A winning wave, deserving note,
In the tempestuous petticoat:
A careless shoe-string, in whose tie
I see a wild civility:
Do more bewitch me than when art
Is too precise in every part.

Upon Julia's Clothes

Whenas in silks my Julia goes,
Then, then, methinks, how sweetly flows
The liquefaction of her clothes!

Next, when I cast mine eyes and see
That brave vibration each way free,
– O how that glittering taketh me!

Upon the Nipples of Julia's Breast

Have ye beheld (with much delight)
A red rose peeping through a white?
Or else a cherry (double grac'd)
Within a lily? Centre plac'd?
Or ever mark'd the pretty beam,
A strawberry shows, half drown'd in cream?
Or seen rich rubies blushing through
A pure smooth pearl, and orient too?
So like to this, nay all the rest,
Is each neat niplet of her breast.

JOHN SUCKLING

Out upon It, I Have Lov'd

Out upon it, I have lov'd
   Three whole days together;
And am like to love three more,
   If it prove fair weather.

Time shall moult away his wings
   Ere he shall discover
In the whole wide world again
   Such a constant lover.

But the spite on't is, no praise
  Is due at all to me:
Love with me had made no stays
  Had it any been but she.

Had it any been but she
  And that very face,
There had been at least ere this
  A dozen dozen in her place.

SAMUEL BUTLER

From *Hudibras*

He was in logic a great critic,
Profoundly skill'd in analytic.
He could distinguish, and divide
A hair 'twixt South and South-West side:
On either which he would dispute,
Confute, change hands, and still confute.
He'd undertake to prove by force
Of argument, a man's no horse.
He'd prove a buzzard is no fowl,
And that a lord may be an owl,
A calf an Alderman, a goose a Justice,
And rooks Committee-men, and Trustees;
He'd run in debt by disputation,
And pay with ratiocination.
All this by syllogism, true
In mood and figure, he would do.
For rhetoric he could not ope
His mouth, but out there flew a trope:
And when he happened to break off
I' th' middle of his speech, or cough,
H' had hard words, ready to shew why,
And tell what rules he did it by.

Else when with greatest art he spoke,
You'd think he talk'd like other folk,
For all a rhetorician's rules,
Teach nothing but to name his tools,
His ordinary rate of speech
In loftiness of sound was rich,
A Babylonish dialect,
Which learned pedants much affect.
It was a parti-colour'd dress
Of patch'd and pyball'd languages:
'Twas English cut on Greek and Latin,
Like fustian heretofore on satin.
It had an odd promiscuous tone,
As if h' had talk'd three parts in one.
Which made some think when he did gabble,
Th' had heard three labo'rers of Babel;
Or Cerberus himself pronounce
A leash of languages at once.
This he as volubly would vent
As if his stock would ne'er be spent.
And truly to support that charge
He had supplies as vast and large.
For he could coin or counterfeit
New words with little or no wit:
Words so debas'd and hard, no stone
Was hard enough to touch them on.
And when with hasty noise he spoke 'em,
The ignorant for current took 'em.
That had the orator who once
Did fill his mouth with pebble stones
When he harangu'd, but known his phrase,
He would have us'd no other ways.

. . . .

Beside he was a shrewd philosopher,
And had read every text and gloss over:

What e'er the crabbed'st author hath
He understood b' implicit faith,
What ever sceptic could inquire for;
For every why he had a wherefore;
Knew more than forty of them do,
As far as words and terms could go.
All which he understood by rote,
And as occasion serv'd, would quote;
No matter whether right or wrong:
They might be either said or sung.
His notions fitted things so well,
That which was which he could not tell;
But oftentimes mistook th' one
For th' other, as great clerks have done.
He could reduce all things to acts,
And knew their natures by abstracts,
Where entity and quiddity
The ghosts of defunct bodies fly;
Where truth in person does appear,
Like words congeal'd in northern air.
He knew what's what, and that's as high
As metaphysic wit can fly,
In school divinity as able
As he that hight Irrefragable;
Profound in all the nominal
And real ways beyond them all;
And with as delicate a hand,
Could twist as tough a rope of sand,
And weave fine cobwebs, fit for skull
That's empty when the moon is full;
Such as take lodgings in a head
That's to be let unfurnished.
He could raise scruples dark and nice,
And after solve 'em in a trice:
As if divinity had catch'd
The itch, of purpose to be scratch'd;

Or, like a mountebank, did wound
And stab her self with doubts profound,
Only to shew with how small pain
The sores of faith are cur'd again;
Although by woeful proof we find,
They always leave a scar behind.
He knew the seat of Paradise,
Could tell in what degree it lies:
And as he was dispos'd, could prove it,
Below the moon, or else above it.
What Adam dreamt of when his bride
Came from her closet in his side:
Whether the Devil tempted her
By a High Dutch interpreter:
If either of them had a navel;
Who first made music malleable:
Whether the serpent at the fall
Had cloven feet, or none at all.
All this without a gloss or comment,
He would unriddle in a moment:
In proper terms, such as men smatter
When they throw out and miss the matter.
For his religion it was fit
To match his learning and his wit:
'Twas Presbyterian true blue,
For he was of that stubborn crew
Of errant saints, whom all men grant
To be the true Church Militant:
Such as do build their faith upon
The holy text of pike and gun;
Decide all controversies by
Infallible artillery;
And prove their doctrine orthodox
By apostolic blows and knocks;
Call fire and sword and desolation,
A godly-thorough-Reformation,

Which always must be carry'd on,
And still be doing, never done:
As if religion were intended
For nothing else but to be mended.
A sect, whose chief devotion lies
In odd perverse antipathies;
In falling out with that or this,
And finding somewhat still amiss:
More peevish, cross, and splenetic,
Than dog distract, or monkey sick.
That with more care keep Holy-day
The wrong, than others the right way:
Compound for sins, they are inclin'd to;
By damning those they have no mind to;
Still so perverse and opposite,
As if they worshipp'd God for spite,
The self-same thing they will abhor
One way, and long another for.
Free-will they one way disavow,
Another, nothing else allow.
All piety consists therein
In them, in other men all sin.
Rather than fail, they will defy
That which they love most tenderly,
Quarrel with minc'd pies, and disparage
Their best and dearest friend, plum-porridge;
Fat pig and goose itself oppose,
And blaspheme custard through the nose.
Th' Apostles of this fierce Religion,
Like Mahomet's, were ass and widgeon,
To whom our Knight, by fast instinct
Of wit and temper was so linked,
As if hypocrisy and non-sense
Had got th' advowson of his conscience.

THOMAS JORDAN

The Epicure

Sung by one in the Habit of a Town Gallant

Let us drink and be merry, dance, joke, and rejoice,
With Claret and Sherry, Theorbo and Voice;
The changeable world to our joy is unjust,
All treasure uncertain, then down with your dust.
  In frolic dispose your pounds, shillings and pence,
  For we shall be nothing a hundred years hence.

We'll kiss and be free with Nan, Betty, and Philly,
Have oysters and lobsters, and maids by the belly;
Fish-dinners will make a lass spring like a flea,
Dame Venus (Love's goddess) was born of the sea.
  With her and with Bacchus we'll tickle the sense,
  For we shall be past it a hundred years hence.

Your most beautiful bit that hath all eyes upon her,
That her honesty sells for a hogo[1] of honour;
Whose lightness and brightness doth shine in such splendour
That none but the stars are thought fit to attend her,
  Though now she be pleasant and sweet to the sense,
  Will be damnably mouldy a hundred years hence.

Then why should we turmoil in cares and in fears,
Turn all our tranquillity to sighs and to tears?
Let's eat, drink and play till the worms do corrupt us,
'Tis certain that *post mortem nulla Voluptas.*[2]
  Let's deal with our damsels, that we may from thence
  Have broods to succeed us a hundred years hence . . .

[1]a taint or flavour [2]after death there is no Pleasure

ANDREW MARVELL

The Mower to the Glow-worms

Ye living lamps, by whose dear light
The nightingale does sit so late,
And studying all the summer-night,
Her matchless songs does meditate;

Ye country comets, that portend
No war, nor prince's funeral,
Shining unto no higher end
Than to presage the grass's fall;

Ye glow-worms, whose officious flame
To wand'ring mowers shows the way,
That in the night have lost their aim,
And after foolish fires do stray;

Your courteous lights in vain you waste,
Since Juliana here is come,
For she my mind hath so displac'd
That I shall never find my home.

The Character of Holland

Holland, that scarce deserves the name of land,
As but the off-scouring of the British sand,
And so much earth as was contributèd
By English pilots when they heaved the lead,
Or what by the ocean's slow alluvion fell,
Of shipwrecked cockle and the mussel-shell;
This indigested vomit of the sea
Fell to the Dutch by just propriety.

Glad then, as miners that have found the ore,
They with mad labour fished the land to shore,
And dived as desperately for each piece
Of earth, as if't had been of ambergris;
Collecting anxiously small loads of clay,
Less than what building swallows bear away;
Or than those pills which sordid beetles roll,
Transfusing into them their dunghill soul.
How did they rivet, with gigantic piles,
Thorough the centre their new-catchèd miles,
And to the stake a struggling country bound,
Where barking waves still bait the forcèd ground;
Building their watery Babel far more high
To reach the sea, than those to scale the sky.
Yet still his claim the injured ocean laid,
And oft at leap-frog o'er their steeples played:
As if on purpose it on land had come
To show them what's their *Mare Liberum.*
A daily deluge over them does boil;
The earth and water play at level-coil;
The fish oft-times the burgher dispossessed,
And sat not as a meat but as a guest;
And oft the tritons and the sea-nymphs saw
Whole shoals of Dutch served up for Cabilliau;[1]
Or as they over the new level ranged
For pickled herring, pickled *Heeren* changed.
Nature, it seemed, ashamed of her mistake,
Would throw their land away at duck and drake.
Therefore Necessity, that first made Kings,
Something like Government among them brings.
For as with pygmies who best kills the crane,[2]
Among the hungry he that treasures grain,

[1]cod [2]in Greek mythology the Cranes and the Pygmies were always at war

Among the blind the one-eyed blinkard reigns,
So rules among the drownèd he that drains.
Not who first see the rising sun commands,
But who could first discern the rising lands.
Who best could know to pump an earth so leak
Him they their lord and country's father speak.
To make a bank was a great plot of state;
Invent a shovel and be a magistrate.
Hence some small Dyke-grave[3] unperceived invades
The power, and grows as 'twere a King of Spades.
But for less envy some joint states endures,
Who look like a commission of the sewers.
For these Half-anders, half wet and half dry,
Nor bear strict service, nor pure liberty.
'Tis probable Religion after this
Came next in order; which they could not miss.
How could the Dutch but be converted, when
The Apostles were so many fishermen?
Besides the waters of themselves did rise,
And, as their land, so them did re-baptize.
Though herring for their God few voices missed,
And Poor-John to have been the Evangelist,
Faith, that could never twins conceive before,
Never so fertile, spawned upon this shore:
More pregnant than their Margaret, that laid down
For Hans-in-Kelder of a whole Hans-Town.
Sure when Religion did itself embark,
And from the east would westward steer its ark,
It struck, and splitting on this unknown ground,
Each one thence pillaged the first piece he found:
Hence Amsterdam, Turk-Christian-Pagan-Jew,
Staple of sects and mint of schism grew;
That bank of conscience, where not one so strange

[3] a joke; like a landgrave (a German count)

Opinion but finds credit and exchange.
In vain for Catholics ourselves we bear;
The universal Church is only there.
Nor can Civility there want for tillage,
Where wisely for their court they chose a village.
How fit a title cloths their Governors,
Themselves the hogs[4] as all their subjects boars!
  Let it suffice to give their country fame
That it had one Civilis called by name
Some fifteen hundred and more years ago,
But surely never any that was so.
  See but their mermaids with their tails of fish,
Reeking at church over the chafing-dish.
A vestal turf enshrined in earthenware
Fumes through the loop-holes of a wooden square.
Each to the temple with these altars tend,
But still does place it at her western end,
While the fat steam of female sacrifice
Fills the priest's nostrils and puts out his eyes . . .
  But when such amity at home is showed,
What then are their confederacies abroad?
Let this one courtesy witness all the rest;
When their whole navy they together pressed,
Not Christian captives to redeem from bands,
Or intercept the western golden sands,
No, but all ancient rights and leagues must vail,
Rather than to the English strike their sail;
To whom their weather-beaten province owes
Itself, when as some greater vessel tows
A cock-boat tossed with the same wind and fate;
We buoyed so often up their sinking state.
  Was this *Jus Belli & Pacis?*[5] Could this be
Cause why their burgomaster of the sea

[4]hoog means high in Dutch [5]a Law for War and Peace

Rammed with gunpowder, flaming with brand-wine,
Should raging hold his linstock to the mine?
While, with feigned treaties, they invade by stealth
Our sore new circumcisèd Commonwealth.
  Yet of his vain attempt no more he sees
Than of case-butter shot and bullet-cheese;
And the torn navy staggered with him home,
While the sea laughed itself into a foam,
'Tis true since that (as fortune kindly sports)
A wholesome danger drove us to our ports,
While half their banished keels the tempest tossed,
Half bound at home in prison to the frost:
That ours meantime at leisure might careen,
In a calm winter, under skies serene.
As the obsequious air and waters rest,
Till the dear halcyon hatch out all its nest.
The Commonwealth doth by its losses grow;
And, like its own seas, only ebbs to flow.
Besides that very agitation laves,
And purges out the corruptible waves.
  And now again our armèd *Bucentaur*[6]
Doth yearly their sea-nuptials restore.
And now the hydra of seven provinces
Is strangled by our infant Hercules.
Their tortoise wants its vainly stretchèd neck,
Their navy all our conquest or our wreck:
Or, what is left, their Carthage overcome
Would render fain unto our better Rome . . .
  For now of nothing may our state despair,
Darling of Heaven, and of men the care;
Provided that they be what they have been,
Watchful abroad, and honest still within.

[6]The ship used by the Venetians in the ceremony of 'wedding the sea'

For while our *Neptune* doth a trident shake,
Steeled with those piercing heads, Dean, Monck and Blake,
And while Jove governs in the highest sphere,
Vainly in hell let Pluto domineer.

JOHN DRYDEN

Song from *Marriage-à-la-Mode*

Whil'st *Alexis* lay prest
In her Arms he lov'd best,
With his hands round her neck,
And his head on her breast,
He found the fierce pleasure too hasty to stay,
And his soul in the tempest just flying away.

When *Celia* saw this,
With a sigh, and a kiss,
She cry'd, Oh my dear, I am robb'd of my bliss;
'Tis unkind to your Love, and unfaithfully done,
To leave me behind you, and die all alone.

The Youth, though in haste,
And breathing his last,
In pity dy'd slowly, while she dy'd more fast;
Till at length she cry'd, Now, my dear, now let us go,
Now die, my *Alexis*, and I will die too.

Thus intranc'd they did lie,
Till *Alexis* did try
To recover new breath, that again he might die:
Then often they di'd; but the more they did so,
The Nymph di'd more quick, and the Shepherd more slow.

Song from *An Evening's Love*

After the pangs of a desperate Lover,
When day and night I have sigh'd all in vain,
Ah what a pleasure it is to discover
In her eyes pity, who causes my pain!

When with unkindness our love at a stand is,
And both have punish'd our selves with the pain,
Ah what a pleasure the touch of her hand is,
Ah what a pleasure to press it again!

When the denyal comes fainter and fainter,
And her eyes give what her tongue does deny,
Ah what a trembling I feel when I venture,
Ah what a trembling does usher my joy!

When, with a Sigh, she accords me the blessing,
And her eyes twinkle 'twixt pleasure and pain;
Ah what a joy 'tis beyond all expressing,
Ah what a joy to hear, shall we again!

Prologue to *Secret Love*

He who wrote this, not without pains and thought
From French and English theatres has brought
Th'exactest rules by which a play is wrought:

The unities of action, place, and time;
The scenes unbroken; and a mingled chime
Of Jonson's humour with Corneillë's rhyme.

But while dead colours he with care did lay,
He fears his wit or plot he did not weigh,
Which are the living beauties of a play.

Plays are like towns, which, howe'er fortified
By engineers, have still some weaker side
By the o'er-seen defendant unespied.

And with that art you make approaches now;
Such skilful fury in assaults you show,
That every poet without shame may bow.

Ours therefore humbly would attend your doom,
If, soldier-like, he may have terms to come
With flying colours and with beat of drum.

Mac Flecknoe

All human things are subject to decay,
And, when Fate summons, monarchs must obey:
This Flecknoe found, who, like Augustus, young
Was called to empire and had governed long:
In prose and verse was owned, without dispute
Through all the realms of Nonsense, absolute.
This aged prince now flourishing in peace,
And blest with issue of a large increase,
Worn out with business, did at length debate
To settle the succession of the state;
And pond'ring which of all his sons was fit
To reign, and wage immortal war with wit,
Cried, ''Tis resolved; for Nature pleads that he
Should only rule, who most resembles me;
Shadwell alone my perfect image bears,
Mature in dulness from his tender years;
Shadwell alone of all my sons is he
Who stands confirmed in full stupidity.
The rest to some faint meaning make pretence,
But Shadwell never deviates into sense.

Some beams of wit on other souls may fall,
Strike through and make a lucid interval;
But Shadwell's genuine night admits no ray,
His rising fogs prevail upon the day:
Besides, his goodly fabric fills the eye
And seems designed for thoughtless Majesty:
Thoughtless as Monarch Oaks that shade the plain,
And, spread in solemn state, supinely reign.
Heywood and Shirley were but types of thee,
Thou last great prophet of tautology:
Even I, a dunce of more renown than they,
Was sent before but to prepare thy way:
And coarsely clad in Norwich drugget came
To teach the nations in thy greater name.
My warbling lute, the lute I whilom strung,
When to King John of Portugal I sung,
Was but the prelude to that glorious day,
When thou on silver Thames did'st cut thy way,
With well timed oars before the Royal Barge,
Swelled with the pride of thy celestial charge;
And, big with Hymn, commander of an host,
The like was ne'er in Epsom blankets tost.
Methinks I see the new Arion sail,
The lute still trembling underneath thy nail.
At thy well sharpened thumb from shore to shore
The treble squeaks for fear, the basses roar:
Echoes from Pissing-Alley, Shadwell call,
And Shadwell they resound from Aston hall.
About thy boat the little fishes throng,
As at the morning toast that floats along.
Sometimes as prince of thy harmonious band,
Thou wield'st thy papers in thy threshing hand.
St. André's feet ne'er kept more equal time,
Not ev'n the feet of thy own Psyche's rhyme:
Though they in number as in sense excel,
So just, so like tautology they fell

That, pale with envy, Singleton forswore
The lute and sword which he in triumph bore,
And vowed he ne'er would act Villerius more.'
Here stopped the good old sire; and wept for joy,
In silent raptures of the hopeful boy.
All arguments, but most his plays, persuade
That for anointed dulness he was made.
Close to the walls which fair Augusta bind,
(The fair Augusta much to fears inclin'd)
An ancient fabric raised t'inform the sight,
There stood of yore, and Barbican it hight:
A watch tower once, but now, so fate ordains,
Of all the pile an empty name remains.
From its old ruins brothel-houses rise,
Scenes of lewd loves, and of polluted joys,
Where their vast courts the mother-strumpets keep,
And, undisturb'd by watch, in silence sleep.
Near these a Nursery erects its head,
Where queens are formed, and future heroes bred:
Where unfledged actors learn to laugh and cry,
Where infant punks their tender voices try,
And little Maximins the gods defy.
Great Fletcher never treads in buskins here,
Nor greater Jonson dares in socks appear.
But gentle Simkin just reception finds
Amid this monument of vanished minds;
Pure clinches, the suburbian Muse affords;
And Panton waging harmless war with words.
Here Flecknoe, as a place to fame well known,
Ambitiously designed his Shadwell's throne.
For ancient Decker prophesied long since,
That in this pile should reign a mighty prince,
Born for a scourge of wit, and flail of sense,
To whom true dulness should some Psyches owe,
But worlds of misers from his pen should flow;
Humorists and hypocrites it should produce,

Whole Raymond families and tribes of Bruce.
Now Empress Fame had published the renown
Of Shadwell's coronation through the town.
Rous'd by report of fame, the nations meet,
From near Bun-Hill and distant Watling-Street,
No Persian carpets spread th' imperial way,
But scattered limbs of mangled poets lay;
From dusty shops neglected authors come,
Martyrs of pies and relics of the bum.
Much Heywood, Shirley, Ogleby there lay,
But loads of Shadwell almost choked the way.
Bilked stationers for yeomen stood prepar'd
And Herringman was captain of the guard.
The hoary prince in majesty appear'd,
High on a throne of his own labours rear'd.
At his right hand our young Ascanius sat
Rome's other hope and pillar of the state.
His brows thick fogs, instead of glories, grace,
And lambent dulness played around his face.
As Hannibal did to the altars come,
Sworn by his sire a mortal foe to Rome;
So Shadwell swore, nor should his vow be vain,
That he till death true dulness would maintain;
And, in his father's right, and realm's defence.
Ne'er to have peace with wit, nor truce with sense.
The king himself the sacred unction made,
As king by office, and as priest by trade:
In his sinister hand, instead of ball,
He placed a mighty mug of potent ale;
Love's kingdom to his right he did convey,
At once his sceptre and his rule of sway;
Whose righteous lore the prince had practis'd young
And from whose loins recorded Psyche sprung.
His temples, last, with poppies were o'erspread,
That nodding seemed to consecrate his head:
Just at that point of time, if fame not lie,

On his left hand twelve reverend owls did fly.
So Romulus, 'tis sung, by Tiber's Brook,
Presage of sway from twice six vultures took.
Th'admiring throng loud acclamations make
And omens of his future empire take.
The sire then shook the honours of his head,
And from his brows damps of oblivion shed
Full on the filial dulness: long he stood,
Repelling from his breast the raging god;
At length burst out in his prophetic mood:
'Heavens bless my son, from Ireland let him reign
To far Barbadoes on the western main;
Of his dominion may no end be known,
And greater than his father's be his throne.
Beyond love's kingdom let him stretch his pen';
He paused, and all the people cried 'Amen'.
Then thus continued he, 'My son, advance
Still in new impudence, new ignorance.
Success let others teach, learn thou from me
Pangs without birth, and fruitless industry.
Let Virtuosos in five years be writ;
Yet not one thought accuse thy toil of wit.
Let gentle George in triumph tread the stage,
Make Dorimant betray, and Loveit rage;
Let Cully, Cockwood, Fopling, charm the pit,
And in their folly show the writer's wit.
Yet still thy fools shall stand in thy defence
And justify their author's want of sense.
Let 'em be all by thy own model made
Of dulness and desire no foreign aid,
That they to future ages may be known,
Not copies drawn, but issue of thy own.
Nay let thy men of wit too be the same,
All full of thee, and differing but in name;
But let no alien Sedley interpose
To lard with wit thy hungry Epsom prose.

And when false flowers of rhetoric thou would'st cull,
Trust Nature, do not labour to be dull;
But write thy best, and top; and in each line
Sir Formal's oratory will be thine.
Sir Formal, though unsought, attends thy quill,
And does thy northern dedications fill.
Nor let false friends seduce thy mind to fame,
By arrogating Jonson's hostile name,
Let Father Flecknoe fire thy mind with praise
And Uncle Ogleby thy envy raise.
Thou art my blood, where Jonson has no part:
What share have we in Nature or in Art?
Where did his wit on learning fix a brand
And rail at arts he did not understand?
Where made he love in Prince Nicander's vein,
Or swept the dust in Psyche's humble strain?
Where sold he bargains, "Whip-stich, kiss my arse,"
Promis'd a play and dwindled to a farce?
When did his muse from Fletcher scenes purloin,
As thou whole Etheredge dost transfuse to thine?
But so transfused as oils on waters flow,
His always floats above, thine sinks below.
This is thy province, this thy wondrous way,
New humours to invent for each new play:
This is that boasted bias of thy mind,
By which one way, to dulness, 'tis inclined.
Which makes thy writings lean on one side still,
And, in all changes, that way bends thy will.
Nor let thy mountain belly make pretence
Of likeness: thine's a tympany of sense.
A tun of man in thy large bulk is writ,
But sure thou'rt but a kilderkin of wit.
Like mine thy gentle numbers feebly creep;
Thy tragic muse gives smiles, thy comic sleep.
With whate'er gall thou sett'st thy self to write,
Thy inoffensive satires never bite.

In thy felonious heart though venom lies,
It does but touch thy Irish pen, and dies.
Thy genius calls thee not to purchase fame
In keen iambics, but mild anagram:
Leave writing plays, and choose for thy command
Some peaceful province in acrostic land.
There thou mayest wings display, and altars raise,
And torture one poor word ten thousand ways;
Or, if thou would'st thy different talents suit,
Set thy own songs, and sing them to thy lute.'
He said, but his last words were scarcely heard,
For Bruce and Longvil had a trap prepar'd,
And down they sent the yet declaiming bard,
Sinking he left his drugget robe behind,
Borne upwards by a subterranean wind,
The mantle fell to the young prophet's part
With double portion of his father's art.

ANONYMOUS

Hares on the Mountain

Young women they'll run like hares on the mountain
Young women they'll run like hares on the mountain
If I was but a young man I'd soon go a-hunting
To my right fol diddle dero, to my right fol diddle dee.

Young women they sing like birds in the bushes
Young women they sing like birds in the bushes
If I was a young man I'd go and bang the bushes
To my right fol diddle dero, to my right fol diddle dee.

Young women they'll swim like ducks in the water
Young women they'll swim like ducks in the water
If I was a young man I'd go and swim all after
To my right fol diddle dero, to my right fol diddle dee.

THOMAS FLATMAN

On Marriage

How happy a thing were a wedding,
And a bedding,
If a man might purchase a wife
For a twelvemonth and a day;
But to live with her all a man's life,
For ever and for aye,
Till she grow as grey as a cat,
Good faith, Mr Parson, I thank you for that!

JOHN WILMOT, EARL OF ROCHESTER

Song

Love a woman? You're an ass!
'Tis a most insipid passion
To choose out for your happiness
The silliest part of God's creation.

Let the porter and the groom,
Things designed for dirty slaves,
Drudge in fair Aurelia's womb
To get supplies for age and graves.

Farewell, woman! I intend
Henceforth every night to sit
With my lewd, well-natured friend,
Drinking to engender wit.

Then give me health, wealth, mirth, and wine,
And, if busy love entrenches,
There's a sweet, soft page of mine
Does the trick worth forty wenches.

Impromptu on Charles II

God bless our good and gracious King,
Whose promise none relies on;
Who never said a foolish thing,
Nor ever did a wise one.

A Satire on Charles II

I' th' isle of Britain, long since famous grown
For breeding the best cunts in Christendom,
There reigns, and oh! long may he reign and thrive,
The easiest King and best-bred man alive.
Him no ambition moves to get renown
Like the French fool, that wanders up and down
Serving his people, hazarding his crown.
Peace is his aim, his gentleness is such,
And love he loves, for he loves fucking much.
Nor are his high desires above his strength:
His sceptre and his prick are of a length;
And she may sway the one who plays with th'other,
And make him little wiser than his brother.
Poor prince! thy prick, like thy buffoons at Court,
Will govern thee because it makes thee sport.
'Tis sure the sauciest prick that e'er did swive,
The proudest, peremptoriest prick alive.
Though safety, law, religion, life lay on 't,
'Twould break through all to make its way to cunt.
Restless he rolls about from whore to whore,
A merry monarch, scandalous and poor.
To Carwell, the most dear of all his dears,
The best relief of his declining years,
Oft he bewails his fortune, and her fate:
To love so well, and be beloved so late.

For though in her he settles well his tarse,
Yet his dull, graceless ballocks hang an arse.
This you'd believe, had I but time to tell ye
The pains it cost to poor, laborious Nelly,
Whilst she employs hands, fingers, mouth and thighs
Ere she can raise the member she enjoys.
All monarchs I hate, and the thrones they sit on,
From the hector of France to the cully of Britain.

A Ramble in St James's Park

Much wine had passed, with grave discourse
Of who fucks who, and who does worse
(Such as you usually do hear
From those that diet at the Bear),
When I, who still take care to see
Drunkenness relieved by lechery,
Went out into St James's Park
To cool my head and fire my heart.
But though St James has th'honour on 't,
'Tis consecrate to prick and cunt.
There, by a most incestuous birth,
Strange woods spring from the teeming earth;
For they relate how heretofore,
When ancient Pict began to whore,
Deluded of his assignation
(Jilting, it seems, was then in fashion),
Poor pensive lover, in this place
Would frig upon his mother's face;
Whence rows of mandrakes tall did rise
Whose lewd tops fucked the very skies.
Each imitative branch does twine
In some loved fold of Aretine,
And nightly now beneath their shade
Are buggeries, rapes, and incests made.

Unto this all-sin-sheltering grove
Whores of the bulk[1] and the alcove,
Great ladies, chambermaids and drudges,
The ragpicker, and heiress trudges.
Carmen, divines, great lords, and tailors,
Prentices, poets, pimps, and jailers,
Footmen, fine fops do here arrive,
And here promiscuously they swive.
   Along these hallowed walks it was
That I beheld Corinna pass.
Whoever had been by to see
The proud disdain she cast on me
Through charming eyes, he would have swore
She dropped from heaven that very hour,
Forsaking the divine abode
In scorn of some despairing god.
But mark what creatures women are:
How infinitely vile, when fair!
   Three knights o' th' elbow and the slur[2]
With wriggling tails made up to her.
   The first was of your Whitehall blades,
Near kin t' th' Mother of the Maids;
Graced by whose favour he was able
To bring a friend t' th' Waiters' table,
Where he had heard Sir Edward Sutton
Say how the King loved Banstead mutton;
Since when he'd ne'er be brought to eat
By 's good will any other meat.
   In this, as well as all the rest,
He ventures to do like the best,
But wanting common sense, th'ingredient
In choosing well not least expedient,
Converts abortive imitation
To universal affectation.

[1] shop front   [2] cheating at dice

Thus he not only eats and talks
But feels and smells, sits down and walks
Nay looks, and lives, and loves by rote,
In an old tawdry birthday coat.
  The second was a Grays Inn wit,
A great inhabiter of the pit,
Where critic-like he sits and squints,
Steals pocket handkerchiefs, and hints,
From 's neighbour, and the comedy,
To court, and pay, his landlady.
  The third, a lady's eldest son
Within few years of twenty-one,
Who hopes from his propitious fate,
Against he comes to his estate,
By these two worthies to be made
A most accomplished tearing blade.
  One, in a strain 'twixt tune and nonsense,
Cries, 'Madam, I have loved you long since.
Permit me your fair hand to kiss';
When at her mouth her cunt cries, 'Yes!'
In short, without much more ado,
Joyful and pleased, away she flew,
And with these three confounded asses
From park to hackney coach she passes.
  So a proud bitch does lead about
Of humble curs the amorous rout,
Who most obsequiously do hunt
The savoury scent of salt-swoln cunt.
Some power more patient now relate
The sense of this surprising fate.
Gods! that a thing admired by me
Should fall to so much infamy.
Had she picked out, to rub her arse on,
Some stiff-pricked clown or well-hung parson,
Each job of whose spermatic sluice
Had filled her cunt with wholesome juice,

I the proceeding should have praised
In hope sh' had quenched a fire I raised.
Such natural freedoms are but just:
There's something generous in mere lust.
But to turn damned abandoned jade
When neither head nor tail persuade;
To be a whore in understanding,
A passive pot for fools to spend in!
The devil played booty, sure, with thee
To bring a blot on infamy.
　But why am I, of all mankind,
To so severe a fate designed?
Ungrateful! Why this treachery
To humble, fond, believing me,
Who gave you privilege above
The nice allowances of love?
Did I ever refuse to bear
The meanest part your lust could spare?
When your lewd cunt came spewing home
Drenched with the seed of half the town,
My dram of sperm was supped up after
For the digestive surfeit water.
Full gorgèd at another time
With a vast meal of nasty slime
Which your devouring cunt had drawn
From porters' backs and footmen's brawn,
I was content to serve you up
My ballock-full for your grace cup,
Nor ever thought it an abuse
While you had pleasure for excuse –
You that could make my heart away
For noise and colour, and betray
The secrets of my tender hours
To such knight-errant paramours,
When, leaning on your faithless breast,
Wrapped in security and rest,

Soft kindness all my powers did move,
And reason lay dissolved in love!
  May stinking vapours choke your womb
Such as the men you dote upon!
May your depravèd appetite,
That could in whiffling fools delight,
Beget such frenzies in your mind
You may go mad for the north wind,
And fixing all your hopes upon 't
To have him bluster in your cunt,
Turn up your longing arse t' th' air
And perish in a wild despair!
But cowards shall forget to rant,
Schoolboys to frig, old whores to paint;
The Jesuits' fraternity
Shall leave the use of buggery;
Crab-louse, inspired with grace divine,
From earthly cod to heaven shall climb;
Physicians shall believe in Jesus,
And disobedience cease to please us,
Ere I desist with all my power
To plague this woman and undo her.
But my revenge will best be timed
When she is married that is limed.
In that most lamentable state
I'll make her feel my scorn and hate:
Pelt her with scandals, truth or lies,
And her poor cur with jealousies,
Till I have torn him from her breech,
While she whines like a dog-drawn bitch;
Loathed and despised, kick'd out o' th' Town
Into some dirty hole alone,
To chew the cud of misery
And know she owes it all to me.
  And may no woman better thrive
That dares profane the cunt I swive!

ANONYMOUS

The Maunder's[1] Praise of His Strowling Mort

Doxy, oh! thy glaziers[2] shine
  As glimmar[3] by the Salomon!
No gentry mort[4] hath prats[5] like thine,
  No cove e'er wap'd[6] with such a one.

White thy fambles,[7] red thy gan,[8]
  And thy quarrons[9] dainty is;
Couch a hogshead with me then,
  In the darkmans[10] clip and kiss . . .

WILLIAM WALSH

The Despairing Lover

Distracted with care,
For Phillis the fair,
Since nothing could move her,
Poor Damon, her lover,
Resolves in despair
No longer to languish,
Nor bear so much anguish;
But, mad with his love,
To a precipice goes;
Where, a leap from above
Would soon finish his woes.

  When in rage he came there,
Beholding how steep

[1]beggar [2]eyes [3]fire, light [4]woman [5]buttocks [6]copulated
[7]hands [8]mouth [9]body [10]night

The sides did appear,
And the bottom how deep;
His torments projecting,
And sadly reflecting,
That a lover forsaken
A new love may get;
But a neck, when once broken,
Can never be set;
And, that he could die
Whenever he would;
But, that he could live
But as long as he could;
How grievous soever
The torment might grow,
He scorn'd to endeavour
To finish it so.
But bold, unconcern'd
At thoughts of the pain,
He calmly return'd
To his cottage again.

MATTHEW PRIOR

The Orange

Good people I pray
Throw the Orange away,
'Tis a very sower Fruit, and was first brought in play
When good Judith Wilk[1]
In her pocket brought Milk,
And with Cushings and Warming-pans labour'd to bilk
This same Orange.

[1] Queen Mary's midwife. The story was that the Queen pretended pregnancy and a baby, the son of a tiler, was smuggled in, in a warming pan

When the Army retreats
And the Parliament sits
To Vote our King the true use of his Wits:
'Twill be a sad means
When all he obtains
Is to have his Calves-head[2] dress'd with other mens Brains,
And an Orange.

The sins of his Youth
Made him think of one Truth,
When he spawl'd from his Lungs, and bled twice at the mouth,
That your fresh sort of Food
Does his Carcass more good,
And the damn'd thing that Cur'd his putrefied blood
Was an Orange.

This hopeful young Son
Is surely his own
Because from an Orange it cry'd to be gone
But the Hereticks say
He was got by Dada[3]
For neither King nor the Nuncio dare stay
Near an Orange.

Since *Lewis* was Cut
From his Breech to the Gut,[4]
France fancies an open-arse delicate Fruit;
We wiser than so
Have two strings to our bow
For we've a good Queen that's an open-arse too,
And an Orange.

[2] The Calves-head Club celebrated the execution of Charles I
[3] D'Adda, the Papal Nuncio
[4] Louis XIV was operated on in 1686 for *fistula in ano*

Till *Nanny* writ much
To the Rebels the Dutch
Her Mother, good Woman, ne'er ow'd her a grutch
And the box of the Ear
Made the matter appear,
That the only foul savour the Queen could not bear
Was an Orange.

An honest old Peer[5]
That forsook God last year,
Pull'd off all his Plaisters, and Arm'd for the War;
But his Arms would not do,
And his Aches throbb'd too,
That he wished his own Pox and his Mothers too
On an Orange.

Old Tyburn must groan,
For *Jeffreys*[6] is known
To have perjur'd his Conscience to marry his Son;
And Devonshires cause
Will be try'd by Just Laws,
And *Herbert*[7] must taste a most damnable Sauce
With an Orange.

Lobb, *Penn*,[8] and a score
Of those honest men more
Will find this same Orange exceedingly sowre;
The Queen to be seiz'd
Will be very ill pleas'd,
And so will King Pippin, too dry to be squeez'd
By an Orange.

[5] The Earl of Peterborough, a Catholic convert
[6] The Judge best known for his cruelty in dealing with Monmouth's rebellion (1685) [7] Lord Chief Justice
[8] A Nonconformist and a Quaker, supporters of James II

Mercury and Cupid

In sullen Humour one Day JOVE
Sent HERMES down to IDA's Grove,
Commanding CUPID to deliver
His store of Darts, his total Quiver;
That HERMES shou'd the Weapons break,
Or throw 'em into LETHE's Lake.

HERMES, You know, must do his Errand:
He found his Man, produc'd his Warrant:
CUPID, your Darts – this very Hour –
There's no contending against Power.

How sullen JUPITER, just now
I think I said: and You'll allow,
That CUPID was as bad as He:
Hear but the Youngster's Repartee.

Come Kinsman (said the little God)
Put off your Wings; lay by your Rod;
Retire with Me to yonder Bower;
And rest your self for half an Hour:
'Tis far indeed from hence to Heav'n:
And You fly fast: and 'tis but Seven.
We'll take one cooling Cup of Nectar;
And drink to this Celestial Hector –

He break my Darts, or hurt my Pow'r!
He, LEDA's Swan, and DANAE's Show'r!
Go, bid him his Wife's Tongue restrain;
And mind his Thunder, and his Rain. –
My Darts? O certainly I'll give 'em:
From CLOE's Eyes He shall receive 'em.
There's One, the Best in all my Quiver,
Twang! thro' his very Heart and Liver.

He then shall Pine, and Sigh, and Rave:
Good Lord! What Bustle shall We have!
NEPTUNE must straight be sent to Sea;
And FLORA summon'd twice a-day:
One must find Shells, and t'other Flow'rs,
For cooling Grotts, and frag'rant Bow'rs,
That CLOE may be serv'd in State:
The HOURS must at Her Toilet wait:
Whilst all the reasoning Fools below,
Wonder their Watches go too slow.
LYBS[1] must fly South, and EURUS[2] East,
For Jewels for Her Hair and Breast:
No Matter tho' their cruel Haste
Sink Cities, and lay Forrests waste.
No matter tho' This Fleet be lost;
Or That lie wind-bound on the Coast.

What whisp'ring in my Mother's Ear!
What Care, that JUNO shou'd not hear!
What Work among You Scholar Gods!
PHOEBUS must write Him am'rous Odes:
And Thou, poor Cousin, must compose
His Letters in submissive Prose:
Whilst haughty CLOE, to sustain
The Honour of My mystic Reign,
Shall all his Gifts and Vows disdain;
And laugh at your Old Bully's Pain.

Dear Couz, said HERMES in a Fright,
For Heav'n sake keep Your Darts: Good Night.

[1] South wind [2] South-east wind

A True Maid

No, no: for my Virginity,
When I lose that, says ROSE, I'll dye:
Behind the Elmes, last Night, cry'd DICK,
ROSE, were You not extreamly Sick?[1]

Enigma

By Birth I'm a Slave, yet can give you a Crown;
I dispose of all Honours, my self having none:
I'm obliged by just Maxims to govern my life,
Yet I hang my own Master, and lye with his Wife.
Where Men are a Gaming, I cunningly sneak,
And their Cudgels and Shovels away from 'em take.
Fair Maidens and Ladies I by the Hand get,
And pick off their Diamonds, tho' ne're so well set;
But when I have Comrades, we rob in whole Bands,
Then we presently take off your Lands from your Hands;
But this fury once over, I've such winning Arts,
That you love me much more than you doe your own
Hearts.[1]

Hans Carvel

HANS CARVEL, Impotent and Old,
Married a Lass of LONDON Mould:
Handsome? enough; extreamly Gay:
Lov'd Musick, Company, and Play:

[1] It is an interesting speculation that knowledge of this poem may have inspired Blake to write his famous lyric beginning 'O Rose, thou art sick!'

[1] The Knave of Clubs, or 'Pam at Lantrelu' (according to the Editor of the *Gentleman's Journal* of 1693)

High Flights She had, and Wit at Will:
And so her Tongue lay seldom still:
For in all Visits who but She,
To Argue, or to Repartee?

She made it plain, that Human Passion
Was order'd by Predestination;
That, if weak Women went astray,
Their Stars were more in Fault than They:
Whole Tragedies She had by Heart;
Enter'd into ROXANA's Part:
To Triumph in her Rival's Blood,
The Action certainly was good.
How like a Vine young AMMON curl'd!
Oh that dear Conqu'ror of the World!
She pity'd BETTERTON in Age,
That ridicul'd the God-like Rage.

She, first of all the Town, was told,
Where newest INDIA Things were sold:
So in a Morning, without Bodice,
Slipt sometimes out to Mrs THODY's;
To cheapen Tea, to buy a Screen:
What else cou'd so much Virtue mean?
For to prevent the least Reproach,
BETTY went with Her in the Coach.

But when no very great Affair
Excited her peculiar Care;
She without fail was wak'd at Ten;
Drank Chocolate, then slept again:
At Twelve She rose: with much ado
Her Cloaths were huddl'd on by Two:
Then; Does my Lady Dine at home?
Yes sure; – but is the Colonel come?

Next, how to spend the Afternoon,
And not come Home again too soon;
The Change, the City, or the Play,
As each was proper for the Day;
A Turn in Summer to HYDE-PARK,
When it grew tolerably Dark.

Wife's Pleasure causes Husband's Pain:
Strange Fancies come in HANS's Brain:
He thought of what He did not name;
And wou'd reform; but durst not blame.
At first He therefore Preach'd his Wife
The Comforts of a Pious Life:
Told Her, how Transient Beauty was;
That All must die, and Flesh was Grass:
He bought Her Sermons, Psalms, and Graces;
And doubled down the useful Places.
But still the Weight of worldly Care
Allow'd Her little time for Pray'r:
And CLEOPATRA was read o'er,
While SCOT, and WAKE, and Twenty more,
That teach one to deny one's self,
Stood unmolested on the Shelf.
An untouch'd Bible grac'd her Toilet:
No fear that Thumb of Her's should spoil it.
In short, the Trade was still the same:
The Dame went out: the Colonel came.

What's to be done? poor CARVEL cry'd:
Another Batt'ry must be try'd:
What if to Spells I had Recourse?
'Tis but to hinder something Worse.
The End must justifie the Means:
He only Sins who Ill intends:
Since therefore 'tis to Combat Evil;
'Tis lawful to employ the Devil.

Forthwith the Devil did appear
(For name Him and He's always near)
Not in the Shape in which He plies
At Miss's Elbow when She lies;
Or stands before the Nurs'ry's Doors,
To take the naughty Boy that roars:
But without Sawcer Eye or Claw,
Like a grave Barrister at Law.

HANS CARVEL, lay aside your Grief,
The Devil says: I bring Relief.
Relief, says HANS: pray let me crave
Your Name, sir. – SATAN. – Sir, your Slave:
I did not look upon your Feet:
You'll pardon Me: – Ay, now I see't:
And pray, Sir, when came you from Hell?
Our Friends there, did You leave them well?
All well: but pr'ythee, honest HANS,
(Says SATAN) leave your Complaisance:
The Truth is this: I cannot stay
Flaring in Sun-shine all the Day:
For, *entre Nous*, we Hellish Sprites,
Love more the Fresco of the Nights;
And oft'ner our Receipts convey
In Dreams, than any other Way.
I tell You therefore as a Friend,
E'er Morning dawns, your Fears shall end:
Go then this Ev'ning, Master CARVEL,
Lay down your Fowls, and broach your Barrel;
Let Friends and Wine dissolve your Care;
Whilst I the great Receipt prepare:
To Night I'll bring it, by my Faith;
Believe for once what SATAN saith.

Away went HANS: glad? not a little;
Obey'd the Devil to a Tittle;
Invited Friends some half a Dozen,
The Colonel, and my Lady's Cousin.
The Meat was serv'd; the Bowls were crown'd;
Catches were sung; and Healths went round;
Barbadoes Waters for the Close;
'Till HANS had fairly got his Dose:
The Colonel toasted to the best:
The Dame mov'd off, to be undrest:
The Chimes went Twelve: the Guests withdrew:
But when, or how, HANS hardly knew.
Some Modern Anecdotes aver,
He nodded in his Elbow Chair;
From thence was carry'd off to Bed:
JOHN held his Heels, and NAN his Head.
My Lady was disturb'd: new Sorrow!
Which HANS must answer for to Morrow.

In Bed then view this happy Pair;
And think how HYMEN Triumph'd there.
HANS, fast asleep, as soon as laid:
The Duty of the Night unpaid:
The waking Dame, with Thoughts opprest,
That made Her Hate both Him and Rest:
By Such a Husband, such a Wife!
'Twas ACME's and SEPTIMIUS's Life.
The Lady sigh'd: the Lover snor'd:
The punctual Devil kept his Word:
Appear'd to honest HANS again;
But not at all by Madam seen:
And giving Him a Magick Ring,
Fit for the Finger of a King;
Dear HANS, said He, this Jewel take,
And wear it long for SATAN's Sake:

'Twill do your Business to a Hair:
For long as you this Ring shall wear,
As sure as I look over LINCOLN,
That ne'er shall happen which You think on.

HANS took the Ring with Joy extream;
(All this was only in a Dream)
And thrusting it beyond his Joint,
'Tis done, He cry'd: I've gain'd my Point. –
What Point, said She, You ugly Beast?
You neither give Me Joy nor Rest:
'Tis done. – What's done, You Drunken Bear?
You've thrust your Finger God knows where.

A Paraphrase from the French

In grey-haired Celia's withered arms
  As mighty Louis lay,
She cried 'If I have any charms,
  My dearest, let's away!
For you, my love, is all my fear,
  Hark how the drums do rattle;
Alas, sir! what should you do here
  In dreadful day of battle?
Let little Orange stay and fight,
  For danger's his diversion;
The wise will think you in the right
  Not to expose your person,
Nor vex your thoughts how to repair
  The ruins of your glory:
You ought to leave so mean a care
  To those who pen your story.
Are not Boileau and Corneille paid
  For panegyric writing?
They know how heroes may be made,
  Without the help of fighting.

When foes too saucily approach,
'Tis best to leave them fairly;
Put six good horses in your coach,
And carry me to Marly.
Let Boufflers, to secure your fame,
Go take some town, or buy it;
Whilst you, great sir, at Notre Dame,
Te Deum sing in quiet!'

JONATHAN SWIFT

Mary the Cook-maid's Letter to Doctor Sheridan

Well; if ever I saw such another man, since my mother bound my head,
You a gentleman! Marry come up, I wonder where you were bred?
I am sure such words do not become a man of your cloth,
I would not give such language to a dog, faith and troth.
Yes, you called my master a knave, Fie. Mr Sheridan, 'tis a shame
For a parson, who should know better things, to come out with such a name.

Knave in your teeth, Mr Sheridan, 'tis both a shame and a sin,
And the dean my master is an honester man than you and all your kin:
He has more goodness in his little finger, than you have in your whole body,
My master is a parsonable man, and not a spindle-shanked hoddy doddy.
And now whereby I find you would fain make an excuse,
Because my master one day in anger called you goose.
Which, and I am sure I have been his servant four years since October,

And he never called me worse than sweetheart drunk or sober:
Not that I know his Reverence was ever concerned to my Knowledge,
Though you and your come-rogues keep him out so late in your College.

You say you will eat grass on his grave: a Christian eat grass!
Whereby you now confess yourself to be a goose or an ass:
But that's as much as to say, that my master should die before ye,
Well, well, that's as God pleases, and I don't believe that's a true story,
And so say I told you so, and you may go tell my master; what care I?
And I don't care who knows it, 'tis all one to Mary.
Everybody knows, that I love to tell truth and shame the Devil,
I am but a poor servant, but I think gentlefolks should be civil.

Besides, you found fault with our vittles one day that you was here,
I remember it was upon a Tuesday, of all days in the year.
And Saunders the man says, you are always jesting and mocking,
Mary (said he, one day as I was mending my master's stocking,)
My master is so fond of that minister that keeps the school;
I thought my master a wise man, but that man makes him a fool.
Saunders, said I, I would rather than a quart of ale,
He would come into our kitchen, and I would pin a dishclout to his tail.

And now I must go, and get Saunders to direct this letter,
For I write but a sad scrawl, but my sister Marget she writes better.
Well, but I must run and make the bed before my master comes from prayers,

And see now, it strikes ten, and I hear him coming upstairs:
Whereof I could say more to your verses, if I could write written
hand,
And so I remain in a civil way, your servant to command,
Mary.

Verses on the Death of Dr Swift

Written by Himself: Nov. 1731

The time is not remote, when I
Must by the course of nature die:
When I foresee my special friends,
Will try to find their private ends:
Though it is hardly understood,
Which way my death can do them good;
Yet, thus methinks, I hear them speak:
'See, how the Dean begins to break;
Poor gentleman, he droops apace,
You plainly find it in his face:
That old vertigo in his head
Will never leave him, till he's dead:
Besides, his memory decays,
He recollects not what he says;
He cannot call his friends to mind;
Forgets the place where last he din'd:
Plies you with stories o'er and o'er,
He told them fifty times before.
How does he fancy we can sit,
To hear his out-of-fashion'd wit?
But he takes up with younger folks,
Who for his wine will bear his jokes:
Faith, he must make his stories shorter,
Or change his comrades once a quarter:
In half the time, he talks them round;
There must another set be found.

'For poetry, he's past his prime,
He takes an hour to find a rhyme:
His fire is out, his wit decay'd,
His fancy sunk, his Muse a jade.
I'd have him throw away his pen; –
But there's no talking to some men.'

And then their tenderness appears,
By adding largely to my years:
'He's older than he would be reckon'd,
And well remembers Charles the Second.

'He hardly drinks a pint of wine;
And that, I doubt, is no good sign.
His stomach too begins to fail:
Last year we thought him strong and hale;
But now, he's quite another thing;
I wish he may hold out till spring.'
Then hug themselves, and reason thus:
'It is not yet so bad with us.'
In such a case they talk in tropes,
And, by their fears express their hopes:
Some great misfortune to portend,
No enemy can match a friend;
With all the kindness they profess,
The merit of a lucky guess,
(When daily Howd'y's come of course,
And servants answer; 'Worse and worse')
Would please them better than to tell,
That, 'God be prais'd, the Dean is well.'
Then he who prophesied the best,
Approves his foresight to the rest:
'You know, I always fear'd the worst,
And often told you so at first:'
He'd rather choose that I should die,
Than his prediction prove a lie.

Not one foretells I shall recover;
But all agree to give me over.

. . . .

Behold the fatal day arrive!
'How is the Dean?' 'He's just alive.'
Now the departing prayer is read;
'He hardly breathes.' 'The Dean is dead.'
Before the passing-bell begun,
The news through half the town has run.
'O, may we all for death prepare!
What has he left? and who's his heir?
I know no more than what the news is,
'Tis all bequeath'd to public uses.
To public use! A perfect whim!
What had the public done for him!
Mere envy, avarice, and pride!
He gave it all: – but first he died.
And had the Dean, in all the nation,
No worthy friend, no poor relation?
So ready to do strangers good,
Forgetting his own flesh and blood?'

Now Grub-Street wits are all employ'd;
With elegies the town is cloy'd;
Some paragraph in every paper,
To curse the Dean, or bless the Drapier.

The doctors, tender of their fame,
Wisely on me lay all the blame:
'We must confess his case was nice;
But he would never take advice:
Had he been rul'd, for aught appears,
He might have liv'd these twenty years:
For when we open'd him we found,
That all his vital parts were sound.'

From Dublin soon to London spread,
'Tis told at court, 'The Dean is dead.'
Kind Lady Suffolk in the spleen,
Runs laughing up to tell the Queen.
The Queen, so gracious, mild, and good,
Cries, 'Is he gone! 'tis time he should.
He's dead you say; why let him rot;
I'm glad the medals were forgot.
I promised him, I own; but when?
I only was the Princess then;
But now, as Consort of the King,
You know, 'tis quite a different thing.'
. . . .

Now Curll his shop from rubbish drains;
Three genuine tomes of Swift's remains.
And then to make them pass the glibber,
Revis'd by Tibbalds, Moore, and Cibber.
He'll treat me as he does my betters.
Publish my Will, my Life, my Letters.
Revive the libels born to die;
Which Pope must bear, as well as I.

Here shift the scene, to represent
How those I love, my death lament.
Poor Pope will grieve a month, and Gay
A week; and Arbuthnot a day.
St John himself will scarce forbear,
To bite his pen, and drop a tear.
The rest will give a shrug and cry,
'I'm sorry; but we all must die.'
Indifference clad in Wisdom's guise,
All fortitude of mind supplies:
For how can stony bowels melt,
In those who never pity felt;
When *we* are lash'd, *they* kiss the rod,
Resigning to the will of God.

The fools, my juniors by a year,
Are tortur'd with suspense and fear.
Who wisely thought my age a screen,
When death approached, to stand between:
The screen removed, their hearts are trembling,
They mourn for me without dissembling.

My female friends, whose tender hearts
Have better learn'd to act their parts,
Receive the news in doleful dumps,
'The Dean is dead, (and what is trumps?)
Then, Lord have mercy on his soul.
(Ladies, I'll venture for the vole.)
Six deans they say must bear the pall.
(I wish I knew what king to call.)
Madam, your husband will attend
The funeral of so good a friend.
No madam, 'tis a shocking sight,
And he's engag'd to-morrow night!
My Lady Club would take it ill,
If he should fail her at quadrille.
He lov'd the Dean. (I lead a heart.)
But dearest friends, they say, must part.
His time was come; he ran his race;
We hope he's in a better place.'

Why do we grieve that friends should die?
No loss more easy to supply.
One year is past; a different scene!
No further mention of the Dean;
Who now, alas, no more is missed,
Than if he never did exist.
Where's now the favourite of Apollo?
Departed; and his Works must follow:
Must undergo the common fate;
His kind of wit is out of date.

Some country squire to Lintot goes,
Inquires for Swift in verse and prose:
Says Lintot, 'I have heard the name:
He died a year ago.' 'The same.'
He searcheth all his shop in vain;
'Sir, you may find them in Duck Lane:
I sent them with a load of books,
Last Monday to the pastry-cook's.
To fancy they could live a year!
I find you're but a stranger here.
The Dean was famous in his time;
And had a kind of knack at rhyme;
His way of writing now is past;
The town has got a better taste:
I keep no antiquated stuff;
But, spick and span I have enough.
Pray, do but give me leave to shew 'em;
Here's Colley Cibber's birthday poem.'

. . . .

Suppose me dead; and then suppose
A club assembled at the Rose;
Where from discourse of this and that,
I grow the subject of their chat:
And, while they toss my name about,
With favour some, and some without;
One quite indifferent in the cause,
My character impartial draws:

'The Dean, if we believe report,
Was never ill received at court:
As for his works in verse and prose,
I own myself no judge of those:
Nor can I tell what critics thought 'em;
But this I know, all people bought 'em;
As with a moral view design'd
To cure the vices of mankind:

His vein, ironically grave,
Expos'd the fool, and lash'd the knave:
To steal a hint was never known,
But what he writ was all his own.

'He never thought an honour done him,
Because a duke was proud to own him:
Would rather slip aside, and choose
To talk with wits in dirty shoes:
Despis'd the fools with stars and garters,
So often seen caressing Chartres.
He never courted men in station,
Nor persons had in admiration;
Of no man's greatness was afraid,
Because he sought for no man's aid.
Though trusted long in great affairs,
He gave himself no haughty airs:
Without regarding private ends,
Spent all his credit for his friends:
And only chose the wise and good;
No flatterers; no allies in blood;
But succour'd virtue in distress,
And seldom fail'd of good success;
As numbers in their hearts must own,
Who, but for him, had been unknown.

'With princes kept a due decorum,
But never stood in awe before 'em:
He follow'd David's lesson just,
In princes never put thy trust.
And, would you make him truly sour;
Provoke him with a slave in power:
The Irish senate, if you nam'd,
With what impatience he declaim'd!
Fair LIBERTY was all his cry;
For her he stood prepar'd to die;

For her he boldly stood alone;
For her he oft expos'd his own.
Two kingdoms, just as faction led,
Had set a price upon his head;
But not a traitor could be found,
To sell him for six hundred pound.

'Had he but spar'd his tongue and pen,
He might have rose like other men:
But power was never in his thought;
And wealth he valu'd not a groat:
Ingratitude he often found,
And pitied those who meant the wound:
But kept the tenour of his mind,
To merit well of humankind:
Nor made a sacrifice of those
Who still were true, to please his foes.
He labour'd many a fruitless hour
To reconcile his friends in power;
Saw mischief by a faction brewing,
While they pursu'd each other's ruin.
But, finding vain was all his care,
He left the court in mere despair.

'And, oh! how short are human schemes!
Here ended all our golden dreams.
What St John's skill in state affairs,
What Ormond's valour, Oxford's cares,
To save their sinking country lent,
Was all destroy'd by one event.
Too soon that precious life was ended,
On which alone, our weal depended.

. . . .

'Perhaps I may allow, the Dean
Had too much satire in his vein;

And seem'd determin'd not to starve it,
Because no age could more deserve it.
Yet, malice never was his aim;
He lash'd the vice but spar'd the name.
No individual could resent,
Where thousands equally were meant.
His satire points at no defect,
But what all mortals may correct;
For he abhorred that senseless tribe,
Who call it humour when they gibe:
He spar'd a hump, or crooked nose,
Whose owners set not up for beaux.
True genuine dulness mov'd his pity,
Unless it offer'd to be witty.
Those, who their ignorance confessed,
He ne'er offended with a jest;
But laughed to hear an idiot quote
A verse from Horace, learn'd by rote.

'He knew a hundred pleasant stories,
With all the turns of Whigs and Tories:
Was cheerful to his dying day,
And friends would let him have his way.

'He gave the little wealth he had,
To build a house for fools and mad:
And showed by one satiric touch,
No nation wanted it so much:
That kingdom he hath left his debtor,
I wish it soon may have a better.'

JOHN GAY

Fable: The Mother, the Nurse, and the Fairy

Give me a son. The blessing sent,
Were ever parents more content?
How partial are their doting eyes!
No child is half so fair and wise.
   Waked to the morning's pleasing care,
The Mother rose, and sought her heir.
She saw the Nurse, like one possess'd,
With wringing hands, and sobbing breast;
   Sure some disaster hath befell:
Speak, Nurse; I hope the boy is well.
   Dear Madam, think not me to blame;
Invisible the Fairy came:
Your precious babe is hence convey'd,
And in the place a changeling laid.
Where are the father's mouth and nose?
The mother's eyes as black as sloes?
See here, a shocking awkward creature,
That speaks a fool in ev'ry feature.
   The woman's blind, the Mother cries;
I see wit sparkle in his eyes.
   Lord! madam, what a squinting leer!
No doubt the Fairy hath been here.
   Just as she spoke, a pigmy sprite
Pops through the key-hole, swift as light;
Perch'd on the cradle's top he stands,
And thus her folly reprimands:
   Whence sprung the vain conceited lie,
That we the world with fools supply?
What! give our sprightly race away,
For the dull helpless sons of clay!
Besides, by partial fondness shown,
Like you we dote upon our own.

Where yet was ever found a mother,
Who'd give her booby for another?
And should we change with human breed,
Well might we pass for fools indeed.

Fable: The Poet and the Rose

I hate the man who builds his name
On ruins of another's fame.
Thus prudes, by characters o'erthrown,
Imagine that they raise their own.
Thus scribblers, covetous of praise,
Think slander can transplant the bays.
Beauties and bards have equal pride,
With both all rivals are decried.
Who praises Lesbia's eyes and feature,
Must call her sister awkward creature;
For the kind flatt'ry's sure to charm,
When we some other nymph disarm.
  As in the cool of early day
A Poet sought the sweets of May,
The garden's fragrant breath ascends,
And ev'ry stalk with odour bends.
A rose he pluck'd, he gazed, admired,
Thus singing as the Muse inspired:

Go, Rose, my Chloe's bosom grace;
  How happy should I prove;
Might I supply that envied place
  With never-fading love!
There, Phoenix-like, beneath her eye,
Involved in fragrance, burn and die!

Know, hapless flower, that thou shalt find
  More fragrant roses there;

I see thy with'ring head reclined
  With envy and despair!
One common fate we both must prove;
You die with envy, I with love.

  Spare your comparisons, replied
An angry Rose who grew beside.
Of all mankind, you should not flout us;
What can a Poet do without us?
In ev'ry love-song roses bloom,
We lend you colour and perfume.
Does it to Chloe's charms conduce,
To found her praise on our abuse?
Must we, to flatter her, be made
To wither, envy, pine, and fade?

Newgate's Garland

Being A New Ballad showing how Mr Jonathan Wild's[1] *throat was cut from ear to ear with a penknife by Mr Blake, alias Blueskin, the bold highwayman, as he stood at his Trial in the Old Bailey, 1725.*

Ye gallants of Newgate, whose fingers are nice,
In diving in pockets, or cogging of dice,
Ye sharpers so rich, who can buy off the noose,
Ye honester poor rogues, who die in your shoes,
  Attend and draw near,
  Good news you shall hear,
  How Jonathan's throat was cut from ear to ear;
How Blueskin's sharp penknife hath set you at ease,
And every man round me may rob if he please.

[1] The original of Peachum in *The Beggar's Opera*. He survived Blueskin's attack but was hanged on 24 May 1725

When to the Old Bailey this Blueskin was led,
He held up his hand, his indictment was read,
Loud rattled his chains, near him Jonathan stood,
For full forty pounds was the price of his blood.
  Then hopeless of life
  He drew his penknife,
  And made a sad widow of Jonathan's wife.
But forty pounds paid her, her grief shall appease,
And every man round me may rob if he please.

Some say they are courtiers of highest renown,
Who steal the king's gold, and leave him but a crown;
Some say there are peers, and parliament-men,
Who meet once a year to rob courtiers again;
  Let them all take their swing,
  To pillage the king,
  And get a blue ribbon instead of a string.
Now Blueskin's sharp penknife hath set you at ease,
And every man round me may rob if he please.

Knaves of old, to hide guilt by their cunning inventions,
Call'd briberies grants, and plain robberies pensions;
Physicians and lawyers (who take their degrees
To be learnèd rogues) call'd their pilfering fees;
  Since this happy day,
  Now ev'ry man may
  Rob (as safe as in office) upon the highway.
For Blueskin's sharp penknife hath set you at ease,
And every man round me may rob if he please.

Some cheat in the customs, some rob the excise,
But he who robs both is esteemèd most wise.
Church-wardens, too prudent to hazard the halter,
As yet only venture to steal from the altar:

But now to get gold,
They may be more bold,
And rob on the highway, since Jonathan's cold.
For Blueskin's sharp penknife hath set you at ease,
And every man round me may rob if he please.

Some by public revenues which pass'd through their hands
Have purchased clean houses and bought dirty lands;
Some to steal from a charity think it no sin,
Which at home (says the proverb) does always begin.
But if ever you be
Assign'd a trustee
Treat not orphans like Masters of the Chancery.
But take the highway and more honestly seize,
For every man round me may rob if he please.

What a pother has here been with Wood and his brass
Who would modestly make a few halfpennies pass.
The patent is good, and the precedent's old.
For Diomede changed his copper for gold.
But if Ireland despise
Thy new halfpennies,
With more safety to rob on the road I advise;
For Blueskin's sharp penknife hath set thee at ease,
And every man round me may rob if he please.

Songs from Operas

I

Through all the employments of life,
Each neighbour abuses his brother;
Whore and rogue they call husband and wife;
All professions be-rogue one another.

The priest calls the lawyer a cheat;
 The lawyer be-knaves the divine;
And the statesman, because he's so great,
 Thinks his trade is as honest as mine.

from *The Beggar's Opera*

2

'Tis woman that seduces all mankind!
 By her we first were taught the wheedling
  arts:
Her very eyes can cheat; when most she's kind,
 She tricks us of our money, with our hearts.
For her, like wolves by night, we roam for prey,
 And practise every fraud to bribe her charms;
For suits of love, like law, are won by pay,
 And beauty must be fee'd into our arms.

from *The Beggar's Opera*

3

If any wench Venus' girdle wear,
 Though she be never so ugly;
Lilies and roses will quickly appear,
 And her face look wond'rously smugly.
Beneath the left ear so fit but the cord
 (A rope so charming a zone is!)
The youth in his cart hath the air of a lord,
 And we cry, There dies an Adonis.

from *The Beggar's Opera*

4

Macheath: Were I laid on Greenland's coast,
 And in my arms embraced my lass,
Warm amidst eternal frost,
 Too soon the half-year's night would pass.

Polly: Were I sold on Indian soil,
  Soon as the burning day was closed,
I could mock the sultry toil,
  When on my charmer's breast reposed.

Macheath: And I would love you all the day,
Polly: Every night would kiss and play;
Macheath: If with me you'd fondly stray
Polly: Over the hills and far away.

from *The Beggar's Opera*

5

Thus I stand like the Turk, with his doxies around,
From all sides their glances his passion confound;
For black, brown and fair, his inconstancy burns,
And the different beauties subdue him by turns:
Each calls forth her charms, to provoke his desires,
Though willing to all, with but one he retires;
But think of this maxim, and put off all sorrow,
The wretch of to-day may be happy to-morrow.

from *The Beggar's Opera*

6

Woman's like the flatt'ring ocean,
  Who her pathless ways can find?
Every blast directs her motion;
  Now she's angry, now she's kind.
What a fool's the vent'rous lover,
  Whirl'd and toss'd by every wind!
Can the bark the port recover
  When the silly pilot's blind?

from *Polly*

7

Honour plays a bubble's part
  Ever bilk'd and cheated;
Never in ambition's heart,
  Int'rest there is seated.
Honour was in use of yore,
  Though by want attended:
Since 'twas talked of, and no more;
  Lord, how times are mended!

from *Polly*

8

Soldier, think before you marry;
  If your wife the camp attends,
You but a convenience carry,
  For (perhaps) a hundred friends.
If at home she's left in sorrow,
  Absence is convenient too;
Neighbours now and then may borrow
  What is of no use to you.

from *Achilles*

My Own Epitaph

Life is a jest; and all things show it,
I thought so once; but now I know it.

ANONYMOUS

O No, John!

On yonder hill there stands a creature;
Who she is I do not know.
I'll go court her for her beauty,
She must answer yes or no.
  O no, John! No, John! No, John! No!

On her bosom are bunches of posies,
On her breast where flowers grow;
If I should chance to touch that posy,
She must answer yes or no.
  O no, John! No, John! No, John! No!

Madam I am come for to court you,
If your favour I can gain;
If you will but entertain me,
Perhaps then I might come again.
  O no, John! No, John! No, John! No!

My husband was a Spanish captain,
Went to sea a month ago;
The very last time we kissed and parted,
Bid me always answer no.
  O no, John! No, John! No, John! No!

Madam in your face is beauty,
In your bosom flowers grow;
In your bedroom there is pleasure,
Shall I view it, yes or no?
  O no, John! No, John! No, John! No!

Madam shall I tie your garter,
Tie it a little above your knee;
If my hand should slip a little farther,
Would you think it amiss of me?
  O no, John! No, John! No, John! No!

My love and I went to bed together,
There we lay till cocks did crow;
Unclose your arms my dearest jewel,
Unclose your arms and let me go.
  O no, John! No, John! No, John! No!

ALEXANDER POPE

The Rape of the Lock

Nolueram, Belinda, tuos violare capillos;
Sed juvat, hoc precibus me tribuisse tuis.

MART.

Canto I

What dire offence from am'rous causes springs,
What mighty contests rise from trivial things,
I sing – This verse to CARYL,[1] Muse! is due:
This, ev'n Belinda may vouchsafe to view:
Slight is the subject, but not so the praise,
If She inspire, and He approve my lays.
Say what strange motive, Goddess! could compel
A well-bred Lord t'assault a gentle Belle?
Oh say what stranger cause, yet unexplor'd,
Could make a gentle Belle reject a Lord?
In tasks so bold, can little men engage,
And in soft bosoms dwells such mighty Rage?
Sol thro' white curtains shot a tim'rous ray,
And ope'd those eyes that must eclipse the day:
Now lap-dogs give themselves the rousing shake,
And sleepless lovers, just at twelve, awake:
Thrice rung the bell, the slipper knock'd the ground,
And the press'd watch return'd a silver sound.
Belinda still her downy pillow prest,
Her guardian SYLPH prolong'd the balmy rest:
'Twas he had summon'd to her silent bed
The morning-dream that hover'd o'er her head.
A Youth more glitt'ring than a Birth-night Beau,
(That ev'n in slumber caus'd her cheek to glow)

[1] The gentleman who suggested the subject to Pope, an actual feud between two noble families

Seem'd to her ear his winning lips to lay,
And thus in whispers said, or seem'd to say.
Fairest of mortals, thou distinguish'd care
Of thousand bright Inhabitants of Air!
If e'er one Vision touch'd thy infant thought,
Of all the Nurse and all the Priest have taught;
Of airy Elves by moonlight shadows seen,
The silver token, and the circled green,
Or virgins visited by Angel-pow'rs,
With golden crowns and wreaths of heav'nly flow'rs;
Hear and believe! thy own importance know,
Nor bound thy narrow views to things below.
Some secret truths, from Learnèd Pride conceal'd,
To Maids alone and Children are reveal'd:
What tho' no credit doubting Wits may give?
The Fair and Innocent shall still believe.
Know then, unnumber'd Spirits round thee fly,
The light Militia of the lower sky;
These, tho' unseen, are ever on the wing,
Hang o'er the Box, and hover round the Ring:
Think what an equipage thou hast in Air,
And view with scorn two Pages and a Chair.
As now your own, our beings were of old,
And once inclos'd in Woman's beauteous mold;
Thence, by a soft transition, we repair
From earthly Vehicles to these of air.
Think not, when Woman's transient breath is fled,
That all her vanities at once are dead;
Succeeding vanities she still regards,
And tho' she plays no more, o'erlooks the cards.
Her joy in gilded Chariots, when alive,
And love of Ombre, after death survive.
For when the Fair in all their pride expire,
To their first Elements their Souls retire:
The Sprites of fiery Termagants in Flame
Mount up, and take a Salamander's name.

Soft yielding minds to Water glide away,
And sip, with Nymphs, their elemental Tea.
The graver Prude sinks downward to a Gnome,
In search of mischief still on Earth to roam.
The light Coquettes in Sylphs aloft repair,
And sport and flutter in the fields of Air.
   Know farther yet; whoever fair and chaste
Rejects mankind, is by some Sylph embrac'd:
For Spirits, freed from mortal laws, with ease
Assume what sexes and what shapes they please.
What guards the purity of melting Maids,
In courtly balls, and midnight masquerades,
Safe from the treach'rous friend, the daring spark,
The glance by day, the whisper in the dark,
When kind occasion prompts their warm desires,
When music softens, and when dancing fires?
'Tis but their Sylph, the wise Celestials know,
Tho' Honour is the word with Men below.
   Some nymphs there are, too conscious of their face,
For life predestin'd to the Gnomes' embrace.
These swell their prospects and exalt their pride,
When offers are disdain'd, and love deny'd.
Then gay Idëas crowd the vacant brain,
While Peers and Dukes, and all their sweeping train,
And Garters, Stars, and Coronets appear,
And in soft sounds, Your Grace salutes their ear.
'Tis these that early taint the female soul,
Instruct the eyes of young Coquettes to roll,
Teach Infant-cheeks a bidden blush to know,
And little hearts to flutter at a Beau.
   Oft, when the world imagine women stray,
The Sylphs thro' mystic mazes guide their way,
Thro' all the giddy circle they pursue,
And old impertinence expel by new.
What tender maid but must a victim fall
To one man's Treat, but for another's Ball?

When Florio speaks, what virgin could withstand,
If gentle Damon did not squeeze her hand?
With varying vanities, from ev'ry part,
They shift the moving Toyshop of their heart;
Where wigs with wigs, with sword-knots
  sword-knots strive,
Beaux banish beaux, and coaches coaches drive.
This erring mortals Levity may call,
Oh blind to truth! the Sylphs contrive it all.
  Of these am I, who thy protection claim,
A watchful sprite, and Ariel is my name.
Late, as I rang'd the crystal wilds of air,
In the clear Mirror of thy ruling Star
I saw, alas! some dread event impend,
Ere to the main this morning sun descend,
But heav'n reveals not what, or how, or where:
Warn'd by the Sylph, oh pious maid, beware!
This to disclose is all thy guardian can:
Beware of all, but most beware of Man!
  He said; when Shock, who thought she slept too
  long,
Leap'd up, and wak'd his mistress with his tongue.
'Twas then Belinda, if report say true,
Thy eyes first open'd on a Billet-doux;
Wounds, Charms, and Ardors, were no sooner read,
But all the Vision vanish'd from thy head.
  And now, unveil'd, the Toilet stands display'd,
Each silver Vase in mystic order laid.
First, rob'd in white, the Nymph intent adores,
With head uncover'd, the Cosmetic pow'rs.
A heav'nly Image in the glass appears,
To that she bends, to that her eyes she rears;
Th' inferior Priestess, at her altar's side,
Trembling, begins the sacred rites of Pride.
Unnumber'd treasures ope at once, and here
The various off'rings of the world appear;

From each she nicely culls with curious toil,
And decks the Goddess with the glitt'ring spoil.
This casket India's glowing gems unlocks,
And all Arabia breathes from yonder box.
The Tortoise here and Elephant unite,
Transform'd to Combs, the speckled, and the white.
Here files of Pins extend their shining rows,
Puffs, Powders, Patches, Bibles, Billet-doux.
Now awful Beauty puts on all its arms;
The fair each moment rises in her charms,
Repairs her smiles, awakens ev'ry grace,
And calls forth all the wonders of her face;
Sees by degrees a purer blush arise,
And keener lightnings quicken in her eyes.
The busy Sylphs surround their darling care,
These set the head, and those divide the hair,
Some fold the sleeve, whilst others plait the gown;
And Betty's prais'd for labours not her own.

Canto 2

Not with more glories, in th' etherial plain,
The Sun first rises o'er the purpled main,
Than, issuing forth, the rival of his beams
Launch'd on the bosom of the silver Thames.
Fair Nymphs, and well-drest Youths around her shone,
But ev'ry eye was fix'd on her alone.
On her white breast a sparkling Cross she wore,
Which Jews might kiss, and infidels adore.
Her lively looks a sprightly mind disclose,
Quick as her eyes, and as unfix'd as those:
Favours to none, to all she smiles extends;
Oft she rejects, but never once offends.
Bright as the sun, her eyes the gazers strike,
And, like the sun, they shine on all alike.

Yet graceful ease, and sweetness void of pride
Might hide her faults, if Belles had faults to hide:
If to her share some female errors fall,
Look on her face, and you'll forget 'em all.
  This Nymph, to the destruction of mankind,
Nourish'd two Locks, which graceful hung behind
In equal curls, and well conspir'd to deck
With shining ringlets her smooth iv'ry neck.
Love in these labyrinths his slaves detains,
And mighty hearts are held in slender chains.
With hairy sprindges we the birds betray,
Slight lines of hair surprize the finny prey,
Fair tresses man's imperial race insnare,
And beauty draws us with a single hair.
  Th' advent'rous Baron the bright locks admir'd;
He saw, he wish'd, and to the prize aspir'd.
Resolv'd to win, he meditates the way,
By force to ravish, or by fraud betray;
For when success a Lover's toil attends,
Few ask, if fraud or force attain'd his ends.
  For this, ere Phœbus rose, he had implor'd
Propitious heav'n, and ev'ry pow'r ador'd,
But chiefly Love – to Love an Altar built,
Of twelve vast French Romances, neatly gilt.
There lay three garters, half a pair of gloves;
And all the trophies of his former loves;
With tender Billet-doux he lights the pyre,
And breathes three am'rous sighs to raise the fire.
Then prostrate falls, and begs with ardent eyes
Soon to obtain, and long possess the prize:
The pow'rs gave ear, and granted half his pray'r,
The rest, the winds dispers'd in empty air.
  But now secure the painted vessel glides,
The sun-beams trembling on the floating tides;
While melting music steals upon the sky,
And soften'd sounds along the waters die;

Smooth flow the waves, the Zephyrs gently play,
Belinda smil'd, and all the world was gay.
All but the Sylph – with careful thoughts opprest,
Th' impending woe sat heavy on his breast.
He summons strait his Denizens of air;
The lucid squadrons round the sails repair:
Soft o'er the shrouds aërial whispers breathe,
That seem'd but Zephyrs to the train beneath.
Some to the sun their insect-wings unfold,
Waft on the breeze, or sink in clouds of gold;
Transparent forms, too fine for mortal sight,
Their fluid bodies half dissolv'd in light.
Loose to the wind their airy garments flew,
Thin glitt'ring textures of the filmy dew,
Dipt in the richest tincture of the skies,
Where light disports in ever-mingling dyes,
While ev'ry beam new transient colours flings,
Colours that change whene'er they wave their wings.
Amid the circle, on the gilded mast,
Superior by the head, was Ariel plac'd;
His purple pinions op'ning to the sun,
He rais'd his azure wand, and thus begun.
    Ye Sylphs and Sylphids, to your chief give ear,
Fays, Fairies, Genii, Elves, and Dæmons hear!
Ye know the spheres and various tasks assign'd
By laws eternal to th' aërial kind.
Some in the fields of purest Æther play,
And bask and whiten in the blaze of day.
Some guide the course of wand'ring orbs on high,
Or roll the planets thro' the boundless sky.
Some less refin'd, beneath the moon's pale light
Pursue the stars that shoot athwart the night,
Or suck the mists in grosser air below,
Or dip their pinions in the painted bow,
Or brew fierce tempests on the wintry main,
Or o'er the glebe distil the kindly rain.

Others on earth o'er human race preside,
Watch all their ways, and all their actions guide:
Of these the chief the care of Nations own,
And guard with Arms divine the British Throne.
  Our humbler province is to tend the Fair,
Not a less pleasing, tho' less glorious care;
To save the powder from too rude a gale,
Nor let th' imprison'd essences exhale;
To draw fresh colours from the vernal flow'rs;
To steal from rainbows e'er they drop in show'rs
A brighter wash; to curl their waving hairs,
Assist their blushes, and inspire their airs;
Nay oft, in dreams, invention we bestow,
To change a Flounce, or add a Furbelow.
  This day, black Omens threat the brightest Fair
That e'er deserv'd a watchful spirit's care;
Some dire disaster, or by force, or slight;
But what, or where, the fates have wrapt in night.
Whether the nymph shall break Diana's law,
Or some frail China jar receive a flaw;
Or stain her honour, or her new brocade;
Forget her pray'rs, or miss a masquerade;
Or lose her heart, or necklace, at a ball;
Or whether Heav'n has doom'd that Shock must fall.
Haste then, ye spirits! to your charge repair:
The flutt'ring fan be Zephyretta's care;
The drops to thee, Brillante, we consign;
And, Momentilla, let the watch be thine;
Do thou, Crispissa, tend her fav'rite Lock;
Ariel himself shall be the guard of Shock.
  To fifty chosen Sylphs, of special note,
We trust th' important charge, the Petticoat:
Oft have we known that seven-fold fence to fail,
Tho' stiff with hoops, and arm'd with ribs of whale;
Form a strong line about the silver bound,
And guard the wide circumference around.

Whatever spirit, careless of his charge,
His post neglects, or leaves the fair at large,
Shall feel sharp vengeance soon o'ertake his sins,
Be stop'd in vials, or transfix'd with pins;
Or plung'd in lakes of bitter washes lie,
Or wedg'd whole ages in a bodkin's eye:
Gums and Pomatums shall his flight restrain,
While clog'd he beats his silken wings in vain;
Or Alum styptics with contracting pow'r
Shrink his thin essence like a rivell'd[2] flow'r:
Or, as Ixion fix'd, the wretch shall feel
The giddy motion of the whirling Mill,
In fumes of burning Chocolate shall glow,
And tremble at the sea that froths below!
He spoke; the spirits from the sails descend;
Some, orb in orb, around the nymph extend,
Some thrid the mazy ringlets of her hair,
Some hang upon the pendants of her ear;
With beating hearts the dire event they wait,
Anxious, and trembling for the birth of Fate.

Canto 3

Close by those meads, for ever crown'd with flow'rs,
Where Thames with pride surveys his rising tow'rs,
There stands a structure of majestic frame,
Which from the neighb'ring Hampton takes its name.
Here Britain's statesmen oft the fall foredoom
Of foreign tyrants, and of nymphs at home;
Here thou, great ANNA! whom three realms obey,
Dost sometimes counsel take – and sometimes Tea.
Hither the heroes and the nymphs resort,
To taste awhile the pleasures of a Court;

[2] shrivelled

In various talk th' instructive hours they past,
Who gave the ball, or paid the visit last:
One speaks the glory of the British Queen,
And one describes a charming Indian screen;
A third interprets motions, looks, and eyes;
At ev'ry word a reputation dies.
Snuff, or the fan, supply each pause of chat,
With singing, laughing, ogling, and all that.
  Mean while, declining from the noon of day,
The sun obliquely shoots his burning ray;
The hungry Judges soon the sentence sign,
And wretches hang that jury-men may dine;
The merchant from th' Exchange returns in peace,
And the long labours of the Toilet cease.
Belinda now, whom thirst of fame invites,
Burns to encounter two adventrous Knights,
At Ombre singly to decide their doom;
And swells her breast with conquests yet to come.
Strait the three bands prepare in arms to join,
Each band the number of the sacred nine.
Soon as she spread her hand, th' aërial guard
Descend, and sit on each important card:
First Ariel perch'd upon a Matadore,
Then each, according to the rank they bore;
For Sylphs, yet mindful of their ancient race,
Are, as when women, wondrous fond of place.
  Behold, four Kings in majesty rever'd,
With hoary whiskers and a forky beard;
And four fair Queens whose hands sustain a flow'r,
Th' expressive emblem of their softer pow'r;
Four Knaves in garbs succinct, a trusty band,
Caps on their heads, and halberts in their hand;
And particolour'd troops, a shining train,
Draw forth to combat on the velvet plain.
  The skilful Nymph reviews her force with care:
Let Spades be trumps! she said, and trumps they were.

Now move to war her sable Matadores,
In show like leaders of the swarthy Moors.
Spadillio first, unconquerable Lord!
Led off two captive trumps, and swept the board.
As many more Manillio forc'd to yield,
And march'd a victor from the verdant field.
Him Basto follow'd, but his fate more hard
Gain'd but one trump and one Plebeian card.
With his broad sabre next, a chief in years,
The hoary Majesty of Spades appears,
Puts forth one manly leg, to sight reveal'd,
The rest, his many-colour'd robe conceal'd.
The rebel Knave, who dares his prince engage,
Proves the just victim of his royal rage.
Ev'n mighty Pam, that Kings and Queens o'erthrew
And mow'd down armies in the fights of Lu,[3]
Sad chance of war! now destitute of aid,
Falls undistinguish'd by the victor Spade!
Thus far both armies to Belinda yield;
Now to the Baron fate inclines the field.
His warlike Amazon her host invades,
Th' imperial consort of the crown of Spades.
The Club's black Tyrant first her victim dy'd,
Spite of his haughty mien, and barb'rous pride:
What boots the regal circle on his head,
His giant limbs, in state unwieldy spread;
That long behind he trails his pompous robe,
And, of all monarchs, only grasps the globe?
The Baron now his Diamonds pours apace;
Th' embroidered King who shows but half his face,
And his refulgent Queen, with pow'rs combin'd,
Of broken troops an easy conquest find.

[3] Or Loo, a card game (full name Lanterloo). Pam is the Jack of Clubs.

Clubs, Diamonds, Hearts, in wild disorder seen,
With throngs promiscuous strow the level green.
Thus when dispers'd a routed army runs,
Of Asia's troops, and Afric's sable sons,
With like confusion different nations fly,
Of various habit, and of various dye,
The pierc'd battalions dis-united fall,
In heaps on heaps; one fate o'erwhelms them all.
  The Knave of Diamonds tries his wily arts,
And wins (oh shameful chance!) the Queen of Hearts.
At this, the blood the virgin's cheek forsook,
A livid paleness spreads o'er all her look;
She sees, and trembles at th' approaching ill,
Just in the jaws of ruin, and Codille.
And now, (as oft in some distemper'd State)
On one nice Trick depends the gen'ral fate.
An Ace of Hearts steps forth: The King unseen
Lurk'd in her hand, and mourn'd his captive Queen:
He springs to vengeance with an eager pace,
And falls like thunder on the prostrate Ace.
The nymph exulting fills with shouts the sky;
The walls, the woods, and long canals reply.
  Oh thoughtless mortals! ever blind to fate,
Too soon dejected, and too soon elate.
Sudden, these honours shall be snatch'd away,
And curs'd for ever this victorious day.
  For lo! the board with cups and spoons is crown'd,
The berries crackle, and the mill turns round;[4]
On shining Altars of Japan they raise
The silver lamp; the fiery spirits blaze:
From silver spouts the grateful liquors glide,
While China's earth receives the smoaking tyde:
At once they gratify their scent and taste,
And frequent cups prolong the rich repaste.

[4] The grinding of coffee

Strait hover round the Fair her airy band;
Some, as she sipp'd, the fuming liquor fann'd,
Some o'er her lap their careful plumes display'd,
Trembling, and conscious of the rich brocade.
Coffee, (which makes the politician wise,
And see thro' all things with his half-shut eyes)
Sent up in vapours to the Baron's brain
New stratagems, the radiant Lock to gain.
Ah cease, rash youth! desist ere 'tis too late,
Fear the just Gods, and think of Scylla's Fate!
Chang'd to a bird, and sent to flit in air,
She dearly pays for Nisus' injur'd hair!
 But when to mischief mortals bend their will,
How soon they find fit instruments of ill!
Just then, Clarissa drew with tempting grace
A two-edg'd weapon from her shining case:
So Ladies in Romance assist their Knight,
Present the spear, and arm him for the fight.
He takes the gift with rev'rence, and extends
The little engine on his finger's ends;
This just behind Belinda's neck he spread,
As o'er the fragrant steams she bends her head.
Swift to the Lock a thousand Sprites repair,
A thousand wings, by turns, blow back the hair;
And thrice they twitch'd the diamond in her ear;
Thrice she look'd back, and thrice the foe drew near.
Just in that instant, anxious Ariel sought
The close recesses of the Virgin's thought;
As on the nosegay in her breast reclin'd,
He watch'd th' Idëas rising in her mind,
Sudden he view'd, in spite of all her art,
An earthly Lover lurking at her heart.
Amaz'd, confus'd, he found his pow'r expir'd,
Resign'd to fate, and with a sigh retir'd.
 The Peer now spreads the glitt'ring Forfex wide,
T' inclose the Lock; now joins it, to divide.

Ev'n then, before the fatal engine clos'd,
A wretched Sylph too fondly interpos'd;
Fate urg'd the sheers, and cut the Sylph in twain,
(But airy substance soon unites again)
The meeting points the sacred hair dissever
From the fair head, for ever, and for ever!
  Then flash'd the living lightning from her eyes,
And screams of horror rend th' affrighted skies.
Not louder shrieks to pitying heav'n are cast,
When husbands, or when lapdogs breathe their last,
Or when rich China vessels, fall'n from high,
In glitt'ring dust, and painted fragments lie!
  Let wreaths of triumph now my temples twine,
(The Victor cry'd) the glorious Prize is mine!
While fish in streams, or birds delight in air,
Or in a coach and six the British Fair,
As long as Atalantis[5] shall be read,
Or the small pillow grace a Lady's bed,
While visits shall be paid on solemn days,
When num'rous wax-lights in bright order blaze,
While nymphs take treats, or assignations give,
So long my honour, name, and praise shall live!
What Time would spare, from steel receives its date,
And monuments, like men, submit to fate!
Steel could the labour of the Gods destroy,
And strike to dust th' imperial tow'rs of Troy;
Steel could the works of mortal pride confound,
And hew triumphal arches to the ground.
What wonder then, fair nymph! thy hairs should feel
The conqu'ring force of unresisted steel?

Canto 4

But anxious cares the pensive nymph oppress'd,
And secret passions labour'd in her breast.

[5] A famous book by Mrs Manley, full of Court and Party scandal

Not youthful kings in battle seiz'd alive,
Not scornful virgins who their charms survive,
Not ardent lovers robb'd of all their bliss,
Not ancient ladies when refus'd a kiss,
Not tyrants fierce that unrepenting die,
Not Cynthia when her manteau's pinn'd awry,
E'er felt such rage, resentment, and despair,
As thou, sad Virgin! for thy ravish'd Hair.
  For, that sad moment, when the Sylphs withdrew,
And Ariel weeping from Belinda flew,
Umbriel, a dusky, melancholy sprite,
As ever sully'd the fair face of light,
Down to the central earth, his proper scene,
Repair'd to search the gloomy Cave of Spleen.
  Swift on his sooty pinions flits the Gnome,
And in a vapour reach'd the dismal dome.
No chearful breeze this sullen region knows,
The dreaded East is all the wind that blows.
Here in a grotto, shelter'd close from air,
And screen'd in shades from day's detested glare,
She sighs for ever on her pensive bed,
Pain at her side, and Megrim at her head.
  Two handmaids wait the throne: alike in place,
But diff'ring far in figure and in face.
Here stood Ill-nature like an ancient maid,
Her wrinkled form in black and white array'd;
With store of pray'rs, for mornings, nights, and noons,
Her hand is fill'd; her bosom with lampoons.
  There Affectation, with a sickly mien,
Shows in her cheek the roses of eighteen,
Practis'd to lisp, and hang the head aside,
Faints into airs, and languishes with pride,
On the rich quilt sinks with becoming woe,
Wrapt in a gown, for sickness, and for show.
The fair-ones feel such maladies as these,
When each new night-dress gives a new disease.

A constant Vapour o'er the palace flies;
Strange phantoms rising as the mists arise;
Dreadful, as hermit's dreams in haunted shades,
Or bright, as visions of expiring maids.
Now glaring fiends, and snakes on rolling spires,
Pale spectres, gaping tombs, and purple fires:
Now lakes of liquid gold, Elysian scenes,
And crystal domes, and Angels in machines.
Unnumber'd throngs on ev'ry side are seen,
Of bodies chang'd to various forms by Spleen.
Here living Teapots stand, one arm held out,
One bent; the handle this, and that the spout:
A Pipkin there like Homer's Tripod walks;
Here sighs a Jar, and there a Goose-pye[6] talks;
Men prove with child, as pow'rful fancy works,
And maids turn'd bottles, call aloud for corks.
Safe past the Gnome thro' this fantastic band,
A branch of healing Spleenwort in his hand.
Then thus address'd the pow'r – Hail wayward
Queen!
Who rule the sex to fifty from fifteen:
Parent of vapours and of female wit,
Who give th' hysteric, or poetic fit,
On various tempers act by various ways,
Make some take physic, others scribble plays;
Who cause the proud their visits to delay,
And send the godly in a pet to pray.
A nymph there is, that all thy pow'r disdains,
And thousands more in equal mirth maintains.
But oh! if e'er thy Gnome could spoil a grace,
Or raise a pimple on a beauteous face,
Like Citron-waters matrons' cheeks inflame,
Or change complexions at a losing game;

[6] Alludes to a real fact, a lady of distinction imagined herself in this condition. [Pope's note]

If e'er with airy horns I planted heads,[7]
Or rumpled petticoats, or tumbled beds,
Or caus'd suspicion when no soul was rude,
Or discompos'd the head-dress of a Prude,
Or e'er to costive lap-dog gave disease,
Which not the tears of brightest eyes could ease:
Hear me, and touch Belinda with chagrin;
That single act gives half the world the spleen.
  The Goddess with a discontented air
Seems to reject him, tho' she grants his pray'r.
A wond'rous Bag with both her hands she binds,
Like that where once Ulysses held the winds;
There she collects the force of female lungs,
Sighs, sobs, and passions, and the war of tongues.
A Vial next she fills with fainting fears,
Soft sorrows, melting griefs, and flowing tears.
The Gnome rejoicing bears her gifts away,
Spreads his black wings, and slowly mounts to day.
  Sunk in Thalestris' arms the nymph he found,
Her eyes dejected and her hair unbound.
Full o'er their heads the swelling bag he rent,
And all the Furies issued at the vent.
Belinda burns with more than mortal ire,
And fierce Thalestris fans the rising fire.
O wretched maid! she spread her hands, and cry'd,
(While Hampton's echoes, wretched maid! reply'd)
Was it for this you took such constant care
The bodkin, comb, and essence to prepare?
For this your locks in paper durance bound,
For this with tort'ring irons wreath'd around?
For this with fillets strain'd your tender head,
And bravely bore the double loads of lead?
Gods! shall the ravisher display your hair,
While the Fops envy, and the Ladies stare!

[7] made cuckolds

Honour forbid! at whose unrival'd shrine
Ease, pleasure, virtue, all, our sex resign.
Methinks already I your tears survey,
Already hear the horrid things they say,
Already see you a degraded toast,
And all your honour in a whisper lost!
How shall I, then, your helpless fame defend?
'Twill then be infamy to seem your friend!
And shall this prize, th' inestimable prize,
Expos'd thro' crystal to the gazing eyes,
And heighten'd by the diamond's circling rays,
On that rapacious hand for ever blaze?
Sooner shall grass in Hyde-park Circus grow,
And wits take lodgings in the sound of Bow;
Sooner let earth, air, sea, to Chaos fall,
Men, monkeys, lap-dogs, parrots, perish all!
  She said: then raging to Sir Plume repairs,
And bids her Beau demand the precious hairs:
(Sir Plume of amber snuff-box justly vain,
And the nice conduct of a clouded cane)
With earnest eyes, and round unthinking face,
He first the snuff-box open'd, then the case,
And thus broke out – 'My Lord, why, what the devil?
Z—ds! damn the lock! 'fore Gad, you must be civil!
Plague on't! 'tis past a jest – nay prithee, pox!
Give her the hair' – he spoke, and rapp'd his box.
  It grieves me much (reply'd the Peer again)
Who speaks so well should ever speak in vain.
But by this Lock, this sacred Lock I swear,
(Which never more shall join its parted hair;
Which never more its honours shall renew,
Clip'd from the lovely head where late it grew)
That while my nostrils draw the vital air,
This hand, which won it, shall for ever wear.
He spoke, and speaking, in proud triumph spread
The long-contended honours of her head.

But Umbriel, hateful Gnome! forbears not so;
He breaks the Vial whence the sorrows flow.
Then see! the nymph in beauteous grief appears,
Her eyes half-languishing, half-drown'd in tears;
On her heav'd bosom hung her drooping head,
Which, with a sigh, she rais'd, and thus she said.
For ever curs'd be this detested day,
Which snatched my best, my fav'rite curl away!
Happy! ah ten times happy had I been,
If Hampton-Court these eyes had never seen!
Yet am not I the first mistaken maid,
By love of Courts to num'rous ills betray'd.
Oh had I rather un-admir'd remain'd
In some lone isle, or distant Northern land;
Where the gilt Chariot never marks the way,
Where none learn Ombre, none e'er taste Bohea![8]
There kept my charms conceal'd from mortal eye,
Like roses that in deserts bloom and die.
What mov'd my mind with youthful Lords to roam?
O had I stay'd, and said my pray'rs at home!
'Twas this, the morning omens seem'd to tell;
Thrice from my trembling hand the Patch-box fell;
The tott'ring China shook without a wind,
Nay Poll sat mute, and Shock was most unkind!
A Sylph too warn'd me of the threats of fate,
In mystic visions, now believ'd too late!
See the poor remnants of these slighted hairs!
My hands shall rend what ev'n thy rapine spares:
These in two sable ringlets taught to break
Once gave new beauties to the snowy neck;
The sister-lock now sits uncouth, alone,
And in its fellow's fate foresees its own;
Uncurl'd it hangs, the fatal sheers demands,
And tempts once more thy sacrilegious hands.

[8] The finest black tea from China

Oh hadst thou, cruel! been content to seize
Hairs less in sight, or any hairs but these!

Canto 5

She said: the pitying audience melt in tears.
But Fate and Jove had stopp'd the Baron's ears.
In vain Thalestris with reproach assails,
For who can move when fair Belinda fails?
Not half so fix'd the Trojan could remain,
While Anna begg'd and Dido rag'd in vain.
Then grave Clarissa graceful wav'd her fan;
Silence ensu'd, and thus the nymph began.
  Say why are Beauties prais'd and honour'd most,
The wise man's passion, and the vain man's toast?
Why deck'd with all that land and sea afford,
Why Angels call'd, and Angel-like ador'd?
Why round our coaches crowd the white-glov'd Beaus,
Why bows the side-box from its inmost rows?
How vain are all these glories, all our pains,
Unless good sense preserve what beauty gains:
That men may say, when we the front-box[9] grace,
Behold the first in virtue as in face!
Oh! if to dance all night, and dress all day,
Charm'd the small-pox, or chas'd old-age away;
Who would not scorn what huswife's cares produce,
Or who would learn one earthly thing of use?
To patch, nay ogle, might become a Saint,
Nor could it sure be such a sin to paint.
But since, alas! frail beauty must decay,
Curl'd or uncurl'd, since Locks will turn to grey;
Since painted, or not painted, all shall fade,
And she who scorns a man, must die a maid;

[9] in a theatre

What then remains but well our pow'r to use,
And keep good-humour still whate'er we lose?
And trust me, dear! good-humour can prevail,
When airs, and flights, and screams, and scolding fail.
Beauties in vain their pretty eyes may roll;
Charms strike the sight, but merit wins the soul.
  So spoke the Dame, but no applause ensu'd;
Belinda frown'd, Thalestris call'd her Prude.
To arms, to arms! the fierce Virago cries,
And swift as lightning to the combat flies.
All side in parties and begin th' attack;
Fans clap, silks rustle and tough whalebones crack;
Heroes and Heroines shouts confus'dly rise,
And base, and treble voices strike the skies.
No common weapons in their hands are found,
Like Gods they fight, nor dread a mortal wound.
  So when bold Homer makes the Gods engage,
And heav'nly breasts with human passions rage;
'Gainst Pallas, Mars; Latona, Hermes arms;
And all Olympus rings with loud alarms:
Jove's thunder roars, heav'n trembles all around,
Blue Neptune storms, the bellowing deeps resound:
Earth shakes her nodding tow'rs, the ground gives
    way,
And the pale ghosts start at the flash of day!
  Triumphant Umbriel on a sconce's[10] height
Clap'd his glad wings, and sate to view the fight:
Prop'd on their bodkin spears, the Sprites survey
The growing combat, or assist the fray.
  While thro' the press enrag'd Thalestris flies,
And scatters deaths around from both her eyes,
A Beau and Witling perish'd in the throng,
One dy'd in metaphor, and one in song.

[10] a candlestick

'O cruel nymph! a living death I bear,'
Cry'd Dapperwit, and sunk beside his chair.
A mournful glance Sir Fopling upwards cast,
'Those eyes are made so killing' – was his last.
Thus on Mæander's flow'ry margin lies
Th' expiring Swan, and as he sings he dies.
When bold Sir Plume had drawn Clarissa down,
Chloe stepp'd in, and kill'd him with a frown;
She smil'd to see the doughty hero slain,
But, at her smile, the Beau reviv'd again.
Now Jove suspends his golden scales in air,
Weighs the Men's wits against the Lady's hair;
The doubtful beam long nods from side to side;
At length the wits mount up, the hairs subside.
See fierce Belinda on the Baron flies,
With more than usual lightning in her eyes:
Nor fear'd the Chief th' unequal fight to try,
Who sought no more than on his foe to die.[11]
But this bold Lord with manly strength endu'd,
She with one finger and a thumb subdu'd:
Just where the breath of life his nostrils drew,
A charge of Snuff the wily virgin threw;
The Gnomes direct, to ev'ry atome just,
The pungent grains of titillating dust.
Sudden, with starting tears each eye o'erflows,
And the high dome re-echoes to his nose.
Now meet thy fate, incens'd Belinda cry'd,
And drew a deadly bodkin from her side.
(The same, his ancient personage to deck,
Her great great grandsire wore about his neck
In three seal-rings; which after, melted down,
Form'd a vast buckle for his widow's gown:
Her infant grandame's whistle next it grew,
The bells she jingled, and the whistle blew;

[11] slang [to have an orgasm]

Then in a bodkin grac'd her mother's hairs,
Which long she wore, and now Belinda wears.)
 Boast not my fall (he cry'd) insulting foe!
Thou by some other shalt be laid as low.
Nor think, to die dejects my lofty mind:
All that I dread is leaving you behind!
Rather than so, ah let me still survive,
And burn in Cupid's flames, – but burn alive.
 Restore the Lock! she cries; and all around
Restore the Lock! the vaulted roofs rebound.
Not fierce Othello in so loud a strain
Roar'd for the handkerchief that caus'd his pain.
But see how oft ambitious aims are cross'd,
And chiefs contend 'till all the prize is lost!
The Lock, obtain'd with guilt, and kept with pain,
In ev'ry place is sought, but sought in vain:
With such a prize no mortal must be blest,
So heav'n decrees! with heav'n who can contest?
 Some thought it mounted to the Lunar sphere,
Since all things lost on earth are treasur'd there.
There Hero's wits are kept in pond'rous vases,
And Beau's in snuff-boxes and tweezer-cases.
There broken vows, and death-bed alms are found,
And lovers' hearts with ends of ribband bound,
The courtier's promises, and sick man's pray'rs,
The smiles of harlots, and the tears of heirs,
Cages for gnats, and chains to yoak a flea,
Dry'd butterflies, and tomes of casuistry.
 But trust the Muse – she saw it upward rise,
Tho' mark'd by none but quick, poetic eyes:
(So Rome's great founder to the heav'ns withdrew,
To Proculus alone confess'd in view)
A sudden Star, it shot thro' liquid air,
And drew behind a radiant trail of hair.
Not Berenice's Locks first rose so bright,
The heav'ns bespangling with dishevel'd light.

The Sylphs behold it kindling as it flies,
And pleas'd pursue its progress thro' the skies.
  This the Beau-monde shall from the Mall survey,
And hail with music its propitious ray.
This the blest Lover shall for Venus take,
And send up vows from Rosamonda's lake.
This Partridge[12] soon shall view in cloudless skies,
When next he looks thro' Galilæo's eyes;
And hence th' egregious wizard shall foredoom
The fate of Louis, and the fall of Rome.
  Then cease, bright Nymph! to mourn thy ravish'd hair,
Which adds new glory to the shining sphere!
Not all the tresses that fair head can boast,
Shall draw such envy as the Lock you lost.
For, after all the murders of your eye,
When, after millions slain, yourself shall die;
When those fair suns shall set, as set they must,
And all those tresses shall be laid in dust;
This Lock, the Muse shall consecrate to fame,
And 'midst the stars inscribe Belinda's name.

LADY MARY WORTLEY MONTAGU

Receipt for the Vapours

Written to Lady J—n

Why will *Delia* thus retire,
And languish life away?
While the sighing croud admire,
'Tis too soon for hartshorn tea.

[12] John Partridge was a ridiculous Star-gazer, who in his Almanacks every year never fail'd to predict the downfall of the Pope, and the King of France, then at war with the English. [Pope's note]

All those dismal looks and fretting
Cannot *Damon*'s life restore;
Long ago the worms have eat him,
You can never see him more.

Once again consult your toilet,
In the glass your face review:
So much weeping soon will spoil it,
And no spring your charms renew.

I, like you, was born a woman,
Well I know what vapours mean:
The disease, alas! is common,
Single, we have all the spleen.

All the morals that they tell us
Never cur'd the sorrow yet:
Choose, among the pretty fellows,
One of humour, youth, and wit.

Prythee hear him every morning,
At the least an hour or two;
Once again at night returning,
I believe the dose will do.

JOHN BYROM

Extempore Intended to Allay the Violence of Party Spirit

God bless the king, I mean the faith's defender;
God bless – (no harm in blessing) – the pretender;
But who pretender is, and who is king,
God bless us all – that's quite another thing.

ANONYMOUS

A Present to a Lady

Ladies, I do here present you
With a token Love hath sent you;
'Tis a thing to sport and play with,
Such another pretty thing
For to pass the time away with;
Prettier sport was never seen;

Name I will not, nor define it,
Sure I am you may divine it:
By those modest looks I guess it,
That I need no more express it,
And those eyes so full of fire,
But leave your fancies to admire.

Yet as much of it be spoken
In the praise of this love-token:
'Tis a wash that far surpasseth
For the cleansing of your blood,
All the Saints may bless your faces,
Yet not do you so much good.

Were you ne'er so melancholy,
It will make you blithe and jolly;
Go no more, no more admiring,
When you feel your spleen's amiss,
For all the drinks of Steel and Iron
Never did such cures as this.

It was born in th' Isle of Man
Venus nurs'd it with her hand,

She puffed it up with milk and pap,
And lull'd it in her wanton lap,
So ever since this Monster can
In no place else with pleasure stand.

Colossus like, between two Rocks,
I have seen him stand and shake his locks,
And when I have heard the names
Of the sweet Saterian Dames,
O he's a Champion for a Queen,
'Tis pity but he should be seen.

Nature, that made him, was so wise
As to give him neither tongue nor eyes,
Supposing he was born to be
The instrument of Jealousie,
Yet here he can, as Poets feign,
Cure a Lady's love-sick brain.

He was the first that did betray
To mortal eyes the milky way;
He is the Proteus cunning Ape
That will beget you any shape;
Give him but leave to act his part,
And he'll revive your saddest heart.

Though he want legs, yet he can stand,
With the least touch of your soft hand;
And though, like Cupid, he be blind,
There's never a hole but he can find;
If by all this you do not know it,
Pray, Ladies, give me leave to show it.

Susannah and the Elders

Susannah the fair
With her beauties all bare
Was bathing her, was bathing herself in an arbour;
The Elders stood peeping and pleas'd
With the dipping,
Would fain have steered into her harbour.

But she in a rage
Swore she'd never engage
With monsters, with monsters, with monsters so old and
so feeble.
This caus'd a great rout
Which had ne'er come about
Had the Elders been sprightly and able.

London Bells

Gay go up, and gay go down,
To ring the bells of London town.

Bull's eyes and targets,
Say the bells of St Marg'ret's.

Brickbats and tiles,
Say the bells of St Giles'.

Halfpence and farthings
Say the bells of St Martin's.

Oranges and lemons,
Say the bells of St Clement's.

Pancakes and fritters,
Say the bells of St Peter's.

Two sticks and an apple,
Say the bells at Whitechapel.

Old Father Baldpate,
Say the slow bells at Aldgate.

Maids in white aprons,
Say the bells of St Cath'rine's.

Pokers and tongs,
Say the bells at St John's.

Kettles and pans,
Say the bells at St Ann's.

You owe me ten shillings,
Say the bells at St Helen's.

When will you pay me?
Say the bells at Old Bailey.

When I grow rich,
Say the bells at Fleetditch.

When will that be?
Say the bells at Stepney.

I am sure I don't know,
Says the great bell at Bow.

When I am old,
Say the bells at St Paul's.

Here comes a candle to light you to bed,
And here comes a chopper to chop off your
head.

HENRY FIELDING

Hunting Song

The dusky night rides down the sky,
  And ushers in the morn;
The hounds all join in glorious cry,
  The huntsman winds his horn:
      And a-hunting we will go.

The wife around her husband throws
  Her arms, and begs his stay;
My dear, it rains, and hails, and snows,
  You will not hunt to-day.
      But a-hunting we will go.

A brushing fox in yonder wood,
  Secure to find we seek;
For why, I carried sound and good
  A cartload there last week.
      And a-hunting we will go.

Away he goes, he flies the rout,
  Their steeds all spur and switch;
Some are thrown in, and some thrown out,
  And some thrown in the ditch:
      But a-hunting we will go.

At length his strength to faintness worn,
  Poor Renard ceases flight;
Then hungry, homeward we return,
  To feast away the night:
      Then a-drinking we will go.

SAMUEL JOHNSON

A Short Song of Congratulation

Long-expected one-and-twenty,
Lingering year at last is flown:
Pomp and pleasure, pride and plenty,
Great Sir John, are all your own.

Loosened from the minor's tether,
Free to mortgage or to sell,
Wild as wind and light as feather,
Bid the slaves of thrift farewell.

Call the Betties, Kates, and Jennies,
Every name that laughs at care;
Lavish of your grandsire's guineas,
Show the spirit of an heir.

All that prey on vice and folly
Joy to see their quarry fly;
Here the gamester light and jolly,
There the lender grave and sly.

Wealth, Sir John, was made to wander,
Let it wander as it will;
See the jockey, see the pander,
Bid them come and take their fill.

When the bonny blade carouses,
Pockets full and spirits high,
What are acres? What are houses?
Only dirt, or wet or dry.

If the guardian or the mother
Tell the woes of wilful waste,
Scorn their counsel, scorn their pother:
You can hang or drown at last!

Epigram

If a man who turnips cries
Cry not when his father dies,
Is it not a proof he'd rather
Have a turnip than his father?

Idyll

Hermit hoar, in solemn cell,
  Wearing out life's evening grey,
Strike thy bosom, Sage, and tell
  What is bliss, and which the way.

Thus I spoke, and speaking sighed,
  Scarce repressed the starting tear,
When the hoary sage replied,
  'Come, my lad, and drink some beer.'

THOMAS GRAY

Ode on the Death of a Favourite Cat Drowned in a Tub of Gold Fishes

'Twas on a lofty vase's side,
Where China's gayest art had dyed
  The azure flowers, that blow;
Demurest of the tabby kind,
The pensive Selima reclined,
  Gazed on the lake below.

Her conscious tail her joy declared,
The fair round face, the snowy beard,
  The velvet of her paws,
Her coat, that with the tortoise vies,
Her ears of jet and emerald eyes,
  She saw, and purred applause.

Still had she gazed but 'midst the tide
Two angel forms were seen to glide,
  The Genii of the stream:
Their scaly armour's Tyrian hue
Through richest purple to the view
  Betrayed a golden gleam.

The hapless nymph with wonder saw:
A whisker first and then a claw,
  With many an ardent wish,
She stretched in vain to reach the prize.
What female heart can gold despise?
  What cat's averse to fish?

Presumptuous maid! with looks intent
Again she stretched, again she bent,
  Nor knew the gulf between.
(Malignant Fate sat by, and smiled)
The slippery verge her feet beguiled,
  She tumbled headlong in.

Eight times emerging from the flood
She mewed to every wat'ry god,
  Some speedy aid to send.
No dolphin came, no Nereid stirred:
Nor cruel Tom, nor Susan heard.
  A favourite has no friend!

From hence, ye beauties, undeceived,
Know, one false step is ne'er retrieved,
  And be with caution bold.
Not all that tempts your wandering eyes
And heedless hearts, is lawful prize;
  Nor all that glisters, gold.

JOHN WOLCOT (PETER PINDAR)

The Royal Tour

He[1] reaches Weymouth – treads the Esplanade –
Hark, hark, the jingling bells! the cannonade!
Drums beat, the hurdigurdies grind the air;
Dogs, cats, old women, all upon the stare:
All Weymouth gapes with wonder – hark! huzzas!
The roaring welcome of a thousand jaws!

. . . .

Lo, Pitt arrives! alas, with lantern face!
'What, hæ, Pitt, hæ – what, Pitt, hæ, more disgrace?'

'Ah, Sire, bad news! a second dire defeat!
Vendé undone, and all the Chouans beat!'

'Hæ, hæ – what, what? – beat, beat? – what, beat agen?
Well, well, more money – raise more men, more men.
But mind, Pitt, hæ – mind, huddle up the news,
Coin something, and the growling land amuse:
Make all the Sans-culottes to Paris caper,
And Rose shall print the vict'ry in his Paper.
Let's hear no more, no more of Cornish tales –
I shan't refund a guinea, Pitt, to Wales:

[1] George III

I can't afford it, no – I can't afford:
Wales cost a deal in pocket-cash and board.
Pitt, Pitt, there's Frost, my bailiff Frost – see, see!
Well, Pitt, go back, go back again – b'ye, b'ye:
Keep London still – no matter how they carp –
Well, well, go back, and bid Dundas look sharp.
Must not lose France – no, France must wear a crown:
If France won't swallow, ram a monarch down.
Some crowns are scarce worth sixpences – hæ, Pitt? –'
The Premier smil'd, and left the Royal Wit.

Now Frost approaches – 'Well, Frost, well, Frost, pray,
How, how went sheep a score? – how corn and hay?'
'An't please your Majesty – a charming price:
Corn very soon will be as dear as spice.'

'Thank God! but say, say, do the poor complain?
Hæ, hæ, will wheat be sixpence, Frost, a grain?'

'I hope not, Sire; for great were then my fears,
That Windsor would be pull'd about our ears.'

'Frost, Frost, no politics – no, no, Frost, no:
You, you talk politics! oho, oho!
Windsor come down about our ears! what, what?
D'ye think, hæ, hæ, that I'm afraid of that?
What, what are soldiers good for, but obey?
Macmanus, Townsend, Jealous, hæ, hæ, hæ?
Pull Windsor down? hæ, what? – a pretty job!
Windsor be pull'd to pieces by the mob!
Talk, talk of farming, that's your fort, d'ye see;
And mind, mind, politics belong to me.
Go back, go back, and watch the Windsor chaps;
Count all the poultry; set, set well the traps.
See, see! see! Stacie – here, here, Stacie, here –
Going to market, Stacie? – dear, dear, dear!

I get all my provision by the mail –
Hæ, money plenty, Stacie? don't fear jail.
Rooms, rooms all full? hæ, hæ? no beds to spare?
What, what! give trav'lers, hæ, good fare, good fare?
Good sign, good sign, to have no empty beds!
Shows, shows that people like to see Crown'd Heads.'

The Mail arrives! hark! hark! the cheerful horn,
To Majesty announcing oil and corn;
Turnips and cabbages and soap and candles;
And lo, each article Great Caesar handles!
Bread, cheese, salt, catchup, vinegar, and mustard,
Small beer, and bacon, apple-pie and custard:
All, all, from Windsor greets his frugal Grace,
For Weymouth is a d—mn'd expensive place.

Sal'sb'ry appears, the Lord of stars and strings;
Presents his poem to the best of Kings.
Great Caesar reads it – feels a laughing fit,
And wonders Sal'sb'ry should become a wit.
A batch of bullocks! see Great Caesar run:
He stops the Drover – bargain is begun.
He feels their ribs and rumps – he shakes his head –
'Poor, Drover, poor – poor, very poor indeed.'
Caesar and Drover haggle – diff'rence split –
How much? – a shilling! what a royal hit!
A load of hay in sight! Great Caesar flies –
Smells – shakes his head – 'bad hay – sour hay –' he buys.
'Smell, Courtown – smell – good bargain – lucky load –
Smell, Courtown – sweeter hay was never mow'd.'

A herd of swine goes by! – 'Whose hogs are these?
Hæ, Farmer, hæ?' – 'Yours, Measter, if yow pleaze.'
'Poor, Farmer, poor – lean, lousy, very poor –
Sell, sell, hæ, sell?' – 'Iss, Measter, to be zure:

My pigs were made for zale, but what o' that?
Yow caall mun lean; now, Zur, I caal mun vat –
Measter, I baant a starling – can't be cort;
You think, agosh, to ha the pigs vor nort.'
Lo! Caesar buys the pigs – he slily winks –
'Hæ, Gwinn, the fellow is not caught, he thinks –
Fool, not to know the bargain I have got!
Hæ, Gwinn – nice bargain – lucky, lucky lot!'

Enter the dancing dogs! they take their stations;
They bow, they curtsey to the Lord of Nations.
They dance, they skip, they charm the K— of Fun,
While Courtiers see themselves almost outdone.

Lord Paulet enters on his hands and knees,
Joining the hunts of hares with hunts of fleas.
Enter Sir Joseph! gladd'ning royal eyes!
What holds his hand! a box of butterflies,
Grubs, nests, and eggs of humming-birds, to please;
Newts, tadpoles, brains of beetles, stings of bees.
The noble President without a bib on,
To sport the glories of his blushing ribbon!
The fishermen! the fishermen behold!
A shoal of fish! the men their nets unfold;
Surround the scaly fry – they drag to land:
Caesar and Co. rush down upon the sand;
The fishes leap about – Gods! what a clatter!
Caesar, delighted, jumps into the water –
He marvels at the fish with fins and scales –
He plunges at them – seizes heads and tails;
Enjoys the draught – he capers – laughs aloud,
And shows his captives to the gaping crowd.
He orders them to Glo'ster Lodge – they go:
But are the fishermen rewarded? – NO!!!

Caesar spies Lady Cathcart with a book;
He flies to know what 'tis – he longs to look.
'What's in your hand, my Lady? let me know.'
'A book, an't please your M—y.' 'Oho!
Book's a good thing – good thing – I like a book.
Very good thing, my Lady – let me look –
War of America! my Lady, hæ?
Bad thing, my Lady! fling, fling that away.'

A sailor pops upon the Royal Pair,
On crutches borne – an object of despair:
His squalid beard, pale cheek, and haggard eye,
Though silent, pour for help a piercing cry.

'Who, who are you? what, what? hæ, what are you?'

'A man, my Liege, whom Kindness never knew.'

'A sailor! sailor, hæ? you've lost a leg.'

'I know it, Sir – which forces me to beg.
I've nine poor children, Sir, besides a wife –
God bless them! the sole comforts of my life.'

'Wife and nine children, hæ? – all, all alive?
No, no, no wonder that you cannot thrive.
Shame, shame, to fill your hut with such a train!
Shame to get brats for others to maintain!
Get, get a wooden leg, or one of cork:
Wood's cheapest – yes, get wood, and go to work.
But mind, mind Sailor – hæ, hæ, hæ – hear, hear –
Don't go to Windsor, mind, and cut one there:
That's dangerous, dangerous – there I place my traps –
Fine things, fine things, for legs of thieving chaps:
Best traps, my traps – take care – they bite, they bite,
And sometimes catch a dozen legs a night.'

'Oh! had I money, Sir, to buy a leg!'

'No money, hæ? nor I – go beg – go beg.' –

How sweetly kind to bid the cripple mump,
And cut from other people's trees a stump!
How vastly like our kind Archbishop M—re,
Who loves not beggar tribes at Lambeth door,
Of meaner parsons bids them ask relief –
There, carry their coarse jugs for broth and beef!
'Mine Gote! your Mashesty! – don't hear such stuff.
De Workhouse always geefs de poor enough.
Why make bout dirty leg sush wond'rous fuss? –
And den, what impudence for beg of Us!
In Strelitz, O mine Gote! de beggar skip:
Dere, for a sharity, we geefs a whip.
Money make subshects impudent, I'm sure –
Respect be always where de peepel's poor.'

'How, Sailor, did you lose your leg? – hæ, hæ?'

'I lost it, please your Majesty, at sea,
Hard fighting for my country and my King.'

'Hæ, what? – that's common, very common thing.
Hæ! lucky fellow, that you were not drill'd:
Some lose their heads, and many men are kill'd.
Your parish? where's your parish? hæ – where, where?'

'I serv'd my 'prenticeship in Manchester.'

'Fine town, fine town – full, full of trade and riches –
Hæ, Sailor, hæ, can you make leather breeches?
These come from Manchester – there, there I got 'em!'
On which Great Caesar claps his buckskin bottom.

'Must not encourage vagrants – no, no, no –
Must not make laws, my lad, and break 'em too.
Where, where's your parish, hæ? and where's your pass?
Well, make haste home – I've got, I've got no brass.'

RICHARD BRINSLEY SHERIDAN

Song

Here's to the maiden of bashful fifteen;
Here's to the widow of fifty;
Here's to the flaunting extravagant quean,
And here's to the housewife that's thrifty.

Chorus
Let the toast pass, –
Drink to the lass,
I'll warrant she'll prove an excuse for the glass.

Here's to the charmer whose dimples we prize;
Now to the maid who has none, sir:
Here's to the girl with a pair of blue eyes,
And here's to the nymph with but *one*, sir.

Here's to the maid with a bosom of snow;
Now to her that's as brown as a berry:
Here's to the wife with a face full of woe,
And now to the girl that is merry.

For let 'em be clumsy, or let 'em be slim,
Young or ancient, I care not a feather;
So fill a pint bumper quite up to the brim,
And let us e'en toast them together.

WILLIAM BLAKE

Epigrams

Sir Joshua Reynolds

When Sir Joshua Reynolds died
  All Nature was degraded;
The King dropped a tear into the Queen's ear,
  And all his pictures faded.

A Character

Her whole life is an epigram, smart, smooth, and neatly penned,
Platted quite neat to catch applause, with a hang-noose at the end.

Marriage

When a man has married a wife, he finds out whether
Her knees and elbows are only glued together.

A Petty Sneaking Knave

A petty sneaking knave I knew –
O! Mr Cromek,[1] how do ye do?

Nurse's Song

When the voices of children are heard on the green,
And laughing is heard on the hill,
My heart is at rest within my breast,
And everything else is still.

[1] R. H. Cromek, an engraver who cheated Blake

'Then come home, my children, the sun is gone down,
And the dews of night arise;
Come, come, leave off play, and let us away
Till the morning appears in the skies.'

'No, no, let us play, for it is yet day,
And we cannot go to sleep;
Besides, in the sky the little birds fly,
And the hills are covered with sheep.'

'Well, well, go and play till the light fades away,
And then go home to bed.'
The little ones leaped and shouted and laughed
And all the hills echoèd.

ROBERT BURNS

Tam o'Shanter

A Tale

Of Brownyis and of Bogillis full is this buke.
GAWIN DOUGLAS

When chapman billies[1] leave the street,
And drouthy[2] neebors, neebors meet,
As market-days are wearing late,
An' folk begin to tak the gate;
While we sit bousing at the nappy,[3]
An' getting fou and unco[4] happy,
We think na on the lang Scots miles,
The mosses, waters, slaps,[5] and styles,

[1] packman fellows [2] thirsty [3] ale [4] very [5] gaps in walls

That lie between us and our hame,
Whare sits our sulky sullen dame,
Gathering her brows like gathering storm,
Nursing her wrath to keep it warm.

This truth fand[6] honest Tam o'Shanter,
As he frae Ayr ae night did canter,
(Auld Ayr, wham ne'er a town surpasses,
For honest men and bonny lasses).

O Tam! had'st thou but been sae wise,
As ta'en thy ain wife Kate's advice!
She tauld thee weel thou was a skellum,[7]
A blethering, blustering, drunken blellum;[8]
That frae November till October,
Ae market-day thou was nae sober;
That ilka melder,[9] wi' the miller,
Thou sat as lang as thou had siller;[10]
That ev'ry naig was ca'd a shoe on,[11]
The smith and thee gat roaring fou on;
That at the Lord's house, even on Sunday,
Thou drank wi' Kirkton Jean till Monday.
She prophesied that, late or soon,
Thou would be found deep drown'd in Doon;
Or catch wi' warlocks[12] in the mirk,
By Alloway's auld haunted kirk.

Ah, gentle dames! it gars me greet,[13]
To think how mony counsels sweet,
How mony lengthen'd sage advices,
The husband frae the wife despises!

[6] found [7] rogue [8] chatterer [9] at every meal-grinding [10] money
[11] nag that had a shoe driven on [12] wizards [13] makes me weep

But to our tale: Ae market-night,
Tam had got planted unco right;
Fast by an ingle, bleezing[14] finely,
Wi' reaming swats,[15] that drank divinely;
And at his elbow, Souter[16] Johnny,
His ancient, trusty, drouthy crony;
Tam lo'ed him like a vera brither;
They had been fou for weeks thegither.
The night drave on wi' sangs and clatter;
And ay the ale was growing better:
The landlady and Tam grew gracious,
Wi' favours, secret, sweet, and precious:
The Souter tauld his queerest stories;
The landlord's laugh was ready chorus:
The storm without might rair and rustle,
Tam did na mind the storm a whistle.

Care, mad to see a man sae happy,
E'en drown'd himsel amang the nappy:
As bees flee hame wi' lades[17] o' treasure,
The minutes wing'd their way wi' pleasure:
Kings may be blest, but Tam was glorious,
O'er a' the ills o' life victorious!

But pleasures are like poppies spread,
You seize the flow'r, its bloom is shed;
Or like the snow falls in the river,
A moment white – then melts for ever;
Or like the borealis race,
That flit ere you can point their place;
Or like the rainbow's lovely form
Evanishing amid the storm. –

[14]blazing [15]frothing ale [16]Cobbler [17]loads

Nae man can tether time or tide;
The hour approaches Tam maun ride;
That hour, o' night's black arch the key-stane,
That dreary hour he mounts his beast in;
And sic a night he taks the road in,
As ne'er poor sinner was abroad in.

The wind blew as 'twad blawn its last;
The rattling showers rose on the blast;
The speedy gleams the darkness swallow'd;
Loud, deep, and lang, the thunder bellow'd:
That night, a child might understand,
The Deil had business on his hand.

Weel mounted on his gray mare, Meg,
A better never lifted leg,
Tam skelpit[18] on thro' dub[19] and mire,
Despising wind, and rain, and fire;
Whiles[20] holding fast his gude blue bonnet;
Whiles crooning o'er some auld Scots sonnet;[21]
Whiles glowring round wi' prudent cares,
Lest bogles catch him unawares:
Kirk-Alloway was drawing nigh,
Whare ghaists and houlets[22] nightly cry. –

By this time he was cross the ford,
Whare, in the snaw, the chapman smoor'd;[23]
And past the birks[24] and meikle[25] stane,
Whare drunken Charlie brak's neck-bane;
And thro' the whins,[26] and by the cairn,
Whare hunters fand the murder'd bairn;

[18] dashed [19] puddle [20] Now [21] song [22] owls [23] smothered
[24] birches [25] big [26] furze

And near the thorn, aboon the well,
Whare Mungo's mither hang'd hersel. –
Before him Doon pours all his floods;
The doubling storm roars thro' the woods;
The lightnings flash from pole to pole;
Near and more near the thunders roll:
When, glimmering thro' the groaning trees,
Kirk-Alloway seem'd in a bleeze;
Thro' ilka bore[27] the beams were glancing;
And loud resounded mirth and dancing. –

Inspiring bold John Barleycorn!
What dangers thou canst make us scorn!
Wi' tippeny,[28] we fear nae evil;
Wi' usquabae,[29] we'll face the devil! –
The swats sae ream'd in Tammie's noddle,
Fair play, he car'd na deils a boddle.[30]
But Maggie stood right sair astonish'd,
Till, by the heel and hand admonish'd,
She ventur'd forward on the light;
And, vow! Tam saw an unco[31] sight!
Warlocks and witches in a dance;
Nae cotillion, brent[32] new frae France,
But hornpipes, jigs, strathspeys, and reels,
Put life and mettle in their heels.
A winnock-bunker[33] in the east,
There sat auld Nick, in shape o' beast;
A towzie tyke,[34] black, grim, and large,
To gie them music was his charge:
He screw'd the pipes and gart[35] them skirl,
Till roof and rafters a' did dirl.[36]
Coffins stood round, like open presses,
That shaw'd the dead in their last dresses;

[27] every cranny [28] ale [29] whisky [30] not a farthing [31] wonderful
[32] brand [33] window-seat [34] shaggy dog [35] made [36] rattle

And by some devilish cantraip slight[37]
Each in its cauld hand held a light. –
By which heroic Tam was able
To note upon the haly table,
A murderer's banes in gibbet airns;[38]
Twa span-lang, wee, unchristen'd bairns;
A thief, new-cutted frae a rape,[39]
Wi' his last gasp his gab did gape;
Five tomahawks, wi' blude red-rusted;
Five scymitars, wi' murder crusted;
A garter, which a babe had strangled;
A knife, a father's throat had mangled,
Whom his ain son o' life bereft,
The grey hairs yet stack to the heft;[40]
Wi' mair o' horrible and awefu',
Which even to name wad be unlawfu'.

As Tammie glowr'd,[41] amaz'd, and curious,
The mirth and fun grew fast and furious:
The piper loud and louder blew;
The dancers quick and quicker flew;
They reel'd, they set, they cross'd, they cleekit,[42]
Till ilka carlin[43] swat and reekit,[44]
And coost her duddies[45] to the wark,
And linket[46] at it in her sark![47]

Now, Tam, O Tam! had thae been queans,
A' plump and strapping in their teens,
Their sarks, instead o' creeshie[48] flannen,
Been snaw-white seventeen hunder linnen!

[37] weird trick [38] irons [39] rope [40] haft [41] stared [42] joined hands
[43] witch [44] sweated and steamed [45] rags [46] tripped
[47] shirt, chemise [48] greasy

Thir breeks o' mine, my only pair,
That ance were plush, o' gude blue hair,
I wad hae gi'en them off my hurdies,[49]
For ae blink o' the bonie burdies![50]

But wither'd beldams, auld and droll,
Rigwoodie[51] hags wad spean[52] a foal,
Lowping[53] and flinging on a crummock,[54]
I wonder didna turn thy stomach.

But Tam kend what was what fu' brawlie,
There was ae winsome wench and wawlie,[55]
That night enlisted in the core,[56]
(Lang after kend on Carrick shore;
For mony a beast to dead she shot,
And perish'd mony a bony boat.
And shook baith meikle corn and bear,[57]
And kept the country-side in fear).
Her cutty sark,[58] o' Paisley harn,[59]
That while a lassie she had worn,
In longitude tho' sorely scanty,
It was her best, and she was vauntie.[60] –
Ah! little kend thy reverend grannie,
That sark she coft[61] for her wee Nannie,
Wi' twa pund Scots ('twas a' her riches),
Wad ever grac'd a dance of witches!

But here my Muse her wing maun cour;[62]
Sic flights are far beyond her pow'r;
To sing how Nannie lap and flang,[63]
(A souple jade she was, and strang),

[49]buttocks [50]lasses [51]Lean [52]wean [53]Leaping [54]staff
[55]choice [56]company [57]barley [58]short shift [59]cloth
[60]proud [61]bought [62]stoop [63]leaped and kicked

And how Tam stood, like ane bewitch'd,
And thought his very een enrich'd;
Even Satan glowr'd, and fidg'd fu' fain,[64]
And hotch'd[65] and blew wi' might and main:
Till first ae caper, syne[66] anither,
Tam tint[67] his reason a' thegither,
And roars out, 'Weel done, Cutty-sark!'
And in an instant all was dark:
And scarcely had he Maggie rallied,
When out the hellish legion sallied.

As bees bizz out wi' angry fyke,[68]
When plundering herds[69] assail their byke;[70]
As open pussie's[71] mortal foes,
When, pop! she starts before their nose;
As eager runs the market-crowd,
When 'Catch the thief!' resounds aloud;
So Maggie runs, the witches follow,
Wi' mony an eldritch skreech and hollow.

Ah, Tam! Ah, Tam! thou'll get thy fairin![72]
In hell they'll roast thee like a herrin!
In vain thy Kate awaits thy comin!
Kate soon will be a woefu' woman!
Now, do thy speedy utmost, Meg,
And win the key-stane of the brig;
There at them thou thy tail may toss,
A running stream they dare na cross.
But ere the key-stane she could make,
The fient[73] a tail she had to shake!
For Nannie, far before the rest,
Hard upon noble Maggie prest,

[64] wriggled with delight [65] jerked [66] then [67] lost [68] fret
[69] shepherds [70] hive [71] the hare's [72] deserts [73] devil

And flew at Tam wi' furious ettle;[74]
But little wist she Maggie's mettle –
Ae spring brought off her master hale,[75]
But left behind her ain grey tail:
The carlin claught[76] her by the rump,
And left poor Maggie scarce a stump.

Now, wha this tale o' truth shall read,
Ilk man and mother's son, take heed:
Whene'er to drink you are inclin'd,
Or cutty-sarks run in your mind,
Think, ye may buy the joys o'er dear,
Remember Tam o'Shanter's mare.

The Rantin[1] Dog the Daddie O't

O wha my babie-clouts[2] will buy,
O wha will ten[3] me when I cry;
Wha will kiss me where I lie.
The rantin dog the daddie o't.

O wha will own he did the faut,
O wha will buy the groanin maut,[4]
O wha will tell me how to ca't.[5]
The rantin dog the daddie o't.

When I mount the Creepie-chair,[6]
Wha will sit beside me there,
Gie me Rob, I'll seek nae mair,
The rantin dog the daddie o't.

[74] intent [75] safe [76] clutched
[1] rollicking [2] baby-clothes [3] attend to [4] buy the nurse ale
[5] name it [6] penance-stool

Wha will crack[7] to me my lane;[8]
Wha will mak me fidgin fain;[9]
Wha will kiss me o'er again.
The rantin dog the daddie o't.

Song

TUNE, *Corn rigs are bonie*

I

It was upon a Lammas night,
When corn rigs[1] are bonie,
Beneath the moon's unclouded light,
I held awa to Annie:
The time flew by, wi' tentless[2] heed,
Till, 'tween the late and early;
Wi' sma' persuasions she agreed,
To see me thro' the barley.

II

The sky was blue, the wind was still,
The moon was shining clearly;
I set her down, wi' right good will,
Amang the rigs o' barley:
I ken't her heart was a' my ain;
I lov'd her most sincerely;
I kiss'd her owre and owre again,
Amang the rigs o' barley.

III

I lock'd her in my fond embrace;
Her heart was beating rarely:
My blessings on that happy place,
Amang the rigs o' barley!

[7] talk [8] alone [9] tingling with desire
[1] fields [2] careless

But by the moon and stars so bright,
That shone that hour so clearly!
She ay shall bless that happy night,
Amang the rigs o'barley.

IV

I hae been blythe wi' comrades dear;
I hae been merry drinking;
I hae been joyfu' gath'rin gear[3]
I hae been happy thinking:
But a' the pleasures e'er I saw,
Tho' three times doubl'd fairly,
That happy night was worth them a',
Amang the rigs o' barley.

Chorus

Corn rigs, an' barley rigs,
An' corn rigs are bonie:
I'll ne'er forget that happy night,
Amang the rigs wi' Annie.

Green Grow the Rashes

A Fragment

Chorus

Green grow the rashes, O;
Green grow the rashes, O;
The sweetest hours that e'er I spent,
Are spent amang the lasses, O.

I

There's nought but care on ev'ry han',
In every hour that passes, O:

[3] making money

What signifies the life o' man,
An' 'twere na for the lasses, O.

II

The warly[1] race may riches chase,
An' riches still may fly them, O;
An' tho' at last they catch them fast,
Their hearts can ne'er enjoy them, O.

III

But gie me a cannie[2] hour at e'en,
My arms about my Dearie, O;
An' warly cares, an' warly men,
May a' gae tapsalteerie,[3] O!

IV

For you sae douse,[4] ye sneer at this,
Ye're nought but senseless asses, O:
The wisest Man the warl' e'er saw,
He dearly lov'd the lasses, O.

V

Auld Nature swears, the lovely Dears
Her noblest work she classes, O:
Her prentice han' she try'd on man,
An' then she made the lasses, O.

Green Grow the Rashes

(*Another version*)

Green grow the rashes, O,
Green grow the rashes, O;
The sweetest bed that e'er I got,
Was the bellies o' the lasses, O!

[1] worldly [2] quiet [3] topsy-turvy [4] sober

'Twas late yestreen I met wi' ane
  And vow[1] but she was gentle, O;
Ae hand she put to my gravat[2]
  The tither to my pintle, O.

I dought na speak, yet was na fly'd,[3]
  My heart play'd duntie, duntie,[4] O,
A' ceremonie laid aside,
  I fairly found her cuntie, O.

The down-bed, the feather-bed,
  The bed amang the rashes, O;
Yet a' the beds is nae sae saft
  As the bellies o' the lasses, O!

Green grow the rashes, O,
  Green grow the rashes, O;
The lasses they hae wimble bores,[5]
  The widows they hae gashes, O!

RICHARD PORSON

Epigram on an Academic Visit to the Continent

I went to Frankfort, and got drunk
With that most learn'd professor – Brunck:
I went to Worts, and got more drunken
With that more learn'd professor – Ruhncken.

[1] wow! (as in America) [2] cravat [3] scared [4] pitter patter
[5] small holes

GEORGE CANNING

The Dutch

In matters of commerce the fault of the Dutch
Is offering too little and asking too much.

Song of One Eleven Years in Prison

Whene'er with haggard eyes I view
  This Dungeon, that I'm rotting in,
I think of those Companions true
  Who studied with me at the U –
    – NIVERSITY of *Gottingen* –
    – NIVERSITY of *Gottingen.*

(Weeps, and pulls out a blue kerchief, with which he wipes his eyes; gazing tenderly at it, he proceeds)

Sweet kerchief, check'd with heav'nly blue,
  Which once my love sat knotting in! –
Alas! MATILDA *then* was true! –
  At least I thought so at the U –
    – NIVERSITY of *Gottingen* –
    – NIVERSITY of *Gottingen.*

(At the repetition of this Line ROGERO clanks his Chains in cadence.)

Barbs![1] Barbs! alas! how swift you flew
  Her neat Post-Waggon trotting in!

[1] Barbary horses

Ye bore MATILDA from my view.
  Forlorn I languish'd at the U –
    – NIVERSITY of *Gottingen* –
    – NIVERSITY of *Gottingen* –

This faded form! this pallid hue!
  This blood my veins is clotting in.
My years are many – They were few
  When first I entered at the U –
    – NIVERSITY of *Gottingen* –
    – NIVERSITY of *Gottingen* –

There first for thee my passion grew,
  Sweet! sweet MATILDA POTTINGEN!
Thou wast the daughter of my TU –
  – TOR, *Law Professor* at the U –
    – NIVERSITY of *Gottingen* –
    – NIVERSITY of *Gottingen* –

Sun, moon, and thou vain world, adieu,
  That kings and priests are plotting in:
Here doom'd to starve on water-gru –
  – el, never shall I see the U –
    – NIVERSITY of *Gottingen* –
    – NIVERSITY of *Gottingen*.

ANONYMOUS

Solomon Grundy

Solomon Grundy,
Born on a Monday,
Christened on Tuesday,
Married on Wednesday,
Took ill on Thursday,

Worse on Friday,
Died on Saturday,
Buried on Sunday.
This is the end
Of Solomon Grundy.

There was a Crooked Man

There was a crooked man, and he went a crooked mile,
He found a crooked sixpence against a crooked stile:
He bought a crooked cat which caught a crooked mouse,
And they all lived together in a little crooked house.

Tweedledum and Tweedledee

Tweedledum and Tweedledee
  Agreed to have a battle,
For Tweedledum said Tweedledee
  Had spoiled his nice new rattle.
Just then flew down a monstrous crow,
  As black as a tar-barrel,
Which frightened both those heroes so,
  They quite forgot their quarrel.

Jack and Gill

Jack and Gill went up the hill
  To fetch a bottle of water;
Jack fell down and broke his crown,
  And Gill came tumbling after.

Then up Jack got, and home did trot,
  As fast as he could caper,
Dame Gill did the job to plaster his nob
  With vinegar and brown paper.

Scarborough Fair

Where are you going? To Scarborough Fair?
Parsley, sage, rosemary and thyme,
Remember me to a bonny lass there,
For once she was a true lover of mine.

Tell her to make me a cambric shirt,
Parsley, sage, rosemary and thyme,
Without any needle or thread work'd in it,
And she shall be a true lover of mine.

Tell her to wash it in yonder well,
Parsley, sage, rosemary and thyme,
Where water ne'er sprung nor a drop of rain fell,
And she shall be a true lover of mine.

Tell her to plough me an acre of land,
Parsley, sage, rosemary and thyme,
Between the sea and the salt sea strand,
And she shall be a true lover of mine.

Tell her to plough it with one ram's horn,
Parsley, sage, rosemary and thyme,
And sow it all over with one peppercorn,
And she shall be a true lover of mine.

Tell her to reap it with a sickle of leather,
Parsley, sage, rosemary and thyme,
And tie it all up with a tom tit's feather,
And she shall be a true lover of mine.

Tell her to gather it all in a sack,
Parsley, sage, rosemary and thyme,
And carry it home on a butterfly's back,
And then she shall be a true lover of mine.

SAMUEL TAYLOR COLERIDGE

The Devil's Thoughts

From his brimstone bed at break of day
A-walking the Devil is gone,
To visit his little snug farm the earth
And see how his stock goes on.

Over the hill and over the dale,
And he went over the plain,
And backward and forward he switched his long tail
As a gentleman switches his cane.

And how then was the Devil dressed?
Oh! he was in his Sunday best:
His jacket was red and his breeches were blue,
And there was a hole where the tail came through.

He saw a Lawyer killing a Viper
On a dunghill hard by his own stable;
And the Devil smiled, for it put him in mind
Of Cain and his brother, Abel.

He saw an Apothecary on a white horse
Ride by on his vocations,
And the Devil thought of his old Friend
Death in the Revelations.

He saw a cottage with a double coach-house,
A cottage of gentility!
And the Devil did grin, for his darling sin
Is pride that apes humility.

He peeped into a rich bookseller's shop,
Quoth he! we are both of one college,
For I sat myself like a cormorant once
Hard by the tree of knowledge.

Down the river did glide, with wind and tide,
A pig, with vast celerity,
And the Devil looked wise as he saw how the while,
It cut its own throat. 'There!' quoth he with a smile,
'Goes "England's commercial prosperity".'

As he went through Cold-Bath fields he saw
A solitary cell;
And the Devil was pleased, for it gave him a hint
For improving his prisons in Hell.

General —'s burning face
He saw with consternation,
And back to hell his way did he take,
For the Devil thought by a slight mistake
It was general conflagration.

ROBERT SOUTHEY

To a Goose

If thou didst feed on western plains of yore;
Or waddle wide with flat and flabby feet
Over some Cambrian mountain's plashy moor;
Or find in farmer's yard a safe retreat
From gypsy thieves, and foxes sly and fleet;
If thy grey quills, by lawyer guided, trace
Deeds big with ruin to some wretched race,
Or love-sick poet's sonnet, sad and sweet,
Wailing the rigour of his lady fair;

Or if, the drudge of housemaid's daily toil,
Cobwebs and dust thy pinions white besoil,
Departed Goose! I neither know nor care.
But this I know, that we pronounced thee fine,
Seasoned with sage and onions, and port wine.

CHARLES LAMB

Free Thoughts on Several Eminent Composers

Some cry up Haydn, some Mozart,
Just as the whim bites; for my part,
I do not care a farthing candle
For either of them, or for Handel. –
Cannot a man live free and easy,
Without admiring Pergolesi?
Or thro' the world with comfort go,
That never heard of Doctor Blow?
So help me God, I hardly have;
And yet I eat, and drink, and shave,
Like other people, if you watch it,
And know no more of Stave or Crotchet,
Than did the primitive Peruvians;
Or those old ante-queer-Diluvians
That lived in the unwash'd world with Tubal,
Before that dirty blacksmith Jubal
By stroke on anvil, or by summ'at,
Found out, to his great surprise, the gamut.
I care no more for Cimarosa,
Than he did for Salvator Rosa,
Being no painter; and bad luck
Be mine, if I can bear that Gluck!
Old Tycho Brahe, and modern Herschel,
Had something in 'em; but who's Purcel?

The devil, with his foot so cloven,
For aught I care, may take Beethoven;
And, if the bargain does not suit,
I'll throw him Weber in to boot.
There's not the splitting of a splinter
To choose 'twixt him last named, and Winter.
Of Doctor Pepusch old queen Dido
Knew just as much, God knows, as I do.
I would not go four miles to visit
Sebastian Bach (or Batch, which is it?);
No more I would for Bononcini.
As for Novello, or Rossini,
I shall not say a word to grieve 'em,
Because they're living; so I leave 'em.

W. S. LANDOR

Ireland Never was Contented

Ireland never was contented.
Say you so? You are demented.
Ireland was contented when
All could use the sword and pen,
And when Tara rose so high
That her turrets split the sky,
And about her courts were seen
Liveried angels robed in green,
Wearing, by St Patrick's bounty,
Emeralds big as half the county.

Plays

Alas, how soon the hours are over,
Counted us out to play the lover!
And how much narrower is the stage,
Allotted us to play the sage!

But when we play the fool, how wide
The theatre expands! beside,
How long the audience sits before us!
How many prompters! what a chorus!

THOMAS MOORE

The Young May Moon

The young May moon is beaming, love,
The glow-worm's lamp is gleaming, love;
    How sweet to rove
    Through Morna's grove,
When the drowsy world is dreaming, love!
Then awake! – the heavens look bright, my dear,
'Tis never too late for delight, my dear;
    And the best of all ways
    To lengthen our days
Is to steal a few hours from the night, my dear!

Now all the world is sleeping, love,
But the Sage, his star-watch keeping, love,
    And I, whose star
    More glorious far
Is the eye from that casement peeping, love.
Then awake! – till rise of sun, my dear,
The Sage's glass we'll shun, my dear,
    Or in watching the flight
    Of bodies of light
He might happen to take thee for one, my dear!

Did Not

'Twas a new feeling – something more
Than we had dared to own before,
    Which then we hid not:
We saw it in each other's eye,
And wished, in every half-breathed sigh,
    To speak, but did not.

She felt my lips' impassioned touch –
'Twas the first time I dared so much,
    And yet she chid not;
But whispered o'er my burning brow,
'Oh, do you doubt I love you now,'
    Sweet soul! I did not.

Warmly I felt her bosom thrill,
I prest it closer, closer still,
    Though gently bid not,
Till – oh! the world hath seldom heard
Of lovers who so nearly erred,
    And yet, who did not.

The Time I've Lost in Wooing

The time I've lost in wooing,
In watching and pursuing
    The light that dies
    In woman's eyes,
Has been my heart's undoing.
Though Wisdom oft has sought me,
I scorned the lore she brought me,
    My only books
    Were woman's looks,
And folly's all they've taught me.

Her smile when Beauty granted,
I hung with gaze enchanted,
  Like him, the sprite,
  Whom maids by night
Oft meet in glen that's haunted.
Like him, too, Beauty won me,
But while her eyes were on me,
  If once their ray
  Was turned away,
O! winds could not outrun me.

And are those follies going?
And is my proud heart growing
  Too cold or wise
  For brilliant eyes
Again to set it glowing?
No, vain, alas, th'endeavour
From bonds so sweet to sever:
  Poor wisdom's chance
  Against a glance
Is now as weak as ever.

From Miss Biddy Fudge to Miss Dorothy —

(Extract from Letter X, *The Fudge Family in Paris*)

Well, it *isn't* the King, after all, my dear creature!
  But *don't* you go laugh, now – there's nothing to quiz in't –
For grandeur of air and for grimness of feature,
  He *might* be a King, DOLL, though, hang him, he isn't.
At first I felt hurt, for I wish'd it, I own,
If for no other cause but to vex Miss MALONE, –
(The great heiress, you know, of Shandangan, who's here,
Showing off with *such* airs, and a real Cashmere,
While mine's but a paltry old rabbit-skin, dear!)

But Pa says, on deeply considering the thing,
'I am just as well pleas'd it should *not* be the King;
As I think for my BIDDY, so *gentille* and *jolie*,
  Whose charms may their price in an *honest* way fetch,
That a Brandenburgh' – (what is a Brandenburgh,
    DOLLY?) –
  'Would be, after all, no such very great catch.
If the R-G-T[1] indeed' – added he, looking sly –
(You remember that comical squint of his eye)
But I stopp'd him with 'La, Pa, how *can* you say so,
When the R-G-T loves none but old women, you know!
Which is fact, my dear DOLLY – we, girls of eighteen,
And so slim – Lord, he'd think us not fit to be seen;
And would like us much better as old – ay, as old
As that Countess of DESMOND, of whom I've been told
That she liv'd to much more than a hundred and ten,
And was kill'd by a fall from a cherry-tree then!
What a frisky old girl! but – to come to my lover,
  Who, though not a King, is a *hero* I'll swear, –
You shall hear all that's happen'd, just briefly run over,
  Since that happy night, when we whisk'd through the air!

Let me see – 'twas on Saturday – yes, DOLLY, yes –
From that evening I date the first dawn of my bliss,
When we both rattled off in that dear little carriage,
Whose journey, BOB says, is so like Love and Marriage,
'Beginning gay, desperate, dashing, down-hilly,
And ending as dull as a six-inside Dilly!'
Well, scarcely a wink did I sleep the night through;
And, next day, having scribbled my letter to you,
With a heart full of hope this sweet fellow to meet,
I set out with Papa, to see LOUIS DIX-HUIT
Make his bow to some half dozen women and boys,

[1] The Regent, later George IV

Who gets up a small concert of shrill *Vive le Roi*'s –
And how vastly genteeler, my dear, even this is,
Than vulgar Pall-Mall's oratorio of hisses!
The gardens seem'd full – so, of course, we walk'd o'er 'em,
'Mong orange-trees, clipp'd into town-bred decorum,
And daphnes,[2] and vases, and many a statue,
There staring, with not ev'n a stitch on them, at you!

JAMES LEIGH HUNT

Jenny Kissed Me

Jenny kissed me when we met,
  Jumping from the chair she sat in;
Time, you thief, who love to get
  Sweets into your list, put that in!
Say I'm weary, say I'm sad,
  Say that health and wealth have missed me,
Say I'm growing old, but add,
  Jenny kissed me.

Two Sonnets

1 To a Fish

You strange, astonished-looking, angle-faced,
Dreary-mouthed, gaping wretches of the sea,
Gulping salt water everlastingly,
Cold-blooded, though with red your blood be graced,
And mute, though dwellers in the roaring waste;
And you, all shapes beside, that fishy be –
Some round, some flat, some long, all devilry,
Legless, unloving, infamously chaste:

[2] laurels

O scaly, slippery, wet, swift, staring wights,
What is't ye do? What life lead? eh, dull goggles?
How do ye vary your vile days and nights?
How pass your Sundays? Are ye still but joggles
In ceaseless wash? Still nought but gapes, and bites,
And drinks, and stares, diversified with boggles?

2 A Fish Replies

Amazing monster! that, for aught I know,
With the first sight of thee didst make our race
For ever stare! O flat and shocking face,
Grimly divided from the breast below!
Thou that on dry land horribly dost go
With a split body and most ridiculous pace,
Prong after prong, disgracer of all grace,
Long-useless-finned, haired, upright, unwet, slow!

O breather of unbreathable, sword-sharp air,
How canst exist? How bear thyself, thou dry
And dreary sloth? What particle canst share
Of the only blessed life, the watery?
I sometimes see of ye an actual *pair*
Go by, linked fin by fin, most odiously.

THOMAS L. PEACOCK

Rich and Poor, or Saint and Sinner

The poor man's sins are glaring;
In the face of ghostly warning
    He is caught in the fact
    Of an overt act –
Buying greens on Sunday morning.

The rich man's sins are hidden
In the pomp of wealth and station;
    And escape the sight
    Of the children of light,
Who are wise in their generation.

The rich man has a kitchen,
And cooks to dress his dinner;
    The poor who would roast
    To the baker's must post,
And thus becomes a sinner.

The rich man has a cellar,
And a ready butler by him;
    The poor must steer
    For his pint of beer
Where the saint can't choose but spy him.

The rich man's painted windows
Hide the concerts of the quality;
    The poor can but share
    A crack'd fiddle in the air,
Which offends all sound morality.

The rich man is invisible
In the crowd of his gay society;
    But the poor man's delight
    Is a sore in the sight,
And a stench in the nose of piety.

The rich man has a carriage
Where no rude eye can flout him;
    The poor man's bane
    Is a third-class train,
With the daylight all about him.

The rich man goes out yachting,
Where sanctity can't pursue him;
    The poor goes afloat
    In a fourpenny boat,
Where the bishop groans to view him.

LORD BYRON

from *Don Juan*

I

Sagest of women, even of widows, she
  Resolved that Juan should be quite a paragon,
And worthy of the noblest pedigree:
  (His sire was of Castile, his dam from Aragon).
Then for accomplishments of chivalry,
  In case our lord the king should go to war again,
He learned the arts of riding, fencing, gunnery,
And how to scale a fortress – or a nunnery.

But that which Donna Inez most desired,
  And saw into herself each day before all
The learned tutors whom for him she hired,
  Was, that his breeding should be strictly moral:
Much into all his studies she inquired,
  And so they were submitted first to her, all
Arts, sciences, no branch was made a mystery
To Juan's eyes, excepting natural history.

The languages, especially the dead,
  The sciences, and most of all the abstruse,
The arts, at least all such as could be said
  To be the most remote from common use,

In all these he was much and deeply read:
  But not a page of anything that's loose
Or hints continuation of the species,
Was ever suffered, lest he should grow vicious.

His classic studies made a little puzzle,
  Because of filthy loves of gods and goddesses,
Who in the earlier ages raised a bustle,
  But never put on pantaloons or bodices;
His reverend tutors had at times a tussle,
  And for their Aeneids, Iliads, and Odysseys
Were forced to make an odd sort of apology,
For Donna Inez dreaded the mythology.

Ovid's a rake, as half his verses show him,
  Anacreon's morals are a still worse sample,
Catullus scarcely has a decent poem,
  I don't think Sappho's ode a good example,
Although Longinus tells us there is no hymn
  Where the sublime soars forth on wings more ample;
But Virgil's songs are pure, except that horrid one
Beginning with 'Formosum pastor Corydon'.

Lucretius' irreligion is too strong
  For early stomachs, to prove wholesome food.
I can't help thinking Juvenal was wrong,
  Although no doubt his real intent was good,
For speaking out so plainly in his song,
  So much indeed as to be downright rude;
And then what proper person can be partial
To all those nauseous epigrams of Martial?

Juan was taught from out the best edition,
  Expurgated by learnèd men, who place
Judiciously from out the schoolboy's vision
  The grosser parts, but fearful to deface

Too much their modest bard by this omission,
  And pitying sore his mutilated case,
They only add them all in an appendix,
Which saves in fact the trouble of an index;

For there we have them all at one fell swoop,
  Instead of being scattered through the pages;
They stand forth marshalled in a handsome troop,
  To meet the ingenuous youth of future ages,
Till some less rigid editor shall stoop
  To call them back into their separate cages,
Instead of standing staring altogether,
Like garden gods – and not so decent either.

. . . .

Milton's the prince of poets – so we say;
  A little heavy, but no less divine:
An independent being in his day –
  Learnèd, pious, temperate in love and wine;
But his life falling into Johnson's way,
  We're told this great high priest of all the Nine
Was whipt at college – a harsh sire – odd spouse,
For the first Mrs Milton left his house.

All these are, *certes*, entertaining facts,
  Like Shakspeare's stealing deer, Lord Bacon's bribes;
Like Titus' youth and Caesar's earliest acts;
  Like Burns (whom Doctor Currie well describes);
Like Cromwell's pranks; but although truth exacts
  These amiable descriptions from the scribes,
As most essential to their hero's story,
They do not much contribute to his glory.

All are not moralists, like Southey, when
  He prated to the world of 'Pantisocracy';
Or Wordsworth unexcised, unhired, who then
  Seasoned his pedlar poems with dèmocracy;

Or Coleridge, long before his flighty pen
  Let to the Morning Post its aristocracy;
When he and Southey, following the same path,
Espoused two partners (milliners of Bath).

II

If ever I should condescend to prose,
  I'll write poetical commandments, which
Shall supersede beyond all doubt all those
  That went before; in these I shall enrich
My text with many things that no one knows,
  And carry precept to the highest pitch:
I'll call the work 'Longinus o'er a Bottle;
Or, Every Poet, his *own* Aristotle'.

Thou shalt believe in Milton, Dryden, Pope;
  Thou shalt not set up Wordsworth, Coleridge, Southey;
Because the first is crazed beyond all hope,
  The second drunk, the third so quaint and mouthey:
With Crabbe it may be difficult to cope,
  And Campbell's Hippocrene is somewhat drouthy:
Thou shalt not steal from Samuel Rogers, nor
Commit – flirtation with the muse of Moore.

Thou shalt not covet Mr Sotheby's muse,
  His Pegasus, nor anything that's his;
Thou shalt not bear false witness like 'the Blues' –
  (There's one, at least, is very fond of this);
Thou shalt not write, in short, but what I choose;
  This is true criticism, and you may kiss –
Exactly as you please, or not – the rod;
But if you don't, I'll lay it on, by G—d!

III

In the great world – which, being interpreted,
Meaneth the west or worst end of a city,
And about twice two thousand people, bred
By no means to be very wise or witty,
But to sit up while others lie in bed,
And look down on the universe with pity –
Juan, as an inveterate patrician,
Was well received by persons of condition.

He was a bachelor, which is a matter
Of import both to virgin and to bride,
The former's hymeneal hopes to flatter;
And (should she not hold fast by love or pride)
'Tis also of some moment to the latter:
A rib's a thorn in a wed gallant's side,
Requires decorum, and is apt to double
The horrid sin – and, what's still worse, the trouble.

But Juan was a bachelor – of arts,
And parts, and hearts: he danced and sung and had
An air as sentimental as Mozart's
Softest of melodies, and could be sad
Or cheerful, without any 'flaws or starts',
Just at the proper time; and though a lad,
Had seen the world – which is a curious sight,
And very much unlike what people write.

Fair virgins blush'd upon him; wedded dames
Bloom'd also in less transitory hues;
For both commodities dwell by the Thames,
The painting and the painted: youth, ceruse,[1]

[1]White lead, used as a cosmetic

Against his heart preferr'd their usual claims,
  Such as no gentleman can quite refuse:
Daughters admired his dress, and pious mothers
Inquired his income, and if he had brothers.

The milliners who furnish 'drapery misses',
  Throughout the season, upon speculation
Of payment ere the honeymoon's last kisses
  Have waned into a crescent's coruscation,
Thought such an opportunity as this is,
  Of a rich foreigner's initiation,
Not to be overlook'd – and gave such credit,
That future bridegrooms swore, and sigh'd, and paid it.

The Blues, that tender tribe, who sigh o'er sonnets,
  And with the pages of the last Review
Line the interior of their heads or bonnets,
  Advanced in all their azure's highest hue;
They talk'd bad French or Spanish, and upon its
  Late authors ask'd him for a hint or two;
And which was softest, Russian or Castilian;
And whether in his travels he saw Ilion?

Juan, who was a little superficial,
  And not in literature a great Drawcansir,[2]
Examined by this learned and especial
  Jury of matrons, scarce knew what to answer,
His duties, warlike, loving, or official,
  His steady application as a dancer,
Had kept him from the brink of Hippocrene,
Which now he found was blue instead of green.

[2]A character in George Villiers' (the Earl of Buckingham) play, *The Rehearsal*, who was ready to fight anybody with the slightest excuse

However, he replied at hazard, with
  A modest confidence and calm assurance,
Which lent his learned lucubrations pith,
  And pass'd for arguments of good endurance.
That prodigy, Miss Araminta Smith
  (Who at sixteen translated *Hercules Furens*
Into as furious English), with her best look,
Set down his sayings in her commonplace book.

Juan knew several languages – as well
  He might – and brought them up with skill, in time
To save his fame with each accomplish'd belle,
  Who still regretted that he did not rhyme.
There wanted but this requisite to swell
  His qualities (with them) into sublime;
Lady Fitz-Frisky, and Miss Mævia Mannish,
Both long'd extremely to be sung in Spanish.

However, he did pretty well, and was
  Admitted as an aspirant to all
The coteries, and, as in Banquo's glass,
  At great assemblies or in parties small,
He saw ten thousand living authors pass,
  That being about their average numeral:
Also the eighty 'greatest living poets',
As every paltry magazine can show *its*.

In twice five years the 'greatest living poet',
  Like to the champion in the fisty ring,
Is call'd on to support his claim, or show it,
  Although 'tis an imaginary thing.
Even I – albeit I'm sure I did not know it,
  Nor sought of foolscap subjects to be king –
Was reckon'd a considerable time,
The grand Napoleon of the realms of rhyme.

But Juan was my Moscow, and Faliero
  My Leipsic, and my Mount Saint Jean seems Cain:
La Belle Alliance of dunces down at zero,
  Now that the lion's fall'n, may rise again;
But I will fall at least as fell my hero;
  Nor reign at all, or as a *monarch* reign;
Or to some lonely isle of jailors go,
With turncoat Southey for my turnkey Lowe.

Sir Walter reign'd before me; Moore and Campbell
  Before and after: but now grown more holy,
The muses upon Sion's hill must ramble
  With poets almost clergymen, or wholly;
And Pegasus has a psalmodic amble
  Beneath the very Reverend Rowley Powley,
Who shoes the glorious animals with stilts,
A modern Ancient Pistol – by the hilts!

Still he excels that artificial hard
  Labourer in the same vineyard, though the vine
Yields him but vinegar for his reward –
  That neutralized dull Dorus of the Nine;
That swarthy Sporus, neither man nor bard;
  That ox of verse, who *ploughs* for every line: –
Cambyses' roaring Romans beat at least
The howling Hebrews of Cybele's priest. –

Then there's my gentle Euphues, who, they say,
  Sets up for being a sort of *moral me*:
He'll find it rather difficult some day
  To turn out both, or either, it may be.
Some persons think that Coleridge hath the sway,
  And Wordsworth hath supporters two or three;
And that deep-mouth'd Bœotian, 'Savage Landor',
Has taken for a swan rogue Southey's gander.

John Keats, who was kill'd off by one critique,
  Just as he really promised something great,
If not intelligible, without Greek,
  Contrived to talk about the gods of late,
Much as they might have been supposed to speak.
  Poor fellow! his was an untoward fate;
'Tis strange the mind, that very fiery particle,
Should let itself be snuff'd out by an article.

The list grows long of live and dead pretenders
  To that which none will gain – or none will know
The conqueror at least; who, ere Time renders
  His last award, will have the long grass grow
Above his burnt-out brain and sapless cinders.
  If I might augur, I should rate but low
Their chances: they are too numerous, like the thirty
Mock tyrants, when Rome's annals wax'd but dirty.

This is the literary *lower* empire,
  Where the prætorian bands take up the matter; –
A 'dreadful trade', like his who 'gathers samphire',
  The insolent soldiery to soothe and flatter,
With the same feelings as you'd coax a vampire.
  Now, were I once at home, and in good satire,
I'd try conclusions with those Janizaries,
And show them *what* an intellectual war is.

I think I know a trick or two would turn
  Their flanks; – but it is hardly worth my while
With such small gear to give myself concern:
  Indeed, I've not the necessary bile;
My natural temper's really aught but stern,
  And even my Muse's worst reproof's a smile;
And then she drops a brief and modern curtsey,
And glides away, assured she never hurts ye.

My Juan, whom I left in deadly peril
  Amongst live poets and blue ladies, past
With some small profit through that field so sterile,
  Being tired in time, and neither least nor last,
Left it before he had been treated very ill;
  And henceforth found himself more gaily class'd
Amongst the higher spirits of the day,
The sun's true son, no vapour, but a ray.

His morns he pass'd in business – which dissected,
  Was like all business, a laborious nothing,
That leads to lassitude, the most infected
  And Centaur Nessus garb of mortal clothing,
And on our sofas makes us lie dejected,
  And talk in tender horrors of our loathing
All kinds of toil, save for our country's good –
Which grows no better, though 'tis time it should.

His afternoons he pass'd in visits, luncheons,
  Lounging, and boxing; and the twilight hour
In riding round those vegetable puncheons
  Call'd 'Parks', where there is neither fruit nor flower,
Enough to gratify a bee's slight munchings;
  But, after all, it is the only 'bower'
(In Moore's phrase) where the fashionable fair
Can form a slight acquaintance with fresh air.

Then dress, then dinner, then awakes the world;
  Then glare the lamps, then whirl the wheels, then roar
Through street and square fast flashing chariots hurl'd
  Like harness'd meteors; then along the floor
Chalk mimics painting; then festoons are twirl'd;
  Then roll the brazen thunders of the door,
Which opens to the thousand happy few,
An earthly paradise of 'Or Molu'.

There stands the noble hostess, nor shall sink
 With the three thousandth curtsey; there the waltz,
The only dance which teaches girls to think,
 Makes one in love even with its very faults.
Saloon, room, hall, o'erflow beyond their brink,
 And long the latest of arrivals halts,
'Midst royal dukes, and dames condemn'd to climb,
And gain an inch of staircase at a time.

Thrice happy he who, after a survey
 Of the good company, can win a corner,
A door that's *in*, or boudoir *out*, of the way,
 Where he may fix himself like small 'Jack Horner',
And let the Babel round run as it may,
 And look on as a mourner, or a scorner,
Or an approver, or a mere spectator,
Yawning a little as the night grows later.

But this won't do, save by and by; and he
 Who, like Don Juan, takes an active share,
Must steer with care through all that glittering sea
 Of gems, and plumes, and pearls, and silks, to where
He deems it is his proper place to be;
 Dissolving in the waltz, to some soft air,
Or proudlier prancing, with mercurial skill,
Where Science marshals forth her own quadrille.

Or, if he dance not, but hath higher views
 Upon an heiress or his neighbour's bride,
Let him take care that that which he pursues
 Is not at once too palpably descried.
Full many an eager gentleman oft rues
 His haste: impatience is a blundering guide,
Amongst a people famous for reflection,
Who like to play the fool with circumspection.

But if you can contrive, get next at supper;
  Or, if forestall'd, get opposite and ogle: –
Oh, ye ambrosial moments! always upper
  In mind, a sort of sentimental bogle
Which sits for ever upon memory's crupper,
  The ghost of vanish'd pleasures once in vogue! Ill
Can tender souls relate the rise and fall
Of hopes and fears which shake a single ball.

But these precautionary hints can touch
  Only the common run, who must pursue,
And watch and ward; whose plans a word too much
  Or little overturns; and not the few
Or many (for the number's sometimes such)
  Whom a good mien, especially if new,
Or fame, or name, for wit, war, sense, or nonsense,
Permits whate'er they please, or *did* not long since.

Our hero, as a hero, young and handsome,
  Noble, rich, celebrated, and a stranger,
Like other slaves, of course must pay his ransom,
  Before he can escape from so much danger
As will environ a conspicuous man. Some
  Talk about poetry, and 'rack and manger',
And ugliness, disease, as toil and trouble; –
I wish they knew the life of a young noble.

They are young, but know not youth – it is anticipated;
  Handsome but wasted, rich without a sou;
Their vigour in a thousand arms is dissipated;
  Their cash comes *from*, their wealth goes *to*, a Jew:
Both senates see their nightly votes participated
  Between the tyrant's and the tribunes' crew;
And having voted, dined, drunk, gamed, and w—d,
The family vault receives another lord.

'Where is the world ?' cries Young, at *eighty*. 'Where
  The world in which a man was born?' Alas,
Where is the world of *eight* years past? '*Twas there* –
  I look for it – 'tis gone, a globe of glass!
Crack'd, shiver'd, vanish'd, scarcely gazed on, ere
  A silent change dissolves the glittering mass.
Statesmen, chiefs, orators, queens, patriots, kings,
And dandies, all are gone on the wind's wings.

Where is Napoleon the Grand? God knows:
  Where little Castlereagh? The devil can tell:
Where Grattan, Curran, Sheridan, all those
  Who bound the bar or senate in their spell?
Where is the unhappy Queen, with all her woes?
  And where the Daughter, whom the Isles loved well?
Where are those martyr'd saints, the Five per Cents?
And where – oh, where the devil are the Rents?

Where's Brummel? Dish'd. Where's Long Pole Wellesley?
    Diddled.
  Where's Whitbread? Romilly? Where's George the
    Third?
Where is his will? (That's not so soon unriddled.)
  And where is 'Fum' the Fourth, our 'royal bird'?
Gone down, it seems, to Scotland, to be fiddled
  Unto by Sawney's violin, we have heard:
'Caw me, caw thee' – for six months had been hatching
This scene of royal itch and royal scratching.

Where is Lord This, and where my Lady That?
  The Honourable Mistresses and Misses?
Some laid aside, like an old opera hat,
  Married, unmarried, and remarried: (this is
An evolution oft performed of late:)
  Where are the Dublin shouts – and London hisses?
Where are the Grenvilles? Turn'd, as usual. Where
My friends the Whigs? Exactly where they were.

Where are the Lady Carolines and Franceses?
  Divorced, or doing thereanent. Ye annals
So brilliant, where the lists of routs and dances is –
  Thou *Morning Post*, sole record of the panels
Broken in carriages, and all the phantasies
  Of fashion – say what streams now fill those channels?
Some die, some fly, some languish on the Continent,
Because the times have hardly left them *one* tenant.

Some, who once set their caps at cautious dukes,
  Have taken up at length with younger brothers:
Some heiresses have bit at sharpers' hooks:
  Some maids have been made wives, some merely
    mothers,
Others have lost their fresh and fairy looks:
  In short, the list of alterations bothers.
There's little strange in this, but something strange is
The unusual quickness of these common changes.

Talk not of seventy years as age: in seven
  I have seen more changes, down from monarchs to
The humblest individual under heaven,
  Than might suffice a modern century through.
I knew that nought was lasting, but now even
  Change grows too changeable, without being new;
Nought's permanent among the human race,
Except the Whigs *not* getting into place.

I have seen Napoleon, who seem'd quite a Jupiter,
  Shrink to a Saturn. I have seen a Duke
(No matter which) turn politician stupider,
  If that can well be, than his wooden look.
But it is time that I should hoist my 'Blue Peter',
  And sail for a new theme: – I have seen, and shook
To see it – the king hiss'd, and then caress'd;
But don't pretend to settle which was best.

I have seen the Landholders without a rap –
  I have seen Joanna Southcote – I have seen
The House of Commons turn'd to a tax-trap –
  I have seen that sad affair of the late Queen –
I have seen crowns worn instead of a fool's cap –
  I have seen a Congress doing all that's mean –
I have seen some nations, like o'erloaded asses,
Kick off their burthens – meaning the high classes –

I have seen small poets, and great prosers, and
  Interminable – *not eternal* – speakers –
I have seen the funds at war with house and land –
  I have seen the country gentlemen turn squeakers –
I have seen the people ridden o'er, like sand,
  By slaves on horseback – I have seen malt liquors
Exchanged for 'thin potations' by John Bull;
I have seen John half detect himself a fool. –

But *carpe diem*, Juan, *carpe*, *carpe!*
  To-morrow sees another race as gay
And transient, and devour'd by the same harpy.
  'Life's a poor player' – then 'play out the play,
Ye villains!' and, above all, keep a sharp eye
  Much less on what you do than what you say;
Be hypocritical, be cautious, be
Not what you *seem*, but always what you *see*.

JOHN KEATS

Lines Rhymed in a Letter Received (by J. H. R.) from Oxford

The Gothic looks solemn,
The plain Doric column
Supports an old Bishop and Crosier;
The mouldering arch,
Shaded o'er by a larch,
Stands next door to Wilson the Hosier.

Vicè – that is, by turns, –
O'er pale faces mourns
The black tassell'd trencher and common hat;
The Chantry boy sings,
The Steeple-bell rings,
And as for the Chancellor – *dominat.*

There are plenty of trees,
And plenty of ease,
And plenty of fat deer for Parsons;
And when it is venison,
Short is the benison, –
Then each on a leg or thigh fastens.

Dawlish Fair

From a letter to James Rice, 24 March 1818

Over the hill and over the dale,
And over the bourn to Dawlish –
Where Gingerbread Wives have a scanty sale
And gingerbread nuts are smallish.

Rantipole Betty she ran down a hill
And kicked up her petticoats fairly
Says I I'll be Jack if you will be Gill.
So she sat on the Grass debonnairly.

Here's somebody coming, here's somebody coming!
  Says I 'tis the Wind at a parley
So without any fuss any hawing and humming
  She lay on the grass debonnairly.

Here's somebody here and here's somebody there!
  Says I hold your tongue you young Gipsey.
So she held her tongue and lay plump and fair
  And dead as a venus tipsy.

O who wouldn't hie to Dawlish fair
  O who wouldn't stop in a Meadow
O who would not rumple the daisies there
  And make the wild fern for a bed do.

Sharing Eve's Apple

O blush not so! O blush not so!
  Or I shall think you knowing;
And if you smile the blushing while,
  Then maidenheads are going.

There's a blush for won't, and a blush for shan't,
  And a blush for having done it:
There's a blush for thought and a blush for naught,
  And a blush for just begun it.

O sigh not so! O sigh not so!
  For it sounds of Eve's sweet pippin;
By these loosened lips you have tasted the pips
  And fought in an amorous nipping.

Will you play once more at nice-cut-core,
For it only will last our youth out,
And we have the prime of the kissing time,
We have not one sweet tooth out.

There's a sigh for yes, and a sigh for no,
And a sigh for I can't bear it!
O what can be done, shall we stay or run?
O cut the sweet apple and share it!

HARTLEY COLERIDGE

Wordsworth Unvisited

He lived amidst th' untrodden ways
To Rydal Lake that lead; –
A bard whom there were none to praise,
And very few to read.

Behind a cloud his mystic sense,
Deep-hidden, who can spy?
Bright as the night when not a star
Is shining in the sky.

Unread his works – his 'Milk White Doe'
With dust is dark and dim;
It's still in Longman's shop, and oh!
The difference to him!

ALARIC A. WATTS

An Austrian Army

An Austrian army awfully array'd,
Boldly by battery besieged Belgrade.
Cossack commanders cannonading come
Dealing destruction's devastating doom:
Every endeavour engineers essay,
For fame, for fortune fighting-furious fray!
Generals 'gainst generals grapple, gracious God!
How Heaven honours heroic hardihood!
Infuriate – indiscriminate in ill –
Kinsmen kill kindred – kindred kinsmen kill:
Labour low levels loftiest, longest lines,
Men march 'mid mounds, 'mid moles, 'mid murd'rous
mines:
Now noisy noxious numbers notice nought
Of outward obstacles, opposing ought –
Poor patriots – partly purchased – partly press'd
Quite quaking, quickly 'Quarter! quarter!' quest:
Reason returns, religious right redounds,
Suwarrow stops such sanguinary sounds.
Truce to thee, Turkey, triumph to thy train,
Unwise, unjust, unmerciful Ukraine!
Vanish, vain victory! Vanish, victory vain!
Why wish we warfare? Wherefore welcome were
Xerxes, Ximenes, Xanthus, Xavier?
Yield, yield, ye youths, ye yeomen, yield your yell:
Zeno's, Zimmermann's, Zoroaster's zeal,
Again attract; arts against arms appeal!

ANONYMOUS

Soldier, Won't You Marry Me?

Soldier, soldier, won't you marry me?
It's O a fife and drum.
How can I marry such a pretty girl as you
When I've got no hat to put on?

Off to the tailor she did go
As hard as she could run,
Brought him back the finest was there.
Now, soldier, put it on.

Soldier, soldier, won't you marry me?
It's O a fife and drum.
How can I marry such a pretty girl as you
When I've got no coat to put on?

Off to the tailor she did go
As hard as she could run,
Brought him back the finest was there.
Now soldier, put it on.

Soldier, soldier, won't you marry me?
It's O a fife and drum.
How can I marry such a pretty girl as you
When I've got no shoes to put on?

Off to the shoe shop she did go
As hard as she could run,
Brought him back the finest was there.
Now, soldier, put them on.

Soldier, soldier, won't you marry me?
It's O a fife and drum.
How can I marry such a pretty girl as you
And a wife and baby at home?

THOMAS HOOD

To Minerva

My temples throb, my pulses boil,
  I'm sick of Song, and Ode, and Ballad –
So, Thyrsis, take the Midnight Oil,
  And pour it on a lobster salad.

My brain is dull, my sight is foul,
  I cannot write a verse, or read, –
Then, Pallas, take away thine Owl,
  And let us have a lark instead.

Miss Kilmansegg's Birth

What different dooms our birthdays bring!
For instance, one little mannikin thing
  Survives to wear many a wrinkle;
While Death forbids another to wake,
And a son that it took nine moons to make
  Expires without even a twinkle!

Into this world we come like ships,
Launch'd from the docks, and stocks, and slips,
  For fortune fair or fatal;
And one little craft is cast away
In its very first trip in Babbicome Bay,
  While another rides safe at Port Natal.

What different lots our stars accord!
This babe to be hail'd and woo'd as a Lord!
  And that to be shunned like a leper!
One, to the world's wine, honey, and corn,
Another, like Colchester native, born
  To its vinegar, only, and pepper.

One is littered under a roof
Neither wind nor water proof, –
   That's the prose of Love in a Cottage, –
A puny, naked, shivering wretch,
The whole of whose birthright would not fetch,
Though Robins himself drew up the sketch,
   The bid of 'a mess of pottage'.

Born of Fortunatus's kin,
Another comes tenderly usher'd in
   To a prospect all bright and burnish'd:
No tenant he for life's back slums –
He comes to the world as a gentleman comes
   To a lodging ready furnish'd.

And the other sex – the tender – the fair –
What wide reverses of fate are there!
Whilst Margaret, charm'd by the Bulbul rare,
   In a garden of Gul reposes –
Poor Peggy hawks nosegays from street to street,
Till – think of that, who find life so sweet! –
   She hates the smell of roses!

Not so with the infant Kilmansegg!
She was not born to steal or beg,
   Or gather cresses in ditches;
To plait the straw, or bind the shoe,
Or sit all day to hem and sew,
As females must, and not a few –
   To fill their insides with stitches!

She was not doom'd, for bread to eat,
To be put to her hands as well as her feet –
   To carry home linen from mangles –
Or heavy-hearted, and weary-limb'd,
To dance on a rope in a jacket trimm'd
   With as many blows as spangles.

She was one of those who by Fortune's boon
Are born, as they say, with a silver spoon
  In her mouth, not a wooden ladle:
To speak according to poet's wont,
Plutus as sponsor stood at her font,
  And Midas rock'd the cradle.

At her first *début* she found her head
On a pillow of down, in a downy bed,
  With a damask canopy over.
For although by the vulgar popular saw,
All mothers are said to be 'in the straw',
  Some children are born in clover.

Her very first draught of vital air
It was not the common chameleon fare
  Of plebeian lungs and noses, –
    No – her earliest sniff
    Of this world was a whiff
  Of the genuine Otto of Roses!

When she saw the light – it was no mere ray
Of that light so common – so everyday –
  That the sun each morning launches –
But six wax tapers dazzled her eyes,
From a thing – a gooseberry bush for size –
  With a golden stem and branches.

She was born exactly at half-past two,
As witness'd a timepiece in or-molu
  That stood on a marble table –
Showing at once the time of day,
And a team of gildings running away
  As fast as they were able,
With a golden god with a golden star,
And a golden spear, in a golden car,
  According to Grecian fable.

Like other babes, at her birth she cried;
Which made a sensation far and wide,
  Ay, for twenty miles around her;
For though to the ear 'twas nothing more
Than an infant's squall, it was really the roar
  Of a Fifty-thousand Pounder!
    It shook the next heir
    In his library chair,
  And made him cry, 'Confound her!'

Of signs and omens there was no dearth,
Any more than at Owen Glendower's birth,
  Or the advent of other great people:
    Two bullocks dropp'd dead,
    As if knock'd on the head,
    And barrels of stout
    And ale ran about,
    And the village-bells such a peal rang out,
  That they crack'd the village steeple.

In no time at all, like mushroom spawn,
Tables sprang up all over the lawn;
Not furnish'd scantly or shabbily,
  But on scale as vast
  As that huge repast,
  With its loads and cargoes
  Of drinks and botargoes,[1]
At the Birth of the Babe in Rabelais.

Hundreds of men were turn'd into beasts,
Like the guests of Circe's horrible feasts,
  By the magic of ale and cider:

[1]Relishes made of fish roe

And each country lass, and each country lad,
Began to caper and dance like mad,
And even some old ones appear'd to have had
   A bite from the Naples Spider.

Then as night came on,
   It had scared King John,
Who considered such signs not risible,
   To have seen the maroons,
   And the whirling moons,
   And the serpents of flame,
   And wheels of the same,
That according to some were 'whizzable'.

Oh, happy Hope of the Kilmanseggs!
Thrice happy in head, and body, and legs
   That her parents had such full pockets!
For had she been born of Want and Thrift,
For care and nursing all adrift,
It's ten to one she had had to make shift
   With rickets instead of rockets!

A Butcher

Whoe'er has gone through London Street,
Has seen a Butcher gazing at his meat
   And how he keeps
   Gloating upon a sheep's
Or bullock's personals, as if his own;
   How he admires his halves
   And quarters – and his calves,
As if in truth upon his own legs grown; –

His fat! his suet!
His kidneys peeping elegantly thro' it!
His thick flank!
And his thin!
His shank!
His shin!
Skin of his skin, and bone too of his bone!

With what an air
He stands aloof, across the thoroughfare
Gazing – and will not let a body by,
Tho' buy! buy! buy! be constantly his cry.
Meanwhile with arms a-kimbo, and a pair
Of Rhodian legs he revels in a stare
At his Joint Stock – for one may call it so,
Howbeit, without a Co.
The dotage of self-love was never fonder
Than he of his brute bodies all a-row;
Narcissus in his wave did never ponder
With love so strong,
On his 'portrait charmant'
As our vain Butcher on his carcase yonder.

Look at his sleek, round skull!
How bright his cheek, how rubicund his nose is!
His visage seems to be
Ripe for beef-tea;
Of brutal juices the whole man is full. –
In fact, fulfilling the metempsychosis,
The Butcher is already half a Bull.

A Nocturnal Sketch

Even is come; and from the dark Park, hark,
The signal of the setting sun – one gun!

And six is sounding from the chime, prime time
To go and see the Drury-Lane Dane slain, –
Or hear Othello's jealous doubt spout out, –
Or Macbeth raving at that shade-made blade,
Denying to his frantic clutch much touch; –
Or else to see Ducrow with wide stride ride
Four horses as no other man can span;
Or in the small Olympic Pit, sit split
Laughing at Liston, while you quiz his phiz.
Anon Night comes, and with her wings brings things
Such as with his poetic tongue, Young sung;
The gas up-blazes with its bright white light,
And paralytic watchmen prowl, howl, growl,
About the streets and take up Pall-Mall Sal,
Who, hasting to her nightly jobs, robs fobs.
Now thieves to enter for your cash, smash, crash,
Past drowsy Charley, in a deep sleep, creep,
But frightened by Policeman B 3, flee,
And while they're going, whisper low, 'No Go!'
Now puss, while folk are in their beds, treads leads,
And sleepers waking, grumble – 'drat that cat!'
Who in the gutter catterwauls, squalls, mauls
Some feline foe, and screams in shrill ill-will.

Now Bulls of Bashan, of a prize size, rise
In childish dreams, and with a roar gore poor
Georgy or Charley, or Billy, willy-nilly; –
But Nursemaid, in a nightmare rest, chest-pressed,
Dreameth of one of her old flames, James Games,
And that she hears – what faith is man's – Ann's banns
And his, from Reverend Mr Rice, twice, thrice:
White ribbons flourish, and a stout shout out,
That upward goes, shows Rose knows those bows'
woes!

Epicurean Reminiscences of a Sentimentalist

'My *Tables*! *Meat* it is, *I set it* down!' *Hamlet*

I think it was Spring – but not certain I am –
  When my passion began first to work;
But I know we were certainly looking for lamb,
  And the season was over for pork.

'Twas at Christmas, I think, when I met with Miss Chase,
  Yes, – for Morris had asked me to dine, –
And I thought I had never beheld such a face,
  Or so noble a turkey and chine.

Placed close to her side, it made others quite wild,
  With sheer envy to witness my luck;
How she blushed as I gave her some turtle, and smiled
  As I afterwards offered some duck.

I looked and I languished, alas, to my cost,
  Through three courses of dishes and meats;
Getting deeper in love – but my heart was quite lost,
  When it came to the trifle and sweets!

With a rent-roll that told of my houses and land
  To her parents I told my designs –
And then to herself I presented my hand,
  With a very fine pottle of pines![1]

I asked her to have me for weal or for woe,
  And she did not object in the least:
I can't tell the date – but we married, I know,
  Just in time to have game at the feast.

[1] basket of pineapples

We went to —, it certainly was the seaside;
  For the next, the most blessed of morns,
I remember how fondly I gazed at my bride,
  Sitting down to a plateful of prawns.

Oh, never may mem'ry lose sight of that year,
  But still hallow the time as it ought,
That season the 'grass'[2] was remarkably dear,
  And the peas at a guinea a quart.

So happy, like hours, all our days seemed to haste,
  A fond pair, such as poets have drawn,
So united in heart – so congenial in taste,
  We were both of us partial to brawn!

A long life I looked for of bliss with my bride,
  But then Death – I ne'er dreamt about that!
Oh, there's nothing certain in life, as I cried,
  When my turbot eloped with the cat!

My dearest took ill at the turn of the year,
  But the cause no physician could nab;
But something it seemed like consumption, I fear,
  It was just after supping on crab.

In vain she was doctored, in vain she was dosed,
  Still her strength and her appetite pined;
She lost relish for what she had relished the most,
  Even salmon she deeply declined.

For months still I lingered in hope and in doubt,
  While her form it grew wasted and thin;
But the last dying spark of existence went out,
  As the oysters were just coming in!

[2] asparagus

She died, and she left me the saddest of men
  To indulge in a widower's moan;
Oh, I felt all the power of solitude then,
  As I ate my first natives alone!

But when I beheld Virtue's friends in their cloaks,
  And with sorrowful crape on their hats,
Oh, my grief poured a flood! and the out-of-door folks
  Were all crying – I think it was sprats!

Domestic Asides
or, Truth in Parentheses

'I really take it very kind,
This visit, Mrs Skinner!
I have not seen you such an age –
(The wretch has come to dinner!)

'Your daughters, too, what loves of girls –
What heads for painters' easels!
Come here and kiss the infant, dears –
(And give it p'rhaps the measles!)

'Your charming boys I see are home
From Reverend Mr Russell's;
'Twas very kind to bring them both –
(What boots for my new Brussels!)

'What! little Clara left at home?
Well now I call that shabby:
I should have loved to kiss her so –
(A flabby, dabby, babby!)

'And Mr S., I hope he's well,
Ah! though he lives so handy,
He never now drops in to sup –
(The better for our brandy!)

'Come, take a seat – I long to hear
About Matilda's marriage;
You're come of course to spend the day!
(Thank Heaven, I hear the carriage!)

'What! Must you go? next time I hope
You'll give me longer measure;
Nay – I shall see you down the stairs –
(With most uncommon pleasure!)

'Good-bye! good-bye! remember all,
Next time you'll take your dinners!
(Now, David, mind I'm not at home
In future to the Skinners!)'

ANONYMOUS

A Maiden There Lived

A maiden there lived in a large market-town,
Whose skin was much fairer – than any that's brown –
Her eyes were as dark as the coals in the mine,
And when they weren't shut, why they always would
shine.
With a black eye, blue eye, blear eye, pig's eye,
swivel eye, and squinting.

Between her two eyes an excrescence arose,
Which the vulgar call snout, but which I call a nose;
An emblem of sense, it should seem to appear,
For without one we'd look very foolish and queer:
With your Roman, Grecian, snub-nose, pug-nose,
snuffling snout, and sneezing.

Good-natured she look'd, that's when out of a frown,
And blush'd like a rose – when the paint was put on;
At church ev'ry morning her prayers she could scan,
And each night sigh and think of – the duty of man,
    With her groaning, moaning, sighing, dying,
    tabernacle – love-feasts.

The follies of youth she had long given o'er,
For the virgin I sing of – was turn'd fifty-four:
Yet suitors she had, who, with words sweet as honey
Strove hard to possess the bright charms of her money,
  With her household, leasehold, freehold, and her
    copyhold and tenement.

The first who appear'd on this am'rous list,
Was a tailor, who swore by his thimble and twist,
That if his strong passion she e'er should refuse,
He'd depart from the world, shop, cabbage, and goose,
  With his waistcoat, breeches, measures, scissors,
    button-holes, and buckram.

The next was a butcher, of slaughter-ox fame,
A very great boor, and Dick Hog was his name;
He swore she was lamb – but she laugh'd at his pains,
For she hated calf's head – unless served up with brains.
  With his sheep's head, lamb's fry, chitterlins –
    his marrow-bones and cleavers.

After many debates, which occasion'd much strife,
'Mongst love-sick admirers to make her their wife,
To end each dispute came a man out of breath,
Who eloped with the maid, and his name was grim Death.
  With his pick-axe, sexton, coffin, funeral, skeleton,
    and bone-house.

The Lincolnshire Poacher

When I was bound apprentice, in famous Lincolnshire,
Full well I served my master for more than seven year,
Till I took up to poaching, as you shall quickly hear:
Oh, 'tis my delight on a shining night, in the season of the
year.

As me and my companions were setting of a snare,
'Twas then we spied the game-keeper, for him we did not
care.
For we can wrestle and fight, my boys, and jump out any
where;
Oh, 'tis my delight on a shining night, in the season of the
year.

As me and my companions were setting four or five,
And, taking on 'em up again, we caught a hare alive.
We took the hare alive, my boys, and through the wood
did steer:
Oh, 'tis my delight on a shining night, in the season of the
year.

I threw him on my shoulder, and then we trudgèd home,
We took him to a neighbour's house and sold him for a
crown,
We sold him for a crown, my boys, but I did not tell you
where:
Oh, 'tis my delight on a shining night, in the season of the
year.

Success to every gentleman that lives in Lincolnshire,
Success to every poacher that wants to sell a hare,
Bad luck to every game-keeper that will not sell his deer:
Oh, 'tis my delight on a shining night, in the season of the
year.

The Fair Maid of Amsterdam

In Amsterdam there dwelt a maid,
Mark well what I do say;
In Amsterdam there dwelt a maid,
And she was mistress of her trade.
And I'll go no more a-roving
With you, fair maid.
A-roving, a-roving,
Since roving's been my ru-i-n,
I'll go no more a-roving
With you, fair maid.

Her cheeks was red, her eyes was brown,
Mark well what I do say;
Her cheeks was red, her eyes was brown,
Her hair like glow-worms hanging down,
And I'll go no more a-roving
With you, fair maid.
A-roving, a-roving,
Since roving's been my ru-i-n,
I'll go no more a-roving
With you, fair maid.

LORD MACAULAY

The Country Clergyman's Trip to Cambridge

An Election Ballad, 1827

As I sat down to breakfast in state,
At my living of Tithing-cum-Boring,
With Betty beside me to wait,
Came a rap that almost beat the door in.

I laid down my basin of tea,
   And Betty ceased spreading the toast,
'As sure as a gun, sir,' said she,
   'That must be the knock of the post.'

A letter – and free – bring it here –
   I have no correspondent who franks.
No! yes! can it be? Why my dear,
   'Tis our glorious, our Protestant Bankes.
'Dear sir, as I know you desire
   That the Church should receive due protection,
I humbly presume to require
   Your aid at the Cambridge election.

'It has lately been brought to my knowledge,
   That the Ministers fully design
To suppress each cathedral and college,
   And eject every learned divine.
To assist this detestable scheme
   Three nuncios from Rome are come over;
They left Calais on Monday by steam,
   And landed to dinner at Dover.

'An army of grim Cordeliers,
   Well furnished with relics and vermin,
Will follow, Lord Westmoreland fears,
   To effect what their chiefs may determine.
Lollards' bower, good authorities say,
   Is again fitting up as a prison;
And a wood-merchant told me to-day
   'Tis a wonder how faggots have risen.

'The finance scheme of Canning contains
   A new Easter-offering tax;
And he means to devote all the gains
   To a bounty on thumb-screws and racks.

Your living, so neat and compact –
  Pray, don't let the news give you pain! –
Is promised, I know for a fact,
  To an olive-faced Padre from Spain.'

I read, and I felt my heart bleed,
  Sore wounded with horror and pity;
So I flew, with all possible speed,
  To our Protestant champion's committee.
True gentlemen, kind and well-bred!
  No fleering! no distance! no scorn!
They asked after my wife, who is dead,
  And my children who never were born.

They then, like high-principled Tories,
  Called our Sovereign unjust and unsteady,
And assailed him with scandalous stories,
  Till the coach for the voters was ready.
That coach might be well called a casket
  Of learning and brotherly love:
There were parsons in boot and in basket;
  There were parsons below and above.

There were Sneaker and Griper, a pair
  Who stick to Lord Mulesby like leeches;
A smug chaplain of plausible air,
  Who writes my Lord Goslingham's speeches;
Dr Buzz, who alone is a host,
  Who, with arguments weighty as lead,
Proves six times a week in the Post
  That flesh somehow differs from bread;

Dr Nimrod, whose orthodox toes
  Are seldom withdrawn from the stirrup;
Dr Humdrum, whose eloquence flows,
  Like droppings of sweet poppy syrup;

Dr Rosygill puffing and fanning,
  And wiping away perspiration,
Dr Humbug, who proved Mr Canning
  The beast in St John's Revelation.

A layman can scarce form a notion
  Of our wonderful talk on the road;
Of the learning, the wit, and devotion,
  Which almost each syllable showed:
Why divided allegiance agrees
  So ill with our free constitution;
How Catholics swear as they please,
  In hope of the priest's absolution;

How the Bishop of Norwich had bartered
  His faith for a legate's commission;
How Lyndhurst, afraid to be martyred,
  Had stooped to a base coalition;
How Papists are cased from compassion
  By bigotry, stronger than steel;
How burning would soon come in fashion,
  And how very bad it must feel.

We were all so much touched and excited
  By a subject so direly sublime,
That the rules of politeness were slighted,
  And we all of us talked at a time;
And in tones, which each moment grew louder,
  Told how we should dress for the show,
And where we should fasten the powder,
  And if we should bellow or no.

Thus from subject to subject we ran,
  And the journey passed pleasantly o'er,
Till at last Dr Humdrum began;
  From that time I remember no more.

At Ware he commenced his prelection,
In the dullest of clerical drones:
And when next I regained recollection
We were rumbling o'er Trumpington stones.

WILLIAM BARNES

A Bit o' Sly Coorten

John and Fanny

John: Now, Fanny, 'tis too bad, you teazèn maïd!
How leäte you be a'come! Where have ye staÿ'd?
How long you have a-meäde me waït about!
I thought you werden gwaïn to come ageän;
I had a mind to goo back hwome ageän.
This idden when you promis'd to come out.

Fanny: Now 'tidden any good to meäke a row,
Upon my word, I cooden come till now.
Vor I've a-been kept in all day by mother,
At work about woone little job an' t'other.
If you want to goo though, don't ye staÿ
Vor me a minute longer, I do praÿ.

John: I thought you mid be out wi' Jemmy Bleäke.

Fanny: An' why be out wi' him, for goodness' seäke?

John: You walk'd o' Zunday evenèn wi'n, d'ye know,
You went vrom church a-hitch'd up in his eärm.

Fanny: Well, if I did, that werden any harm.
Lauk! that *is* zome'at to teäke notice o'.

John: He took ye roun' the middle at the stile,
An' kiss'd ye twice within the half a mile.

Fanny: Ees, at the stile, because I shou'den vall,
He took me hold to help me down, that's all;
An' I can't zee what very mighty harm
He could ha' done a-lendèn me his eärm.
An' as for kissen o' me, if he did,
I didden ax en to, nor zay he mid:
An' if he kiss'd me dree times, or a dozen,
What harm wer it? Why, idden he my cousin?
An' I can't zee, then, what there is amiss
In Cousin Jem's jist gi'en me a kiss.

John: Well, he shan't kiss ye, then; you shan't be kiss'd
By his gre't ugly chops, a lanky houn'!
If I do zee'n, I'll jist wring up my vist
An' knock en down.
I'll squot his gre't pug-nose, if I don't miss en;
I'll warn' I'll spweil his pretty lips vor kissèn!

Fanny: Well, John, I'm sure I little thought to vind
That you had ever sich a jealous mind.
What then! I s'pose that I must be a dummy,
An' mussen goo about nor wag my tongue
To any soul, if he's a man, an' young;
Or else you'll work yourself up mad wi' passion,
An' talk away o' gi'en vo'k a drashèn,
An' breakèn bwones, and beäten heads to pummy!
If you've a-got sich jealous ways about ye,
I'm sure I should be better off 'ithout ye.

John: Well, if gre't Jemmy have a-won your heart,
We'd better break the coortship off, and peärt.

Fanny: He won my heart! There, John, don't talk sich stuff;
Don't talk noo mwore, vor you've a-zaid enough.
If I'd a-liked another mwore than you,
I'm sure I shou'den come to meet ye zoo;
Vor I've a-twold to father many a storry,
An' took o' mother many a scwolden vor ye.
(*weeping*)
But 'twull be over now, vor you shan't zee me.
Out wi' ye noo mwore, to pick a quarrel wi' me.

John: Well, Fanny, I woon't zay noo mwore, my dear.
Let's meäke it up. Come, wipe off thik there tear.
Let's goo an' zit o' top o' theäse here stile,
An' rest, an' look about a little while.
Fanny: Now goo away, you crabbed jealous chap!
You shan't kiss me – you shan't! I'll gi' ye a slap.

John: Then you look smilen; don't you pout an' toss
Your head so much, an look so very cross.

Fanny: Now, John! don't squeeze me roun' the middle zoo.
I woon't stop here noo longer if you do.
Why, John! be quiet, wull ye? Fie upon it!
Now zee how you've a-wrumpled up my bonnet.
Mother'ill zee it after I'm at hwome,
An' gi'e a guess directly how it come.

John: Then don't you zay that I be jealous, Fanny.

Fanny: I wull; vor you *be* jealous, Mister Jahnny.
There's zomebody a-comèn down the groun'
Towards the stile. Who is it? Come, get down.
I must run hwome, upon my word then, now;
If I do staÿ, they'll kick up sich a row.
Good night. I can't staÿ now.

John: Then good night, Fanny!
Come out a-bit to-morrow evenen, can ye?

W. M. PRAED

Good Night to the Season

Good night to the Season! 'Tis over!
Gay dwellings no longer are gay;
The courtier, the gambler, the lover,
Are scattered like swallows away:
There's nobody left to invite one
Except my good uncle and spouse;
My mistress is bathing at Brighton,
My patron is sailing at Cowes:
For want of a better employment,
Till Ponto and Don can get out,
I'll cultivate rural enjoyment,
And angle immensely for trout.

Good night to the Season! – the lobbies,
Their changes, and rumours of change,
Which startled the rustic Sir Bobbies,
And made all the Bishops look strange;
The breaches, and battles, and blunders,
Performed by the Commons and Peers;
The Marquis's eloquent blunders,
The Baronet's eloquent ears;
Denouncings of Papists and treasons,
Of foreign dominion and oats;
Misrepresentations of reasons,
And misunderstandings of notes.

Good night to the Season! – the buildings
Enough to make Inigo sick;
The paintings, and plasterings, and gildings
Of stucco, and marble, and brick;

The orders deliciously blended,
  From love of effect, into one;
The club-houses only intended,
  The palaces only begun;
The hell, where the fiend in his glory
  Sits staring at putty and stones,
And scrambles from story to story,
  To rattle at midnight his bones.

Good night to the Season! – the dances,
  The fillings of hot little rooms,
The glancings of rapturous glances,
  The fancyings of fancy costumes;
The pleasures which fashion makes duties,
  The praisings of fiddles and flutes,
The luxury of looking at Beauties,
  The tedium of talking to mutes;
The female diplomatists, planners
  Of matches for Laura and Jane;
The ice of her Ladyship's manners,
  The ice of his Lordship's champagne.

Good night to the Season! – the rages
  Led off by the chiefs of the throng,
The Lady Matilda's new pages,
  The Lady Eliza's new song;
Miss Fennel's macaw, which at Boodle's
  Was held to have something to say;
Mrs Splenetic's musical poodles,
  Which bark '*Batti Batti*' all day;
The pony Sir Araby sported,
  As hot and as black as a coal,
And the Lion his mother imported,
  In bearskins and grease, from the Pole.

Good night to the Season! – the Toso,
  So very majestic and tall;
Miss Ayton, whose singing was so-so,
  And Pasta, divinest of all;
The labour in vain of the ballet,
  So sadly deficient in stars;
The foreigners thronging the Alley,
  Exhaling the breath of cigars;
The *loge* where some heiress (how killing!)
  Environed with exquisites sits,
The lovely one out of her drilling,
  The silly ones out of their wits.

Good night to the Season! – the splendour
  That beamed in the Spanish Bazaar;
Where I purchased – my heart was so tender –
  A card-case, a pasteboard guitar,
A bottle of perfume, a girdle,
  A lithographed Riego, full-grown,
Whom bigotry drew on a hurdle
  That artists might draw him on stone;
A small panorama of Seville,
  A trap for demolishing flies,
A caricature of the Devil,
  And a look from Miss Sheridan's eyes.

Good night to the Season! – the flowers
  Of the grand horticultural fête,
When boudoirs were quitted for bowers,
  And the fashion was – not to be late;
When all who had money and leisure
  Grew rural o'er ices and wines,
All pleasantly toiling for pleasure,
  All hungrily pining for pines,

And making of beautiful speeches,
   And marring of beautiful shows,
And feeding on delicate peaches,
   And treading on delicate toes.

Good night to the Season! – Another
   Will come, with its trifles and toys,
And hurry away, like its brother,
   In sunshine, and odour, and noise.
Will it come with a rose or a briar?
   Will it come with a blessing or curse?
Will its bonnets be lower or higher?
   Will its morals be better or worse?
Will it find me grown thinner or fatter,
   Or fonder of wrong or of right,
Or married – or buried? – no matter:
   Good night to the Season – good night!

A Letter of Advice

From Miss Medora Trevilian, at Padua,
to Miss Araminta Vavasour, in London

Enfin, monsieur, un homme aimable;
Voilà pourquoi je ne saurais l'aimer. SCRIBE

You tell me you're promised a lover,
   My own Araminta, next week;
Why cannot my fancy discover
   The hue of his coat and his cheek?
Alas! if he look like another,
   A vicar, a banker, a beau,
Be deaf to your father and mother,
   My own Araminta, say 'No!'

Miss Lane, at her Temple of Fashion,
  Taught us both how to sing and to speak,
And we loved one another with passion,
  Before we had been there a week:
You gave me a ring for a token;
  I wear it wherever I go;
I gave you a chain, – is it broken?
  My own Araminta, say 'No!'

O think of our favourite cottage,
  And think of our dear Lalla Rookh!
How we shared with the milkmaids their pottage,
  And drank of the stream from the brook:
How fondly our loving lips faltered
  'What further can grandeur bestow?'
My heart is the same; – is yours altered?
  My own Araminta, say 'No!'

Remember the thrilling romances
  We read on the bank in the glen;
Remember the suitors our fancies
  Would picture for both of us then.
They wore the red cross on their shoulder,
  They had vanquished and pardoned their foe –
Sweet friend, are you wiser or colder?
  My own Araminta, say 'No!'

You know, when Lord Rigmarole's carriage
  Drove off with your cousin Justine,
You wept, dearest girl, at the marriage,
  And whispered 'How base she has been!'
You said you were sure it would kill you,
  If ever your husband looked so;
And you will not apostatize, – will you?
  My own Araminta, say 'No!'

When I heard I was going abroad, love,
  I thought I was going to die;
We walked arm in arm to the road, love,
  We looked arm in arm to the sky;
And I said 'When a foreign postilion
  Has hurried me off to the Po,
Forget not Medora Trevilian:
  My own Araminta, say "No!"'

We parted! but sympathy's fetters
  Reach far over valley and hill;
I muse o'er your exquisite letters,
  And feel that your heart is mine still;
And he who would share it with me, love, –
  The richest of treasures below –
If he's not what Orlando should be, love,
  My own Araminta, say 'No!'

If he wears a top-boot in his wooing,
  If he comes to you riding a cob,
If he talks of his baking or brewing,
  If he puts up his feet on the hob,
If he ever drinks port after dinner,
  If his brow or his breeding is low,
If he calls himself 'Thompson' or 'Skinner',
  My own Araminta, say 'No!'

If he studies the news in the papers
  While you are preparing the tea,
If he talks of the damps or the vapours
  While moonlight lies soft on the sea,
If he's sleepy while you are capricious,
  If he has not a musical 'Oh!'
If he does not call Werther delicious, –
  My own Araminta, say 'No!'

If he ever sets foot in the City
  Among the stockbrokers and Jews,
If he has not a heart full of pity,
  If he don't stand six feet in his shoes,
If his lips are not redder than roses,
  If his hands are not whiter than snow,
If he has not the model of noses, –
  My own Araminta, say 'No!'

If he speaks of a tax or a duty,
  If he does not look grand on his knees,
If he's blind to a landscape of beauty,
  Hills, valleys, rocks, waters, and trees,
If he dotes not on desolate towers,
  If he likes not to hear the blast blow,
If he knows not the language of flowers, –
  My own Araminta, say 'No!'

He must walk – like a god of old story
  Come down from the home of his rest;
He must smile – like the sun in his glory
  On the buds he loves ever the best;
And oh! from its ivory portal
  Like music his soft speech must flow! –
If he speak, smile, or walk like a mortal,
  My own Araminta, say 'No!'

Don't listen to tales of his bounty,
  Don't hear what they say of his birth,
Don't look at his seat in the county,
  Don't calculate what he is worth;
But give him a theme to write verse on,
  And see if he turns out his toe;
If he's only an excellent person, –
  My own Araminta, say 'No!'

The Talented Man

Dear Alice! you'll laugh when you know it, –
  Last week, at the Duchess's ball,
I danced with the clever new poet, –
  You've heard of him, – Tully St Paul.
Miss Jonquil was perfectly frantic;
  I wish you had seen Lady Anne!
It really was very romantic,
  He *is* such a talented man!

He came up from Brazenose College,
  Just caught, as they call it, this spring;
And his head, love, is stuffed full of knowledge
  Of every conceivable thing.
Of science and logic he chatters,
  As fine and as fast as he can;
Though I am no judge of such matters,
  I'm sure he's a talented man.

His stories and jests are delightful; –
  Not stories or jests, dear, for you;
The jests are exceedingly spiteful,
  The stories not always *quite* true.
Perhaps to be kind and veracious
  May do pretty well at Lausanne;
But it never would answer, – good gracious!
  Chez nous – in a talented man.

He sneers, – how my Alice would scold him! –
  At the bliss of a sigh or a tear;
He laughed – only think! – when I told him
  How we cried o'er Trevelyan last year;
I vow I was quite in a passion;
  I broke all the sticks of my fan;
But sentiment's quite out of fashion,
  It seems, in a talented man.

Lady Bab, who is terribly moral,
  Has told me that Tully is vain,
And apt – which is silly – to quarrel,
  And fond – which is sad – of champagne.
I listened, and doubted, dear Alice,
  For I saw, when my Lady began,
It was only the Dowager's malice; –
  She *does* hate a talented man!

He's hideous, I own it. But fame, love,
  Is all that these eyes can adore;
He's lame, – but Lord Byron was lame, love,
  And dumpy, – but so is Tom Moore.
Then his voice, – *such* a voice! my sweet creature,
  It's like your Aunt Lucy's toucan:
But oh! what's a tone or a feature,
  When once one's a talented man?

My mother, you know, all the season,
  Has talked of Sir Geoffrey's estate;
And truly, to do the fool reason,
  He *has* been less horrid of late.
But today, when we drive in the carriage,
  I'll tell her to lay down her plan; –
If ever I venture on marriage,
  It must be a talented man!

P.S. – I have found, on reflection,
  One fault in my friend, – *entre nous*;
Without it, he'd just be perfection; –
  Poor fellow, he has not a *sou*!
And so, when he comes in September
  To shoot with my uncle, Sir Dan,
I've promised mamma to remember
  He's *only* a talented man!

Arrivals at a Watering-Place

'I play a spade. – Such strange new faces
  Are flocking in from near and far;
Such frights! – (Miss Dobbs holds all the aces) –
  One can't imagine who they are:
The lodgings at enormous prices, –
  New donkeys, and another fly;
And Madame Bonbon out of ices,
  Although we're scarcely in July:
We're quite as sociable as any,
  But one old horse can scarcely crawl;
And really, where there are so many,
  We can't tell where we ought to call.

'Pray who has seen the odd old fellow
  Who took the Doctor's house last week? –
A pretty chariot, – livery yellow,
  Almost as yellow as his cheek;
A widower, sixty-five, and surly,
  And stiffer than a poplar-tree;
Drinks rum and water, gets up early
  To dip his carcass in the sea;
He's always in a monstrous hurry,
  And always talking of Bengal;
They say his cook makes noble curry; –
  I think, Louisa, we should call.

'And so Miss Jones, the mantua-maker,
  Has let her cottage on the hill! –
The drollest man, – a sugar-baker
  Last year imported from the till;
Prates of his '*orses* and his '*oney*,
  Is quite in love with fields and farms;
A horrid Vandal, – but his money
  Will buy a glorious coat of arms;

Old Clyster makes him take the waters;
  Some say he means to give a ball;
And after all, with thirteen daughters,
  I think, Sir Thomas, you might call.

'That poor young man! – I'm sure and certain
  Despair is making up his shroud;
He walks all night beneath the curtain
  Of the dim sky and murky cloud;
Draws landscapes, – throws such mournful glances;
  Writes verses, – has such splendid eyes;
An ugly name, – but Laura fancies
  He's some great person in disguise! –
And since his dress is all the fashion,
  And since he's very dark and tall,
I think that out of pure compassion,
  I'll get Papa to go and call.

'So Lord St Ives is occupying
  The whole of Mr Ford's hotel!
Last Saturday his man was trying
  A little nag I want to sell.
He brought a lady in the carriage;
  Blue eyes, – eighteen, or thereabouts; –
Of course, you know, we *hope* it's marriage,
  But yet the *femme de chambre* doubts.
She looked so pensive when we met her.
  Poor thing! – and such a charming shawl! –
Well! till we understand it better,
  It's quite impossible to call!

'Old Mr Fund, the London Banker,
  Arrived to-day at Premium Court;
I would not, for the world, cast anchor
  In such a horrid dangerous port;

Such dust and rubbish, lath and plaster, –
   (Contractors play the meanest tricks) –
The roof's as crazy as its master,
   And he was born in fifty-six;
Stairs creaking – cracks in every landing, –
   The colonnade is sure to fall;
We shan't find post or pillar standing,
   Unless we make great haste to call.

'Who was that sweetest of sweet creatures
   Last Sunday in the Rector's seat?
The finest shape, – the loveliest features, –
   I never saw such tiny feet!
My brother, – (this is quite between us)
   Poor Arthur, – 'twas a sad affair;
Love at first sight! – she's quite a Venus,
   But then she's poorer far than fair;
And so my father and my mother
   Agreed it would not do at all;
And so, – I'm sorry for my brother! –
   It's settled that we're not to call.

'And there's an author, full of knowledge;
   And there's a captain on half-pay;
And there's a baronet from college,
   Who keeps a boy and rides a bay;
And sweet Sir Marcus from the Shannon,
   Fine specimen of brogue and bone;
And Doctor Calipee, the canon,
   Who weighs, I fancy, twenty stone:
A maiden lady is adorning
   The faded front of Lily Hall: –
Upon my word, the first fine morning,
   We'll make a round, my dear, and call.'

Alas! disturb not, maid and matron,
   The swallow in my humble thatch;
Your son may find a better patron,
   Your niece may meet a richer match:
I can't afford to give a dinner,
   I never was on Almack's list;
And, since I seldom rise a winner,
   I never like to play at whist:
Unknown to me the stocks are falling,
   Unwatched by me the glass may fall:
Let all the world pursue its calling, –
   I'm not at home if people call.

Every-day Characters: Portrait of a Lady

What are you, Lady? – naught is here
   To tell us of your name or story,
To claim the gazer's smile or tear,
   To dub you Whig, or damn you Tory;
It is beyond a poet's skill
   To form the slightest notion, whether
We e'er shall walk through one quadrille,
   Or look upon one moon together.

You're very pretty! – all the world
   Are talking of your bright brow's splendour,
And of your locks, so softly curled,
   And of your hands, so white and slender;
Some think you're blooming in Bengal;
   Some say you're blowing in the city;
Some know you're nobody at all:
   I only feel – you're very pretty.

But bless my heart! it's very wrong;
   You're making all our belles ferocious;
Anne 'never saw a chin so long;'
   And Laura thinks your dress 'atrocious;'

And Lady Jane, who now and then
  Is taken for the village steeple,
Is sure you can't be four feet ten,
  And 'wonders at the taste of people'.

Soon pass the praises of a face;
  Swift fades the very best vermilion;
Fame rides a most prodigious pace;
  Oblivion follows on the pillion;
And all who in these sultry rooms
  Today have stared, and pushed, and fainted,
Will soon forget your pearls and plumes,
  As if they never had been painted.

You'll be forgotten – as old debts
  By persons who are used to borrow;
Forgotten – as the sun that sets,
  When shines a new one on the morrow;
Forgotten – like the luscious peach
  That blessed the schoolboy last September;
Forgotten – like a maiden speech,
  Which all men praise, but none remember.

Yet, ere you sink into the stream
  That whelms alike sage, saint, and martyr,
And soldier's sword, and minstrel's theme,
  And Canning's wit, and Gatton's charter,
Here, of the fortunes of your youth,
  My fancy weaves her dim conjectures,
Which have, perhaps, as much of truth
  As passion's vows, or Cobbett's lectures.

Was't in the north or in the south
  That summer breezes rocked your cradle?
And had you in your baby mouth
  A wooden or a silver ladle?

And was your first unconscious sleep,
  By Brownie banned, or blessed by Fairy?
And did you wake to laugh or weep?
  And were you christened Maud or Mary?

And was your father called 'your grace'?
  And did he bet at Ascot races?
And did he chat of commonplace?
  And did he fill a score of places?
And did your lady-mother's charms
  Consist in picklings, broilings, bastings?
Or did she prate about the arms
  Her brave forefathers wore at Hastings?

Where were you *finished*? tell me where!
  Was it at Chelsea, or at Chiswick?
Had you the ordinary share
  Of books and backboard, harp and physic?
And did they bid you banish pride,
  And mind your Oriental tinting?
And did you learn how Dido died,
  And who found out the art of printing?

And are you fond of lanes and brooks –
  A votary of the sylvan Muses?
Or do you con the little books
  Which Baron Brougham and Vaux diffuses?
Or do you love to knit and sew –
  The fashionable world's Arachne?
Or do you canter down the Row
  Upon a very long-tailed hackney?

And do you love your brother James?
  And do you pet his mares and setters?
And have your friends romantic names?
  And do you write them long long letters?

And are you – since the world began
  All women are – a little spiteful?
And don't you dote on Malibran?
  And don't you think Tom Moore delightful?

I see they've brought you flowers to-day;
  Delicious food for eyes and noses;
But carelessly you turn away
  From all the pinks, and all the roses;
Say, is that fond look sent in search
  Of one whose look as fondly answers?
And is he, fairest, in the Church?
  Or is he – ain't he – in the Lancers?

And is your love a motley page
  Of black and white, half joy, half sorrow?
Are you to wait till you're of age?
  Or are you to be his to-morrow?
Or do they bid you, in their scorn,
  Your pure and sinless flame to smother?
Is he so very meanly born?
  Or are you married to another?

Whate'er you are, at last, adieu!
  I think it is your bounden duty
To let the rhymes I coin for you
  Be prized by all who prize your beauty.
From you I seek nor gold nor fame;
  From you I fear no cruel strictures;
I wish some girls that I could name
  Were half as silent as their pictures!

ANONYMOUS

The Lover's Arithmetic

In love to be sure what disasters we meet,
  what torment what grief and vexation;
I've crosses encountered my hopes to defeat,
  will scarcely admit NUMERATION.
I courted a maid, and I called her divine,
  and begged she would change her condition;
For I thought that her fortune united to mine,
  would make a most handsome ADDITION.
    Heigho, dot and go one,
    Fal lal de ral de ra, &c.

When married, a plaguy SUBTRACTION I found,
  her debts wanted much liquidation;
And we couldn't, so badly our wishes were crowned,
  get forward in MULTIPLICATION.
DIVISION in wedlock is common they say,
  and both being fond of the suction;
I very soon had to exclaim 'Lack-a-day!
  my fortune's got into REDUCTION.'
    Heigho, dot and go one, &c.

The RULES OF PROPORTION Dame Nature forgot
  when my Deary she formed – so the fact is,
And she had a tongue to embitter my lot,
  which she never could keep out of PRACTICE,
One day after breaking my head with a stool,
  said I, 'Ma'am, if these are your actions,
I'm off; for you know I've been so long at school
  I don't want to learn VULGAR FRACTIONS.'
    Heigho, dot and go one, &c.

ALFRED, LORD TENNYSON

Hendecasyllabics

O you chorus of indolent reviewers,
Irresponsible, indolent reviewers,
Look, I come to the test, a tiny poem
All composed in a metre of Catullus,
All in quantity, careful of my motion,
Like the skater on ice that hardly bears him,
Lest I fall unawares before the people,
Waking laughter in indolent reviewers.
Should I flounder awhile without a tumble
Thro' this metrification of Catullus,
They should speak to me not without a welcome,
All that chorus of indolent reviewers.
Hard, hard, hard is it, only not to tumble,
So fantastical is the dainty metre.
Wherefore slight me not wholly, nor believe me
Too presumptuous, indolent reviewers.
O blatant Magazines, regard me rather –
Since I blush to belaud myself a moment –
As some rare little rose, a piece of inmost
Horticultural art, or half coquette-like
Maiden, not to be greeted unbenignly.

To Christopher North

You did late review my lays,
  Crusty Christopher;
You did mingle blame and praise,
  Rusty Christopher.
When I learnt from whom it came,
I forgave you all the blame,
  Musty Christopher;
I could *not* forgive the praise,
  Fusty Christopher.

W. M. THACKERAY

The Sorrows of Werther

Werther had a love for Charlotte
   Such as words could never utter;
Would you know how first he met her?
   She was cutting bread and butter.

Charlotte was a married lady,
   And a moral man was Werther,
And for all the wealth of Indies,
   Would do nothing for to hurt her.

So he sighed and pined and ogled,
   And his passion boiled and bubbled,
Till he blew his silly brains out,
   And no more was by it troubled.

Charlotte, having seen his body
   Borne before her on a shutter,
Like a well-conducted person,
   Went on cutting bread and butter.

EDWARD LEAR

By Way of Preface

'How pleasant to know Mr Lear!'
   Who has written such volumes of stuff!
Some think him ill-tempered and queer,
   But a few think him pleasant enough.

His mind is concrete and fastidious,
  His nose is remarkably big;
His visage is more or less hideous,
  His beard it resembles a wig.

He has ears, and two eyes, and ten fingers,
  Leastways if you reckon two thumbs;
Long ago he was one of the singers,
  But now he is one of the dumbs.

He sits in a beautiful parlour,
  With hundreds of books on the wall;
He drinks a great deal of Marsala,
  But never gets tipsy at all.

He has many friends, laymen and clerical,
  Old Foss is the name of his cat:
His body is perfectly spherical,
  He weareth a runcible hat.

When he walks in a waterproof white,
  The children run after him so!
Calling out, 'He's come out in his night-
  gown, that crazy old Englishman, oh!'

He weeps by the side of the ocean,
  He weeps on the top of the hill;
He purchases pancakes and lotion,
  And chocolate shrimps from the mill.

He reads but he cannot speak Spanish,
  He cannot abide ginger-beer:
Ere the days of his pilgrimage vanish,
  How pleasant to know Mr Lear!

The Jumblies

I

They went to sea in a Sieve, they did,
  In a Sieve they went to sea:
In spite of all their friends could say,
On a winter's morn, on a stormy day,
  In a Sieve they went to sea!
And when the Sieve turned round and round,
And every one cried, 'You'll all be drowned!'
They called aloud, 'Our Sieve ain't big,
But we don't care a button! we don't care a fig!
  In a Sieve we'll go to sea!'
    Far and few, far and few,
      Are the lands where the Jumblies live;
    Their heads are green, and their hands are blue,
      And they went to sea in a Sieve.

II

They sailed away in a Sieve, they did,
  In a Sieve they sailed so fast,
With only a beautiful pea-green veil
Tied with a riband by way of a sail,
  To a small tobacco-pipe mast;
And every one said, who saw them go,
'O won't they be soon upset, you know!
For the sky is dark, and the voyage is long,
And happen what may, it's extremely wrong
  In a Sieve to sail so fast!'
    Far and few, far and few,
      Are the lands where the Jumblies live;
    Their heads are green, and their hands are blue,
      And they went to sea in a Sieve.

III

The water it soon came in, it did,
  The water it soon came in;
So to keep them dry, they wrapped their feet
In a pinky paper all folded neat,
  And they fastened it down with a pin.
And they passed the night in a crockery-jar,
And each of them said, 'How wise we are!
Though the sky be dark, and the voyage be long,
Yet we never can think we were rash or wrong,
  While round in our Sieve we spin!'
    Far and few, far and few,
      Are the lands where the Jumblies live;
    Their heads are green, and their hands are blue,
      And they went to sea in a Sieve.

IV

And all night long they sailed away;
  And when the sun went down,
They whistled and warbled a moony song
To the echoing sound of a coppery gong,
  In the shade of the mountains brown.
'O Timballo! How happy we are,
When we live in a Sieve and a crockery-jar,
And all night long in the moonlight pale,
We sail away with a pea-green sail,
  In the shade of the mountains brown!'
    Far and few, far and few,
      Are the lands where the Jumblies live;
    Their heads are green, and their hands are blue,
      And they went to sea in a Sieve.

V

They sailed to the Western Sea, they did,
  To a land all covered with trees,

And they bought an Owl, and a useful Cart,
And a pound of Rice, and a Cranberry Tart,
  And a hive of silvery Bees.
And they bought a Pig, and some green Jack-daws,
And a lovely Monkey with lollipop paws,
And forty bottles of Ring-Bo-Ree,
  And no end of Stilton Cheese.
    Far and few, far and few,
      Are the lands where the Jumblies live;
    Their heads are green, and their hands are blue,
      And they went to sea in a Sieve.

VI

And in twenty years they all came back,
  In twenty years or more,
And every one said, 'How tall they've grown!
For they've been to the Lakes, and the Torrible Zone,
  And the hills of the Chankly Bore';
And they drank their health, and gave them a feast
Of dumplings made of beautiful yeast;
And every one said, 'If we only live,
We too will go to sea in a Sieve, –
  To the hills of the Chankly Bore!'
    Far and few, far and few,
      Are the lands where the Jumblies live;
    Their heads are green, and their hands are blue,
      And they went to sea in a Sieve.

The Owl and the Pussy Cat

The Owl and the Pussy Cat went to sea
  In a beautiful pea-green boat.
They took some honey, and plenty of money
  Wrapped up in a five-pound note.

The Owl looked up to the stars above,
  And sang to a small guitar,
'O lovely Pussy! O Pussy, my love,
What a beautiful Pussy you are,
    You are,
    You are!
What a beautiful Pussy you are!'

Pussy said to the Owl, 'You elegant fowl!
  How charmingly sweet you sing!
O let us be married! too long we have tarried:
  But what shall we do for a ring?'
They sailed away, for a year and a day,
  To the land where the Bong-Tree grows,
And there in a wood a Piggy-wig stood,
With a ring at the end of his nose,
    His nose,
    His nose!
With a ring at the end of his nose.

'Dear Pig, are you willing to sell for one shilling
  Your ring?' Said the Piggy, 'I will.'
So they took it away, and were married next day
  By the Turkey who lives on the hill.
They dinèd on mince, and slices of quince,
  Which they ate with a runcible spoon;
And hand in hand, on the edge of the sand
  They danced by the light of the moon,
    The moon,
    The moon,
  They danced by the light of the moon.

Limericks

1

There was a Young Lady of Ryde,
Whose shoe-strings were seldom untied;
She purchased some clogs
And some small spotty dogs,
And frequently walked about Ryde.

2

There was a young person of Smyrna
Whose Grandmother threatened to burn her;
But she seized on the cat,
And said, 'Granny, burn that!
You incongruous Old Woman of Smyrna.'

3

There was a Young Lady of Portugal,
Whose ideas were excessively nautical;
She climbed up a tree
To examine the sea,
But declared she would never leave Portugal.

4

There was an Old Man with a beard,
Who said, 'It is just as I feared! –
Two Owls and a Hen,
Four Larks and a Wren,
Have all built their nests in my beard!'

5

There was an Old Man who said, 'Hush!
I perceive a young bird in this bush!'
When they said – 'Is it small?'
He replied – 'Not at all!
It is four times as big as the bush!'

ROBERT BROWNING

The Pied Piper of Hamelin

I

Hamelin Town's in Brunswick,
By famous Hanover city;
The river Weser, deep and wide,
Washes its wall on the southern side;
A pleasanter spot you never spied;
But, when begins my ditty,
Almost five hundred years ago,
To see the townsfolk suffer so
From vermin, was a pity.

II

Rats!
They fought the dogs and killed the cats,
And bit the babies in the cradles,
And ate the cheeses out of the vats,
And licked the soup from the cooks' own ladles,
Split open the kegs of salted sprats,
Made nests inside men's Sunday hats,
And even spoiled the women's chats,
By drowning their speaking
With shrieking and squeaking
In fifty different sharps and flats.

III

At last the people in a body
To the Town Hall came flocking:
''Tis clear,' cried they, 'our Mayor's a noddy;
'And as for our Corporation – shocking!
'To think we buy gowns lined with ermine
'For dolts that can't or won't determine
'What's best to rid us of our vermin!

'You hope, because you're old and obese,
'To find in the furry civic robe ease?
'Rouse up, sirs! Give your brains a racking
'To find the remedy we're lacking,
'Or, sure as fate, we'll send you packing!'
At this the Mayor and Corporation
Quaked with a mighty consternation.

IV

An hour they sate in council,
　At length the Mayor broke silence:
'For a guilder I'd my ermine gown sell;
　'I wish I were a mile hence!
'It's easy to bid one rack one's brain –
'I'm sure my poor head aches again,
'I've scratched it so, and all in vain.
'Oh for a trap, a trap, a trap!'
Just as he said this, what should hap
At the chamber door but a gentle tap?
'Bless us,' cried the Mayor, 'what's that?'
(With the Corporation as he sat,
Looking little though wondrous fat;
Nor brighter was his eye, nor moister
Than a too-long-opened oyster,
Save when at noon his paunch grew mutinous
For a plate of turtle green and glutinous)
'Only a scraping of shoes on the mat?
'Anything like the sound of a rat
'Makes my heart go pit-a-pat!'

V

'Come in!' – the Mayor cried, looking bigger:
And in did come the strangest figure!
His queer long coat from heel to head
Was half of yellow and half of red,

And he himself was tall and thin,
With sharp blue eyes, each like a pin,
And light loose hair, yet swarthy skin,
No tuft on cheek nor beard on chin,
But lips where smiles went out and in;
There was no guessing his kith and kin;
And nobody could enough admire
The tall man and his quaint attire.
Quoth one: 'It's as if my great-grandsire,
'Starting up at the Trump of Doom's tone,
'Had walked this way from his painted tombstone!'

VI

He advanced to the council-table:
And, 'Please your honours,' said he, 'I'm able,
'By means of a secret charm, to draw
'All creatures living beneath the sun,
'That creep or swim or fly or run,
'After me so as you never saw!
'And I chiefly use my charm
'On creatures that do people harm,
'The mole and toad and newt and viper;
'And people call me the Pied Piper.'
(And here they noticed round his neck
A scarf of red and yellow stripe,
To match with his coat of the self-same cheque;
And at the scarf's end hung a pipe;
And his fingers they noticed were ever straying
As if impatient to be playing
Upon his pipe, as low it dangled
Over his vesture so old-fangled.)
'Yet,' said he, 'poor Piper as I am,
'In Tartary I freed the Cham,
'Last June, from his huge swarms of gnats,
'I eased in Asia the Nizam
'Of a monstrous brood of vampyre-bats:

'And as for what your brain bewilders,
'If I can rid your town of rats
'Will you give me a thousand guilders?'
'One? fifty thousand!' – was the exclamation
Of the astonished Mayor and Corporation.

VII

Into the street the Piper stept,
  Smiling first a little smile,
As if he knew what magic slept
  In his quiet pipe the while;
Then, like a musical adept,
To blow the pipe his lips he wrinkled,
And green and blue his sharp eyes twinkled,
Like a candle-flame where salt is sprinkled;
And ere three shrill notes the pipe uttered,
You heard as though an army muttered;
And the muttering grew to a grumbling;
And the grumbling grew to a mighty rumbling;
And out of the houses the rats came tumbling.
Great rats, small rats, lean rats, brawny rats,
Brown rats, black rats, grey rats, tawny rats,
Grave old plodders, gay young friskers,
  Fathers, mothers, uncles, cousins,
Cocking tails and pricking whiskers,
  Families by tens and dozens,
Brothers, sisters, husbands, wives –
Followed the Piper for their lives.
From street to street he piped advancing,
And step for step they followed dancing,
Until they came to the river Weser
Wherein all plunged and perished!
– Save one who, stout as Julius Caesar,
Swam across and lived to carry
(As he, the manuscript he cherished)
To Rat-land home his commentary:

Which was, 'At the first shrill notes of the pipe
'I heard a sound as of scraping tripe,
'And putting apples, wondrous ripe,
'Into a cider-press's gripe:
'And moving away of pickle-tub-boards,
'And leaving ajar of conserve-cupboards,
'And a drawing the corks of train-oil-flasks,
'And a breaking the hoops of butter-casks:
'And it seemed as if a voice
'(Sweeter far than by harp or psaltery
'Is breathed) called out, "Oh rats, rejoice!
'"The world is grown to one vast drysaltery!
'"So munch on, crunch on, take your nuncheon,
'"Breakfast, supper, dinner, luncheon!"
'And just as a bulky sugar-puncheon,
'All ready staved, like a great sun shone
'Glorious scarce an inch before me,
'Just as methought it said, "Come, bore me!"
'– I found the Weser rolling o'er me.'

VIII

You should have heard the Hamelin people
Ringing the bells till they rocked the steeple!
'Go!' cried the Mayor, 'and get long poles,
'Poke out the nests and block up the holes!
'Consult with carpenters and builders,
'And leave in our town not even a trace
'Of the rats!' – when suddenly, up the face
Of the Piper perked in the market-place,
With a, 'First, if you please, my thousand guilders!'

IX

A thousand guilders! The Mayor looked blue;
So did the Corporation too.
For council dinners made rare havoc
With Claret, Moselle, Vin-de-Grave, Hock;

And half the money would replenish
Their cellar's biggest butt with Rhenish.
To pay this sum to a wandering fellow
With a gipsy coat of red and yellow!
'Beside,' quoth the Mayor with a knowing wink,
'Our business was done at the river's brink;
'We saw with our eyes the vermin sink,
'And what's dead can't come to life, I think.
'So, friend, we're not the folks to shrink
'From the duty of giving you something to drink,
'And a matter of money to put in your poke;
'But as for the guilders, what we spoke
'Of them, as you very well know, was in joke.
'Beside, our losses have made us thrifty.
'A thousand guilders! Come, take fifty!'

X

The Piper's face fell, and he cried,
'No trifling! I can't wait, beside!
'I've promised to visit by dinner-time
'Bagdad, and accept the prime
'Of the Head-Cook's pottage, all he's rich in,
'For having left, in the Caliph's kitchen,
'Of a nest of scorpions no survivor:
'With him I proved no bargain-driver,
'With you, don't think I'll bate a stiver!
'And folks who put me in a passion
'May find me pipe after another fashion.'

XI

'How?' cried the Mayor, 'd'ye think I brook
'Being worse treated than a Cook?
'Insulted by a lazy ribald
'With idle pipe and vesture piebald?

'You threaten us, fellow? Do your worst,
'Blow your pipe there till you burst!'

XII

Once more he stept into the street
  And to his lips again
Laid his long pipe of smooth straight cane;
And ere he blew three notes (such sweet
Soft notes as yet musician's cunning
  Never gave the enraptured air)
There was a rustling, that seemed like a bustling
Of merry crowds justling at pitching and hustling,
Small feet were pattering, wooden shoes clattering,
Little hands clapping and little tongues chattering,
And, like fowls in a farm-yard when barley is scattering,
  Out came the children running.
  All the little boys and girls,
  With rosy cheeks and flaxen curls,
  And sparkling eyes and teeth like pearls,
  Tripping and skipping, ran merrily after
  The wonderful music with shouting and laughter.

XIII

The Mayor was dumb, and the Council stood
As if they were changed into blocks of wood,
Unable to move a step, or cry
To the children merrily skipping by.
– Could only follow with the eye
That joyous crowd at the Piper's back,
But how the Mayor was on the rack,
And the wretched Council's bosoms beat,
As the Piper turned from the High Street
To where the Weser rolled its waters
Right in the way of their sons and daughters!
However he turned from South to West,
And to Koppelberg Hill his steps addressed,

And after him the children pressed;
Great was the joy in every breast.
'He never can cross that mighty top!
'He's forced to let the piping drop,
'And we shall see our children stop!'
When, lo, as they reached the mountain-side,
A wondrous portal opened wide,
As if a cavern was suddenly hollowed;
And the Piper advanced and the children followed.
And when all were in to the very last,
The door in the mountain-side shut fast.
Did I say, all? No! One was lame,
And could not dance the whole of the way;
And in after years, if you would blame
His sadness, he was used to say, –
'It's dull in our town since my playmates left!
'I can't forget that I'm bereft
'Of all the pleasant sights they see,
'Which the Piper also promised me.
'For he led us, he said, to a joyous land,
'Joining the town and just at hand,
'Where waters gushed and fruit-trees grew
'And flowers put forth a fairer hue,
'And everything was strange and new;
'The sparrows were brighter than peacocks here,
'And their dogs outran our fallow deer,
'And honey-bees had lost their stings,
'And horses were born with eagles' wings:
'And just as I became assured
'My lame foot would be speedily cured,
'The music stopped and I stood still,
'And found myself outside the hill,
'Left alone against my will,
'To go now limping as before,
'And never hear of that country more!'

XIV

Alas, alas for Hamelin!

There came into many a burgher's pate
A text which says that Heaven's gate
Opes to the rich at as easy a rate
As the needle's eye takes a camel in!
The Mayor sent East, West, North, and South,
To offer the Piper, by word of mouth,
Wherever it was men's lot to find him,
Silver and gold to his heart's content,
If he'd only return the way he went,
And bring the children behind him.
But when they saw 'twas a lost endeavour,
And Piper and dancers were gone for ever,
They made a decree that lawyers never
Should think their records dated duly
If, after the day of the month and year,
These words did not as well appear,
'And so long after what happened here
'On the Twenty-second of July,
'Thirteen hundred and seventy-six:'
And the better in memory to fix
The place of the children's last retreat,
They called it, the Pied Piper's Street –
Where any one playing on pipe or tabor,
Was sure for the future to lose his labour.
Nor suffered they hostelry or tavern
To shock with mirth a street so solemn;
But opposite the place of the cavern
They wrote the story on a column,
And on the great church-window painted
The same, to make the world acquainted
How their children were stolen away,
And there it stands to this very day.
And I must not omit to say

That in Transylvania there's a tribe
Of alien people that ascribe
The outlandish ways and dress
On which their neighbours lay such stress,
To their fathers and mothers having risen
Out of some subterranean prison
Into which they were trepanned
Long ago in a mighty band
Out of Hamelin town in Brunswick land,
But how or why, they don't understand.

XV

So, Willy, let me and you be wipers
Of scores out with all men – especially pipers!
And, whether they pipe us free from rats or from mice,
If we've promised them aught, let us keep our promise!

ARTHUR HUGH CLOUGH

From *The Bothie of Tober-Na-Vuolich*

Then was the dinner served, and the Minister prayed for a
    blessing,
And to the viands before them with knife and with fork they
    beset them;
Venison, the red and the roe, with mutton; and grouse
    succeeding;
Such was the feast, with whisky of course, and at top and
    bottom
Small decanters of Sherry, not overchoice, for the gentry.
So the viands before them with laughter and chat they beset
    them.
And, when on flesh and on fowl had appetite duly been sated,
Up rose the Catholic Priest and returned God thanks for the
    dinner.

Then on all tables were set black bottles of well-mixed toddy,
And, with the bottles and glasses before them, they sat,
digesting,
Talking, enjoying, but chiefly awaiting the toasts and
speeches.
Spare me, O great Recollection! for words to the task were
unequal,
Spare me, O mistress of Song! nor bid me remember
minutely
All that was said and done o'er the well-mixed tempting
toddy;
How were healths proposed and drunk 'with all the honours',
Glasses and bonnets waving, and three-times-three thrice over,
Queen, and Prince, and Army, and Landlords all, and
Keepers;
Bid me not, grammar defying, repeat from grammar-defiers
Long constructions strange and plusquam-Thucydidean,
Tell how, as sudden torrent in time of speat in the mountain
Hurries six ways at once, and takes at last to the roughest,
Or as the practised rider at Astley's or Franconi's
Skilfully, boldly bestrides many steeds at once in the gallop,
Crossing from this to that, with one leg here, one yonder,
So, less skilful, but equally bold, and wild as the torrent,
All through sentences six at a time, unsuspecting of syntax,
Hurried the lively good-will and garrulous tale of Sir Hector.
Left to oblivion be it, the memory, faithful as ever,
How the Marquis of Ayr, with wonderful gesticulation,
Floundering on through game and mess-room recollections,
Gossip of neighbouring forest, praise of targeted gillies,
Anticipation of royal visit, skits at pedestrians,
Swore he would never abandon his country, nor give up
deer-stalking;
How, too, more brief, and plainer in spite of the Gaelic
accent,
Highland peasants gave courteous answer to flattering nobles.
Two orations alone the memorial song will render;

For at the banquet's close spake thus the lively Sir Hector,
Somewhat husky with praises exuberant, often repeated,
Pleasant to him and to them, of the gallant Highland soldiers
Whom he erst led in the fight; – somewhat husky, but ready, though weary,
Up to them rose and spoke the grey but gladsome chieftain:—
Fill up your glasses, my friends, once more, – With all the honours!
There was a toast I forgot, which our gallant Highland homes have
Always welcomed the stranger, delighted, I may say, to see such
Fine young men at my table – My friends! are you ready? the Strangers.

From *Amours de Voyage*

Claude to Eustace

Now supposing the French or the Neapolitan soldier
Should by some evil chance come exploring the Maison Serny
(Where the family English are all to assemble for safety),
Am I prepared to lay down my life for the British female?
Really, who knows? One has bowed and talked, till, little by little,
All the natural heat has escaped of the chivalrous spirit.
Oh, one conformed, of course; but one doesn't die for good manners,
Stab or shoot, or be shot, by way of a graceful attention.
No, if it should be at all, it should be on the barricades there;
Should I incarnadine ever this inky pacifical finger,
Sooner far should it be for this vapour of Italy's freedom,
Sooner far by the side of the d—d and dirty plebeians.
Ah, for a child in the street I could strike; for the full-blown lady –
Somehow, Eustace, alas! I have not felt the vocation.

Yet these people of course will expect, as of course, my protection,
Vernon in radiant arms stand forth for the lovely Georgina,
And to appear, I suppose, were but common civility. Yes, and
Truly I do not desire they should either be killed or offended.
Oh, and of course you will say, 'When the time comes, you will be ready.'
Ah, but before it comes, am I to presume it will be so?
What I cannot feel now, am I to suppose that I shall feel?
Am I not free to attend for the ripe and indubious instinct?
Am I forbidden to wait for the clear and lawful perception?
Is it the calling of man to surrender his knowledge and insight
For the mere venture of what may, perhaps, be the virtuous action?
Must we, walking our earth, discerning a little and hoping
Some plain visible task shall yet for our hands be assigned us, –
Must we abandon the future for fear of omitting the present,
Quit our own fireside hopes at the alien call of a neighbour,
To the mere possible shadow of Deity offer the victim?
And is all this, my friend, but a weak and ignoble refining,
Wholly unworthy the head or the heart of Your Own Correspondent?

From *Dipsychus*

The Public Garden

Dipsychus: Assuredly, a lively scene!
And, ah, how pleasant, something green!
With circling heavens one perfect rose
Each smoother patch of water glows,
Hence to where, o'er the full tide's face,
We see the Palace and the Place,
And the White Dome. Beauteous but hot.
Where in the meantime is the spot,

My favourite, where by masses blue
And white cloud-folds, I follow true
The great Alps, rounding grandly o'er,
Huge arc, to the Dalmatian shore?

Spirit: This rather stupid place to-day,
It's true, is most extremely gay;
And rightly – the Assunzione
Was always a *gran' funzione.*

Dipsychus: What is this persecuting voice that haunts me?
What? whence? of whom? How am I to detect?
Myself or not myself? My own bad thoughts,
Or some external agency at work,
To lead me who knows whither?

Spirit: Eh?
We're certainly in luck today:
What lots of boats before us plying –
Gay parties, singing, shouting, crying,
Saluting others past them flying!
What numbers at the landing lying!
What lots of pretty girls, too, hieing
Hither and thither – coming, going,
And with what satisfaction showing,
To our male eyes unveiled and bare
Their dark exuberance of hair,
Black eyes, rich tints, and sundry graces
Of classic pure Italian faces!

2 Temptation

Spirit: In Paris, at the Opera
In the *coulisses* – but ah, aha!
There was a glance, I saw you spy it –
So! shall we follow suit and try it?

Pooh! what a goose you are! quick, quick!
This hesitation makes me sick.
You simpleton! what's your alarm?
She'd merely thank you for your arm.

Dipsychus: Sweet thing! ah well! but yet I am not sure.
Ah no. I think she did not mean it. No.

Spirit: Plainly, unless I much mistake,
She likes a something in your make:
She turned her head – another glance –
She really gives you every chance.

Dipsychus: Ah, pretty thing – well, well. Yet should I go?
Alas, I cannot say. What should I do?

Spirit: What should you do? well, that is funny!
I think you are supplied with money.

Dipsychus: No, no – it may not be. I could, I would –
And yet I would not – cannot. To what end?

Spirit: Trust her for teaching! Go but you,
She'll quickly show you what to do.
Well, well! It's too late now – they're gone;
Some wise youth is coming on.

. . . .

You'd like another turn, I see.
Yes, yes, a little quiet turn.
By all means let us live and learn.
Here's many a lady still waylaying,
And sundry gentlemen purveying.
And if 'twere only just to see
The room of an Italian *fille*,
'Twere worth the trouble and the money.

You'll like to find – I found it funny –
The chamber *où vous faites votre affaire*
Stand nicely fitted up for prayer;
While dim you trace along one end
The Sacred Supper's length extend.
The calm Madonna o'er your head
Smiles, *col bambino*, on the bed
Where – but your chaste ears I must spare –
Where, as we said, *vous faites votre affaire.*
They'll suit you, these Venetian pets!
So natural, not the least coquettes –
Really at times one quite forgets –
Well, would you like perhaps to arrive at
A pretty creature's home in private?
We can look in, just say goodnight,
And, if you like to stay, all right.
Just as you fancy – is it well?

Dipsychus: O folly, folly, folly! To the Hotel!

Spectator ab Extra

I

As I sat at the Café I said to myself,
They may talk as they please about what they call pelf,
They may sneer as they like about eating and drinking,
But help it I cannot, I cannot help thinking
  How pleasant it is to have money, heigh-ho!
  How pleasant it is to have money.

I sit at my table *en grand seigneur*,
And when I have done, throw a crust to the poor;
Not only the pleasure itself of good living,
But also the pleasure of now and then giving:
  So pleasant it is to have money, heigh-ho!
  So pleasant it is to have money.

They may talk as they please about what they call pelf,
And how one ought never to think of one's self,
How pleasures of thought surpass eating and drinking, –
My pleasure of thought is the pleasure of thinking
  How pleasant it is to have money, heigh-ho!
  How pleasant it is to have money.

2

Le Diner

Come along, 'tis the time, ten or more minutes past,
And he who came first had to wait for the last;
The oysters ere this had been in and been out;
Whilst I have been sitting and thinking about
  How pleasant it is to have money, heigh-ho!
  How pleasant it is to have money.

A clear soup with eggs; *voilà tout*; of the fish
The *filets de sole* are a moderate dish
A la Orly, but you're for red mullet, you say:
By the gods of good fare, who can question to-day
  How pleasant it is to have money, heigh-ho!
  How pleasant it is to have money.

After oysters, sauterne; then sherry; champagne,
Ere one bottle goes, comes another again;
Fly up, thou bold cork, to the ceiling above,
And tell to our ears in the sound that they love
  How pleasant it is to have money, heigh-ho!
  How pleasant it is to have money.

I've the simplest of palates; absurd it may be,
But I almost could dine on a *poulet-au-riz*,
Fish and soup and omelette and that – but the deuce –
There were to be woodcocks, and not *Charlotte Russe*!
  So pleasant it is to have money, heigh-ho!
  So pleasant it is to have money.

Your chablis is acid, away with the hock,
Give me the pure juice of the purple médoc:
St Peray is exquisite; but, if you please,
Some burgundy just before tasting the cheese.
  So pleasant it is to have money, heigh-ho!
  So pleasant it is to have money.

As for that, pass the bottle, and d—n the expense,
I've seen it observed by a writer of sense,
That the labouring classes could scarce live a day,
If people like us didn't eat, drink, and pay.
  So useful it is to have money, heigh-ho!
  So useful it is to have money.

One ought to be grateful, I quite apprehend,
Having dinner and supper and plenty to spend,
And so suppose now, while the things go away,
By way of a grace we all stand up and say
  How pleasant it is to have money, heigh-ho!
  How pleasant it is to have money.

3

Parvenant

I cannot but ask, in the park and the streets
When I look at the number of persons one meets,
What e'er in the world the poor devils can do
Whose fathers and mothers can't give them a *sou*.
  So needful it is to have money, heigh-ho!
  So needful it is to have money.

I ride, and I drive, and I care not a d—n,
The people look up and they ask who I am;
And if I should chance to run over a cad,
I can pay for the damage, if ever so bad.
  So useful it is to have money, heigh-ho!
  So useful it is to have money.

It was but this winter I came up to town,
And already I'm gaining a sort of renown;
Find my way to good houses without much ado,
Am beginning to see the nobility too.
  So useful it is to have money, heigh-ho!
  So useful it is to have money.

O dear what a pity they ever should lose it,
Since they are the people that know how to use it;
So easy, so stately, such manners, such dinners,
And yet, after all, it is we are the winners.
  So needful it is to have money, heigh-ho!
  So needful it is to have money.

It's all very well to be handsome and tall,
Which certainly makes you look well at a ball;
It's all very well to be clever and witty,
But if you are poor, why it's only a pity.
  So needful it is to have money, heigh-ho!
  So needful it is to have money.

There's something undoubtedly in a fine air,
To know how to smile and be able to stare.
High breeding is something, but well-bred or not,
In the end the one question is, what have you got.
  So needful it is to have money, heigh-ho!
  So needful it is to have money.

And the angels in pink and the angels in blue,
In muslins and moirés so lovely and new,
What is it they want, and so wish you to guess.
But if you have money, the answer is Yes.
  So needful, they tell you, is money, heigh-ho!
  So needful it is to have money.

FREDERICK LOCKER-LAMPSON

Our Photograph

She played me false, but that's not why
I haven't quite forgiven Di,
Although I've tried:
This curl was hers, so brown, so bright,
She gave it me one blissful night,
And – more beside!

In photo we were grouped together;
She wore the darling hat and feather
That I adore;
In profile by her side I sat
Reading my poetry – but that
She'd heard before.

Why, after all, Di threw me over
I never knew, and can't discover,
Or even guess:
Maybe Smith's lyrics, she decided,
Were sweeter than the sweetest I did –
I acquiesce.

A week before their wedding-day
When Smith was called in haste away
To join the Staff,
Di gave to him, with tearful mien,
Our only photograph. I've seen
That photograph.

I've seen it in Smith's album-book!
Just think! her hat – her tender look,
Are now that brute's!

Before she gave it, off she cut
My body, head and lyrics, but
She was obliged, the little slut,
        To leave my boots.

ANONYMOUS

Polly Perkins

I am a broken-hearted milkman, in grief I'm arrayed,
Through keeping of the company of a young servant maid,
Who lived on board and wages the house to keep clean
In a gentleman's family near Paddington Green.

Chorus:

She was as beautiful as a butterfly
  And as proud as a Queen
Was pretty little Polly Perkins of
  Paddington Green.

She'd an ankle like an antelope and a step like a deer,
A voice like a blackbird, so mellow and clear,
Her hair hung in ringlets so beautiful and long,
I thought that she loved me but I found I was wrong.

When I'd rattle in a morning and cry 'milk below',
At the sound of my milk-cans her face she would show
With a smile upon her countenance and a laugh in her eye,
If I thought she'd have loved me, I'd have laid down to die.

When I asked her to marry me she said 'Oh! what stuff',
And told me to 'drop it, for she had quite enough
Of my nonsense' – at the same time I'd been very kind,
But to marry a milkman she didn't feel inclined.

'Oh, the man that has me must have silver and gold,
A chariot to ride in and be handsome and bold,
His hair must be curly as any watch spring,
And his whiskers as big as a brush for clothing.'

The words that she uttered went straight through my heart,
I sobbed, I sighed, and straight did depart;
With a tear on my eyelid as big as a bean,
Bidding good-bye to Polly and Paddington Green.

In six months she married, – this hard-hearted girl, –
But it was not a Wi-count, and it was not a Nearl,
It was not a 'Baronite', but a shade or two wuss,
It was a bow-legged conductor of a twopenny bus.

ROBERT BARNABAS BROUGH

My Lord Tomnoddy

My Lord Tomnoddy is the son of an Earl;
His hair is straight, but his whiskers curl:
His Lordship's forehead is far from wide,
But there's plenty of room for the brains inside.
He writes his name with indifferent ease,
He's rather uncertain about the *d*'s;
But what does it matter, if three or one,
To the Earl of Fitzdotterel's eldest son?

My Lord Tomnoddy to College went;
Much time he lost, much money he spent;
Rules, and windows, and heads, he broke –
Authorities wink'd – young men will joke!

He never peep'd inside of a book:
In two years' time a degree he took,
And the newspapers vaunted the honours won
By the Earl of Fitzdotterel's eldest son.

My Lord Tomnoddy came out in the world:
Waists were tighten'd and ringlets curl'd.
Virgins languish'd, and matrons smil'd –
'Tis true, his Lordship is rather wild;
In very queer places he spends his life;
There's talk of some children by nobody's wife –
But we mustn't look close into what is done
By the Earl of Fitzdotterel's eldest son.

My Lord Tomnoddy prefers the Guards,
(The House is a bore) so, it's on the cards!
My Lord's a Lieutenant at twenty-three,
A Captain at twenty-six is he:
He never drew sword, except on drill;
The tricks of parade he has learnt but ill;
A full-blown Colonel at thirty-one
Is the Earl of Fitzdotterel's eldest son!

My Lord Tomnoddy is thirty-four;
The Earl can last but a few years more.
My Lord in the Peers will take his place:
Her Majesty's councils his words will grace.
Office he'll hold, and patronage sway;
Fortunes and lives he will vote away;
And what are his qualifications? – ONE!
He's the Earl of Fitzdotterel's eldest son.

C. S. CALVERLEY

Companions, a Tale of a Grandfather

By the Author of 'Dewy Memories', etc.

I know not of what we ponder'd
  Or made pretty pretence to talk
As, her hand within mine, we wander'd
  Tow'rd the pool by the limetree walk,
While the dew fell in showers from the passion flowers
  And the blush-rose bent on her stalk.

I cannot recall her figure:
  Was it regal as Juno's own?
Or only a trifle bigger
  Than the elves who surround the throne
Of the Faëry Queen, and are seen, I ween,
  By mortals in dreams alone?

What her eyes were like, I know not:
  Perhaps they were blurr'd with tears;
And perhaps in your skies there glow not
  (On the contrary) clearer spheres.
No! as to her eyes I am just as wise
  As you or the cat, my dears.

Her teeth, I presume, were 'pearly':
  But which was she, brunette or blonde?
Her hair, was it quaintly curly,
  Or as straight as a beadle's wand?
That I fail'd to remark; – it was rather dark
  And shadowy round the pond.

Then the hand that reposed so snugly
  In mine – was it plump or spare?

Was the countenance fair or ugly?
  Nay, children, you have me there!
My eyes were p'raps blurr'd; and besides I'd heard
  That it's horribly rude to stare.

And I – was I brusque and surly?
  Or oppressively bland and fond?
Was I partial to rising early?
  Or why did we twain abscond,
All breakfastless too, from the public view
  To prowl by a misty pond?

What pass'd, what was felt or spoken –
  Whether anything pass'd at all –
And whether the heart was broken
  That beat under that shelt'ring shawl –
(If shawl she had on, which I doubt) – has gone,
  Yes, gone from me past recall.

Was I haply the lady's suitor?
  Or her uncle? I can't make out –
Ask your governess, dears, or tutor.
  For myself, I'm in hopeless doubt
As to why we were there, who on earth we were,
  And what this is all about.

The Schoolmaster Abroad with his Son

O what harper could worthily harp it,
  Mine Edward! this wide-stretching wold
(Look out *wold*) with its wonderful carpet
  Of emerald, purple, and gold!
Look well at it – also look sharp, it
      Is getting so cold.

The purple is heather (*erica*);
  The yellow, gorse – call'd sometimes 'whin.'
Cruel boys on its prickles might spike a
  Green beetle as if on a pin.
You may roll in it, if you would like a
    Few holes in your skin.

You wouldn't? Then think of how kind you
  Should be to the insects who crave
Your compassion – and then, look behind you
  At yon barley-ears! Don't they look brave
As they undulate (*undulate*, mind you,
    From *unda*, *a wave*).

The noise of those sheep-bells, how faint it
  Sounds here – (on account of our height)!
And this hillock itself – who could paint it,
  With its changes of shadow and light?
Is it not – (never, Eddy, say 'ain't it') –
    A marvellous sight?

Then yon desolate eerie morasses,
  The haunts of the snipe and the hern –
(I shall question the two upper classes
  On *aquatiles*, when we return) –
Why, I see on them absolute masses
    Of *filix* or fern.

How it interests e'en a beginner
  (Or *tiro*) like dear little Ned!
Is he listening? As I am a sinner
  He's asleep – he is wagging his head.
Wake up! I'll go home to my dinner,
    And you to your bed.

The boundless ineffable prairie;
  The splendour of mountain and lake
With their hues that seem ever to vary;
  The mighty pine-forests which shake
In the wind, and in which the unwary
    May tread on a snake;

And this wold with its heathery garment
  Are themes undeniably great.
But – although there is not any harm in't –
  It's perhaps little good to dilate
On their charms to a dull little varmint
    Of seven or eight.

In the Gloaming

In the Gloaming to be roaming, where the crested waves are foaming,
  And the shy mermaidens combing locks that ripple to their feet;
When the Gloaming is, I never made the ghost of an endeavour
  To discover – but whatever were the hour, it would be sweet.

'To their feet,' I say, for Leech's sketch indisputably teaches
  That the mermaids of our beaches do not end in ugly tails,
Nor have homes among the corals; but are shod with neat balmorals,
  An arrangement no one quarrels with, as many might with scales.

Sweet to roam beneath a shady cliff, of course with some young lady,
  Lalage, Neæra, Haidee, or Elaine, or Mary Ann:

Love, you dear delusive dream, you! Very sweet your victims
 deem you,
 When, heard only by the seamew, they talk all the stuff one
 can.

Sweet to haste, a licensed lover, to Miss Pinkerton the glover,
 Having managed to discover what is dear Neæra's 'size':
P'raps to touch that wrist so slender, as your tiny gift you
 tender,
 And to read you're no offender, in those laughing hazel
 eyes.

Then to hear her call you 'Harry,' when she makes you fetch
 and carry –
 O young men about to marry, what a blessed thing it is!
To be photograph'd – together – cased in pretty Russian
 leather –
 Hear her gravely doubting whether they have spoilt your
 honest phiz!

Then to bring your plighted fair one first a ring – a rich and
 rare one –
 Next a bracelet, if she'll wear one, and a heap of things
 beside;
And serenely bending o'er her, to inquire if it would bore her
 To say when her own adorer may aspire to call her bride!

Then, the days of courtship over, with your WIFE to start for
 Dover
 Or Dieppe – and live in clover evermore, whate'er befalls:
For I've read in many a novel that, unless they've souls that
 grovel,
 Folks *prefer* in fact a hovel to your dreary marble halls:

To sit, happy married lovers; Phillis trifling with a plover's
 Egg, while Corydon uncovers with a grace the Sally Lunn,

Or dissects the lucky pheasant – that, I think, were passing
pleasant;
As I sit alone at present, dreaming darkly of a Dun.

On the Rhine

On, on the vessel steals;
Round go the paddle-wheels,
And now the tourist feels
As he should;
For king-like rolls the Rhine,
And the scenery's divine,
And the victuals and the wine
Rather good.

From every crag we pass'll
Rise up some hoar old castle;
The hanging fir-groves tassel
Every slope;
And the vine her lithe arm stretches
Over peasants singing catches –
And you'll make no end of sketches,
I should hope.

We've a nun here (called Therèse),
Two couriers out of place,
One Yankee with a face
Like a ferret's:
And three youths in scarlet caps
Drinking chocolate and schnapps –
A diet which perhaps
Has its merits.

And day again declines:
In shadow sleep the vines,
And the last ray thro' the pines
    Feebly glows,
Then sinks behind yon ridge;
And the usual evening midge
Is settling on the bridge
    Of my nose.

And keen's the air and cold,
And the sheep are in the fold,
And Night walks sable-stoled
    Thro' the trees;
And on the silent river
The floating starbeams quiver; –
And now, the saints deliver
    Us from fleas.

'Hic Vir, Hic Est'

Often, when o'er tree and turret,
  Eve a dying radiance flings,
By that ancient pile I linger
  Known familiarly as 'King's'.
And the ghosts of days departed
  Rise, and in my burning breast
All the undergraduate wakens,
  And my spirit is at rest.

What, but a revolting fiction,
  Seems the actual result
Of the Census's enquiries
  Made upon the 15th ult.?
Still my soul is in its boyhood;
  Nor of year or changes recks,
Though my scalp is almost hairless,
  And my figure grows convex.

Backward moves the kindly dial;
  And I'm numbered once again
With those noblest of their species
  Called emphatically 'Men':
Loaf, as I have loafed aforetime,
  Through the streets, with tranquil mind,
And a long-backed fancy-mongrel
  Trailing casually behind:

Past the Senate-house I saunter,
  Whistling with an easy grace;
Past the cabbage-stalks that carpet
  Still the beefy market-place;
Poising evermore the eye-glass
  In the light sarcastic eye,
Lest, by chance, some breezy nursemaid
  Pass, without a tribute, by.

Once, an unassuming Freshman,
  Through these wilds I wandered on,
Seeing in each house a College,
  Under every cap a Don:
Each perambulating infant
  Had a magic in its squall,
For my eager eye detected
  Senior Wranglers in them all.

By degrees my education
  Grew, and I became as others;
Learned to blunt my moral feelings
  By the aid of Bacon Brothers;[1]

[1]Tobacconists

Bought me tiny boots of Mortlock,
  And colossal prints of Roe;
And ignored the proposition
  That both time and money go.

Learned to work the wary dogcart
  Artfully thro' King's Parade;
Dress, and steer a boat, and sport with
  Amaryllis in the shade:
Struck, at Brown's, the dashing hazard;
  Or (more curious sport than that)
Dropped, at Callaby's, the terrier
  Down upon the prisoned rat.

I have stood serene on Fenner's
  Ground, indifferent to blisters,
While the Buttress of the period
  Bowled me his peculiar twisters:
Sung 'We won't go home till morning';
  Striven to part my backhair straight;
Drunk (not lavishly) of Miller's
  Old dry wines at 78/–:—

When within my veins the blood ran,
  And the curls were on my brow,
I did, oh ye undergraduates,
  Much as ye are doing now.
Wherefore bless ye, O beloved ones:—
  Now unto mine inn must I,
Your 'poor moralist', betake me,
  In my 'solitary fly'.

ANONYMOUS

Casey Jones

Come all you rounders if you want to hear
The story of a brave engineer;
Casey Jones was the hogger's name,
On a big eight-wheeler, boys, he won his fame.
Caller called Casey at half-past four,
He kissed his wife at the station door,
Mounted to the cabin with orders in his hand,
And took his farewell trip to the promised land.

Casey Jones, he mounted to the cabin,
Casey Jones, with his orders in his hand!
Casey Jones, he mounted to the cabin,
Took his farewell trip into the promised land.

Put in your water and shovel in your coal,
Put your head out the window, watch the drivers roll,
I'll run her till she leaves the rail,
'Cause we're eight hours late with the Western Mail!
He looked at his watch and his watch was slow,
Looked at the water and the water was low,
Turned to his fireboy and said,
'We'll get to 'Frisco, but we'll all be dead!'
(*Refrain*)

Casey pulled up Reno Hill,
Tooted for the crossing with an awful shrill,
Snakes all knew by the engine's moans
That the hogger at the throttle was Casey Jones.
He pulled up short two miles from the place,
Number Four stared him right in the face,
Turned to his fireboy, said 'You'd better jump,
'Cause there's two locomotives going to bump!'
(*Refrain*)

Casey said, just before he died,
'There's two more roads I'd like to ride.'
Fireboy said, 'What can they be?'
'The Rio Grande and the Old S.P.'
Mrs Jones sat on her bed a-sighing,
Got a pink that Casey was dying,
Said, 'Go to bed, children; hush your crying,
'Cause you'll get another papa on the Salt Lake Line.'

Casey Jones! Got another papa!
Casey Jones, on the Salt Lake Line!
Casey Jones! Got another papa!
Got another papa on the Salt Lake Line!

The Foggy, Foggy Dew

When I was a bachelor, I lived by myself
And I worked at the weaver's trade;
The only, only thing that I ever did wrong
Was to woo a fair young maid.
I wooed her in the winter time,
And in the summer too;
And the only, only thing that I ever did wrong
Was to keep her from the foggy, foggy dew.

One night she came to my bedside
Where I lay fast asleep;
She laid her head upon my bed,
And then began to weep.
She sighed, she cried, she damn near died,
She said – 'What shall I do?' –
So I hauled her into bed and I covered up her head,
Just to save her from the foggy, foggy dew.

Oh, I am a bachelor, I live with my son,
And we work at the weaver's trade;
And every, every time that I look into his eyes,
He reminds me of that maid.
He reminds me of the winter time,
And of the summer too;
And the many, many times that I held her in my arms,
Just to keep her from the foggy, foggy dew.

LEWIS CARROLL

'You are Old, Father William'

'You are old, Father William,' the young man said,
  'And your hair has become very white;
And yet you incessantly stand on your head –
  Do you think, at your age, it is right?'

'In my youth,' Father William replied to his son,
  'I feared it might injure the brain;
But, now that I'm perfectly sure I have none,
  Why, I do it again and again.'

'You are old,' said the youth, 'as I mentioned before,
  And have grown most uncommonly fat;
Yet you turned a back-somersault in at the door –
  Pray, what is the reason of that?'

'In my youth,' said the sage, as he shook his grey locks,
  'I kept all my limbs very supple
By the use of this ointment – one shilling the box –
  Allow me to sell you a couple?'

'You are old,' said the youth, 'and your jaws are too weak
For anything tougher than suet;
Yet you finished the goose, with the bones and the beak –
Pray, how did you manage to do it?'

'In my youth,' said his father, 'I took to the law,
And argued each case with my wife;
And the muscular strength, which it gave to my jaw,
Has lasted the rest of my life.'

'You are old,' said the youth, 'one would hardly suppose
That your eye was as steady as ever;
Yet you balance an eel on the end of your nose –
What made you so awfully clever?'

'I have answered three questions, and that is enough,'
Said his father. 'Don't give yourself airs!
Do you think I can listen all day to such stuff?
Be off, or I'll kick you down-stairs!'

'Tis the Voice of the Lobster

I

''Tis the voice of the Lobster: I heard him declare
"You have baked me too brown, I must sugar my hair."
As a duck with its eyelids, so he with his nose
Trims his belt and his buttons, and turns out his toes.
When the sands are all dry, he is gay as a lark,
And will talk in contemptuous tones of the Shark:
But, when the tide rises and sharks are around,
His voice has a timid and tremulous sound.'

II

I passed by his garden, and marked, with one eye,
How the Owl and the Panther were sharing a pie:
The Panther took pie-crust, and gravy, and meat,
While the Owl had the dish as its share of the treat.
When the pie was all finished, the Owl, as a boon,
Was kindly permitted to pocket the spoon:
While the Panther received knife and fork with a growl.
And concluded the banquet by –

Jabberwocky

'Twas brillig, and the slithy toves
  Did gyre and gimble in the wabe;
All mimsy were the borogoves,
  And the mome raths outgrabe.

'Beware the Jabberwock, my son!
  The jaws that bite, the claws that catch!
Beware the Jubjub bird, and shun
  The frumious Bandersnatch!'

He took his vorpal sword in hand:
  Long time the manxome foe he sought –
So rested he by the Tumtum tree,
  And stood awhile in thought.

And as in uffish thought he stood,
  The Jabberwock, with eyes of flame,
Came whiffling through the tulgey wood,
  And burbled as it came!

One, two! One, two! And through and through
  The vorpal blade went snicker-snack!
He left it dead, and with its head
  He went galumphing back.

'And hast thou slain the Jabberwock!
  Come to my arms, my beamish boy!
O frabjous day! Callooh! Callay!'
  He chortled in his joy.

'Twas brillig, and the slithy toves
  Did gyre and gimble in the wabe;
All mimsy were the borogoves,
  And the mome raths outgrabe.

The Walrus and the Carpenter

The sun was shining on the sea,
  Shining with all his might:
He did his very best to make
  The billows smooth and bright –
And this was odd, because it was
  The middle of the night.

The moon was shining sulkily,
  Because she thought the sun
Had got no business to be there
  After the day was done –
'It's very rude of him,' she said,
  'To come and spoil the fun!'

The sea was wet as wet could be,
  The sands were dry as dry.
You could not see a cloud, because
  No cloud was in the sky:
No birds were flying overhead –
  There were no birds to fly.

The Walrus and the Carpenter
   Were walking close at hand:
They wept like anything to see
   Such quantities of sand:
'If this were only cleared away,'
   They said, 'it *would* be grand!'

'If seven maids with seven mops
   Swept it for half a year,
Do you suppose,' the Walrus said,
   'That they could get it clear?'
'I doubt it,' said the Carpenter,
   And shed a bitter tear.

'O Oysters, come and walk with us!'
   The Walrus did beseech.
'A pleasant walk, a pleasant talk,
   Along the briny beach:
We cannot do with more than four,
   To give a hand to each.'

The eldest Oyster looked at him,
   But not a word he said:
The eldest Oyster winked his eye,
   And shook his heavy head –
Meaning to say he did not choose
   To leave the oyster-bed.

But four young Oysters hurried up,
   All eager for the treat:
Their coats were brushed, their faces washed
   Their shoes were clean and neat –
And this was odd, because, you know,
   They hadn't any feet.

Four other Oysters followed them,
   And yet another four;
And thick and fast they came at last,
   And more, and more, and more –
All hopping through the frothy waves,
   And scrambling to the shore.

The Walrus and the Carpenter
   Walked on a mile or so,
And then they rested on a rock
   Conveniently low:
And all the little Oysters stood
   And waited in a row.

'The time has come,' the Walrus said,
   'To talk of many things:
Of shoes – and ships – and sealing wax –
   Of cabbages – and kings –
And why the sea is boiling hot –
   And whether pigs have wings.'

'But wait a bit,' the Oysters cried,
   'Before we have our chat;
For some of us are out of breath,
   And all of us are fat!'
'No hurry!' said the Carpenter.
   They thanked him much for that.

'A loaf of bread,' the Walrus said,
   'Is what we chiefly need:
Pepper and vinegar besides
   Are very good indeed –
Now, if you're ready, Oysters dear,
   We can begin to feed.'

'But not on us!' the Oysters cried,
  Turning a little blue.
'After such kindness that would be
  A dismal thing to do!'
'The night is fine,' the Walrus said,
  'Do you admire the view?

'It was so kind of you to come,
  And you are very nice!'
The Carpenter said nothing but
  'Cut us another slice.
I wish you were not quite so deaf –
  I've had to ask you twice!'

'It seems a shame,' the Walrus said,
  'To play them such a trick.
After we've brought them out so far,
  And made them trot so quick!'
The Carpenter said nothing but
  'The butter's spread too thick!'

'I weep for you,' the Walrus said:
  'I deeply sympathize.'
With sobs and tears he sorted out
  Those of the largest size,
Holding his pocket-handkerchief
  Before his streaming eyes.

'O Oysters,' said the Carpenter,
  'You've had a pleasant run!
Shall we be trotting home again?'
  But answer came there none –
And this was scarcely odd, because
  They'd eaten every one.

The White Knight's Song

I'll tell thee everything I can;
  There's little to relate.
I saw an aged aged man,
  A-sitting on a gate.
'Who are you, aged man?' I said.
  'And how is it you live?'
And his answer trickled through my head
  Like water through a sieve.

He said 'I look for butterflies
  That sleep among the wheat:
I make them into mutton-pies,
  And sell them in the street.
I sell them unto men,' he said,
  'Who sail on stormy seas;
And that's the way I get my bread –
  A trifle, if you please.'

But I was thinking of a plan
  To dye one's whiskers green,
And always use so large a fan
  That they could not be seen.
So, having no reply to give
  To what the old man said,
I cried 'Come, tell me how you live!'
  And thumped him on the head.

His accents mild took up the tale:
  He said 'I go my ways,
And when I find a mountain-rill,
  I set it in a blaze;
And thence they make a stuff they call
  Rowland's Macassar-Oil –
Yet twopence-halfpenny is all
  They give me for my toil.'

But I was thinking of a way
   To feed oneself on batter,
And so go on from day to day
   Getting a little fatter.
I shook him well from side to side,
   Until his face was blue:
'Come, tell me how you live,' I cried,
   'And what it is you do!'

He said 'I hunt for haddocks' eyes
   Among the heather bright,
And work them into waistcoat-buttons
   In the silent night.
And these I do not sell for gold
   Or coin of silvery shine,
But for a copper halfpenny,
   And that will purchase nine.

'I sometimes dig for buttered rolls,
   Or set limed twigs for crabs;
I sometimes search the grassy knolls
   For wheels of Hansom-cabs.
And that's the way' (he gave a wink)
   'By which I get my wealth –
And very gladly will I drink
   Your Honour's noble health.'

I heard him then, for I had just
   Completed my design
To keep the Menai bridge from rust
   By boiling it in wine.
I thanked him much for telling me
   The way he got his wealth,
But chiefly for his wish that he
   Might drink my noble health.

And now, if e'er by chance I put
  My fingers into glue,
Or madly squeeze a right-hand foot
  Into a left-hand shoe,
Or if I drop upon my toe
  A very heavy weight,
I weep, for it reminds me so
Of that old man I used to know –
Whose look was mild, whose speech was slow,
Whose hair was whiter than the snow,
Whose face was very like a crow,
With eyes, like cinders, all aglow,
Who seemed distracted with his woe,
Who rocked his body to and fro,
And muttered mumblingly and low,
As if his mouth were full of dough,
Who snorted like a buffalo –
That summer evening long ago
  A-sitting on a gate.

Humpty Dumpty's Song

In winter, when the fields are white,
I sing this song for your delight –

*

In spring, when woods are getting green,
I'll try and tell you what I mean.

*

In summer, when the days are long,
Perhaps you'll understand the song:

*

In autumn, when the leaves are brown,
Take pen and ink, and write it down.

*

I sent a message to the fish:
I told them 'This is what I wish.'

The little fishes of the sea
They sent an answer back to me.

The little fishes' answer was
'We cannot do it, Sir, because –'

*

I sent to them again to say
'It will be better to obey.'

The fishes answered with a grin
'Why, what a temper you are in!'

I told them once, I told them twice:
They would not listen to advice.

I took a kettle large and new,
Fit for the deed I had to do.

My heart went hop, my heart went thump;
I filled the kettle at the pump.

Then some one came to me and said
'The little fishes are in bed.'

I said to him, I said it plain,
'Then you must wake them up again'.

I said it very loud and clear;
I went and shouted in his ear.

*

But he was very stiff and proud;
He said 'You needn't shout so loud!'

And he was very proud and stiff;
He said 'I'd go and wake them, if –'

I took a corkscrew from the shelf:
I went to wake them up myself.

And when I found the door was locked,
I pulled and pushed and kicked and knocked.

And when I found the door was shut
I tried to turn the handle, but –

Evidence Read at the Trial of the Knave of Hearts

They told me you had been to her,
  And mentioned me to him:
She gave me a good character,
  But said I could not swim.

He sent them word I had not gone,
  (We know it to be true:)
If she should push the matter on,
  What would become of you?

I gave her one, they gave him two,
  You gave us three or more;
They all returned from him to you,
  Though they were mine before.

If I or she should chance to be
   Involved in this affair,
He trusts to you to set them free,
   Exactly as we were.

My notion was that you had been
   (Before she had this fit)
An obstacle that came between
   Him, and ourselves, and it.

Don't let him know she liked them best,
   For this must ever be
A secret, kept from all the rest,
   Between yourself and me.

Little Birds are Playing

Little Birds are playing
      Bagpipes on the shore,
      Where the tourists snore:
'Thanks!' they cry. ''Tis thrilling!
Take, oh, take, this shilling!
      Let us have no more!'

Little Birds are bathing
      Crocodiles in cream,
      Like a happy dream:
Like, but not so lasting –
Crocodiles, when fasting,
      Are not all they seem!

Little Birds are choking
      Baronets with bun,
      Taught to fire a gun:

Taught, I say, to splinter
Salmon in the winter –
        Merely for the fun.

Little Birds are hiding
        Crimes in carpet-bags,
        Blessed by happy stags:
Blessed, I say, though beaten –
Since our friends are eaten
        When the memory flags.

Little Birds are tasting
        Gratitude and gold,
        Pale with sudden cold;
Pale, I say, and wrinkled –
When the bells have tinkled,
        And the Tale is told.

Hiawatha's Photographing

From his shoulder Hiawatha
Took the camera of rosewood –
Made of sliding, folding rosewood –
Neatly put it all together.
        In its case it lay compactly,
Folded into nearly nothing;
But he opened out its hinges,
Pushed and pulled the joints and hinges
Till it looked all squares and oblongs,
Like a complicated figure
In the second book of Euclid.
        This he perched upon a tripod,
And the family, in order,
Sat before him for their pictures –
Mystic, awful, was the process.

First, a piece of glass he coated
With collodion, and plunged it
In a bath of lunar caustic
Carefully dissolved in water –
There he left it certain minutes.
Secondly, my Hiawatha
Made with cunning hand a mixture
Of the acid pyrro-gallic,
And of glacial-acetic,
And of alcohol and water –
This developed all the picture.
Finally, he fixed each picture
With a saturate solution
Which was made of hyposulphite
Which, again, was made of soda.
(Very difficult the name is
For a metre like the present
But periphrasis has done it.)
All the family, in order,
Sat before him for their pictures;
Each in turn, as he was taken,
Volunteered his own suggestions –
His invaluable suggestions.
First, the governor – the father –
He suggested velvet curtains
Looped about a massy pillar,
And the corner of a table –
Of a rosewood dining table.
He would hold a scroll of something –
Hold it firmly in his left hand;
He would keep his right hand buried
(Like Napoleon) in his waistcoat;
He would gaze upon the distance –
(Like a poet seeing visions,
Like a man that plots a poem,
In a dressing gown of damask,

At 12.30 in the morning,
Ere the servants bring in luncheon) –
With a look of pensive meaning,
As of ducks that die in tempests.
  Grand, heroic was the notion:
Yet the picture failed entirely,
Failed because he moved a little –
Moved because he couldn't help it.
  Next his better half took courage –
She would have her picture taken:
She came dressed beyond description,
Dressed in jewels and in satin,
Far too gorgeous for an empress.
Gracefully she sat down sideways,
With a simper scarcely human,
Holding in her hand a nosegay
Rather larger than a cabbage.
  All the while that she was taking,
Still the lady chattered, chattered,
Like a monkey in the forest.
'Am I sitting still?' she asked him;
'Is my face enough in profile?
Shall I hold the nosegay higher?
Will it come into the picture?'
And the picture failed completely.
  Next the son, the stunning Cantab—
He suggested curves of beauty,
Curves pervading all his figure,
Which the eye might follow onward
Till it centred in the breast-pin –
Centred in the golden breast-pin.
He had learnt it all from Ruskin,
(Author of *The Stones of Venice*,
Seven Lamps of Architecture,
Modern Painters, and some others) –
And perhaps he had not fully

Understood the author's meaning;
But, whatever was the reason,
All was fruitless, as the picture
Ended in a total failure.
After him the eldest daughter:
She suggested very little,
Only begged she might be taken
With her look of 'passive beauty'.
Her idea of passive beauty
Was a squinting of the left eye,
Was a drooping of the right eye,
Was a smile that went up sideways
To the corner of the nostrils.
Hiawatha, when she asked him,
Took no notice of the question,
Looked as if he hadn't heard it;
But, when pointedly appealed to,
Smiled in a peculiar manner,
Coughed, and said it 'didn't matter',
Bit his lips, and changed the subject.
Nor in this was he mistaken,
As the picture failed completely.
So, in turn, the other daughters:
All of them agreed on one thing,
That their pictures came to nothing,
Though they differed in their causes,
From the eldest, Grinny-haha,
Who, throughout her time of taking,
Shook with sudden, ceaseless laughter,
With a silent fit of laughter,
To the youngest, Dinny-wawa,
Shook with sudden, causeless weeping –
Anything but silent weeping:
And their pictures failed completely.
Last, the youngest son was taken:
'John' his Christian name had once been;

But his overbearing sisters
Called him names he disapproved of –
Called him Johnny, 'Daddy's Darling' –
Called him Jacky, 'Scrubby Schoolboy'.
Very rough and thick his hair was,
Very dusty was his jacket,
Very fidgetty his manner,
And, so fearful was the picture,
In comparison the others
Might be thought to have succeeded –
To have partially succeeded.
　　Finally, my Hiawatha
Tumbled all the tribe together
('Grouped' is not the right expression),
And, as happy chance would have it,
Did at last obtain a picture
Where the faces all succeeded:
Each came out a perfect likeness.
　　Then they joined and all abused it –
Unrestrainedly abused it –
As 'the worst and ugliest picture
That could possibly be taken
Giving one such strange expressions!
Sulkiness, conceit, and meanness!
Really any one would take us
(Any one who did not know us)
For the most unpleasant people!'
(Hiawatha seemed to think so –
Seemed to think it not unlikely).
All together rang their voices –
Angry, hard, discordant voices –
As of dogs that howl in concert,
As of cats that wail in chorus.
　　But my Hiawatha's patience,
His politeness and his patience,
Unaccountably had vanished,

And he left that happy party.
Neither did he leave them slowly,
With the calm deliberation,
The intense deliberation
Of a photographic artist:
But he left them in a hurry,
Left them in a mighty hurry,
Stating that he would not stand it,
Stating in emphatic language
What he'd be before he'd stand it.
Hurriedly he packed his boxes:
Hurriedly the porter trundled
On a barrow all his boxes:
Hurriedly he took his ticket:
Hurriedly the train received him:
Thus departed Hiawatha.

GEORGE A. STRONG

The Modern Hiawatha

He killed the noble Mudjokivis,
With the skin he made him mittens,
Made them with the fur side inside,
Made them with the skin side outside,
He, to get the warm side inside,
Put the inside skin side outside:
He, to get the cold side outside,
Put the warm side fur side inside:
That's why he put the fur side inside,
Why he put the skin side outside
Why he turned them inside outside.

SAMUEL BUTLER

O God! O Montreal!

Stowed away in a Montreal lumber room
The Discobolus standeth and turneth his face to the wall;
Dusty, cobweb-covered, maimed and set at naught,
Beauty lieth in an attic and no man regardeth:
O God! O Montreal!

Beautiful by night and day, beautiful in summer and winter,
Whole or maimed, always and alike beautiful –
He preacheth gospel of grace to the skins of owls
And to one who seasoneth the skins of Canadian owls;
O God! O Montreal!

When I saw him I was wroth and I said, 'O Discobolus!
Beautiful Discobolus, a Prince both among Gods and men,
What doest thou here, how camest thou hither, Discobolus,
Preaching gospel in vain to the skins of owls?'
O God! O Montreal!

And I turned to the man of skins and said unto him, 'O
thou man of skins,
Wherefore hast thou done thus to shame the beauty of the
Discobolus?'
But the Lord had hardened the heart of the man of skins,
And he answered, 'My brother-in-law is haberdasher to
Mr Spurgeon.'
O God! O Montreal!

'The Discobolus is put here because he is vulgar,
He has neither vest nor pants with which to cover his
limbs;
I, Sir, am a person of most respectable connections –
My brother-in-law is haberdasher to Mr Spurgeon.'
O God! O Montreal!

Then I said, 'O brother-in-law to Mr Spurgeon's
haberdasher,
Who seasonest also the skins of Canadian owls,
Thou callest trousers "pants", whereas I call them
"trousers",
Therefore, thou art in hell-fire and may the Lord pity
thee!'
O God! O Montreal!

'Preferrest thou the gospel of Montreal to the gospel of
Hellas,
The gospel of thy connection with Mr Spurgeon's
haberdashery to the gospel of the Discobolus?'
Yet none the less blasphemed he beauty saying, 'The
Discobolus hath no gospel,
But my brother-in-law is haberdasher to Mr Spurgeon.'
O God! O Montreal!

W. S. GILBERT

The Nightmare

When you're lying awake with a dismal headache, and
repose is taboo'd by anxiety,
I conceive you may use any language you choose to
indulge in, without impropriety;
For your brain is on fire – the bedclothes conspire of usual
slumber to plunder you:
First your counterpane goes, and uncovers your toes, and
your sheet slips demurely from under you;
Then the blanketing tickles – you feel like mixed pickles –
so terribly sharp is the pricking,
And you're hot, and you're cross, and you tumble and toss
till there's nothing 'twixt you and the ticking.

Then the bedclothes all creep to the ground in a heap, and
you pick 'em all up in a tangle;
Next your pillow resigns and politely declines to remain at
its usual angle!
Well, you get some repose in the form of a doze, with hot
eye-balls and head ever aching,
But your slumbering teems with such horrible dreams that
you'd very much better be waking;
For you dream you are crossing the Channel, and tossing
about in a steamer from Harwich –
Which is something between a large bathing machine and
a very small second-class carriage –
And you're giving a treat (penny ice and cold meat) to a
party of friends and relations –
They're a ravenous horde – and they all came on board at
Sloane Square and South Kensington Stations.
And bound on that journey you find your attorney (who
started that morning from Devon);
He's a bit undersized, and you don't feel surprised when he
tells you he's only eleven.
Well, you're driving like mad with this singular lad
(by-the-bye the ship's now a four-wheeler),
And you're playing round games, and he calls you bad
names when you tell him that 'ties pay the dealer';
But this you can't stand, so you throw up your hand, and
you find you're as cold as an icicle,
In your shirt and your socks (the black silk with gold
clocks), crossing Salisbury Plain on a bicycle:
And he and the crew are on bicycles too – which they've
somehow or other invested in –
And he's telling the tars, all the particu*lars* of a company
he's interested in –
It's a scheme of devices, to get at low prices, all goods from
cough mixtures to cables
(Which tickled the sailors) by treating retailers, as though
they were all vege*ta*bles –

You get a good spadesman to plant a small tradesman,
(first take off his boots with a boot-tree),
And his legs will take root, and his fingers will shoot, and
they'll blossom and bud like a fruit-tree –
From the greengrocer tree you get grapes and green pea,
cauliflower, pineapple, and cranberries,
While the pastrycook plant, cherry brandy will grant,
apple puffs, and three-corners, and banberries –
The shares are a penny, and ever so many are taken by
Rothschild and Baring,
And just as a few are allotted to you, you awake with a
shudder despairing –
You're a regular wreck, with a crick in your neck, and no
wonder you snore, for your head's on the floor, and
you've needles and pins from your soles to your shins,
and your flesh is a-creep for your left leg's asleep, and
you've cramp in your toes, and a fly on your nose,
and some fluff in your lung, and a feverish tongue,
and a thirst that's intense, and a general sense that you
haven't been sleeping in clover;
But the darkness has passed, and it's daylight at last, and
the night has been long – ditto ditto my song – and
thank goodness they're both of them over!

The Policeman's Lot

When a felon's not engaged in his employment
Or maturing his felonious little plans,
His capacity for innocent enjoyment
Is just as great as any honest man's.
Our feelings we with difficulty smother
When constabulary duty's to be done:
Ah, take one consideration with another,
A policeman's lot is not a happy one!

When the enterprising burglar isn't burgling,
  When the cut-throat isn't occupied in crime,
He loves to hear the little brook a-gurgling,
  And listen to the merry village chime.
When the coster's finished jumping on his mother,
  He loves to lie a-basking in the sun:
Ah, take one consideration with another,
  The policeman's lot is not a happy one!

The First Lord's Song

When I was a lad I served a term
As office boy to an Attorney's firm,
I cleaned the windows and I swept the floor,
And I polished up the handle of the big front door.
Chorus: He polished up the handle of the big front door.
Solo: I polished up that handle so carefullee
That now I am the ruler of the Queen's Navee!
Chorus: He polished up that handle so carefullee
That now he is the ruler of the Queen's Navee!

Solo: As office boy I made such a mark
That they gave me the post of a junior clerk.
I served all the writs with a smile so bland,
And I copied all the letters in a big round hand.
Chorus: He copied all the letters in a big round hand.
Solo: I copied all the letters in a hand so free
That now I am the ruler of the Queen's Navee!
Chorus: He copied all the letters in a hand so free
That now he is the ruler of the Queen's Navee!

Solo: In serving writs I made such a name
That an articled clerk I soon became;
I wore clean collars and a brand new suit
For the pass examination at the Institute.

Chorus: For the pass examination at the Institute.
Solo: That pass examination did so well for me
That now I am the ruler of the Queen's Navee!
Chorus: That pass examination did so well for he
That now he is the ruler of the Queen's Navee!

Solo: Of legal knowledge I acquired such a grip
That they took me into the partnership.
And that junior partnership I ween
Was the only ship that I ever had seen.
Chorus: Was the only ship that he ever had seen.
Solo: But that kind of ship so suited me
That now I am the ruler of the Queen's Navee!
Chorus: But that kind of ship so suited he
That now he is the ruler of the Queen's Navee!

Solo: I grew so rich that I was sent
By a pocket borough into Parliament.
I always voted at my party's call
And I never thought of thinking for myself at all.
Chorus: He never thought of thinking for himself at all.
Solo: I thought so little, they rewarded me
By making me the ruler of the Queen's Navee!
Chorus: He thought so little they rewarded he
By making him the ruler of the Queen's Navee!

Solo: Now landsmen all, whoever you may be,
If you want to rise to the top of the tree,
If your soul isn't fettered to an office stool,
Be careful to be guided by this golden rule:
Chorus: Be careful to be guided by this golden rule:
Solo: Stick close to your desks and never go to sea
And you all may be rulers of the Queen's Navee!
Chorus: Stick close to your desks and never go to sea
And you all may be rulers of the Queen's Navee!

from *H.M.S. Pinafore*

The Rival Curates

List while the poet trolls
   Of MR CLAYTON HOOPER,
Who had a cure of souls
   At Spiffton-extra-Sooper.

He lived on curds and whey,
   And daily sang their praises,
And then he'd go and play
   With buttercups and daisies.

Wild croquet HOOPER banned,
   And all the sports of Mammon,
He warred with cribbage, and
   He exorcized backgammon.

His helmet was a glance
   That spoke of holy gladness;
A saintly smile his lance;
   His shield a tear of sadness.

His Vicar smiled to see
   This armour on him buckled;
With pardonable glee
   He blessed himself and chuckled.

'In mildness to abound
   My curate's sole design is;
In all the country round
   There's none so mild as mine is!'

And HOOPER, disinclined
   His trumpet to be blowing,
Yet didn't think you'd find
   A milder curate going.

A friend arrived one day
   At Spiffton-extra-Sooper,
And in this shameful way
   He spoke to MR HOOPER:

'You think your famous name
   For mildness can't be shaken,
That none can blot your fame –
   But, HOOPER, you're mistaken!

'Your mind is not so blank
   As that of HOPLEY PORTER,
Who holds a curate's rank
   At Assesmilk-cum-Worter.

'*He* plays the airy flute,
   And looks depressed and blighted,
Doves round about him "toot",
   And lambkins dance delighted.

'*He* labours more than you
   At worsted work, and frames it;
In old maids' albums, too,
   Sticks seaweed – yes, and names it!'

The tempter said his say,
   Which pierced him like a needle –
He summoned straight away
   His sexton and his beadle.

(These men were men who could
   Hold liberal opinions:
On Sundays they were good –
   On week-days they were minions.)

'To Hopley Porter go,
Your fare I will afford you –
Deal him a deadly blow,
And blessings shall reward you.

'But stay – I do not like
Undue assassination,
And so, before you strike,
Make this communication:

'I'll give him this one chance –
If he'll more gaily bear him,
Play croquet, smoke, and dance,
I willingly will spare him.'

They went, those minions true,
To Assesmilk-cum-Worter,
And told their errand to
The Reverend Hopley Porter.

'What?' said that reverend gent,
'Dance through my hours of leisure?
Smoke? – bathe myself with scent? –
Play croquet? Oh, with pleasure!

'Wear all my hair in curl?
Stand at my door, and wink – so –
At every passing girl?
My brothers, I should think so!'

ANONYMOUS

Driving in the Park

Of all the pleasant ways
To pass an afternoon,
Is in a pony chaise
One sultry day in June.
To drive between the trees
In Hyde Park round and round,
It brings a pleasant sense of ease
In spinning o'er the ground.
The men raise hats to me,
I mean, the men I know,
They smile, kiss hands, then laugh to see
The flying pony go.
And then I come in sight
Of one against the rails
Whose handsome face lights up so bright
As he my presence hails.

Driving in the Park,
Driving in the Park;
Love may haunt the drive,
And no one ever mark.
Glances meet with joy,
Alighting with love's spark.
Sweet one. Naughty boy.
Driving in the Park.

And very nice it seems
Among the beats I know,
When early sunlight gleams,
To gallop round the Row.

At ten some breezy morn
All care away I fling,
Luxurious days of rest I scorn,
The gallop is the thing.
I challenge all my friends
To run a race with me,
And when the madcap scamper ends,
The blood flows fresh and free.
And nicer yet to walk
The horse while some one near
Engages me with tender talk,
So very sweet to hear.

Riding in the Park,
Riding in the Park;
Love may haunt the Row
And no one ever mark.
Love may bend his bow,
Make two hearts his mark,
No one ever know –
Riding in the Park.

GODFREY TURNER

The Journal of Society

Oh, have you seen the *Tattlesnake* and have you read what's in it,
About – dear me! Tut! What's his name? I'll tell you in a minute.
Thwaites? No, not Thwaites. McCorquodale? No. Gillingwater? Coutts?
The man who wears a high-crowned hat and patent-leather boots.
In philanthropic circles he is known as 'Ready Bob';
I think he lives out Kilburn way and rides a chestnut cob.

He gets it in the *Tattlesnake*! I wonder how he feels
When all his friends their shoulders shrug and turn upon their heels.
We thought him such a thoroughbred! And now it's all found out.
They'd hardly dare to write like that, if there were any doubt.
Besides, 'twixt you and me, you know, there *was* a something queer
About his early history, I think I used to hear.
You don't remember? Well, I do; although I could not say
Precisely what the story was, at such a distant day.
These things will always hang about a fellow's after-life.
Oh, now I know! Yes. Was there not some talk about his wife?
Or else it was his sister, or his mother, or his aunt:
Though if I'm asked to give the facts, I frankly say I can't.
But get the *Tattlesnake*, my boy; you'll find it worth the money,
Unless, that is, you're one of those who don't think scandal funny.
That class of writing lacks, I own, the literary zeal
To add a charm to Addison, or polish put on Steele.
Between the *Tattlesnake* and *them* it's not a case of choosing;
But personality, if dull, is in its way amusing;
Although the way's not that of wit, nor graciousness, nor grammar.
You would not have a rapier-point upon a blacksmith's hammer!
But what of that? On certain ears wit blunted tells the best,
And satire glads the public heart when as a libel dressed.
Of course I don't defend the thing: it's bad in many ways;
But is not this the 'golden' age? And I suppose it pays.
So get the *Tattlesnake*. – It's dead? Bless me! You don't mean that?

Well, after all, I'm not surprised. I thought it rather flat.
By chance I saw it once or twice, and then I found it slow;
That shameful article I read about a month ago.
But still some dirt will always stick; and, long as he may
 live,
That that same dirt had not been flung a thousand pounds
 he'd give; –
When all his old acquaintance cut and every urchin hoots
The man who wears the high-crowned hat and
 patent-leather boots.

BRET HARTE

Plain Language from Truthful James

Which I wish to remark,
 And my language is plain,
That for ways that are dark
 And for tricks that are vain,
The heathen Chinee is peculiar,
 Which the same I would rise to explain.

Ah Sin was his name;
 And I shall not deny
In regard to the same,
 What that name might imply;
But his smile it was pensive and childlike,
 As I frequent remarked to Bill Nye.

It was August the third;
 And quite soft was the skies;
Which it might be inferred
 That Ah Sin was likewise;
Yet he played it that day upon William
 And me in a way I despise.

Which we had a small game,
  And Ah Sin took a hand:
It was Euchre. The same
  He did not understand;
But he smiled as he sat by the table,
  With the smile that was childlike and bland.

Yet the cards they were stocked
  In a way that I grieve,
And my feelings were shocked
  At the state of Nye's sleeve:
Which was stuffed full of aces and bowers,
  And the same with intent to deceive.

But the hands that were played
  By that heathen Chinee,
And the points that he made,
  Were quite frightful to see, –
Till at last he put down a right bower,[1]
  Which the same Nye had dealt unto me.

Then I looked up at Nye,
  And he gazed upon me;
And he rose with a sigh,
  And said, 'Can this be?
We are ruined by Chinese cheap labour, –'
  And he went for that heathen Chinee.

In the scene that ensued
  I did not take a hand,
But the floor it was strewed
  Like the leaves on the strand
With the cards that Ah Sin had been hiding,
  In the game 'he did not understand.'

[1]The knave of the trump suit, the highest card in the game of euchre

In his sleeves, which were long,
  He had twenty-four packs, –
Which was coming it strong,
  Yet I state but the facts;
And we found on his nails, which were taper,
  What is frequent in tapers, – that's wax.

Which is why I remark,
  And my language is plain,
That for ways that are dark,
  And for tricks that are vain,
The heathen Chinee is peculiar, –
  Which the same I am free to maintain.

E. H. PALMER

The Parterre

I don't know any greatest treat
As sit him in a gay parterre,
And sniff one up the perfume sweet
Of every roses buttoning there.

It only want my charming miss
Who make to blush the self red rose;
Oh! I have envy of to kiss
The end's tip of her splendid nose.

Oh! I have envy of to be
What grass 'neath her pantoffle push,
And too much happy seemeth me
The margaret which her vestige crush.

But I will meet her nose at nose,
And take occasion for her hairs,
And indicate her all my woes,
That she in fine agree my prayers.

I don't know any greatest treat
As sit him in a gay parterre,
With Madame who is too more sweet
Than every roses buttoning there.

THOMAS HARDY

Liddell and Scott

On the completion of their Lexicon

(Written after the death of Liddell in 1898. Scott had died some ten years earlier)

'Well, though it seems
Beyond our dreams,'
Said Liddell to Scott,
'We've really got
To the very end,
All inked and penned
Blotless and fair
Without turning a hair,
This sultry summer day, A.D.
Eighteen hundred and forty-three.

'I've often, I own,
Belched many a moan
At undertaking it,
And dreamt forsaking it.

– Yes, on to Pi,
When the end loomed nigh,
And friends said: "You've as good as done,"
I almost wished we'd not begun.
Even now, if people only knew
My sinkings, as we slowly drew
Along through Kappa, Lambda, Mu,
They'd be concerned at my misgiving,
And how I mused on a College living
Right down to Sigma,
But feared a stigma
If I succumbed, and left old Donnegan
For weary freshmen's eyes to con again:
And how I often, often wondered
What could have led me to have blundered
So far away from sound theology
To dialects and etymology;
Words, accents not to be breathed by men
Of any country ever again!'

'My heart most failed,
Indeed, quite quailed,'
Said Scott to Liddell,
'Long ere the middle! . . .
'Twas one wet dawn
When, slippers on,
And a cold in the head anew,
Gazing at Delta
I turned and felt a
Wish for bed anew,
And to let supersedings
Of Passow's readings
In dialects go.
"That German has read
More than we!" I said;
Yea, several times did I feel so! . . .

'O that first morning, smiling bland,
With sheets of foolscap, quills in hand,
To write ἀάατος and ἀαγής,
Followed by fifteen hundred pages,
        What nerve was ours
        So to back our powers,
Assured that we should reach ὠώδης
While there was breath left in our bodies!'

Liddell replied: 'Well, that's past now;
The job's done, thank God, anyhow.'

        'And yet it's not,'
        Considered Scott,
        'For we've to get
        Subscribers yet
        We must remember;
        Yes; by September.'

'O Lord; dismiss that. We'll succeed.
Dinner is my immediate need.
I feel as hollow as a fiddle,
Working so many hours,' said Liddell.

The Ruined Maid

'O 'Melia, my dear, this does everything crown!
Who could have supposed I should meet you in Town?
And whence such fair garments, such prosperi-ty?' –
'O didn't you know I'd been ruined?' said she.

– 'You left us in tatters, without shoes or socks,
Tired of digging potatoes, and spudding up docks;
And now you've gay bracelets and bright feathers three!' –
'Yes: that's how we dress when we're ruined,' said she.

– 'At home in the barton you said "thee" and "thou",
And "thik oon", and "theäs oon", and "t'other"; but now
Your talking quite fits 'ee for high compa-ny!' –
'Some polish is gained with one's ruin,' said she.

– 'Your hands were like paws then, your face blue and bleak
But now I'm bewitched by your delicate cheek,
And your little gloves fit as on any la-dy!'
'We never do work when we're ruined,' said she.

– 'You used to call home-life a hag-ridden dream,
And you'd sigh, and you'd sock; but at present you seem
To know not of megrims or melancho-ly!' –
'True. One's pretty lively when ruined,' said she.

– 'I wish I had feathers, a fine sweeping gown,
And a delicate face, and could strut about Town!' –
'My dear – a raw country girl, such as you be,
Cannot quite expect that. You ain't ruined,' said she.

Wagtail and Baby

A baby watched a ford, whereto
   A wagtail came for drinking;
A blaring bull went wading through,
   The wagtail showed no shrinking.

A stallion splashed his way across,
   The birdie nearly sinking;
He gave his plumes a twitch and toss,
   And held his own unblinking.

Next saw the baby round the spot
   A mongrel slowly slinking;
The wagtail gazed, but faltered not
   In dip and sip and prinking.

A perfect gentleman then neared;
  The wagtail, in a winking,
With terror rose and disappeared;
  The baby fell a-thinking.

ANONYMOUS

Poem by a Perfectly Furious Academician

I takes and I paints,
Hears no complaints,
And sells before I'm dry;
Till savage Ruskin
He sticks his tusk in,
Then nobody will buy.

ANDREW LANG

Brahma

If the wild bowler thinks he bowls,
  Or if the batsman thinks he's bowled,
They know not, poor misguided souls,
  They too shall perish unconsoled.
I am the batsman and the bat,
  I am the bowler and the ball,
The umpire, the pavilion cat,
  The roller, pitch, and stumps, and all.

SAMUEL C. BUSHNELL

Boston

I come from the city of Boston,
The home of the bean and the cod,
Where Cabots speak only to Lowells,
And Lowells speak only to God.

J. K. STEPHEN

On a Rhine Steamer

Republic of the West
  Enlightened, free, sublime,
Unquestionably best
  Production of our time,

The telephone is thine,
  And thine the Pullman car,
The caucus, the divine
  Intense electric star.

To thee we likewise owe
  The venerable names
Of Edgar Allan Poe,
  And Mr Henry James.

In short it's due to thee,
  Thou kind of Western star,
That we have come to be
  Precisely what we are.

But every now and then,
   It cannot be denied,
You breed a kind of men
   Who are not dignified,

Or courteous or refined,
   Benevolent or wise,
Or gifted with a mind
   Beyond the common size,

Or notable for tact,
   Agreeable to me,
Or anything, in fact,
   That people ought to be.

Drinking Song

There are people, I know, to be found,
   Who say, and apparently think,
That sorrow and care may be drowned
   By a timely consumption of drink.

Does not man, these enthusiasts ask,
   Most nearly approach the divine,
When engaged in the soul-stirring task
   Of filling his body with wine?

Have not beggars been frequently known,
   When satisfied, soakèd and replete,
To imagine their bench was a throne
   And the civilised world at their feet?

Lord Byron has finely described
   The remarkably soothing effect
Of liquor, profusely imbibed,
   On a soul that is shattered and wrecked.

In short, if your body or mind
   Or your soul or your purse come to grief,
You need only get drunk, and you'll find
   Complete and immediate relief.

For myself, I have managed to do
   Without having recourse to this plan,
So I can't write a poem for you,
   And you'd better get someone who can.

To R.K.

> As long I dwell on some stupendous
> And tremendous (Heaven defend us!)
> Monstr'-inform'-ingens-horrendous
> Demoniaco-seraphic
> Penman's latest piece of graphic.
>
> BROWNING

Will there never come a season
Which shall rid us from the curse
Of a prose which knows no reason
And an unmelodious verse:
When the world shall cease to wonder
At the genius of an Ass,
And a boy's eccentric blunder
Shall not bring success to pass:
When mankind shall be delivered
From the clash of magazines,
And the inkstand shall be shivered
Into countless smithereens:
When there stands a muzzled stripling,
Mute, beside a muzzled bore:
When the Rudyards cease from Kipling
And the Haggards Ride no more.

A Sonnet

Two voices are there: one is of the deep;
It learns the storm-cloud's thunderous melody,
Now roars, now murmurs with the changing sea,
Now bird-like pipes, now closes soft in sleep:
And one is of an old half-witted sheep
Which bleats articulate monotony,
And indicates that two and one are three,
That grass is green, lakes damp, and mountains steep:
And, Wordsworth, both are thine: at certain times
Forth from the heart of thy melodious rhymes,
The form and pressure of high thoughts will burst:
At other times – good Lord! I'd rather be
Quite unacquainted with the ABC
Than write such hopeless rubbish as thy worst.

FRANCIS THOMPSON

At Lord's

It is little I repair to the matches of the Southron folk,
  Though my own red roses there may blow;
It is little I repair to the matches of the Southron folk,
  Though the red roses crest the caps, I know.
For the field is full of shades as I near the shadowy coast,
And a ghostly batsman plays to the bowling of a ghost,
And I look through my tears on a soundless-clapping host
  As the run-stealers flicker to and fro,
    To and fro:
  O my Hornby and my Barlow long ago!

It is Glo'ster coming North, the irresistible,
  The Shire of the Graces, long ago!
It is Gloucestershire up North, the irresistible,
  And new-risen Lancashire the foe!
A Shire so young that has scarce impressed its traces,
Ah, how shall it stand before all-resistless Graces?
O, little red rose, their bats are as maces
  To beat thee down, this summer long ago!

This day of seventy-eight they are come up North against
    thee
  This day of seventy-eight, long ago!
The champion of the centuries, he cometh up against thee,
  With his brethren, every one a famous foe!
The long-whiskered Doctor, that laugheth rules to scorn,
While the bowler, pitched against him, bans the day that he
    was born;
And G.F. with his science makes the fairest length forlorn;
  They are come from the West to work thee woe!

It is little I repair to the matches of the Southron folk,
  Though my own red roses there may blow;
It is little I repair to the matches of the Southron folk,
  Though the red roses crest the caps, I know.
For the field is full of shades as I near the shadowy coast,
And a ghostly batsman plays to the bowling of a ghost,
And I look through my tears on a soundless-clapping host
  As the run-stealers flicker to and fro,
    To and fro:
  O my Hornby and my Barlow long ago!

A. E. HOUSMAN

Infant Innocence

The Grizzly Bear is huge and wild;
He has devoured the infant child.
The infant child is not aware
He has been eaten by the bear.

Fragment of a Greek Tragedy

Alcmaeon, Chorus

Chorus: O suitably-attired-in-leather-boots
Head of a traveller, wherefore seeking whom
Whence by what way how purposed art thou come
To this well-nightingaled vicinity?
My object in enquiring is to know,
But if you happen to be deaf and dumb
And do not understand a word I say,
Then wave your hand, to signify as much.
Alcmaeon: I journeyed hither a Bœotian road.
Chorus: Sailing on horseback, or with feet for oars?
Alcmaeon: Plying with speed my partnership of legs.
Chorus: Beneath a shining or a rainy Zeus?
Alcmaeon: Mud's sister, not himself, adorns my shoes.
Chorus: To learn your name would not displease me much.
Alcmaeon: Not all that men desire do they obtain.
Chorus: Might I then hear at what your presence shoots?
Alcmaeon: A shepherd's questioned mouth informed me that –
Chorus: What? for I know not yet what you will say –
Alcmaeon: Nor will you ever, if you interrupt.

Chorus: Proceed, and I will hold my speechless tongue.
Alcmaeon: – This house was Eriphyla's, no one's else.
Chorus: Nor did he shame his throat with hateful lies.
Alcmaeon: May I then enter, passing through the door?
Chorus: Go, chase into the house a lucky foot,
And, O my son, be, on the one hand, good,
And do not, on the other hand, be bad;
For that is very much the safest plan.
Alcmaeon: I go into the house with heels and speed.

Chorus: In speculation *Strophe*
I would not willingly acquire a name
For ill-digested thought;
But after pondering much
To this conclusion I at last have come:
Life is uncertain.
This truth I have written deep
In my reflective midriff
On tablets not of wax,
Nor with a pen did I inscribe it there,
For many reasons: *Life, I say, is not*
A stranger to uncertainty.
Not from the flight of omen-yelling fowls
This fact did I discover.
Nor did the Delphic tripod bark it out,
Nor yet Dodona.
Its native ingenuity sufficed
My self-taught diaphragm.

Why should I mention *Antistrophe*
The Inachean daughter, loved of Zeus?
Her whom of old the gods,
More provident than kind,
Provided with four hoofs, two horns, one tail,
A gift not asked for,

And sent her forth to learn
The unfamiliar science
Of how to chew the cud.
She therefore, all about the Argive fields,
Went cropping pale green grass and nettle-tops,
Nor did they disagree with her.
But yet, howe'er nutritious, such repasts
I do not hanker after:
Never may Cypris for her seat select
My dappled liver!
Why should I mention Io! Why indeed?
I have no notion why.

But now does my boding heart, *Epode*
Unhired, unaccompanied, sing
A strain not meet for the dance.
Yea even the palace appears
To my yoke of circular eyes
(The right, nor omit I the left)
Like a slaughterhouse, so to speak,
Garnished with woolly deaths
And many shipwrecks of cows.
I therefore in a Cissian strain lament;
And to the rapid,
Loud, linen-tattering thumps upon my chest
Resounds in concert
The battering of my unlucky head.

ERIPHYLA (*within*). O, I am smitten with a hatchet's jaw;
And that in deed and not in word alone.
Chorus: I thought I heard a sound within the house
Unlike the voice of one that jumps for joy.
Eriphyla: He splits my skull, not in a friendly way,
One more: he purposes to kill me dead.
Chorus: I would not be reputed rash, but yet
I doubt if all be gay within the house.

Eriphyla: O! O! another stroke! that makes the third.
He stabs me to the heart against my wish.
Chorus: If that be so, thy state of health is poor;
But thine arithmetic is quite correct.

Occasional Poem

When Adam day by day
Woke up in Paradise,
He always used to say
'Oh, this is very nice.'

But Eve from scenes of bliss
Transported him for life.
The more I think of this
The more I beat my wife.

Hallelujah!

'Hallelujah!' was the only observation
That escaped Lieutenant-Colonel Mary Jane,
When she tumbled off the platform in the station,
And was cut in little pieces by the train.
Mary Jane, the train is through yer:
Hallelujah, Hallelujah!
We will gather up the fragments that remain.

Balliol Rhymes

I

First come I; my name is Jowett.
There's no knowledge but I know it.
I am Master of this college:
What I don't know isn't knowledge.

H. C. Beeching

2

My name is George Nathaniel Curzon,
I am a most superior person.
My face is pink, my hair is sleek.
I dine at Blenheim once a week.

Anonymous

ANONYMOUS

The Tale of Lord Lovell

Lord Lovell he stood at his own front door,
  Seeking the hole for the key;
His hat was wrecked, and his trousers bore
  A rent across either knee,
When down came the beauteous Lady Jane
  In fair white draperie.

'Oh, where have you been, Lord Lovell?' she said,
  'Oh, where have you been?' said she;
'I have not closed an eye in bed,
  And the clock has just struck three.
Who has been standing you on your head
  In the ash-barrel, pardie?'

'I am not drunk, Lad' Shane,' he said:
  'And so late it cannot be;
The clock struck one as I enterèd –
  I heard it two times or three;
It must be the salmon on which I fed
  Has been too many for me.'

'Go tell your tale, Lord Lovell,' she said,
 'To the maritime cavalree,
To your grandmother of the hoary head –
 To any one but me:
The door is not used to be openèd
 With a cigarette for a key.'

The Ballad of William Bloat

In a mean abode in the Shankill Road
 Lived a man named William Bloat;
Now he had a wife, the plague of his life,
 Who continually got his goat,
And one day at dawn, with her night-shift on,
 He slit her bloody throat.

With a razor-gash he settled her hash –
 Oh, never was death so quick;
But the steady drip on the pillowslip
 Of her life-blood turned him sick,
And the pool of gore on the bedroom floor
 Grew clotted and cold and thick.

Now he was right glad he had done as he had
 As his wife lay there so still,
When a sudden awe of the mighty Law
 Struck his heart with an icy chill,
And, to finish the fun so well begun,
 He resolved himself to kill.

He took the sheet from his wife's cold feet
 And knotted it into a rope,
And hanged himself from the pantry shelf –
 An easy death, let's hope.
In the jaws of death with his latest breath
 Said he, 'To Hell with the Pope'.

But the strangest turn of the whole concern
  Is only just beginning:
He went to Hell, but his wife got well
  And is still alive and sinning,
For the razor-blade was Dublin-made
  But the sheet was Belfast linen.

WALTER RALEIGH

Wishes of an Elderly Man

I wish I loved the Human Race;
I wish I loved its silly face;
I wish I liked the way it walks;
I wish I liked the way it talks;
And when I'm introduced to one
I wish I thought *What Jolly Fun!*

OWEN SEAMAN

A Plea for Trigamy

I've been trying to fashion a wifely ideal,
  And find that my tastes are so far from concise
That, to marry completely, no fewer than three'll
    Suffice.

I've subjected my views to severe atmospheric
  Compression, but still, in defiance of force,
They distinctly fall under three heads, like a cleric
    Discourse.

My *first* must be fashion's own fancy-bred daughter,
Proud, peerless, and perfect – in fact, *comme il faut;*
A waltzer and wit of the very first water –
For *show.*

But these beauties that serve to make all the men
jealous,
Once face them alone in the family cot,
Heaven's angels incarnate (the novelists tell us)
They're *not.*

But so much for appearances. Now for my *second*,
My lover, the wife of my home and my heart:
Of all fortune and fate of my life to be reckon'd
A part.

She must know all the needs of a rational being,
Be skilled to keep council, to comfort, to coax;
And, above all things else, be accomplished at seeing
My jokes.

I complete the ménage by including one other
With all the domestic prestige of a hen:
As my housekeeper, nurse, or it may be, a mother
Of men.

Total *three!* and the virtues all well represented;
With fewer than this such a thing can't be done;
Though I've known married men who declare
they're contented
With one.

Would you hunt during harvest, or hay-make in
winter?
And how can one woman expect to combine
Certain qualifications essentially inter-
necine?

You may say that my prospects are (legally) sunless;
I state that I find them as clear as can be: –
I will marry *no* wife, since I can't do with one less
Than three.

To a Boy-Poet of the Decadence

(Showing curious reversal of epigram – '*La nature l'a fait sanglier; la civilisation l'a réduit à l'état de cochon.*')

But my good little man, you have made a mistake
If you really are pleased to suppose
That the Thames is alight with the lyrics you make;
We could all do the same if we chose.

From Solomon down, we may read, as we run,
Of the ways of a man and a maid;
There is nothing that's new to us under the sun,
And certainly not in the shade.

The erotic affairs that you fiddle aloud
Are as vulgar as coin of the mint;
And you merely distinguish yourself from the crowd
By the fact that you put 'em in print.

You're a 'prentice, my boy, in the primitive stage,
And you itch, like a boy, to confess:
When you know a bit more of the arts of the age
You will probably talk a bit less.

For your dull little vices we don't care a fig,
It is *this* that we deeply deplore;
You were cast for a common or usual pig,
But you play the invincible bore.

OLIVER HERFORD

The Smile of the Goat

The Smile of the Goat has a meaning that few
  Will mistake, and explains in a measure
The Censor attending a risqué Revue
  And combining Stern Duty with pleasure.

The Platypus

My child, the Duck-billed Plat-y-pus
A sad ex-am-ple sets for us
From him we learn how in-de-ci-sion
Of char-ac-ter pro-vokes De-ri-sion.
This vac-il-lat-ing Thing, you see,
Could not de-cide which he would be,
Fish, Flesh, or Fowl, and chose all three.
The sci-en-tists were sore-ly vexed
To clas-si-fy him; so per-plexed
Their brains that they, with Rage at bay,
Called him a hor-rid name one day –
A name that baf-fles, frights, and shocks us –
Or-ni-tho-rhyn-chus Par-a-dox-us.

A. T. QUILLER-COUCH

Lady Jane

Sapphics

Down the green hillside fro' the castle window
Lady Jane spied Bill Amaranth a-workin';
Day by day watched him go about his ample
          Nursery garden.

Cabbages thriv'd there, wi' a mort o' green-stuff –
Kidney beans, broad beans, onions, tomatoes,
Artichokes, seakale, vegetable marrows,
Early potatoes.

Lady Jane cared not very much for all these:
What she cared much for was a glimpse o' Willum
Strippin' his brown arms wi' a view to horti-
Cultural effort.

Little guessed Willum, never extra-vain, that
Up the green hillside, i' the gloomy castle,
Feminine eyes could so delight to view his
Noble proportions.

Only one day while, in an innocent mood,
Moppin' his brow ('cos 'twas a trifle sweaty)
With a blue kerchief – lo, he spies a white 'un
Coyly responding.

Oh, delightsome Love! Not a jot do *you* care
For the restrictions set on human inter-
Course by cold-blooded social refiners;
Nor do I, neither.

Day by day, peepin' fro' behind the bean sticks,
Willum observed that scrap o' white a-wavin',
Till his hot sighs outgrowin' all repression
Busted his weskit.

Lady Jane's guardian was a haughty Peer, who
Clung to old creeds and had a nasty temper;
Can we blame William that he hardly cared to
Risk a refusal?

Year by year found him busy 'mid the bean sticks,
Wholly uncertain how on earth to take steps.
Thus for eighteen years he beheld the maiden
Wave fro' her window.

But the nineteenth spring, i' the Castle post bag,
Came by book post Bill's catalogue o' seedlings
Mark'd wi' blue ink at 'Paragraphs relatin'
Mainly to Pumpkins.'

'W.A. can,' so the Lady Jane read,
'Strongly commend that very noble Gourd, the
Lady Jane, first-class medal, ornamental;
Grows to a great height.'

Scarce a year arter, by the scented hedgerows –
Down the mown hillside, fro' the castle gateway –
Came a long train and, i' the midst, a black bier,
Easily shouldered.

'Whose is yon corse that, thus adorned wi' gourd leaves,
Forth ye bear with slow step?' A mourner answer'd,
'Tis the poor clay-cold body Lady Jane grew
Tired to abide in.'

'Delve my grave quick, then, for I die tomorrow.
Delve it one furlong fro' the kidney bean sticks,
Where I may dream she's goin' on precisely
As she was used to.'

Hardly died Bill when, fro' the Lady Jane's grave,
Crept to his white deathbed a lovely pumpkin:
Climb'd the house wall and overarched his head wi'
Billowy verdure.

Simple this tale! – but delicately perfumed
As the sweet roadside honeysuckle. That's why,
Difficult though its metre was to tackle,
I'm glad I wrote it.

GEORGE ADE

R-E-M-O-R-S-E

The cocktail is a pleasant drink,
It's mild and harmless, I don't think.
When you've had one, you call for two,
And then you don't care what you do.
Last night I hoisted twenty-three
Of these arrangements into me;
My wealth increased, I swelled with pride;
I was pickled, primed and ossified.

R-E-M-O-R-S-E!
Those dry martinis did the work for me;
Last night at twelve I felt immense;
Today I feel like thirty cents.
At four I sought my whirling bed,
At eight I woke with such a head!
It is no time for mirth or laughter –
The cold, gray dawn of the morning after

If ever I want to sign the pledge,
It's the morning after I've had an edge;
When I've been full of the oil of joy
And fancied I was a sporty boy.
This world was one kaleidoscope
Of purple bliss, transcendent hope.
But now I'm feeling mighty blue –
Three cheers for the W.C.T.U.!

R-E-M-O-R-S-E!
The water wagon is the place for me;
I think that somewhere in the game,
I wept and told my maiden name.
My eyes are bleared, my coppers hot;
I try to eat, but I can not;
It is no time for mirth or laughter –
The cold, gray dawn of the morning after.

ANTHONY C. DEANE

The Cult of the Celtic

When the eager squadrons of day are faint and disbanded,
  And under the wind-swept stars the reaper gleans
The petulant passion flowers – although, to be candid,
  I haven't the faintest notion what that means –

Surely the Snow-White Bird makes melody sweeter
  High in the air than skimming the clogging dust.
(Yes, there's certainly something queer about this metre,
  But, as it's Celtic, you and I must take it on trust.)

And oh, the smile of the Slave as he shakes his fetters!
  And oh, the Purple Pig as it roams afar!
And oh, the – something or other in capital letters –
  As it yields to the magic spell of a wind-swept star!

And look at the tricksy Elves, how they leap and frolic,
  Ducking the Bad Banshee in the moonlit pool,
Celtic, yet fully content to be 'symbolic',
  Never a thought in their head about Home Rule!

But the wind-swept star – you notice it has to figure,
   Taking an average merely, in each alternate verse
Of every Celtic poem – smiles with a palpable snigger,
   While the Yellow Wolf-Hound bays his blighting curse,

And the voices of dead desires in sufferers waken,
   And the voice of the limitless lake is harsh and rough,
And the voice of the reader, too, unless I'm mistaken,
   Is heard to remark that he's had about enough.

But since the critics have stated with some decision
   That stanzas very like these are simply grand
Showing 'a sense of beauty and intimate vision',
   Proving a 'Celtic Renaissance' close at hand;

Then, although I admit it's a terrible tax on
   Powers like mine, yet I sincerely felt
My task, as an unintelligent Saxon,
   Was, at all hazards, to try to copy the Celt!

EDWIN ARLINGTON ROBINSON

Miniver Cheevy

Miniver Cheevy, child of scorn,
   Grew lean while he assailed the seasons;
He wept that he was ever born,
   And he had reasons.

Miniver loved the days of old
   When swords were bright and steeds were prancing;
The vision of a warrior bold
   Would set him dancing.

Miniver sighed for what was not,
  And dreamed, and rested from his labours;
He dreamed of Thebes and Camelot,
  And Priam's neighbours.

Miniver mourned the ripe renown
  That made so many a name so fragrant;
He mourned Romance, now on the town,
  And Art, a vagrant.

Miniver loved the Medici.
  Albeit he had never seen one;
He would have sinned incessantly
  Could he have been one.

Miniver cursed the commonplace
  And eyed a khaki suit with loathing;
He missed the medieval grace
  Of iron clothing.

Miniver scorned the gold he sought,
  But sore annoyed was he without it;
Miniver thought, and thought, and thought,
  And thought about it.

Miniver Cheevy, born too late,
  Scratched his head and kept on thinking;
Miniver coughed, and called it fate,
  And kept on drinking.

HILAIRE BELLOC

Lord Lundy

Lord Lundy from his earliest years
Was far too freely moved to Tears.
For instance, if his Mother said,
'Lundy! It's time to go to Bed!'
He bellowed like a Little Turk.
Or if his father, Lord Dunquerque,
Said, 'Hi!' in a Commanding Tone,
'Hi, Lundy! Leave the Cat alone!'
Lord Lundy, letting go its tail,
Would raise so terrible a wail
As moved His Grandpapa the Duke
To utter the severe rebuke:
'When I, Sir! was a little Boy,
An Animal was not a Toy!'
His father's Elder Sister, who
Was married to a Parvenoo,
Confided to Her Husband, 'Drat!
The Miserable, Peevish Brat!
Why don't they drown the Little Beast?'
Suggestions which, to say the least,
Are not what we expect to hear
From Daughters of an English Peer.
His grandmamma, His Mother's Mother,
Who had some dignity or other,
The Garter, or no matter what,
I can't remember all the Lot!
Said, 'Oh! that I were Brisk and Spry
To give him that for which to cry!'
(An empty wish, alas! for she
Was Blind and nearly ninety-three.)
The Dear Old Butler thought – but there!
I really neither know nor care

For what the Dear Old Butler thought!
In my opinion, Butlers ought
To know their place, and not to play
The Old Retainer night and day.
I'm getting tired and so are you,
Let's cut the Poem into two!

Second Canto

It happened to Lord Lundy then,
As happens to so many men:
Towards the age of twenty-six,
They shoved him into politics;
In which profession he commanded
The income that his rank demanded
In turn as Secretary for
India, the Colonies, and War.
But very soon his friends began
To doubt if he were quite the man:
Thus, if a member rose to say
(As members do from day to day),
'Arising out of that reply . . . !'
Lord Lundy would begin to cry.
A Hint at harmless little jobs
Would shake him with convulsive sobs.
While as for Revelations, these
Would simply bring him to his knees,
And leave him whimpering like a child.
It drove his Colleagues raving wild!
They let him sink from Post to Post,
From fifteen hundred at the most
To eight, and barely six – and then
To be Curator of Big Ben! . . .
And finally there came a Threat
To oust him from the Cabinet!

The Duke – his aged grandsire – bore
The shame till he could bear no more.
He rallied his declining powers,
Summoned the youth to Brackley Towers,
And bitterly addressed him thus –
'Sir! you have disappointed us!
We had intended you to be
The next Prime Minister but three:
The stocks were sold; the Press was squared;
The Middle Class was quite prepared.
But as it is! . . . My language fails!
Go out and govern New South Wales!'

*

The Aged Patriot groaned and died:
And gracious! how Lord Lundy cried!

Lord Finchley

Lord Finchley tried to mend the Electric Light
Himself. It struck him dead: And serve him right!
It is the business of the wealthy man
To give employment to the artisan.

Jim

Who ran away from his Nurse, and was eaten by a Lion.

There was a Boy whose name was Jim;
His Friends were very good to him.
They gave him Tea, and Cakes, and Jam,
And slices of delicious Ham,
And Chocolate with pink inside,
And little tricycles to ride,
And read him stories through and through,
And even took him to the Zoo –
But there it was the dreadful Fate
Befell him, which I now relate.

You know – at least you *ought* to know,
For I have often told you so –
That Children never are allowed
To leave their Nurses in a Crowd;
Now this was Jim's especial foible,
He ran away when he was able,
And on this inauspicious day
He slipped his hand and ran away!
He hadn't gone a yard when –
Bang!
With open Jaws, a Lion sprang,
And hungrily began to eat
The Boy: beginning at his feet.

Now just imagine how it feels
When first your toes and then your heels,
And then by gradual degrees,
Your shins and ankles, calves and knees,
Are slowly eaten, bit by bit.
No wonder Jim detested it!
No wonder that he shouted 'Hi!'
The Honest Keeper heard his cry,
Though very fat, he almost ran
To help the little gentleman.
'Ponto!' he ordered as he came
(For Ponto was the Lion's name),
'Ponto!' he cried, with angry Frown.
'Let go, Sir! Down, Sir! Put it down!'

The Lion made a sudden stop,
He let the Dainty Morsel drop,
And slunk reluctant to his Cage,
Snarling with Disappointed Rage.
But when he bent him over Jim,
The Honest Keeper's Eyes were dim.

The Lion having reached his Head,
The Miserable Boy was dead!

When Nurse informed his Parents, they
Were more Concerned than I can say: –
His Mother, as She dried her eyes,
Said, 'Well – it gives me no surprise,
He would not do as he was told!'
His Father, who was self-controlled,
Bade all the children round attend
To James' miserable end,
And always keep a-hold of Nurse
For fear of finding something worse.

Henry King

Who chewed bits of String, and was early cut off in Dreadful Agonies.

The Chief Defect of Henry King
Was chewing little bits of String.
At last he swallowed some which tied
Itself in ugly Knots inside.

Physicians of the Utmost Fame
Were called at once; but when they came
They answered, as they took their Fees,
'There is no Cure for this Disease.
Henry will very soon be dead.'
His Parents stood about his Bed
Lamenting his Untimely Death,
When Henry, with his Latest Breath,
Cried – 'Oh, my Friends, be warned by me,
That Breakfast, Dinner, Lunch and Tea
Are all the Human Frame requires . . .'
With that, the Wretched Child expires.

MAX BEERBOHM

A Police Station Ditty

Then it's collar 'im tight,
  In the name of the Law!
'Ustle 'im, shake 'im till 'e's sick!
  Wot, 'e *would*, would 'e? Well,
  Then yer've got ter give 'im 'Ell,
An' it's trunch, trunch, truncheon does the trick!

A Luncheon (Thomas Hardy Entertains the Prince of Wales)

Lift latch, step in, be welcome, Sir,
Albeit to see you I'm unglad
And your face is fraught with a deathly shyness
Bleaching what pink it may have had,
Come in, come in, Your Royal Highness.

Beautiful weather? – Sir, that's true,
Though the farmers are casting rueful looks
At tilth's and pasture's dearth of spryness. –
Yes, Sir, I've written several books. –
A little more chicken, Your Royal Highness?

Lift latch, step out, your car is there,
To bear you hence from this ancient vale.
We are both of us aged by our strange brief nighness,
But each of us lives to tell the tale.
Farewell, farewell, Your Royal Highness.

WALTER DE LA MARE

Hi!

Hi! handsome hunting man,
Fire your little gun.
Bang! Now the animal
Is dead and dumb and done.
Never more to peep again, creep again, leap again,
Eat or sleep or drink again. Oh, what fun!

Pooh!

Dainty Miss Apathy
Sat on a sofa,
Dangling her legs,
And with nothing to do;
She looked at a drawing of
Old Queen Victoria,
At a rug from far Persia –
An exquisite blue;
At a bowl of bright tulips;
A needlework picture
Of doves caged in wicker
You could almost hear coo;
She looked at the switch
That evokes e-
Lectricity;
At the coals of an age
B.C. millions and two –
When the trees were like ferns
And the reptiles all flew;
She looked at the cat
Asleep on the hearthrug,
At the sky at the window –
The clouds in it, too;

And a marvellous light
From the West burning through:
And the one silly word
In her desolate noddle
As she dangled her legs,
Having nothing to do,
Was not, as you'd guess,
Of dumfoundered felicity,
But contained just four letters,
And these pronounced *Pooh!*

G. K. CHESTERTON

Variations on an Air Composed on Having to Appear in a Pageant as Old King Cole

After Walt Whitman

Me clairvoyant,
Me conscious of you, old camarado,
Needing no telescope, lorgnette, field-glass, opera-glass, pince-nez,
Me piercing two thousand years with eye naked and not ashamed;
The crown cannot hide you from me;
Musty old feudal-heraldic trappings cannot hide you from me,
I perceive that you drink.
(I am drinking with you. I am as drunk as you are.)
I see you are inhaling tobacco, puffing, smoking, spitting
(I do not object to your spitting),
You prophetic of American largeness,
You anticipating the broad masculine manners of these States;
I see in you also there are movements, tremors, tears, desire for the melodious,
I salute your three violinists, endlessly making vibrations,
Rigid, relentless, capable of going on for ever;

They play my accompaniment; but I shall take no notice of any accompaniment;
I myself am a complete orchestra.
So long.

After Swinburne

In the time of old sin without sadness
And golden with wastage of gold,
Like the gods that grow old in their gladness
Was the king that was glad, growing old;
And with sound of loud lyres from his palace
The voice of his oracles spoke,
And the lips that were red from his chalice
Were splendid with smoke.

When the weed was as flame for a token
And the wine was as blood for a sign;
And upheld in his hands and unbroken
The fountains of fire and of wine.
And a song without speech, without singer,
Stung the soul of a thousand in three
As the flesh of the earth has to sting her,
The soul of the sea.

HARRY GRAHAM

Ruthless Rhymes

The Stern Parent

Father heard his Children scream,
So he threw them in the stream,
Saying, as he drowned the third,
'Children should be seen, *not* heard!'

Tender-Heartedness

Billy, in one of his nice new sashes,
Fell in the fire and was burnt to ashes;
Now, although the room grows chilly,
I haven't the heart to poke poor Billy.

The Englishman's Home

I was playing golf the day
That the Germans landed;
All our troops had run away,
All our ships were stranded;
And the thought of England's shame
Altogether spoilt my game.

Calculating Clara

O'er the rugged mountain's brow
Clara threw the twins she nursed,
And remarked, 'I wonder now
Which will reach the bottom first?'

Mr Jones

'There's been an accident!' they said,
'Your servant's cut in half; he's dead!'
'Indeed!' said Mr Jones, 'and please
Send me the half that's got my keys.'

Necessity

Late last night I slew my wife,
Stretched her on the parquet flooring;
I was loth to take her life,
But I *had* to stop her snoring!

Compensation

Weep not for little Léonie,
Abducted by a French *Marquis*!
Though loss of honour was a wrench,
Just think how it's improved her French!

L'Enfant Glacé

When Baby's cries grew hard to bear
I popped him in the Frigidaire.
I never would have done so if
I'd known that he'd be frozen stiff.
My wife said: 'George, I'm so unhappé!
Our darling's now completely *frappé*!'

Opportunity

When Mrs Gorm (Aunt Eloïse)
Was stung to death by savage bees,
Her husband (Prebendary Gorm)
Put on his veil, and took the swarm.
He's publishing a book, next May,
On 'How to Make Bee-keeping Pay.'

Lord Gorbals

Once, as old Lord Gorbals motored
  Round his moors near John o' Groats,
He collided with a goatherd
  And a herd of forty goats.
By the time his car got through
They were all defunct but two.

Roughly he addressed the goatherd:
  'Dash my whiskers and my corns!
Can't you teach your goats, you dotard,
  That they ought to sound their horns?
Look, my A.A. badge is bent!
I've a mind to raise your rent!'

ROBERT FROST

Departmental

An ant on the tablecloth
Ran into a dormant moth
Of many times his size.
He showed not the least surprise.
His business wasn't with such.
He gave it scarcely a touch,
And was off on his duty run.
Yet if he encountered one
Of the hive's inquiry squad
Whose work is to find out God
And the nature of time and space,
He would put him onto the case.
Ants are a curious race;
One crossing with hurried tread
The body of one of their dead
Isn't given a moment's arrest –
Seems not even impressed.
But he no doubt reports to any
With whom he crosses antennae,
And they no doubt report
To the higher-up at court.
Then word goes forth in Formic:
'Death's come to Jerry McCormic,
Our selfless forager Jerry.

Will the special Janizary
Whose office it is to bury
The dead of the commissary
Go bring him home to his people.
Lay him in state on a sepal.
Wrap him for shroud in a petal.
Embalm him with ichor of nettle.
This is the word of your Queen.'
And presently on the scene
Appears a solemn mortician;
And taking formal position
With feelers calmly atwiddle,
Seizes the dead by the middle,
And heaving him high in air,
Carries him out of there.
No one stands round to stare.
It is nobody else's affair.

It couldn't be called ungentle.
But how thoroughly departmental.

E. C. BENTLEY

(*Clerihews*)

Lord Clive

What I like about Clive
Is that he is no longer alive.
There is a great deal to be said
For being dead.

The Art of Biography

The Art of Biography
Is different from Geography.
Geography is about Maps,
But Biography is about Chaps.

J. S. Mill

John Stuart Mill,
By a mighty effort of will,
Overcame his natural bonhomie
And wrote 'Principles of Political Economy'.

George III

George the Third
Ought never to have occurred.
One can only wonder
At so grotesque a blunder.

Sir Christopher Wren

Sir Christopher Wren
Said, 'I am going to dine with some men.
If anybody calls
Say I am designing St Paul's.'

JAMES JOYCE

The Ballad of Persse O'Reilly

Have you heard of one Humpty Dumpty
How he fell with a roll and a rumble
And curled up like Lord Olofa Crumple
By the butt of the Magazine Wall,
Chorus Of the Magazine Wall,
Hump, helmet and all?

He was one time our King of the Castle
Now he's kicked about like a rotten old parsnip.
And from Green street he'll be sent by order of His Worship
To the penal jail of Mountjoy
Chorus To the jail of Mountjoy!
Jail him and joy.

He was fafafather of all schemes for to bother us
Slow coaches and immaculate contraceptives for the populace,
Mare's milk for the sick, seven dry Sundays a week,
Openair love and religion's reform,
Chorus And religious reform,
Hideous in form.

Arrah, why, says you, couldn't he manage it?
I'll go bail, my fine dairyman darling,
Like the bumping bull of the Cassidys
All your butter is in your horns.
Chorus His butter is in his horns.
Butter his horns!

Repeat Hurrah there, Hosty, frosty Hosty, change that shirt on ye,
Rhyme the rann, the king of all ranns!

Balbaccio, balbuccio!
We had chaw chaw chops, chairs, chewing gum, the chicken-pox
and china chambers
Universally provided by this soffsoaping salesman.
Small wonder He'll Cheat E'erawan our local lads nicknamed
him
When Chimpden first took the floor
Chorus With his bucketshop store
Down Bargainweg, Lower.

So snug he was in his hotel premises sumptuous
But soon we'll bonfire all his trash, tricks and trumpery
And 'tis short till sheriff Clancy'll be winding up his unlimited
company
With the bailiff's bom at the door,
Chorus Bimbam at the door.
Then he'll bum no more.

Sweet bad luck on the waves washed to our island
The hooker of that hammerfast viking
And Gall's curse on the day when Eblana bay
Saw his black and tan man-o'-war.
Chorus Saw his man-o'-war.
On the harbour bar.

Where from? roars Poolbeg. Cookingha'pence, he bawls
Donnez-moi scampitle, wick an wipin'fampiny
Fingal Mac Oscar Onesine Bargearse Boniface
Thok's min gammelhole Norveegickers moniker
Og as ay are at gammelhore Norveegickers cod.
Chorus A Norwegian camel old cod.
He is, begod.

Lift it, Hosty, lift it, ye devil ye! up with the rann, the rhyming
rann!

It was during some fresh water garden pumping
Or, according to the *Nursing Mirror*, while admiring the monkeys
That our heavyweight heathen Humpharey
Made bold a maid to woo
Chorus Woohoo, what'll she doo!
The general lost her maidenloo!

He ought to blush for himself, the old hayheaded philosopher
For to go and shove himself that way on top of her
Begob, he's the crux of the catalogue
Of our antediluvial zoo,
Chorus Messrs Billing and Coo.
Noah's larks, good as noo.

He was joulting by Wellinton's monument
Our rotorious hippopopotamuns
When some bugger let down the backtrap of the omnibus
And he caught his death of fusiliers,
Chorus With his rent in his rears.
Give him six years.

'Tis sore pity for his innocent poor children
But look out for his missus legitimate!
When that frew gets a grip of old Earwicker
Won't there be earwigs on the green?
Chorus Big earwigs on the green,
The largest ever you seen.

Suffoclose! shikespower! Seudodanto! Anonymoses!

Then we'll have a free trade Gaels' band and mass meeting
For to sod the brave son of Scandiknavery.
And we'll bury him down in Oxmanstown
Along with the devil and Danes,
Chorus With the deaf and dumb Danes,
And all their remains.

And not all the king's men nor his horses
Will resurrect his corpus
For there's no true spell in Connacht or hell
bis That's able to raise a Cain.

from *Finnegans Wake*

D. H. LAWRENCE

Don'ts

Fight your little fight, my boy,
fight and be a man.
Don't be a good little, good little boy
being as good as you can
and agreeing with all the mealy-mouthed, mealy-mouthed
truths that the sly trot out
to protect themselves and their greedy-mouthed, greedy-mouthed
cowardice, every old lout.

Don't live up to the dear little girl who costs
you your manhood, and makes you pay.
Nor the dear old mater who so proudly boasts
that you'll make your way.

Don't earn golden opinions, opinions golden,
or at least worth Treasury notes,
from all sorts of men; don't be beholden
to the herd inside the pen.

Don't long to have dear little, dear little boys
whom you'll have to educate
to earn their living; nor yet girls, sweet joys
who will find it so hard to mate.

Nor a dear little home, with its cost, its cost
that you have to pay,
earning your living while your life is lost
and dull death comes in a day.

Don't be sucked in by the su-superior,
don't swallow the culture bait,
don't drink, don't drink and get beerier and beerier,
do learn to discriminate.

Do hold yourself together, and fight
with a hit-hit here and a hit-hit there,
and a comfortable feeling at night
that you've let in a little air.

A little fresh air in the money sty,
knocked a little hole in the holy prison,
done your own little bit, made your own little try
that the risen Christ should be risen.

EZRA POUND

Ancient Music

Winter is icummen in,
Lhude sing Goddamm,
Raineth drop and staineth slop,
And how the wind doth ramm!
                                        Sing: Goddamm.
Skiddeth bus and sloppeth us,
An ague hath my ham.
Freezeth river, turneth liver,
                                        Damn you, sing: Goddamm.
Goddamm, Goddamm, 'tis why I am, Goddamm,
                                        So 'gainst the winter's balm.

Sing goddamm, damm, sing Goddamm,
Sing Goddamm, sing Goddamm, DAMM.

Note: This is not folk music, but Dr Ker writes that the tune is to be found under the Latin words of a very ancient canon. [E.P.]

M. E. HARE

Limerick

There once was a man who said, 'Damn!
It is borne in upon me I am
An engine that moves
In predestinate grooves:
I'm not even a bus I'm a tram.'

ANONYMOUS

Limerick

There was an old man of Boulogne
Who sang a most topical song.
It wasn't the words
Which frightened the birds,
But the horrible double-entendre.

SIEGFRIED SASSOON

The Blues at Lord's

Near-neighboured by a blandly boisterous Dean
Who 'hasn't missed the match since '92',
Proposing to perpetuate the scene
I concentrate my eyesight on the cricket.

The game proceeds, as it is bound to do
Till tea-time or the fall of the next wicket.

Agreeable sunshine fosters greensward greener
Than College lawns in June. Tradition-true,
The stalwart teams, capped with contrasted blue,
Exert their skill; adorning the arena
With modest, manly, muscular demeanour –
Reviving memories in ex-athletes who
Are superannuated from agility –
And (while the five-ounce fetish they pursue)
Admired by gloved and virginal gentility.

My intellectual feet approach this function
With tolerance and Public-School compunction;
Aware that, whichever side bats best,
Their partisans are equally well-dressed.
For, though the Government has gone vermilion
And, as a whole, is weak in Greek and Latin,
The fogies harboured by the august Pavilion
Sit strangely similar to those who sat in
The edifice when first the Dean went pious –
For possible preferment sacrificed
His hedonistic and patrician bias,
And offered his complacency to Christ.

Meanwhile some Cantab slogs a fast half-volley
Against the ropes. 'Good shot, sir! O good shot!'
Ejaculates the Dean in accents jolly . . .
Will Oxford win? Perhaps. Perhaps they'll not.
Can Cambridge lose? Who knows? One fact seems sure;
That, while the Church approves, Lord's will endure.

RUPERT BROOKE

Wagner

Creeps in half wanton, half asleep,
   One with a fat wide hairless face.
He likes love-music that is cheap;
   Likes women in a crowded place;
      And wants to hear the noise they're making.

His heavy eyelids droop half-over,
   Great pouches swing beneath his eyes.
He listens, thinks himself the lover,
   Heaves from his stomach wheezy sighs;
      He likes to feel his heart's a-breaking.

The music swells. His gross legs quiver.
   His little lips are bright with slime.
The music swells. The women shiver.
   And all the while, in perfect time,
His pendulous stomach hangs a-shaking.

Sonnet Reversed

Hand trembling towards hand; the amazing lights
Of heart and eye. They stood on supreme heights.

Ah, the delirious weeks of honeymoon!
   Soon they returned, and, after strange adventures,
Settled at Balham by the end of June.
   Their money was in Can. Pacs. B. Debentures,
And in Antofagastas. Still he went
   Cityward daily; still she did abide
At home. And both were really quite content
   With work and social pleasures. Then they died.

They left three children (besides George, who drank):
  The eldest Jane, who married Mr Bell,
William, the head-clerk in the County Bank,
  And Henry, a stock-broker, doing well.

ANONYMOUS

The Dying Airman

A handsome young airman lay dying,
And as on the aerodrome he lay,
To the mechanics who round him came sighing,
These last dying words he did say:

'Take the cylinders out of my kidneys,
The connecting-rod out of my brain,
Take the cam-shaft from out of my backbone,
And assemble the engine again.'

T. S. ELIOT

Two Five-finger Exercises

1 *Lines to Ralph Hodgson Esqre*

How delightful to meet Mr Hodgson!
  (Everyone wants to know *him*)
With his musical sound
And his Baskerville Hound
Which, just at a word from his master
Will follow you faster and faster
And tear you limb from limb.
How delightful to meet Mr Hodgson!
Who is worshipped by all waitresses
(They regard him as something apart)
While on his palate fine he presses
The juice of the gooseberry tart.

How delightful to meet Mr Hodgson!
  (Everyone wants to know *him*).
He has 999 canaries
And round his head finches and fairies
In jubilant rapture skim.
How delightful to meet Mr Hodgson!
  (Everyone wants to meet *him*.)

2 *Lines for Cuscuscaraway and Mirza Murad Ali Beg*

How unpleasant to meet Mr Eliot!
With his features of clerical cut,
And his brow so grim
And his mouth so prim
And his conversation, so nicely
Restricted to What Precisely
And If and Perhaps and But.
How unpleasant to meet Mr Eliot!
With a bobtail cur
In a coat of fur
And a porpentine cat
And a wopsical hat;
How unpleasant to meet Mr Eliot!
  (Whether his mouth be open or shut).

Macavity: The Mystery Cat

Macavity's a Mystery Cat: he's called the Hidden Paw –
For he's the master criminal who can defy the Law.
He's the bafflement of Scotland Yard, the Flying Squad's despair:
For when they reach the scene of crime – *Macavity's not there*!

Macavity, Macavity, there's no one like Macavity,
He's broken every human law, he breaks the law of gravity.
His powers of levitation would make a fakir stare,
And when you reach the scene of crime – *Macavity's not there*!

You may seek him in the basement, you may look up in the air –
But I tell you once and once again, *Macavity's not there*!

Macavity's a ginger cat, he's very tall and thin;
You would know him if you saw him, for his eyes are sunken in.
His brow is deeply lined with thought, his head is highly domed;
His coat is dusty from neglect, his whiskers are uncombed.
He sways his head from side to side, with movements like a snake;
And when you think he's half asleep, he's always wide awake.

Macavity, Macavity, there's no one like Macavity,
For he's a fiend in feline shape, a monster of depravity.
You may meet him in a by-street, you may see him in the square –
But when a crime's discovered, then *Macavity's not there*!

He's outwardly respectable. (They say he cheats at cards.)
And his footprints are not found in any file of Scotland Yard's.
And when the larder's looted, or the jewel-case is rifled,
Or when the milk is missing, or another Peke's been stifled,
Or the greenhouse glass is broken, and the trellis past repair –
Ay, there's the wonder of the thing! *Macavity's not there*!

And when the Foreign Office find a Treaty's gone astray,
Or the Admiralty lose some plans and drawings by the way,
There may be a scrap of paper in the hall or on the stair –
But it's useless to investigate – *Macavity's not there*!
And when the loss has been disclosed, the Secret Service say:
'It *must* have been Macavity!' – but he's a mile away.
You'll be sure to find him resting, or a-licking of his thumbs,
Or engaged in doing complicated long division sums.

Macavity, Macavity, there's no one like Macavity,
There never was a Cat of such deceitfulness and suavity.

He always has an alibi, and one or two to spare:
At whatever time the deed took place – MACAVITY WASN'T
THERE!
And they say that all the Cats whose wicked deeds are widely
known
(I might mention Mungojerrie, I might mention Griddlebone)
Are nothing more than agents for the Cat who all the time
Just controls their operations: the Napoleon of Crime!

Cat Morgan Introduces Himself

I once was a Pirate what sailed the 'igh seas –
But now I've retired as a com-mission-aire:
And that's how you find me a-takin' my ease
And keepin' the door in a Bloomsbury Square.

I'm partial to partridges, likewise to grouse,
And I favour that Devonshire cream in a bowl;
But I'm allus content with a drink on the 'ouse
And a bit o' cold fish when I done me patrol.

I ain't got much polish, me manners is gruff,
But I've got a good coat, and I keep meself smart;
And everyone says, and I guess that's enough:
'You can't but like Morgan, 'e's got a kind 'art.'

I got knocked about on the Barbary Coast,
And me voice it ain't no sich melliferous horgan;
But yet I can state, and I'm not one to boast,
That some of the gals is dead keen on old Morgan.

So if you 'ave business with Faber – or Faber –
I'll give you this tip, and it's worth a lot more:
You'll save yourself time, and you'll spare yourself
labour
If jist you make friends with the Cat at the door.

– *Morgan*

NEWMAN LEVY

Thaïs

One time in Alexandria, in wicked Alexandria,
Where nights were wild with revelry and life was but a game,
There lived, so the report is, an adventuress and courtesan,
The pride of Alexandria, and Thaïs was her name.

Nearby, in peace and piety, avoiding all society,
There dwelt a band of holy men who'd built a refuge there:
And in the desert's solitude they spurned all earthly folly to
Devote their days to holy works, to fasting and to prayer.

Now one monk whom I solely mention of this group of holy
men
Was known as Athanael; he was famous near and far.
At fasting bouts or prayer with him no other could compare
with him;
At ground and lofty praying he could do the course in par.

One night while sleeping heavily (from fighting with the devil
he
Had gone to bed exhausted while the sun was shining still),
He had a vision Freudian, and though he was annoyed he an-
Alyzed it in the well-known style of Doctors Jung and Brill.

He dreamed of Alexandria, of wicked Alexandria;
A crowd of men were cheering in a manner rather rude
At Thaïs, who was dancing there, and Athanael, glancing there,
Observed her do the shimmy in what artists call The Nude.

Said he, 'This dream fantastical disturbs my thoughts monastical;
Some unsuppressed desire, I fear, has found my monkish cell.
I blushed up to the hat o' me to view that girl's anatomy.
I'll go to Alexandria and save her soul from Hell.'

So, pausing not to wonder where he'd put his summer underwear,
He quickly packed his evening clothes, his toothbrush and a vest.
To guard against exposure he threw in some woollen hosiery,
And bidding all the boys goodbye, he started on his quest.

The monk, though warned and fortified, was deeply shocked and mortified
To find, on his arrival, wild debauchery in sway.
While some lay in a stupor, sent by booze of more than two per cent,
The others were behaving in a most immoral way.

Said he to Thaïs, 'Pardon me. Although this job is hard on me,
I gotta put you wise to what I came down here to tell.
What's all this sousin' gettin' you? Cut out this pie-eyed retinue;
Let's hit the trail together, kid, and save yourself from Hell.'

Although this bold admonishment caused Thaïs some astonishment,
She coyly answered, 'Say, you said a heaping mouthful, bo,
This burg's a frost, I'm telling you. The brand of hooch they're selling you
Ain't like the stuff we used to get, so let's pack up and go.'

So forth from Alexandria, from wicked Alexandria,
Across the desert sands they go beneath the blazing sun;
Till Thaïs, parched and sweltering, finds refuge in the sheltering
Seclusion of a convent, and the habit of a nun.

But now the monk is terrified to find his fears are verified:
His holy vows of chastity have cracked beneath the strain.
Like one who has a jag on he cries out in grief and agony,
'I'd sell my soul to see her do the shimmy once again.'

Alas! his pleadings clamorous, the passionate and amorous,
Have come too late; the courtesan has danced her final dance.
The monk says, 'That's a joke on me, for that there dame to
croak on me.
I hadn't oughter passed her up the time I had the chance.'

CONRAD AIKEN

Limberick

It's time to make love. Douse the glim.
The fireflies twinkle and dim.
The stars lean together
Like birds of a feather,
And the loin lies down with the limb.

ANONYMOUS

Limericks

I

There was a young lady of Kew
Who filled her vagina with glue
As she said with a grin
'If they pay to get in
They must pay to get out again too!'

2

Young men who frequent picture palaces
Haven't heard of our psycho-analysis,
They've never read Freud
But they feel overjoyed
As they cling to their long-standing fallacies.

3

There was a young man of St John's
Who wanted to bugger the swans
So he went to the porter
Who said 'Have my daughter!
The swans are reserved for the dons.'

4

An epicure dining at Crewe
Found quite a large mouse in his stew.
Said the waiter 'Don't shout
And wave it about!
Or the rest will be wanting one too.'

5

There was a young lady of Exeter
So pretty, young men craned their necks at her.
One went so far
As to wave from his car
The distinguishing mark of his sex at her.

All Anonymous

6

There was a young lady named Bright
Whose speed was far faster than light;
She went out one day
In a relative way
And returned home the previous night.

Arthur Buller

7

There was an old man of St Bees,
Who was stung in the arm by a wasp.
When asked 'Does it hurt?'
He replied 'No, it doesn't,
I'm so glad it wasn't a hornet.'

W. S. Gilbert

COLE PORTER

Let's Do It, Let's Fall In Love

When the little Bluebird,
Who has never said a word,
Starts to sing 'Spring, spring';
When the little Bluebell,
At the bottom of the dell,
Starts to ring: 'Ding, ding';
When the little blue clerk,
Sitting sadly in the park,
Starts a tune to the moon up above,
It is nature, that's all,
Simply telling us to fall in love.

And that's why Chinks do it, Japs do it,
Up in Lapland, little Laps do it,
  Let's do it, let's fall in love.
In Spain the best upper sets do it,
Lithuanians and Letts do it,
  Let's do it, let's fall in love.

The Dutch in old Amsterdam do it,
  Not to mention the Finns,
Folks in Siam do it –
  Think of Siamese twins.

Some Argentines, without means, do it,
People say, in Boston, even beans do it,
  Let's do it, let's fall in love.

The nightingales, in the dark, do it,
Larks, karazy for a lark, do it,
  Let's do it, let's fall in love.
Canaries caged in the house do it,
When they're out of season, grouse do it,
  Let's do it, let's fall in love.

The most sedate barnyard fowls do it,
  When a chantecleer cries;
High-brow'd old owls do it –
  They're supposed to be wise.
Penguins in flocks on the rocks do it,
Even little cuckoos in the clocks do it,
  Let's do it, let's fall in love.

Romantic sponges, they say, do it,
Oysters down in Oyster Bay do it,
  Let's do it, let's fall in love.
Cold Cape Cod clams, 'gainst their wish, do it,
Even lazy jellyfish do it,
  Let's do it, let's fall in love.

The most refined schools of cod do it,
  Though it shocks them, I fear,
Sturgeons, thank God, do it –
  Have some caviare, dear!
In shallow shoals Dover soles do it,
Goldfish in the privacy of bowls do it,
  Let's do it, let's fall in love.

The dragonflies in their eaves do it,
Sentimental-scented leaves do it,
  Let's do it, let's fall in love,

Mosquitoes (Heaven forbid) do it,
So does every katydid do it,
  Let's do it, let's fall in love.

The most refined lady bugs do it,
  When a gentleman calls,
Moths in your rugs do it –
  What's the use of moth-balls?
Locusts in trees do it, bees do it,
Even super-educated fleas do it,
  Let's do it, let's fall in love.

The chimpanzees in the Zoos do it,
Some courageous kangaroos do it,
  Let's do it, let's fall in love.
And, sure, giraffes from the sky do it,
Heavens! Hippopotami do it!
  Let's do it, let's fall in love.

Old sloths who hang down from twigs do it
  Though the effort is great.
Sweet guinea-pigs do it –
  Buy a couple and wait!
We know that bears in their pits do it,
Even Pekineses at the Ritz do it,
  Let's do it, let's fall in love!

D. B. WYNDHAM LEWIS

Sapphics

Exquisite torment, dainty Mrs Hargreaves
Trips down the High Street, slaying hearts a-plenty;
Stricken and doomed are all who meet her eye-shots!
      Bar Mr Hargreaves.

Grocers a-tremble bash their brassy scales down,
Careless of weight and hacking cheese regardless;
Postmen shoot letters in the nearest ashcan,
    Dogs dance in circles.

Leaving their meters, gas-inspectors gallop,
Water Board men cease cutting off the water;
Florists are strewing inexpensive posies
    In Beauty's pathway.

'O cruel fair!' groan butchers at their chopping,
'Vive la belle Hargreaves!' howls a pallid milkman;
Even the Vicar shades his eyes and mutters:
    'O dea certe.'

Back to 'Balmoral' trips the goddess lightly;
Night comes at length, and Mr Hargreaves with it,
Casting his bowler glumly on the sideboard:
    'Gimme my dinner.'

MORRIS BISHOP

The Naughty Preposition

I lately lost a preposition:
    It hid, I thought, beneath my chair.
And angrily I cried: 'Perdition!
    Up from out of in under there!'

Correctness is my vade mecum,
    And straggling phrases I abhor;
And yet I wondered: 'What should he come
    Up from out of in under for?'

e. e. cummings

may i feel said he

may i feel said he
(i'll squeal said she
just once said he)
it's fun said she

(may i touch said he
how much said she
a lot said he)
why not said she

(let's go said he
not too far said she
what's too far said he
where you are said she)

may i stay said he
(which way said she
like this said he
if you kiss said she

may i move said he
is it love said she)
if you're willing said he
(but you're killing said she

but it's life said he
but your wife said she
now said he)
ow said she

(tiptop said he
don't stop said she
oh no said he)
go slow said she

(cccome? said he
ummm said she)
you're divine! said he
(you are Mine said she)

Poem, or Beauty Hurts Mr Vinal

take it from me kiddo
believe me
my country, 'tis of

you, land of the Cluett
Shirt Boston Garter and Spearmint
Girl With the Wrigley Eyes (of you
land of the Arrow Ide
And Earl &
Wilson
Collars) of you i
sing: land of Abraham Lincoln and Lydia E. Pinkham,
land above all of Just Add Hot Water And Serve –
from every B.V.D.

let freedom ring

amen. i do however protest, anent the un
-spontaneous and otherwise scented merde which
greets one (Everywhere Why) as divine poesy per
that and this radically defunct periodical. i would

suggest that certain ideas gestures
rhymes, like Gillette Razor Blades
having been used and reused
to the mystical moment of dullness emphatically are
Not To Be Resharpened. (Case in point

if we are to believe these gently O so sweetly
melancholy trillers amid the thrillers
these crepuscular violinists among my and your
skyscrapers – Helen & Cleopatra were Just Too Lovely,
The Snail's On The Thorn enter Morn and God's
In His andsoforth
do you get me?) according
to such supposedly indigenous
throstles Art is O World O Life
a formula example, Turn Your Shirttails Into
Drawers and If It Isn't An Eastman It Isn't A
Kodak therefore my friends let
us now sing each and all fortissimo A-
mer
i

ca. I
love,
You. And there're a
hun-dred-mil-lion-oth-ers, like
all of you successfully if
delicately gelded (or spaded)
gentlemen (and ladies) – pretty

littleliverpill –
hearted-Nujolneeding-There's-A-Reason
americans (who tensetendoned and with
upward vacant eyes, painfully
perpetually crouched, quivering, upon the
sternly allotted sandpile
– how silently
emit a tiny violetflavoured nuisance: Odor?

ono.
comes out like a ribbon lies flat on the brush

she being Brand

-new; and you
now consequently a
little stiff i was
careful of her and(having

thoroughly oiled the universal
joint tested my gas felt of
her radiator made sure her springs were O.

K.)i went right to it flooded-the-carburetor cranked her

up, slipped the
clutch(and then somehow got into reverse she
kicked what
the hell)next
minute i was back in neutral tried and

again slo-wly; bare,ly nudg.   ing(my

lev-er Right-
oh and her gears being in
A 1 shape passed
from low through
second-in-to-high like
greasedlightning)just as we turned the corner of Divinity

avenue i touched the accelerator and give

her the juice, good

(it
was the first ride and believe i we was
happy to see how nice she acted right up to
the last minute coming back down by the Public
Gardens i slammed on
the
internalexpanding
&
externalcontracting
brakes Bothatonce and

brought her allofher tremB
-ling
to a:dead

stand-
;Still)

ygUDuh

ydoan
yunnuhstan

ydoan o
yunnuhstan dem
yguduh ged

yunnuhstan dem doidee
yguduh ged riduh
ydoan o nudn
LISNbudLISN
dem
gud
am

lidl yelluh bas
tuds weer goin
duhSIVILEYEzum

ROBERT GRAVES

'¡Wellcome, to the Caves of Artá!'

'They are hollowed out in the see coast at the municipal terminal of Capdepera, at nine kilometer from the town of Artá in the Island of Mallorca, with a suporizing infinity of graceful colums of 21 meter and by downward, wich prives the spectator of all animacion and plunges in dumbness. The way going is very picturesque, serpentine between style mountains, til the arrival at the esplanade of the vallee, called 'The Spider'. There are good enlacements of the railroad with autobuses of excursion, many days of the week, today actually Wednesday and Satturday. Since many centuries renown foreing visitors have explored them and wrote their eulogy about, included Nort-American geoglogues.' (*from a Tourist leaflet*)

Such subtile filigranity and nobless of construccion
Here fraternise in harmony, that respiracion stops.
While all admit their impotence (though autors most formidable)
To sing in words the excellence of Nature's underprops,
Yet stalactite and stalagmite together with dumb language
Make hymnes to God wich celebrate the strength of water drops.

¿You, also, are you capable to make precise in idiom
Consideracions magic of ilusions very wide?
Alraedy in the Vestibule of these Grand Caves of Artá
The spirit of the human verb is darked and stupefyed;
So humildy you trespass trough the forest of the colums
And listen to the grandess explicated by the guide.

From darkness into darkness, but at measure, now descending
   You remark with what esxactitude he designates each bent;
'The Saloon of Thousand Banners', or 'The Tumba of Napoleon',
   'The Grotto of the Rosary', 'The Club', 'The Camping Tent'.
And at 'Cavern of the Organ' there are knocking streange formacions
Wich give a nois particular pervoking wonderment.

¡Too far do not adventure, sir! For, further as you wander,
   The every of the stalactites will make you stop and stay.
Grand peril amenaces now, your nostrills aprehending
   An odour least delicious of lamentable decay
It is some poor touristers, in the depth of obscure cristal,
   Wich deceased of their emocion on a past excursion day.

'The General Elliott'

He fell in victory's fierce pursuit,
   Holed through and through with shot;
A sabre sweep had hacked him deep
   'Twixt neck and shoulder-knot.

The potman cannot well recall,
   The ostler never knew,
Whether that day was Malplaquet,
   The Boyne or Waterloo.

But there he hangs, a tavern sign,
   With foolish bold regard
For cock and hen and loitering men
   And wagons down the yard.

Raised high above the hayseed world
He smokes his china pipe;
And now surveys the orchard ways,
The damsons clustering ripe –

Stares at the churchyard slabs beyond,
Where country neighbours lie:
Their brief renown set lowly down,
But his invades the sky.

He grips a tankard of brown ale
That spills a generous foam:
Often he drinks, they say, and winks
At drunk men lurching home.

No upstart hero may usurp
That honoured swinging seat;
His seasons pass with pipe and glass
Until the tale's complete –

And paint shall keep his buttons bright
Though all the world's forgot
Whether he died for England's pride
By battle or by pot.

Allie

Allie, call the birds in,
The birds from the sky!
Allie calls, Allie sings,
Down they all fly:
First there came
Two white doves,
Then a sparrow from his nest,
Then a clucking bantam hen,
Then a robin red-breast.

Allie, call the beasts in,
  The beasts, everyone!
Allie calls, Allie sings,
  In they run:
First there came
Two black lambs,
  Then a grunting Berkshire sow,
Then a dog without a tail,
  Then a red and white cow.

Allie, call the fish up,
  The fish from the stream!
Allie calls, Allie sings,
  Up they all swim:
First there came
Two goldfish,
  A minnow and a miller's thumb,
Then a school of little trout,
  Then the twisting eels come.

Allie, call the children,
  Call them from the green!
Allie calls, Allie sings,
  Soon they run in:
First there came
Tom and Madge,
  Kate and I who'll not forget
How we played by the water's edge
  Till the April sun set.

The Legs

There was this road,
And it led up-hill,
And it led down-hill,
And round and in and out.

And the traffic was legs,
Legs from the knee down,
Coming and going,
Never pausing.

And the gutters gurgled
With the rain's overflow,
And the sticks on the pavement
Blindly tapped and tapped.

What drew the legs along
Was the never-stopping,
And the senseless, frightening
Fate of being legs.

Legs for the road,
The road for legs,
Resolutely nowhere
In both directions.

My legs at least
Were not in that rout:
On grass by the road-side
Entire I stood,

Watching the unstoppable
Legs go by
With never a stumble
Between step and step.

Though my smile was broad
The legs could not see,
Though my laugh was loud
The legs could not hear.

My head dizzied, then:
I wondered suddenly,
Might I too be a walker
From the knees down?

Gently I touched my shins.
The doubt unchained them:
They had run in twenty puddles
Before I regained them.

Two Grotesques

I

Dr Newman with the crooked pince-nez
Had studied in Vienna and Chicago.
Chess was his only relaxation.
And Dr Newman remained unperturbed
By every nastier manifestation
Of plutodemocratic civilization:
All that was cranky, corny, ill-behaved,
Unnecessary, askew or orgiastic
Would creep unbidden to his side-door (hidden
Behind a poster in the Tube Station,
Nearly half-way up the moving-stairs),
Push its way in, to squat there undisturbed
Among box-files and tubular steel chairs.
He was once seen at the Philharmonic Hall
Noting the reactions of two patients,
With pronounced paranoiac tendencies,
To old Dutch music. He appeared to recall
A tin of lozenges in his breast-pocket,
Put his hand confidently in –
And drew out a black imp, or sooterkin,
Six inches long, with one ear upside-down,
Licking at a vanilla ice-cream cornet –
Then put it back again with a slight frown.

2

Sir John addressed the Snake God in his temple,
Which was full of bats, not as a votary
But with the somewhat cynical courtesy,
Just short of condescension,
He might have paid the Governor-General
Of a small, hot, backward colony.
He was well versed in primitive religion,
But found this an embarrassing occasion:
The God was immense, noisy and affable,
Began to tickle him with a nervous chuckle,
Unfobbed a great gold clock for him to listen,
Hissed like a snake, and swallowed him at one mouthful.

Flying Crooked

The butterfly, a cabbage-white,
(His honest idiocy of flight)
Will never now, it is too late,
Master the art of flying straight,
Yet has – who knows so well as I? –
Just sense of how not to fly:
He lurches here and here by guess
And God and hope and hopelessness.
Even the aerobatic swift
Has not his flying-crooked gift.

1805

At Viscount Nelson's lavish funeral,
  While the mob milled and yelled about St Paul's,
A General chatted with an Admiral:

'One of your colleagues, Sir, remarked today
  That Nelson's *exit*, though to be lamented,
Falls not inopportunely, in its way.'

'He was a thorn in our flesh,' came the reply –
    'The most bird-witted, unaccountable,
Odd little runt that ever I did spy.

'One arm, one peeper, vain as Pretty Poll,
    A meddler, too, in foreign politics
And gave his heart in pawn to a plain moll.

'He would dare lecture us Sea Lords, and then
    Would treat his ratings as though men of honour
And play at leap-frog with his midshipmen!

'We tried to box him down, but up he popped,
    And when he'd banged Napoleon at the Nile
Became too much the hero to be dropped.

'You've heard that Copenhagen 'blind eye' story?
    We'd tied him to Nurse Parker's apron-strings –
By G—d, he snipped them through and snatched the glory!'

'Yet,' cried the General, 'six-and-twenty sail
    Captured or sunk by him off Trafalgar –
That writes a handsome *finis* to the tale.'

'Handsome enough. The seas are England's now.
    That fellow's foibles need no longer plague us.
He died most creditably, I'll allow.'

'And, Sir, the secret of his victories?'
    'By his unServicelike, familiar ways, Sir,
He made the whole Fleet love him, damn his eyes!'

L. A. G. STRONG

The Brewer's Man

Have I a wife? Bedam I have!
  But we was badly mated:
I hit her a great clout one night,
  And now we're separated.

And mornin's, going to my work,
  I meets her on the quay:
'Good mornin' to ye, ma'am,' says I;
  'To hell with ye,' says she.

NOEL COWARD

Mad Dogs and Englishmen

In tropical climes there are certain times of day,
When all the citizens retire
To tear their clothes off and perspire.
It's one of those rules that the greatest fools obey,
Because the sun is much too sultry
And one must avoid its ultry-violet ray. . .
The natives grieve when the white men leave their huts,
Because they're obviously definitely nuts!

Mad dogs and Englishmen
Go out in the midday sun.
The Japanese don't care to,
The Chinese wouldn't dare to,
Hindoos and Argentines sleep firmly from twelve to one,
But Englishmen detest a
Siesta.
In the Philippines there are lovely screens
To protect you from the glare.

In the Malay States there are hats like plates
Which the Britishers won't wear.
At twelve noon
The natives swoon
And no further work is done,
But mad dogs and Englishmen
Go out in the midday sun.

It's such a surprise for the Eastern eyes to see,
That though the English are effete
They're quite impervious to heat.
When the white man rides every native hides in glee,
Because the simple creatures hope he
Will impale his solar topee on a tree. . .
It seems such a shame when the English claim the earth
That they give rise to such hilarity and mirth.

Mad dogs and Englishmen
Go out in the midday sun.
The toughest Burmese bandit
Can never understand it.
In Rangoon the heat of noon
Is just what the natives shun.
They put their Scotch or rye down
And lie down.
In a jungle town
Where the sun beats down
To the rage of man and beast,
The English garb
Of the English sahib
Merely gets a bit more creased.
In Bangkok
At twelve o'clock
They foam at the mouth and run,
But mad dogs and Englishmen
Go out in the midday sun.

Mad dogs and Englishmen
Go out in the midday sun.
The smallest Malay rabbit
Deplores this foolish habit.
In Hong Kong
They strike a gong
And fire off a noonday gun,
To reprimand each inmate
Who's in late.
In the mangrove swamps
Where the python romps
There is peace from twelve to two.
Even caribous
Lie around and snooze,
For there's nothing else to do.
In Bengal
To move at all
Is seldom, if ever done,
But mad dogs and Englishmen
Go out in the midday sun.

Any Part of Piggy

Any part of piggy
Is quite all right with me
Ham from Westphalia, ham from Parma
Ham as lean as the Dalai Lama
Ham from Virginia, ham from York,
Trotters, sausages, hot roast pork.
Crackling crisp for my teeth to grind on
Bacon with or without the rind on
Though humanitarian
I'm not a vegetarian.
I'm neither crank nor prude nor prig
And though it may sound infra dig
Any part of darling pig
Is perfectly fine with me.

A Room with a View

I've been cherishing
Through the perishing winter nights and days
A funny little phrase,
That means
Such a lot to me
That you've got to be
With me heart and soul,
For on you the whole thing leans.

Come with me and leave behind the noisy crowds,
When night shines on earth above the clouds!

Please don't turn away or my dream will stay
Hidden out of sight
Among a lot of might-have-beens!

A room with a view and you,
And no one to worry us,
No one to hurry us through
This dream we've found.
We'll gaze at the sky and try
To guess what it's all about.
Then we will figure out why the world is round.

We'll be as happy and contented
As birds upon a tree,
High above the mountains and sea.

We'll bill and we'll coo-oo-oo,
And sorrow will never come.
Oh, will it ever come true?
Our room with a view!

A room with a view and you,
And no one to give advice,
That kind of paradise you
Would deign to choose.
With fingers entwined we'll find
Relief from the preachers who
Always beseech us to mind
Our P's and Q's.

We'll watch the whole world pass before us
While we are sitting still,
Leaning on our own windowsill.

We'll bill and we'll coo-oo-oo,
And maybe a stork will bring
This, that and 'tother thing to
A room with a view!

VLADIMIR NABOKOV

A Literary Dinner

Come here, said my hostess, her face making room
for one of those pink introductory smiles
that link, like a valley of fruit trees in bloom,
the slopes of two names.
I want you, she murmured, to eat Dr James.

I was hungry. The Doctor looked good. He had read
the great book of the week and had liked it, he said,
because it was powerful. So I was brought
a generous helping. His mauve-bosomed wife
kept showing me, very politely, I thought,
the tenderest bits with the point of her knife.
I ate – and in Egypt the sunsets were swell;

The Russians were doing remarkably well:
had I met a Prince Poprinsky, whom he had known
in Caparabella, or was it Mentone?
They had traveled extensively, he and his wife;
her hobby was People, his hobby was Life.
All was good and well cooked, but the tastiest part
was his nut-flavored, crisp cerebellum. The heart
resembled a shiny brown date,
and I stowed all the studs on the edge of my plate.

ROY CAMPBELL

On Some South African Novelists

You praise the firm restraint with which they write –
I'm with you there, of course:
They use the snaffle and the curb all right,
But where's the bloody horse?

OGDEN NASH

Family Court

One would be in less danger
From the wiles of the stranger
If one's own kin and kith
Were more fun to be with.

England Expects

Let us pause to consider the English,
Who when they pause to consider themselves get all reticently thrilled and tinglish,
Because every Englishman is convinced of one thing, viz:
That to be an Englishman is to belong to the most exclusive club there is:
A club to which benighted bounders of Frenchmen and Germans and Italians et cetera cannot even aspire to belong,
Because they don't even speak English, and the Americans are worst of all because they speak it wrong.
Englishmen are distinguished by their traditions and ceremonials,
And also by their affection for their colonies and their contempt for the colonials.
When foreigners ponder world affairs, why sometimes by doubts they are smitten,
But Englishmen know instinctively that what the world needs most is whatever is best for Britain.
They have a splendid navy and they conscientiously admire it,
And every English schoolboy knows that John Paul Jones was an unfair American pirate.
English people disclaim sparkle and verve,
But speak without reservations of their Anglo-Saxon reserve.
After listening to little groups of English ladies and gentlemen at cocktail parties and in hotels and Pullmans, of defining Anglo-Saxon reserve I despair,
But I think it consists of assuming that nobody else is there,
And I shudder to think where Anglo-Saxon reserve ends when I consider where it begins,
Which is in a few high-pitched statements of what one's income is and just which foods give one a rash and whether one and one's husband or wife sleep in a double bed or twins.
All good Englishmen go to Oxford or Cambridge and they all write and publish books before their graduation,

And I often wondered how they did it until I realized that they have to do it because their genteel accents are so developed that they can no longer understand each other's spoken words so the written word is their only means of intercommunication.
England is the last home of the aristocracy, and the art of protecting the aristocracy from the encroachments of commerce has been raised to quite an art.
Because in America a rich butter-and-egg man is only a rich butter-and-egg man or at most an honorary LLD of some hungry university, but in England he is Sir Benjamin Buttery, Bart.
Anyhow, I think the English people are sweet,
And we might as well get used to them because when they slip and fall they always land on their own or somebody else's feet.

Peekaboo, I Almost See You

Middle-aged life is merry, and I love to lead it,
But there comes a day when your eyes are all right, but your arm isn't long enough to hold the telephone book where you can read it,
And your friends get jocular, so you go to the oculist,
And of all your friends he is the joculist,
So over his facetiousness let us skim,
Only noting that he had been waiting for you ever since you said Good Evening to his grandfather clock under the impression that it was him.
And you look at his chart and it says SHRDLU QWERTYOP, and you say Well, why SHRDNTLU QWERTYOP? and he says one set of glasses won't do.
You need two,
One for reading Erle Stanley Gardner's Perry Mason and Keats's 'Endymion' with,

And the other for walking around without saying Hallo to
strange wymion with.
So you spend your time taking off your seeing glasses to put on
your reading glasses, and then remembering that your
reading glasses are upstairs or in the car,
And then you can't find your seeing glasses again because
without them you can't see where they are.
Enough of such mishaps, they would try the patience of an ox,
I prefer to forget both pairs of glasses and pass my declining
years saluting strange women and grandfather clocks.

Reflections on Ice-breaking

Candy
is dandy
But liquor
is quicker.

The Canary

The song of canaries
Never varies,
And when they're moulting
They're pretty revolting.

Lines Written to Console Those Ladies Distressed by the Lines 'Men Never Make Passes, etc.'[1]

A girl who is bespectacled
Don't even get her nectacled
But safety pins and bassinets
Await the girl who fascinets.

[1]A reference to a poem by Dorothy Parker

WILLIAM PLOMER

A Right-of-Way: 1865

An old bass-viol was lately bought for a few shillings at a farm sale not a thousand miles from Mellstock. Pasted on the inside of it was the following poem in a well-known handwriting. It is regretted that technical difficulties prevent its reproduction in facsimile.

Decades behind me
When courting took more time,
In Tuphampton ewe-leaze I mind me
Two trudging afore time:
A botanist he, in quest of a sought-after fleabane,
Wheedling his leman with 'Do you love *me*, Jane?'

Yestreen with bowed back
(To hike now is irksome),
Hydroptic and sagging the cloud wrack,
I spied in the murk some
Wayfarer myopic Linnaeus-wise quizzing the quitches
And snooping at simples and worts in the ditches.

Remarked he, 'A path here
I seek to discover,
A right-of-way bang through this garth here,
Where elsewhiles a lover
I prinked with a pocket herbarium, necked I and cuddled:
Now I'm all mud-besprent, bored and be-puddled.

'I'm long past my noon-time.
The Unsweeting Planner
Again proffers bale for one's boon-time
By tossing a spanner
Or crowbar into the works without reckoning the cost, sir.
At eighty,' intoned he, 'life is a frost, sir.'

'When erst here I tarried
I knew not my steady
Had coolly, concurrently married
Three husbands already,
Nor learnt I till later, what's more, that all three were brothers,
Though sprang they, it seems, of disparate mothers.

'Well, we two inspected
The flora of Wessex;
More specimens had we collected
Had she pondered less sex;
We botanized little that year . . . But I must be wending;
My analyst hints at amnesia impending.'

EARLE BIRNEY

Sestina for the Ladies of Tehuántepec

'*Teh.* has six claims to fame: its numerous hotsprings
(*radioactive*, *therapeutic*); moderate earthquakes
(*none in several years*); herbivorous iguanas
(*eaten stewed*); Dictator Porfirio Diaz
(*d. 1911*); its hundred-mile-wide isthmus;
and the commanding beauty of its Indian women.'

Stately still and tall as gillyflowers the women
though they no longer glide unwary past the hotsprings
naked as sunlight to each slender softer isthmus
now that ogling busloads (*Greyhound*) make their earth
quake
And still skirt-bright before the flaking palace of old Diaz
(*hotel*) they gravely offer up their cold iguanas

Their furtive men (*unfamed*) who snare iguanas
sliding on tree-limbs olive-smooth as are their women's
have fallen out of peonage to landlord Diaz
into an air more active than their tepid hotsprings
more prompt with tremors than the obsolete earthquakes
rumbling through their intercontinental isthmus

From the stone music of their past the only isthmus
from astronomic shrines fantastic as iguanas
to this unlikely world (*3 bil.*) that waits its earthquake
is their long matriarchal ritual of women
whose eyes from fires more stubborn than under hotsprings
flash out a thousand Mayan years before a Diaz

Goldnecklaced turbaned swaying in the square of Diaz
volute and secret as the orchids in their isthmus
braids black and luminous as obsidian by hotsprings
beneath their crowns of fruit and crested live iguanas
rhythmic and Zapotecan-proud the classic women
dance (*v. marimbas*) their ancient therapy for earthquakes

O dance and hurl flamboya till the cobbled earth quakes
let your strong teeth shine out in the plaza lost to Diaz
toss your soaring sunflower plumes sunflowering women!
Hold for all men yet your supple blossoming isthmus
lest we be noosed consumed with all iguanas
and leave the radiant leaping of the lonely hotsprings

Beneath all hotsprings lie the triggered earthquakes
Within this gray iguana coils another Diaz
Is there a green isthmus walking yet in women?

Salina Cruz, Mexico 1956

Earle Birney

A Small Faculty Stag for the Visiting Poet

but a large quantity of brandy
                                        on whisky
                                        on sherry

At one table's end the Necessary Dean
has broken out cigars
At the other the Oxonian Canon
splotchfaced now
is putting us all down with naughty quotes
from Persius we're too slow to get
– except the Czech professor and the Hungarian
who dig everything
so civilised they're savage with disappointment
in us all & no doubt saying so this moment
safely across my chest in at least 2 languages

somewhere in the smoke the Librarian
is heard toasting the cummunwealth
and feck the Yenks
The Padre winces & gradually
like Yahweh in the Zohar withdraws his presence
leaving behind that vacuum of Evil
which is us

The Physics Department's chief cultural exhibit
also a very anthropological Native Son
have just asked me unanswerable questions
simultaneously from across the centrepiece

I am the dead eye of this verbal typhoon
I am the fraudulent word-doctor
stripped to dumbness by their tribal ritual
I am neither civilised nor savage but also Necessary
                                        grinning
                                        & stoned
                                        & desolate

Australia 1968

Canada: Case History: 1973

No more the highschool land
deadset in loutishness
This cat's turned cool
the gangling's gone
guffaws are for the peasants

Inside his plastic igloo now
he watches gooks and yankees bleed
in colour on the telly
But under a faded Carnaby shirt
ulcers knife the rounding belly

Hung up on rye and nicotine and sex-
y flicks, kept off the snow and grass
he teeters tiptoe on his arctic roof
(ten brittle legs, no two together)
baring his royal canadian ass
white and helpless in the global winds

Schizoid from birth, and still a sado-masochist
this turkey thinks that for his sins
he should be carved while still alive:
legs to Québec, the future Vietnam;
the rest, self-served and pre-digested,
to make a Harvest Home for Uncle Sam . . .

Teeth shot and memory going
(except for childhood grudges),
one moment murderous, the next depressed,
this youth, we fear, has moved from adolescence
into what looks like permanent senescence.

Toronto

Sinalóa

Si señor, is halligators here, your guidebook say it,
si, jaguar in the montañas, maybe helephants, quién sabe?
You like, dose palmas in the sunset? Certamente very nice,
it happen each night in the guia tourista
But who de hell eat jaguar, halligator, you heat em?
Mira my fren, wat dis town need is muy big breakwater –
  I like take hax to dem jeezly palmas.

So you wan buy machete? Por favor I give you
sousand machetes you give me one grand bulldozer, hey?
Wat dis country is lack, señor, is real good goosin,
is need pinehapple shove hup her bottom
(sure, sure is bella all dose water-ayacints)
si need drains for sugar cane in dem pitoresco swamps –
  and shoot all dem anarquista egrets.

Hokay, you like bugambilla, ow you say, flower-hung cliffs?
Is ow old, de Fort? Is Colhuan, muy viejo, before Moses, no?
Is for you, señor, take em away, send us helevator for w'eat.
It like me to see all dem fine boxcar stuff full rice,
sugar, flax, rollin down to dose palmstudded ports
were Cortés and all dat crap (you heat history?) –
  and bugger de pink flamingos.

Amigo, we make you present all dem two-wheel hoxcart,
you send em Québec, were my brudder was learn to be padre –
we take ditchdiggers, tractors, Massey-Arris yes?
Sinalóa want ten tousand mile irrigation canals,
absolutamente. Is fun all dat organ-cactus fence?
Is for de birds, señor, is more better barbwire, verdad?
  and chingar dose cute little burros.

Sin argumento, my fren, is a beautiful music,
all dem birds. Pero, wy you no like to hear combos,
refrigerator trucks? Is wonderful on straight new ighway,
jampack wit melons, peppers, bananas, tomatoes, si, si . . .
Chirrimoyas? Mangos? You like! Is for Indios, solamente,
is bruise, no can ship, is no bueno, believe me, señor –
and defecar on dose goddam guidebook.

Mazatlán, Mexico 1956

Toronto Board of Trade Goes Abroad

George ! I dunno how you do it George . . .

Wy, eat all at *stuff*, all at horses *doovers* after all we had for *lunch* ! I bet you dunno wat half it *is*! *Raw fish* fer gossake I betitis you wanna *watch* that stuff George. Fellah in *Mexico* told me theres *worms* in it . . .

Gossake George I wish I had your *appetite* I can't *eat* I cant eat *any*thin . . .

Naw *I'm* not worryin . . . *Crisis*?! Hell George I *never* got the wind up and you know *wy* George? Because I allus *knew* that sonofabitch *Kroo*shef had no *guts* . . .

Naw George its I gotta terrible *thirst*. Its them uh Pis—? Them . . .

Yeah *Pisscoes* ! *Thats* wot they give us at lunch, yeah *hell* I thought they was kinda mild mar*teen*ies but theyre straight *al*cohol George – an an redi*stilled*! *Wow*! . . .

Four a them . . .

Yeah, so wat wouldn't I give *now* for, for you know *wat* George? For jus, jus a liddle drink of *wa*ter because you know somethin George? George? This the *longest bar* ina *world* . . .

Well I bet in Southa Merica anyway . . .

You take a *look*, hunderd twenny five *mee*tres fellah over there told me, blongsta Club, wy thas – how much *is* that George?

Yeah well thasa lot eh? an George every *yard* of its *piled* with *licker* analla this greazer *chow* yer eatin and you jes try finda drinka *water* on it! . . .

O sure sure but how you gonna trustim? They doenoe *ing*lish George these waiters. Anyway watta *they* care if its cont*am*inated maybe *loaded* with you know *wat* George, wat *you* got in Per*oo* George!

Well now doan get me *wrong* I wouldn let *them* hear me I'm not criticizin hell *no* these things doan really *matter* itsa great *country* and we all got somethin in *common* Canadians Chileans because you know *wot*? you know wattis we got in common? we're all A*meri*cans thas wat eh George? thas watta tellem but jussa same George I'd – George I'd give ten *bucks* this *min*ute for *one glass* of good old *Lake Ontario tapwater* thas wat – George? . . . George?! . . .

Now where the hell did *he* git to?

Union Club, Santiago de Chile, October 1962

ANONYMOUS

Limericks

1

A vice most obscene and unsavoury
Holds the Bishop of Balham in slavery:
With maniacal howls
He rogers young owls
Which he keeps in an underground aviary.

2

A lesbian girl of Khartoum
Took a pansy-boy up to her room;
As they turned out the light
She said, 'Let's get this right –
Who does what, and with which, and to whom?'

PHYLLIS McGINLEY

Trial and Error

A lady is smarter than a gentleman, maybe.
She can sew a fine seam, she can have a baby,
She can use her intuition instead of her brain,
But she can't fold a paper on a crowded train.

ANONYMOUS

The Soldier's Tale

A Rugger Song[1]

Oh, a soldier told me, before he died,
How once there was a woman with a cunt so wide
That she could never be satisfied . . .

So they built a machine with a bloody great wheel,
Two brass balls and a prick of steel;
The two brass balls were filled with cream
And the whole fucking issue was driven by steam.

Round and round went the bloody great wheel,
In and out went the prick of steel
Until, at last, the maiden cried:
'Enough! Enough! I'm satisfied!'

But this is a tale of the biter bit –
There was no way of stopping it
And she was rent from cunt to tit
And the whole fucking issue was covered in shit!

JOHN BETJEMAN

Tea with the Poets

Three pink Hampstead intellectuals,
  Three thin *passé* Bloomsbury dons
Sit discussing Manley Hopkins
  Over Mr Grogley's dainty scones.

[1]Although the words are crude and even scarifying, the effect of this song, when sung in Officers' Messes and Rugger Clubs, is quite benign.

Three great hunks of bread and butter,
   Three great lumps of Cheddar cheese,
Big legs sprawling in the roadway
   Friends of Stephen Spender lie at ease.

Tucking in at whipped cream walnuts,
   Blue shorts bursting under green,
C. Day Lewis brings his wolf cubs
   Safe into the full canteen.

But when the major lets the net down,
   When I see that cotton dress,
When we move to the verandah,
   When I put my racket in its press –

Then comes the tea time of all I like best
With my long-leggèd, blubber-lipped,
      carefree, uncorsetted,
      fun-freckled
      PRIMULA GUEST.

Our Padre

Our padre is an old sky pilot,
   Severely now they've clipped his wings,
But still the flagstaff in the Rect'ry garden
   Points to Higher Things.

Still he has got a hearty handshake;
   Still he wears medals and a stole;
His voice would reach to Heaven, *and* make
   The Rock of Ages roll.

He's too sincere to join the high church,
  Worshipping idols for the Lord,
And, though the lowest church is my church
  Our padre's Broad.

Our padre is an old sky pilot,
  He's tied a reef knot round my heart,
We'll be rock'd up to Heaven on a rare old tune –
  Come on – take part!

Chorus (*sung*)

Pull for the shore, sailor, pull for the shore!
Heed not the raging billow, bend to the oar!

Bend to the oar before the padre!
  Proud, with the padre rowing stroke!
Good old padre! God for the Services!
  Row like smoke!

The Flight from Bootle

Lonely in the Regent Palace,
  Sipping her 'Banana Blush',
Lilian lost sight of Alice
  In the honey-coloured rush.

Settled down at last from Bootle,
  Alice whispered, 'Just a min,
While I pop upstairs and rootle
  For another safety pin.'

Dreamy from the band pavilion
  Drops of the *Immortal Hour*
Fell around the lonely Lilian
  Like an ineffectual shower.

Half an hour she sat and waited
   In the honey-coloured lounge,
Till she with herself debated,
   'Time for me to go and scrounge!'

Time enough! or not enough time!
   Lilian, you wait in vain;
Alice will not have a rough time,
   Nor be quite the same again.

WILLIAM EMPSON

Just a Smack at Auden

Waiting for the end, boys, waiting for the end.
What is there to be or do?
What's to become of me or you?
Are we kind or are we true?
Sitting two and two, boys, waiting for the end.

Shall I build a tower, boys, knowing it will rend,
Crack upon the hour, boys, waiting for the end?
Shall I pluck a flower, boys, shall I save or spend?
All turns sour, boys, waiting for the end.

Shall I send a wire, boys? Where is there to send?
All are under fire, boys, waiting for the end.
Shall I turn a sire, boys? Shall I choose a friend?
The fat is in the pyre, boys, waiting for the end.

Shall I make it clear, boys, for all to apprehend,
Those that will not hear, boys, waiting for the end,
Knowing it is near, boys, trying to pretend,
Sitting in cold fear, boys, waiting for the end?

Shall we send a cable, boys, accurately penned,
Knowing we are able, boys, waiting for the end,
Via the Tower of Babel, boys? Christ will not ascend.
He's hiding in his stable, boys, waiting for the end.

Shall we blow a bubble, boys, glittering to distend,
Hiding from our trouble, boys, waiting for the end?
When you build on rubble, boys, Nature will append
Double and re-double, boys, waiting for the end.

Shall we make a tale, boys, that things are sure to mend,
Playing bluff and hale, boys, waiting for the end?
It will be born stale, boys, stinking to offend,
Dying ere it fail, boys, waiting for the end.

Shall we all go wild, boys, waste and make them lend,
Playing at the child, boys, waiting for the end?
It has all been filed, boys, history has a trend,
Each of us enisled, boys, waiting for the end.

What was said by Marx, boys, what did he perpend?
No good being sparks, boys, waiting for the end.
Treason of the clerks, boys, curtains that descend,
Lights becoming darks, boys, waiting for the end.

Waiting for the end, boys, waiting for the end.
Not a chance of blend, boys, things have got to tend.
Think of those who vend, boys, think of how we wend,
Waiting for the end, boys, waiting for the end.

LOUIS MacNEICE

Bagpipe Music

It's no go the merrygoround, it's no go the rickshaw,
All we want is a limousine and a ticket for the peepshow.
Their knickers are made of crêpe-de-chine, their shoes are made of python,
Their halls are lined with tiger rugs and their walls with heads of bison.

John MacDonald found a corpse, put it under the sofa,
Waited till it came to life and hit it with a poker,
Sold its eyes for souvenirs, sold its blood for whisky,
Kept its bones for dumb-bells to use when he was fifty.

It's no go the Yogi-Man, it's no go Blavatsky,
All we want is a bank balance and a bit of skirt in a taxi.

Annie MacDougall went to milk, caught her foot in the heather,
Woke to hear a dance record playing of Old Vienna.
It's no go your maidenheads, it's no go your culture,
All we want is a Dunlop tyre and the devil mend the puncture.

The Laird o' Phelps spent Hogmanay declaring he was sober,
Counted his feet to prove the fact and found he had one foot over.
Mrs Carmichael had her fifth, looked at the job with repulsion,
Said to the midwife 'Take it away; I'm through with over-production'.

It's no go the gossip column, it's no go the ceilidh,
All we want is a mother's help and a sugar-stick for the baby.

Willie Murray cut his thumb, couldn't count the damage,
Took the hide of an Ayrshire cow and used it for a bandage.

His brother caught three hundred cran when the seas were lavish,
Threw the bleeders back in the sea and went upon the parish.

It's no go the Herring Board, it's no go the Bible,
All we want is a packet of fags when our hands are idle.

It's no go the picture palace, it's no go the stadium,
It's no go the country cot with a pot of pink geraniums,
It's no go the Government grants, it's no go the elections,
Sit on your arse for fifty years and hang your hat on a pension.

It's no go my honey love, it's no go my poppet;
Work your hands from day to day, the winds will blow the profit.
The glass is falling hour by hour, the glass will fall for ever,
But if you break the bloody glass you won't hold up the weather.

W. H. AUDEN

Love Song

For what as easy
For what though small,
For what is well
Because between,
To you simply
From me I mean.

Who goes with who
The bedclothes say,
As I and you
Go kissed away,
The data given,
The senses even.

Fate is not late,
Nor the speech rewritten,
Nor one word forgotten,
Said at the start
About heart,
By heart, for heart.

Dedications

I

Let us honour if we can
The vertical man,
Though we value none
But the horizontal one.

2

Private faces in public places
Are wiser and nicer
Than public faces in private places.

Song

– 'O for doors to be open and an invite with gilded edges
To dine with Lord Lobcock and Count Asthma on the platinum benches,
With somersaults and fireworks, the roast and the smacking kisses' –
Cried the cripples to the silent statue,
The six beggared cripples.

– 'And Garbo's and Cleopatra's wits to go astraying,
In a feather ocean with me to go fishing and playing,
Still jolly when the cock has burst himself with crowing' –
Cried the cripples to the silent statue,
The six beggared cripples.

– 'And to stand on green turf among the craning yellow faces
Dependent on the chestnut, the sable, and Arabian horses,
And me with a magic crystal to foresee their places' –
Cried the cripples to the silent statue,
The six beggared cripples.

– 'And this square to be a deck and these pigeons canvas to rig,
And to follow the delicious breeze like a tantony pig
To the shaded feverless islands where the melons are big' –
Cried the cripples to the silent statue,
The six beggared cripples.

– 'And these shops to be turned to tulips in a garden bed,
And me with my crutch to thrash each merchant dead
As he pokes from a flower his bald and wicked head' –
Cried the cripples to the silent statue,
The six beggared cripples.

– 'And a hole in the bottom of heaven, and Peter and Paul
And each smug surprised saint like parachutes to fall,
And every one-legged beggar to have no legs at all' –
Cried the cripples to the silent statue,
The six beggared cripples.

Uncle Henry

When the Flyin' Scot
fills for shootin', I go southward,
wisin' after coffee, leavin'
Lady Starkie.

Weady for some fun,
visit yearly Wome, Damascus,
in Mowocco look for fwesh a-
-musin' places.

Where I'll find a fwend,
don't you know, a charmin' cweature,
like a Gweek God and devoted:
how delicious!

All they have they bwing,
Abdul, Nino, Manfwed, Kosta:
here's to women for they bear such
lovely kiddies!

Calypso

Dríver, drive fáster and máke a good rún
Down the Spríngfield Line únder the shining sún.

Flý like an aéroplane, dón't pull up shórt
Till you bráke for Grand Céntral Státion, New Yórk.

For thére in the míddle of thát waiting-háll
Should be stánding the óne that í love best of áll.

If he's nót there to meét me when í get to tówn,
I'll stánd on the síde-walk with téars rolling dówn.

For hé is the óne that I lóve to look ón,
The ácme of kíndness and pérfectión.

He présses my hánd and he sáys he loves mé,
Which I fínd an admirável pecúliarirtý.

The woóds are bright gréen on both sídes of the líne;
The trées have their lóves though they're dífferent from míne.

But the poór fat old bánker in the sún-parlor cár
Has nó one to lóve him excépt his cigár.

If I were the Heád of the Chúrch or the Státe,
I'd pówder my nóse and just téll them to wáit.

For lóve's more impórtant and pówerful thán
Éven a priést or a pólitición.

Words

Base words are uttered only by the base
And can for such at once be understood,
But noble platitudes: – ah, that's a case
Where the most careful scrutiny is needed
To tell a voice that's genuinely good
From one that's base but merely has succeeded.

Song

When the Sex War ended with the slaughter of the Grandmothers,
They found a bachelor's baby suffocating under them;
Somebody called him George and that was the end of it;
They hitched him up to the Army.
George, you old debutante,
How did you get in the Army?

In the Retreat from Reason he deserted on his rocking-horse
And lived on a fairy's kindness till he tired of kicking her;
He smashed her spectacles and stole her cheque-book and mackintosh
Then cruised his way back to the Army.
George, you old numero,
How did you get in the Army?

Before the Diet of Sugar he was using razor-blades
And exited soon after with an allergy to maidenheads;
He discovered a cure of his own, but no one would patent it,
So he showed up again in the Army.
George, you old flybynight,
How did you get in the Army?

When the Vice Crusades were over he was hired by some Muscovites
Prospecting for deodorants among the Eskimos;
He was caught by a common cold and condemned to the whiskey mines,
But schemozzled back to the Army.
George, you old Emperor,
How did you get in the Army?

Since Peace was signed with Honour he's been minding his business;
But, whoops, here comes His Idleness, buttoning his uniform;
Just in tidy time to massacre the Innocents;
He's come home to roost in the Army.
George, you old matador,
Welcome back to the Army.

Under Which Lyre

A Reactionary Tract for the Times

(Phi Beta Kappa Poem, Harvard, 1946)

Ares at last has quit the field,
The bloodstains on the bushes yield
To seeping showers,
And in their convalescent state
The fractured towns associate
With summer flowers.

Encamped upon the college plain
Raw veterans already train
As freshman forces;
Instructors with sarcastic tongue
Shepherd the battle-weary young
Through basic courses.

Among bewildering appliances
For mastering the arts and sciences
They stroll or run,
And nerves that steeled themselves to slaughter
Are shot to pieces by the shorter
Poems of Donne.

Professors back from secret missions
Resume their proper eruditions,
Though some regret it;
They liked their dictaphones a lot,
They met some big wheels, and do not
Let you forget it.

But Zeus' inscrutable decree
Permits the will-to-disagree
To be pandemic,
Ordains that vaudeville shall preach
And every commencement speech
Be a polemic.

Let Ares doze, that other war
Is instantly declared once more
'Twixt those who follow
Precocious Hermes all the way
And those who without qualms obey
Pompous Apollo.

Brutal like all Olympic games,
Though fought with smiles and Christian names
        And less dramatic,
This dialectic strife between
The civil gods is just as mean,
        And more fanatic.

What high immortals do in mirth
Is life and death on Middle Earth;
        Their a-historic
Antipathy forever gripes
All ages and somatic types,
        The sophomoric

Who face the future's darkest hints
With giggles or with prairie squints
        As stout as Cortez,
And those who like myself turn pale
As we approach with ragged sail
        The fattening forties.

The sons of Hermes love to play,
And only do their best when they
        Are told they oughtn't;
Apollo's children never shrink
From boring jobs but have to think
        Their work important.

Related by antithesis,
A compromise between us is
        Impossible;
Respect perhaps but friendship never:
Falstaff the fool confronts forever
        The prig Prince Hal.

If he would leave the self alone,
Apollo's welcome to the throne,
Fasces and falcons;
He loves to rule, has always done it;
The earth would soon, did Hermes run it,
Be like the Balkans.

But jealous of our god of dreams,
His common-sense in secret schemes
To rule the heart;
Unable to invent the lyre,
Creates with simulated fire
Official art.

And when he occupies a college,
Truth is replaced by Useful Knowledge;
He pays particular
Attention to Commercial Thought,
Public Relations, Hygiene, Sport,
In his curricula.

Athletic, extrovert and crude,
For him, to work in solitude
Is the offence,
The goal a populous Nirvana:
His shield bears this device: *Mens sana*
Qui mal y pense.

Today his arms, we must confess,
From Right to Left have met success,
His banners wave
From Yale to Princeton, and the news
From Broadway to the Book Reviews
Is very grave.

His radio Homers all day long
In over-Whitmanated song
    That does not scan,
With adjectives laid end to end,
Extol the doughnut and commend
    The Common Man.

His, too, each homely lyric thing
On sport or spousal love or spring
    Or dogs or dusters,
Invented by some court-house bard
For recitation by the yard
    In filibusters.

To him ascend the prize orations
And sets of fugal variations
    On some folk-ballad,
While dietitians sacrifice
A glass of prune-juice or a nice
    Marsh-mallow salad.

Charged with his command of sensational
Sex plus some undenominational
    Religious matter,
Enormous novels by co-eds
Rain down on our defenceless heads
    Till our teeth chatter.

In fake Hermetic uniforms
Behind our battle-line, in swarms
    That keep alighting,
His existentialists declare
That they are in complete despair,
    Yet go on writing.

No matter; He shall be defied;
White Aphrodite is on our side:
        What though his threat
To organize us grow more critical?
Zeus willing, we, the unpolitical,
        Shall beat him yet.

Lone scholars, sniping from the walls
Of learned periodicals,
        Our facts defend,
Our intellectual marines,
Landing in little magazines
        Capture a trend,

By night or student Underground
At cocktail parties whisper round
        From ear to ear;
Fat figures in the public eye
Collapse next morning, ambushed by
        Some witty sneer.

In our morale must lie our strength:
So, that we may behold at length
        Routed Apollo's
Battalions melt away like fog,
Keep well the Hermetic Decalogue,
        Which runs as follows: –

Thou shalt not do as the dean pleases,
Thou shalt not write thy doctor's thesis
        On education,
Thou shalt not worship projects nor
Shalt thou or thine bow down before
        Administration.

Thou shalt not answer questionnaires
Or quizzes upon World-Affairs,
    Nor with compliance
Take any test. Thou shalt not sit
With statisticians nor commit
    A social science.

Thou shalt not be on friendly terms
With guys in advertising firms,
    Nor speak with such
As read the Bible for its prose,
Nor, above all, make love to those
    Who wash too much.

Thou shalt not live within thy means
Nor on plain water and raw greens.
    If thou must choose
Between the chances, choose the odd:
Read *The New Yorker*, trust in God:
    And take short views.

LINCOLN KIRSTEIN

Double Date

Myself and Curtis Dean are seniors together, –
  half- and full-backs, junior-varsity teams.
Dean and I have fun, all sortsa weather
  sharing similar sexual dreams.

Curt and I do quite a lota double-dating,
  specially on Saturday nights, –
lotsa heavy-loving, (some x-rating),
  fanTASTic freeform farout delights.

Last Senior Prom he picks me up 7:30.
  We get Jane, – and friend (some unknown dame):
four of us, – crocked. Start talking-dirty,
  kick-off in the double-dating game.

First: breast-fondling. Then light n'lively kissing;
  next: pet-to-climax, (tongue & ear).
Then, partial-stripping. Still, something's missing.
  Jane plays the field; her friend's full o' fear.

Curt, – (he only ASKed her), – just suggesting shyly:
  'Stroke my pecker, please.' (Inside his pants.)
She gets sore: 'I'm a NICE girl!' (A lie.) She
  weeps; we'll miss that old high-school dance.

I laugh like hell, but Curt's bitched and bitter;
  starts up his car; gravel flies, wheels squeal.
Jane takes HER side. I sure coulda hit her.
  Curtis drives fast feeling one real heel.

We walk 'em to their door. They slamit, not speaking.
  Dean says: 'You drive. I'm too pissed to move.'
Must we go home yet? We stall there, seeking
  some real outlet for unrequited love.

Parked on a side-street for more serious-drinking
  Curt grins: 'I'm horny.' 'Beat-off,' I said. –
much the same we both of us were thinking;
  easier when formal-dress is shed.

Dumb simple hand-jobs aren't so all-fired thrilling.
  Dean sighs: 'I'll do you if you do me.'
Chances being caught queer can be chilling;
  we were jet-propelled on liberty.

Agreed on next steps albeit kinda risky;
  stripped bare-ass on that slippery back-seat.
Man o Man! That full-back's prime-time frisky!
  Mutual release is mor'n beating-meat.

But just like it was when those chicks got us started, –
  no chance for rocks-off. Fate interferes.
Headlights spot our tangle. We get us parted.
  Nudity unknots two bare-assed queers.

Flashlight glares hot on our raw frank condition;
  'What's goin' ON here?' inquires this Cop.
'Officer, we're drunk, sir.' Rank submission.
  Cop snaps: 'Curtis Dean! This gotta STOP!'

Yup. We're illegal. Policeman put it clearly:
  (he knows Dean's dad; acts paternally):
'Just pull your pants on,' proposing merely:
  'You're too drunk to drive, boys. Follow me.'

To Curt's house, bingo! Police-escort protection!
  Real motherly is Curt Dean's mother:
'You poor lambs look TIRED!' With no objection
  we bounce to bed. No further bother.

PATRICK BARRINGTON

I Had a Duck-billed Platypus

I had a duck-billed platypus when I was up at Trinity,
With whom I soon discovered a remarkable affinity.
He used to live in lodgings with myself and Arthur Purvis,
And we all went up together for the Diplomatic Service.
I had a certain confidence, I own, in his ability,
He mastered all the subjects with remarkable facility;

And Purvis, though more dubious, agreed that he was clever,
But no one else imagined he had any chance whatever.
I failed to pass the interview, the Board with wry grimaces
Took exception to my boots and then objected to my braces,
And Purvis too was failed by an intolerant examiner
Who said he had his doubts as to his sock-suspenders' stamina.
The bitterness of failure was considerably mollified,
However, by the ease with which our platypus had qualified.
The wisdom of the choice, it soon appeared, was undeniable;
There never was a diplomat more thoroughly reliable.
He never made rash statements his enemies might hold him to,
He never stated anything, for no one ever told him to,
And soon he was appointed, so correct was his behaviour,
Our Minister (without Portfolio) to Trans-Moravia.
My friend was loved and honoured from the Andes to Esthonia
He soon achieved a pact between Peru and Patagonia,
He never vexed the Russians nor offended the Rumanians,
He pacified the Letts and yet appeased the Lithuanians,
Won approval from his masters down in Downing Street so
    wholly, O,
He was soon to be rewarded with the grant of a Portfolio.

When, on the Anniversary of Greek Emancipation,
Alas! He laid an egg in the Bulgarian Legation.
This untoward occurrence caused unheard-of repercussions,
Giving rise to epidemics of sword-clanking in the Prussians.
The Poles began to threaten, and the Finns began to flap at him,
Directing all the blame for this unfortunate mishap at him;
While the Swedes withdrew entirely from the Anglo-Saxon
    dailies
The right of photographing the Aurora Borealis,
And, all efforts at rapprochement in the meantime proving
    barren,
The Japanese in self-defence annexed the Isle of Arran.
My platypus, once thought to be more cautious and more
    tentative

Than any other living diplomatic representative,
Was now a sort of warning to all diplomatic students
Of the risks attached to negligence, the perils of imprudence,
And, branded in the Honours List as 'Platypus, Dame Vera,'
Retired, a lonely figure, to lay eggs at Bordighera.

OSBERT LANCASTER

From *Afternoons with Baedeker*

1 Eireann

The distant Seychelles are not so remote
Nor Ctesiphon as ultimately dead
As this damp square round which tired echoes float
Of something brilliant that George Moore once said:
Where, still, in pitch-pine snugs pale poets quote
Verses rejected by the Bodley Head.
For in this drained aquarium no breeze
Deposits pollen from more fertile shores
Or kills the smell of long unopened drawers
That clings for ever to these dripping trees.
Where Bloom once wandered, gross and ill-at-ease,
Twice-pensioned heroes of forgotten wars
With misplaced confidence demand applause
Shouting stale slogans on the Liffey quays.

2 English

In 1910 a royal princess
Contracted measles here;
Last spring a pregnant stewardess
Was found beneath the pier;
Her throat, according to the Press,
Was slit from ear to ear.

In all the years that passed between
These two distressing dates
Our only tragedy has been
The raising of the rates,
Though once a flying-bomb was seen
Far out across the straits.

Heard on this coast, the music of the spheres
Would sound like something from *The Gondoliers.*

3 French

I shall not linger in that draughty square
Attracted by the art-nouveau hotel
Nor ring in vain the concierge's bell
And then, engulfed by a profound despair
That finds its echo in the passing trains,
Sit drinking in the café, wondering why,
Maddened by love, a butcher at Versailles
On Tuesday evening made to jump his brains.
Nor shall I visit the Flamboyant church,
Three stars in Michelin, yet by some strange fluke
Left unrestored by Viollet-le-Duc,
To carry out some long-desired research.
Too well I know the power to get one down
Exerted by this grey and shuttered town.

4 Manhattan

Here those of us who really understand
Feel that the past is very close at hand.
In that old brownstone mansion 'cross the way,
Copied from one that she had seen by chance
When on her honeymoon in Paris, France,
Mrs Van Dryssel gave her great soirées;
And in the chic apartment house next door
J. Rittenhaus the Second lived – and jumped,
The morning after General Motors slumped,

Down from a love-nest on the thirtieth floor.
Tread softly then, for on this holy ground
You'd hear the 'twenties cry from every stone
And Bye-bye Blackbird on the saxophone
If only History were wired for sound.

STANLEY J. SHARPLESS

In Praise of Cocoa, Cupid's Nightcap

Lines written upon hearing the startling news that cocoa is, in fact, a mild aphrodisiac.

Half past nine – high time for supper;
'Cocoa, love?' 'Of course, my dear.'
Helen thinks it quite delicious,
John prefers it now to beer.
Knocking back the sepia potion,
Hubby winks, says, 'Who's for bed?'
'Shan't be long,' says Helen softly,
Cheeks a faintly flushing red.
For they've stumbled on the secret
Of a love that never wanes,
Rapt beneath the tumbled bedclothes,
Cocoa coursing through their veins.

Does That Answer Your Question, Mr Shakespeare?

Who is Silvia? What a shame
You didn't catch her other name;
There's such a lot of them about:
Silvias sylph-like, Silvias stout,
Silvias cool and Silvias twittery,
Silvias po-faced, Silvias tittery,

Silvias true and Silvias phoney,
Silvias bosomy, Silvias bony,
Silvias nasty, Silvias nice,
Silvias up two floors (knock twice);
There's one comfort, anyway –
In the dark all cats are grey.

Low Church

It was after vespers one evening
When the vicar, inflamed by desire,
Beckoned a lad to the vestry,
Dismissing the rest of the choir.

He said, 'I've got something to show you,'
The boy followed hard on his heels;
Behind the locked door there was silence,
Except for some half-muffled squeals.

The vicar got two years (suspended),
The judge spoke of 'moral decay',
The vicar is sadder and wiser,
But the choir-boy is happy and gay.

Costa Geriatrica

Land of the ding-dong doorbell and trim hedges,
The Lotus Land of over 65's,
Geraniums' fringe of fire on window-ledges,
Seed-packet lawns, and diminished sexual drives.

The golf is good, and once they've past their prime,
Bingo shall succour whom the years condemn;
Plenty of painless ways of killing time,
Until time ('suddenly, at home') kills them.

A Moment of Eschatological Doubt

Happening to pass a Roman Catholic church
He stops and gazes,
And has the sudden thought: if they are right,
I'm wrong to blazes.

ROY FULLER

Dedicatory Epistle, with a Book of 1949

To Jack Clark and Alan Ross

Here's proof – as if one needed any –
Of Fuller's classic parsimony.
One volume, two dedicatees;
So little verse and less to please.
Alan, I hear you say, behind
That manner which is always kind:
'No meat, and where's the bloody gravy?
He wrote much better in the Navy'.
And you, Jack, glancing up from Proust:
'It's compromise come home to roost'.

Hysteria is the destiny
Of those who want, insatiably,
In childhood love; and the condition
Of being wet in bed's ambition.
What kind of pasts must we have led
That now we're neither red nor dead?
We had our fill of love and hunger
When uninhibited and younger:
After we lost the initial breast
We knew a falling off of zest;
And while the workless topped three million
Read Eliot in the pavilion;

For us the Reichstag burned to tones
Of Bach on hand-made gramophones;
We saw the long-drawn fascist trauma
In terms of the poetic drama;
And even the ensuing war
For most was something of a bore.

Dear Clark, it's you to whom I speak,
As one who hovered in that clique:
A wit and cause of wit in others;
Who called the working-class half-brothers;
Easy at Lords or Wigmore Hall;
A nibbler at the off-side ball –
We would have moved, were held, alas,
In the paralysis of class.
We spoke our thoughts not loud and bold
But whispered through the coward's cold;
And all the time, with deadly humour,
Inside us grew the coward's tumour.
Nothing I say can warn, console,
You who've survived the liberal rôle,
And in a world of Camps and Bomb
Wait for the end with false aplomb.

The nineteenth century dream of good
Erecting barricades of wood
And storming keypoints of reaction
To substitute its kindly faction,
Until what's violent and rotten
Withers like warts tied round with cotton –
Such vision fades, and yet our age
Need not become the last blank page,
And though the future may be odd
We shouldn't let it rest with God;
Confused and wrong though things have gone
There is a side we can be on:

Distaste for lasting bread and peace
May thus support a king in Greece,
And trust in General Chiang Kai-shek
Will safely lead to freedom's wreck.

Our dreams no longer guard our sleep:
The noses of the road-drills creep,
With thoughts of death, across the lawn
Out of the swarthy urban dawn.
And one by one, against our will,
The cultured cities vanish till
We see with horror just ahead
The sudden end of history's thread.
Ross, with your innings' lead of years,
Such brooding will not bring your tears.
You lived when doom was not the fashion,
What's sad for you is human passion.
Your verse is sensuous, not spare,
Somerset in, not Lancashire.
We disagree in much, I know:
I'm over-fond of Uncle Joe;
You find in Auden not an era –
Simply a poet who grows queerer;
The working class for you's a fact,
No statue in the final act.
Yet we should never come to blows
On this – that man as artist goes,
And in that rôle, most sane, most free,
Fulfils his spacious infancy;
That truth's half feeling and half style,
And feeling and no style is vile.
About us lie our elder writers,
Small, gritty, barren, like detritus:
Resistance to the epoch's rage
Has not survived their middle age.

The type of ivory tower varies
But all live in the caves of caries.
The younger men, not long from mother,
Write articles about each other,
Examining, in solemn chorus,
Ten poems or a brace of stories.
The treason of the clerks is when
They make a fetish of the pen,
Forget that art has duties to –
As well as to the 'I' – the 'You',
And that its source must always be
What presses most, most constantly.
Since Sarajevo there has been
Only one thing the word could mean,
And each successive crisis shows
That meaning plainer than a nose.
Sassoon found Georgian style napoo
To state what he was going through:
And Owen knew why he was born –
To write the truth and thus to warn.
The poet now must put verse back
Time and again upon the track
That first was cut by Wordsworth when
He said that verse was meant for men,
And ought to speak on all occasions
In language which has no evasions.

Dear friends, I wish this book bore out
More than the bourgeois' fear and doubt.
Alas, my talent and my way
Of life are useless for today.
I might have cut a better figure
When peace was longer, incomes bigger.
The 'nineties would have seen me thrive,
Dyspeptic, bookish, half-alive.

Even between the wars I might
With luck have written something bright.
But now, I feel, the 'thirties gone,
The dim light's out that could have shone.
My richest ambiguity
In nightmares now, not poetry:
After eight lines the latter ends
Unless I'm babbling to my friends.
The arteries and treaties harden,
The shadow falls across the garden,
And down the tunnel of the years
The spectre that we feared appears.
Gazing upon our love or book,
Between the lines or in the look,
We see that choice must fall at last,
And the immortal, lucky past –
Thinking of bed or lying in it –
Cry out and crumble in a minute.
For such times are these poems meant,
A muted, sparse accompaniment,
Until the Wagner we await
Provides a score that's up to date,
And world and way and godheads pass
To vulgar but triumphant brass.

LAWRENCE DURRELL

A Ballad of the Good Lord Nelson

The Good Lord Nelson had a swollen gland,
Little of the scripture did he understand
Till a woman led him to the promised land
  Aboard the Victory, Victory O.

Adam and Eve and a bushel of figs
Meant nothing to Nelson who was keeping pigs,
Till a woman showed him the various rigs
  Aboard the Victory, Victory O.

His heart was softer than a new laid egg,
Too poor for loving and ashamed to beg,
Till Nelson was taken by the Dancing Leg
  Aboard the Victory, Victory O.

Now he up and did up his little tin trunk
And he took to the ocean on his English junk,
Turning like the hour-glass in his lonely bunk
  Aboard the Victory, Victory O.

The Frenchman saw him a-coming there
With the one-piece eye and the valentine hair.
With the safety-pin sleeve and occupied air
  Aboard the Victory, Victory O.

Now you all remember the message he sent
As an answer to Hamilton's discontent –
There were questions asked about it in Parliament
  Aboard the Victory, Victory O.

Now the blacker the berry, the thicker comes the juice.
Think of Good Lord Nelson and avoid self-abuse,
For the empty sleeve was no mere excuse
  Aboard the Victory, Victory O.

'England Expects' was the motto he gave
When he thought of little Emma out on Biscay's wave,
And remembered working on her like a galley-slave
  Aboard the Victory, Victory O.

The finest Great Lord in our English land
To honour the Freudian command,
For a cast in the bush is worth two in the hand
    Aboard the Victory, Victory O.

Now the Frenchman shot him there as he stood
In the rage of battle in a silk-lined hood
And he heard the whistle of his own hot blood
    Aboard the Victory, Victory O.

Now stiff on a pillar with a phallic air
Nelson stylites in Trafalgar Square
Reminds the British what once they were
    Aboard the Victory, Victory O.

If they'd treat their women in the Nelson way
There'd be fewer frigid husbands every day
And many more heroes on the Bay of Biscay
    Aboard the Victory, Victory O.

JULIAN SYMONS

Central Park

A walk in Central Park,
New York friends tell me, is far from being a lark.
If lucky enough to escape attack by muggers
You will attract the more insidious attentions of buggers.
At night it is even more dangerous than the subways,
Those hubways
Of delinquency and violence.
                                        But I walked there at dusk
And felt as safe as if I were in the office of Dean Rusk.
It is a city park, hard cracked and bare
And melancholy, like the brown bear

Who paws at his cage in the Zoo. In places the grass
Looks as if it has received attention from (to quote Cummings)
Lil's white arse.
The lamps are wired over to prevent their destruction
And boys playing baseball are warned: 'Instruction,
Use soft ball only.' The cars move through it, spat out by the great suction
Cleaner on West, sucked in again on East. Trees, greenness are incidental,
For this park is part of the roaring mental
Delirium of the city. Although the prospects please
The park is a place of excitement, not ease.
It is this, and not the assaults of sluggers and huggers
That make a walk in Central Park,
In daylight or after dark,
Something short of a lark.

Harvard

Harvard, Cambridge, Mass.
A fine spring day. On the Charles River boats pass
Under the bridges, urged by the earnest doing their best to fulfil
The exhortation (Nicholas Longworth Anderson Bridge) that they should develop their manhood in the service of the nation's will.
Across the river the Business School and behind
Me colleges and hamburger houses mixed up, a little red brick Georgian and a lot of fake, resigned
To the contiguity of modern blocks where the students like to live.
Watching their casual ease, eagerness, brashness, which derive
From the democratic process, I wonder how much will survive

Of all this as America feels its power
Growing. We are formed by our institutions, they create the flower
We call civilization. But even as we say proudly, *Look*,
Some boy at Harvard is shaping a book
Under the heavy brows of Widener and Lamont, singular and shy,
To assert the opposites of virtue, to deny
The reek of unwanted history in the coils of their embrace,
And to search in petrol station, Hamburger Heaven, high risers, for the reflection of a modern face.

MERVYN PEAKE

The Frivolous Cake

A freckled and frivolous cake there was
That sailed on a pointless sea,
Or any lugubrious lake there was,
In a manner emphatic and free.
How jointlessly, and how jointlessly
The frivolous cake sailed by
On the waves of the ocean that pointlessly
Threw fish to the lilac sky.

Oh, plenty and plenty of hake there was
Of a glory beyond compare,
And every conceivable make there was
Was tossed through the lilac air.

Up the smooth billows and over the crests
Of the cumbersome combers flew
The frivolous cake with a knife in the wake
Of herself and her curranty crew.

Like a swordfish grim it would bounce and skim
  (This dinner knife fierce and blue),
And the frivolous cake was filled to the brim
  With the fun of her curranty crew.

Oh, plenty and plenty of hake there was
  Of a glory beyond compare –
And every conceivable make there was
  Was tossed through the lilac air.

Around the shores of the Elegant Isles
  Where the cat-fish bask and purr
And lick their paws with adhesive smiles
  And wriggle their fins of fur,
They fly and fly 'neath the lilac sky –
  The frivolous cake and the knife
Who winketh his glamorous indigo eye
  In the wake of his future wife.

The crumbs blow free down the pointless sea
  To the beat of a cakey heart
And the sensitive steel of the knife can feel
  That love is a race apart.
In the speed of the lingering light are blown
  The crumbs to the hake above,
And the tropical air vibrates to the drone
  Of a cake in the throes of love.

HENRY REED

Chard Whitlow

(*Mr Eliot's Sunday Evening Postscript*)

As we get older we do not get any younger.
Seasons return, and today I am fifty-five,
And this time last year I was fifty-four,
And this time next year I shall be sixty-two.
And I cannot say I should care (to speak for myself)
To see my time over again – if you can call it time,
Fidgeting uneasily under a draughty stair,
Or counting sleepless nights in the crowded Tube.

There are certain precautions – though none of them
very reliable –
Against the blast from bombs, or the flying splinter,
But not against the blast from Heaven, *vento dei venti*,
The wind within a wind, unable to speak for wind;
And the frigid burnings of purgatory will not be touched
By any emollient.
I think you will find this put,
Better than I could ever hope to express it,
In the words of Kharma: 'It is, we believe,
Idle to hope that the simple stirrup-pump
Can extinguish hell.'
Oh, listeners,
And you especially who have turned off the wireless,
And sit in Stoke or Basingstoke, listening appreciatively
to the silence,
(Which is also the silence of hell) pray, not for yourselves
but your souls.
And pray for me also under the draughty stair.
As we get older we do not get any younger.

And pray for Kharma under the holy mountain.

GEORGE BARKER

Song

Now this bloody war is over
no more soldiering for me.
I can hear the angel in the kitchen
washing up the crockery for tea,
and down the lane the donkeys and the children
splashing through the puddle by the tree
and the daffodils that should have died in April
ostentatiously continuing to be,
so now this bloody war is over
no more soldiering for me.

Us dead are up and dancing in the garden,
us dead are throwing parties every night
and the destiny of man is with the children
daubing every bleeding elephant dead white
and us dead men and the children in the garden
are dancing hand in hand such a helluva saraband
that the Church and State in bed think it's thunder overhead
as the children and us dead dance through the night.

DAVID GASCOYNE

An Unsagacious Animal

or *The Triumph of Art Over Nature*

The Master of *The Monarch of the Glen*
Was making once a sojourn 'neath the roof
Of an admiring Peer, Lord Rivers, when
Occasion rose which put to sternest proof

That intrepidity and tact which had
Secured for him familiar intercourse
With Nature's greatest gentlemen and made
Him reverenced alike by man and horse.
For while his fellow guests one afternoon
Were rapidly gleaning Landseer's dicta, sound
Of lawless canine truculence, which soor
Became intolerable, made him pound
With sudden fist the tea-table and cry:
'What insolence of importuning cur,
What rumour as of kennel mutiny
Is this? Shall Man the Master then defer
To a hound's ill-bred fury? Follow me:
Let's to the stable-yard whence these barks come,
And I will prove to you that Art can be
A force more sure than blows to make dogs dumb.
I who not seldom with forbidding gaze
Have known how to persuade huge Highland kine
To emulate the Southern cow's sweet ways
And made whole shaggy herds hang on the line,
Will there, if it amuse you, demonstrate
A sovereign power yet stronger than the eye's:
That of the Human Voice, which is so great
That it can Lions strike dumb with surprise!'
Some of the painter's intimates had been
Already privileged to hear his skill
In imitation of the less obscene
Sounds with which animals are wont to fill
The atmosphere of jungle, swamp and glade
When moved by meal-time longings or by bliss
To self-expression. For some years he'd made
The feat his study, and could bellow, hiss,
Roar, bark, snarl, with a realism which
Was quite astonishing, till in no part
Of all Victoria's realms was known so rich
A repertoire of Imitative Art

As that perfected by the great RA.
In view of this, it hardly will seem queer
To any that all present there that day
Excitedly accompanied Landseer
Out to the stables, craning and agog,
To watch him stride, masterfully serene,
Towards the kennel out of which the dog
Surveyed defiantly the crowded scene
With jaws aslaver and keen fangs exposed.
Then, not without surprise, they saw him fall
Down on his knees! It was by some supposed
This was in order piously to call
On Providence for aid; but they were wrong.
His aim was to confront the renegade
As man to man (or – dog to dog?). Ere long
That wretched animal's vile din was made
To seem the fretful yap of Pekinese
By an appallingly hyenine bark
Which evidently made the dog's blood freeze,
For his rebellion ceased at once, and stark
Terror replaced the murder in his eye.
The artful mimicry of Landseer proved
So awful that the beast, which recently
Had rivalled Cerberus himself, now moved
With such violence away from the advance
Of the superior barker, that his chain
Snapped, and he crossed the yard swift as a glance,
Leaped o'er the wall, and never was again
Seen anywhere on Lord Rivers' estate.
Landseer, on rising, found that only one
Of those who'd watched him still remained to fête
His triumph. 'Twas his host, who breathed: 'What fun!
How good of you to teach them how, dear old
Dog-lover! But come now, your tea's quite cold.'

GAVIN EWART

Poets

It isn't a very big cake,
some of us won't get a slice,
and that, make no mistake,
can make us not very nice
to one and all – or another
poetical sister or brother.

We all want total praise
for every word we write,
not for a singular phrase;
we're ready to turn and bite
the thick malicious reviewers,
our hated and feared pursuers.

We feel a sad neglect
when people don't buy our books;
it isn't what we expect
and gives rise to dirty looks
at a public whose addiction
is mainly romantic fiction.

We think there's something wrong
with poets that readers *read*,
disdaining our soulful song
for some pretentious screed
or poems pure and simple
as beauty's deluding dimple.

We can't imagine how
portentous nonsense by A
is loved like a sacred cow,

while dons are carried away
by B's more rustic stanzas
and C's banal bonanzas.

We have our minority view
and a sort of trust in Time;
meanwhile in this human zoo
we wander free, or rhyme,
our admirers not very many –
lucky, perhaps, to have any.

Office Friendships

Eve is madly in love with Hugh
And Hugh is keen on Jim.
Charles is in love with very few
And few are in love with him.

Myra sits typing notes of love
With romantic pianist's fingers.
Dick turns his eyes to the heavens above
Where Fran's divine perfume lingers.

Nicky is rolling eyes and tits
And flaunting her wiggly walk.
Everybody is thrilled to bits
By Clive's suggestive talk.

Sex suppressed will go berserk,
But it keeps us all alive.
It's a wonderful change from wives and work
And it ends at half past five.

The Word-Bird

The Word-Bird knows that everybody in Britain is
frightened to death of *words.*
So it flies up to a great height and drops them on people
like turds.
It always chooses large assemblies where all sexes are
present
And some of the words it lets fall are very far from
pleasant
To the Puritan ears they strike with a loud thud –
And among the genteel (for this reason) its name has
always been mud.

When the first four-letter words float down you should see
the commuters quail,
As it chants them confidently and firmly on a descending
scale.
They shake the Church and Chapel-going housewives to
the tits
And the policemen are rocked in their boots as each hot
syllable hits
And knocks their helmets sideways. Each Magistrate and
Judge
Looks as though he is choking in a sea of hot chocolate
fudge,
With bursting purple cheeks and a heart-pounding
waistcoat
And big bulging eyes like a lecherous old goat.

The Word-Bird eats dictionaries and any printed matter
Sufficiently scarifying to make the crowds scatter –
But it also has several medical terms up its sleeve
And their effect on those who understand them you would
scarcely believe.

Words that excite with a wild music, like 'penilingism' and
'cunnilingus',
That pierce the brain like the disturbing notes of Charlie
Parker or Charlie Mingus.

And each night when the day is over the Word-Bird
returns to the nest,
And teaches its chickens a few more juicy dirty words
before it retires to rest.

Fiction: The House Party

Ambrose is an Old Etonian and he
is terribly in love with a girl called Fluffy
who has Lesbian tendencies and is very attracted
to a sophisticated debutante called Angela Fondling
who was once the mistress of old Lord Vintage.

Don and Vi come to stay at The Castle
and neither of them know how looking-glasses aren't mirrors
or what wines go best with fish or even how to
handle a butter knife or talk about horses.
Don makes a joke about being unstable.

Fluffy doesn't know where to look and Ambrose
chokes on his claret. His Lordship is thinking
about a certain incident in 1930
when 'Filthy' Fynes-Pantlebury rode a bay gelding
up the main staircase and into a bathroom.

Angela is writing a book about the middle classes,
she keeps giving Don and Vi gin and depth interviews
and trying like a mad thing to understand Bradford.
Lady Vintage is pathetically faded
but she loves a young criminal in London: Reg. Ratcock.

They sometimes meet in the afternoon, on Fridays,
and smoke a lot of pot in the tenement basement.
Ambrose is thinking of taking Holy Orders,
he usually thinks of Fluffy as a very young choirboy.
Vi wants to go to the loo but she's shy about asking.

Lord Vintage has vanished into several daydreams;
he remembers well how Frank Fondling once shot a beater.
Don is getting very tired of gin. Vi wets her knickers.
Fluffy says to Ambrose: 'But what *is* a chasuble?'
And Angela keeps her tape-recorder running . . .

ROGER WODDIS

All Clear

Nobody put their hand out,
Nobody took a bribe,
Nobody was compromised
By acts you could describe.

Nobody got away with it,
Nobody thought they could,
And all of them were honest men,
And all of them were good.

Nobody bought a silver gift
To please somebody's wife,
Nobody did a single thing
To poison public life.

Nobody bought a cabinet,
Whatever you may hear,
And all of them were honest men,
And all were in the clear.

Nobody did a secret deal,
Nobody was for sale,
Nobody bent the rules at all,
And nobody went to jail.

And all of them were honest men,
As white as driven snow,
And all lived on a higher plane,
And shat on those below.

CHARLES CAUSLEY

Betjeman, 1984

I saw him in the Airstrip Gardens
  (Fahrenheit at 451)
Feeding automative orchids
  With a little plastic bun,
While above his brickwork cranium
  Burned the trapped and troubled sun.

'Where is Piper? Where is Pontefract?
  (Devil take my boiling pate!)
Where is Pam? and where's Myfanwy?
  Don't remind me of the date!
Can it be that I am *really*
  Knocking on for 78?

'In my splendid State Apartment
  Underneath a secret lock
Finger now forbidden treasures
  (Pray for me St Enodoc!):
TV plate and concrete lamp-post
  And a single nylon sock.

'Take your ease, pale-haired admirer,
As I, half the century saner,
Pour a vintage Mazawattee
Through the Marks and Spencer strainer
In a *genuine* British Railways
(Luton Made) cardboard container.

'Though they say my verse-compulsion
Lacks an interstellar drive,
Reading Beverley and Daphne
Keeps *my* sense of words alive.
Lord, but *how* much beauty was there
Back in 1935!'

TED PAUKER

A Grouchy Good Night to the Academic Year

(*with acknowledgements to W. M. P.*)

Good night to the Year Academic,
It finally crept to a close:
Dry fact about physic and chemic,
Wet drip about people and prose.
Emotion was down to a snivel
And reason was pulped to a pap,
Sociologists droning out drivel
And critics all croaking out crap.
For any such doctrine is preachable
In our tolerant Temple of Thought
Where lads that are largely unteachable
Learn subjects that cannot be taught.

Good night to the Session – portentous
Inside the Vice-Chancellor's gown,

The personage who'll represent us
To Public and Party and Crown.
By enthusing for nitwitted novelty
He wheedles the moment'ry Great,
And at influence-dinner or grovel-tea
Further worsens the whims of the State.
So it is that, however much *we* rage,
The glibber of heart and of tongue
Build ladders to reach a life-peerage
From the buzz-sawed-up brains of the young,

Good night to the Session – the Chaplain,
Progressive and Ritualist too,
Who refers to the role of the apple in
Eden as 'under review'.
When the whole situation has ripened
Of his temporal hopes these are chief:
A notable increase in stipend,
And the right to abandon belief.
Meanwhile, his sermons: 'The Wafer –
Is it really the Presence of God?'
'Is the Pill or the French Letter Safer?'
And, 'Does the Biretta look Mod?'

Good night to the Session – what Art meant,
Or Science, no longer seemed plain,
But our new Education Department
Confuses confusion again.
'Those *teach* who can't *do*' runs the dictum,
But for some even that's out of reach:
They can't even teach – so they've picked 'em
To teach other people to teach.
Then alas for the next generation,
For the pots fairly crackle with thorn.
Where psychology meets education
A terrible bullshit is born.

Good night to the Session – the students
So eager to put us all right,
Whose conceit might have taken a few dents
But that ploughing's no longer polite;
So the essays drop round us in torrents
Of jargon a mouldering mound,
All worrying weakly at Lawrence,
All drearily pounding at Pound;
And their knowledge would get them through no test
On Ghana or Greece or Vietnam,
But they've mugged up enough for a Protest
– An easyish form of exam.

Good night to the Session – so solemn,
'Truth' and 'Freedom' their crusader crests,
One hardly knows quite what to call 'em
These children with beards or with breasts.
When from State or parental Golcondas
Treasure trickles to such little boys
They spend it on reefers and Hondas
– That is, upon sweeties and toys;
While girls of delicious proportions
Are thronging to Clinic's front stair,
Some of them seeking abortions
And some a psychiatrist's care.

Good night to the Session – the politics,
So noisy, and nagging, and null.
You can tell how the time-bomb of Folly ticks
By applying your ear to their skull;
Of course, that is only a metaphor,
But they have their metaphors too,
Such as 'Fascist', that's hardly the better for
Being used of a liberal and Jew

– The Prof. of Applied Aeronautics,
For failing such students as try,
With LSD lapping their cortex,
To fub up a fresh way to fly.

Good night to the Session – the Union:
The speeches with epigram packed,
So high upon phatic communion,
So low upon logic and fact.
(Those epigrams?–Oh well, at any rate
By now we're all quite reconciled
To a version that's vastly degenerate
From the Greek, via Voltaire and Wilde.)
Then the bold resolutions devoted
To the praise of a party or state
In *this* context most obviously noted
For its zeal in destroying debate.

Good night to the Session – the sculpture:
A jelly containing a clock;
Where they say, 'From the way that you gulped you're
Therapeutically thrilled by the shock!'
– It's the Shock of, alas, Recognition
At what's yearly presented as new
Since first seen at Duchamps' exhibition
'Des Maudits', in Nineteen-O-Two.
But let's go along to the Happening,
Where an artist can really unwind,
Stuff like 'Rapists should not take the rap' penning
In gamboge on a model's behind.

Good night to the Session – a later
Will come – and the freshmen we'll get!
Their pretensions will be even greater,
Their qualifications worse yet.

– But don't be too deeply depressible
At obtuseness aflame for applause;
The louts that are loudest in decibel
Melt away in post-graduate thaws.
Don't succumb to an anger unreasoned!
Most students are charming, and bright;
And even some dons are quite decent . . .
But good night to the Session, good night!

MARTIN BELL

Senilio's Weather Saw

If Church spire be clëar
Twill be däamp round here

If it be not
Twill be bloody hot

When thee caänt see spire
Church be on fire

And we'll hang parson, squire
And the whole bleeding choir.

With a Presentation Copy of Verses

How nice to know Mr MacBeth,
That Harlequin glinter and frisker!
What a gay air of 'I'm Colonel Death!'
Sets twitching each end of his whisker.

His appearance is feline and elegant.
He is certain of each fact he states.

His spectacles prove he's intelligent.
His degree is a good onė (in Greats).

May the verse-form remove my remarks
A little bit higher than platitude;
Though we're off after different Snarks,
Accept this book, George, with my gratitude.

Hemingway, Jimmy Bond, and D'Annunzio
Are not in my line and you know it –
You would surely have been Papal Nuncio
If you were not (hélas) a good poet.

May History's mischievous glass
Not show us out of our decades,
With me primly holding the pass,
And you at the barricades.

EDWIN MORGAN

The First Men on Mercury

– We come in peace from the third planet.
Would you take us to your leader?

– Bawr stretter! Bawr. Bawr. Stretterhawl?

– This is a little plastic model
of the solar system, with working parts.
You are here and we are there and we
are now here with you, is this clear?

– Gawl horrop. Bawr. Abawrhannahanna!

– Where we come from is blue and white
with brown, you see we call the brown
here 'land', the blue is 'sea', and the white
is 'clouds' over land and sea, we live
on the surface of the brown land,
all round is sea and clouds. We are 'men'.
Men come –

– Glawp men! Gawrbenner menko. Menhawl?

– Men come in peace from the third planet
which we call 'earth'. We are earthmen.
Take us earthmen to your leader.

– Thmen? Thmen? Bawr. Bawrhossop.
Yuleeda tan hanna. Harrabost yuleeda.

– I am the yuleeda. You see my hands,
we carry no benner, we come in peace.
The spaceways are all stretterhawn.

– Glawn peacemen all horrobhanna tantko!
Tan come at'mstrossop. Glawp yuleeda!

– Atoms are peacegawl in our harraban.
Menbat worrabost from tan hannahanna.

– ou men we know bawrhossoptant. Bawr.
We know yuleeda. Go strawg backspetter quick.

– We cantantabawr, tantingko backspetter now!

– Banghapper now! Yes, third planet back.
Yuleeda will go back blue, white, brown
nowhanna! There is no more talk.

– Gawl han fasthapper?

– No. You must go back to your planet.
Go back in peace, take what you have gained
but quickly.

– Stretterworra gawl, gawl . . .

– Of course, but nothing is ever the same,
now is it? You'll remember Mercury.

ROBERT GREACEN

Ten New Commandments

1st. No other God exists than Mighty Me,
2nd. Worship the vulgar idols of TV.
3rd. Say 'God' when laughing or to be provoking.
4th. No Sunday overtime? You must be joking!
5th. Revile your Dad, break Mother's heart,
6th. Remember murder is a necessary art.
7th. Adultery clearly shows sophistication
8th. And theft's the hallmark of a clever nation.
9th. False witness leads to increased dividends,
10th. And envy's the prerogative of friends.

D. J. ENRIGHT

Royalties

As 'Name of individual, partnership, or corporation to
whom paid'
I find my own, followed by (in brackets) 'Faust'.
The amount of income received in this capacity is $3.30
gross,
From which I am glad to see no tax has been withheld.

Egotist as he is
One had never thought the Devil so close-fisted.
He wasn't always:
Gretchen – Helen – contributions to knowledge – all that
real estate . . .
What can have changed him?

And yet, Goethe only lasted a couple of months after
completing his masterpiece,
So I could even be said to be lucky, nearly twenty-four
years after publication, still making \$3.30 out of a
little crib of the Master's epic designed for
non-German-speaking near-dropouts taking the
World Literature course.

None of us, it seems, even though no tax is deducted, gets
much for selling his soul.
The sea took back the land, Gretchen lost her head, Helen
was incorporeal, the scholarship soon discredited;
Faust died the moment he started to enjoy life; and
Goethe's poetry is supplanted by a crib –
It was always a buyer's market, always.

PHILIP LARKIN

Naturally the Foundation Will Bear Your Expenses

Hurrying to catch my Comet
One dark November day,
Which soon would snatch me from it
To the sunshine of Bombay,
I pondered pages Berkeley
Not three weeks since had heard,
Perceiving Chatto darkly
Through the mirror of the Third.

Crowds, colourless and careworn,
   Had made my taxi late,
Yet not till I was airborne
   Did I recall the date –
That day when Queen and Minister
   And Band of Guards and all
Still act their solemn-sinister
   Wreath-rubbish in Whitehall.

It used to make me throw up,
   These mawkish nursery games:
O when will England grow up?
   – But I outsoar the Thames,
And dwindle off down Auster
   To greet Professor Lal
(He once met Morgan Forster),
   My contact and my pal.

Self's the Man

Oh, no one can deny
That Arnold is less selfish than I.
He married a woman to stop her getting away
Now she's there all day,

And the money he gets for wasting his life on work
She takes as her perk
To pay for the kiddies' clobber and the drier
And the electric fire,

And when he finishes supper
Planning to have a read at the evening paper
It's *Put a screw in this wall* –
He has no time at all,

With the nippers to wheel round the houses
And the hall to paint in his old trousers
And that letter to her mother
Saying *Won't you come for the summer.*

To compare his life and mine
Makes me feel a swine:
Oh, no one can deny
That Arnold is less selfish than I.

But wait, not so fast:
Is there such a contrast?
He was out for his own ends
Not just pleasing his friends;

And if it was such a mistake
He still did it for his own sake,
Playing his own game.
So he and I are the same,

Only I'm a better hand
At knowing what I can stand
Without them sending a van –
Or I suppose I can.

Vers de Société

My wife and I have asked a crowd of craps
To come and waste their time and ours: perhaps
You'd care to join us? In a pig's arse, friend.
Day comes to an end.
The gas fire breathes, the trees are darkly swayed.
And so *Dear Warlock-Williams: I'm afraid –*

Funny how hard it is to be alone.
I could spend half my evenings, if I wanted,
Holding a glass of washing sherry, canted
Over to catch the drivel of some bitch
Who's read nothing but *Which*;
Just think of all the spare time that has flown

Straight into nothingness by being filled
With forks and faces, rather than repaid
Under a lamp, hearing the noise of wind,
And looking out to see the moon thinned
To an air-sharpened blade.
A life, and yet how sternly it's instilled

All solitude is selfish. No one now
Believes the hermit with his gown and dish
Talking to God (who's gone too); the big wish
Is to have people nice to you, which means
Doing it back somehow.
Virtue is social. Are, then, these routines

Playing at goodness, like going to church?
Something that bores us, something we don't do well
(Asking that ass about his fool research)
But try to feel, because, however crudely,
It shows us what should be?
Too subtle, that. Too decent, too. Oh hell,

Only the young can be alone freely.
The time is shorter now for company,
And sitting by a lamp more often brings
Not peace, but other things.
Beyond the light stand failure and remorse
Whispering *Dear Warlock-Williams: Why, of course –*

HOWARD MOSS

Tourists

Cramped like sardines on the Queens, and sedated,
The sittings all first, the roommates mismated,

Three nuns at the table, the waiter a barber,
Then dumped with their luggage at some frumpish harbour,

Veering through rapids in a vapid *rapido*
To view the new moon from a ruin on the Lido,

Or a sundown in London from a rundown Mercedes,
Then high-borne to Glyndebourne for Orféo in Hades,

Embarrassed in Paris in Harris tweed, dying to
Get to the next museum piece that they're flying to,

Finding, in Frankfurt, that one indigestible
Comestible makes them too ill for the festival,

Footloose in Lucerne, or taking a pub in in
Glasgow or Belfast, or maudlin in Dublin, in-

sensitive, garrulous, querulous, audible,
Drunk in the Dolomites, tuning a portable,

Homesick in Stockholm, or dressed to toboggan
At the wrong time of year in too dear Copenhagen,

Generally being too genial or hostile –
Too grand at the Grand, too old at the Hostel –

Humdrum conundrums, what's to become of them?
Most will come home, but there will be some of them

Subsiding like Lawrence in Florence, or crazily
Ending up tending shop up in Fiesole.

ANTHONY BRODE

Calypsomania

Now the trouble with SETting down a: written calypso
Is some folks MAY conclude the: printer's a dipso
Maniac, that's partly be:cause of the tmesis
(Cutting words: into pieces)
And also on account of there is: little relation
Between the line enDINGS and the: punctuation.
Calypso, lovely calypso,
It slaps on a chap's lower lip so –
You may believe that IT'S just irregular verse
But the more you want it casual the: more you rehearse.

Well it's certainly good to:be alive,
That's one thing OF: which I'm positIVE,
So THREE cheers for the Government: which subsidizes
Us poor calypso-writers with: annual prIzes!
For I'm bound to SAY more: calypsos would be written
If commissioned by the Arts CounCIL: of Great Britain.

Calypso, lovely calypso,
It can make phraseology trip so –
It doesn't signiFY if the metre is unsure
Because the meaning tends to be to:tally obscure.

Now to all criTICS who: quiver like jelly at
The thought of a calypso by: T. S. Eliot,
I wish to STATE that: there are poets and musicians,
Singers also, with: hidden ambitions –
Operatic calypsos: will get society cheers
If COMposed by Britten and sung by Pears.

Calypso, lovely calypso,
It allows every syllable to slip so –
Many a person who will never be a poet
Is tempted by: calypsos to show it.

ALAN ROSS

Cricket at Oxford

Pedalling between lectures, spokes throwing off
Sun like Catherine wheels, the damp grass
Bestowing its sweetness from a long way off –
Perhaps the Australians were playing
On a May morning, family saloons
Swaying down the Broad en route
For the Parks, the whole city –
It seemed to me then – going about
In a daze, who won the toss,
Who's batting? And arrived,
Breathless from the Taylorian, pockets stuffed
With indecipherable notes on Baudelaire
Les diverses beautés qui parent ta jeunesse
And Rimbaud, it was to exchange
A *fin de siècle* poetry for the more immediate
Mesmeric magic of the scorecard –
Macindoe, Lomas, and hazier behind them
Indelible syllables of those lingering others,
Walford, De Saram, Bosanquet, Pataudi.
All day we would marvel at technique
Exercised, it seemed, for its own sake,
The extending of a tradition, as might
Language be refined: an innings
By McCabe packed with epigrams,
Bradman ruthless as if sacking a city.

'Pick, pack, pock, puck', Joyce's
'Drops of water in a fountain
Falling softly in the brimming bowl.'
Language and stroke play, the honey
Of the bats against the trees
Whose green might have been arranged
By Poussin or Claude, grouped just so –
That park-music, connived at
And returned to how often for solace –
A refrain running through the years,
Faintly discernible, whatever the distance.

KINGSLEY AMIS

A Bookshop Idyll

Between the GARDENING and the COOKERY
  Comes the brief POETRY shelf;
By the Nonesuch Donne, a thin anthology
  Offers itself.

Critical, and with nothing else to do,
  I scan the Contents page,
Relieved to find the names are mostly new;
  No one my age.

Like all strangers, they divide by sex:
  Landscape near Parma
Interests a man, so does *The Double Vortex*,
  So does *Rilke and Buddha*.

'I travel, you see', 'I think' and 'I can read'
  These titles seem to say;
But *I Remember You*, *Love is my Creed*,
  Poem for J.,

The ladies' choice, discountenance my patter
  For several seconds;
From somewhere in this (as in any) matter
  A moral beckons.

Should poets bicycle-pump the human heart
  Or squash it flat?
Man's love is of man's life a thing apart;
  Girls aren't like that.

We men have got love well weighed up; our stuff
  Can get by without it.
Women don't seem to think that's good enough;
  They write about it,

And the awful way their poems lay them open
  Just doesn't strike them.
Women are really much nicer than men:
  No wonder we like them.

Deciding this, we can forget those times
  We sat up half the night
Chockfull of love, crammed with bright thoughts, names,
    rhymes,
  And couldn't write.

ANTHONY HECHT

The Dover Bitch

A Criticism of Life
for Andrews Wanning

So there stood Matthew Arnold and this girl
With the cliffs of England crumbling away behind them,
And he said to her, 'Try to be true to me,
And I'll do the same for you, for things are bad
All over, etc., etc.'
Well now, I knew this girl. It's true she had read
Sophocles in a fairly good translation
And caught that bitter allusion to the sea,
But all the time he was talking she had in mind
The notion of what his whiskers would feel like
On the back of her neck. She told me later on
That after a while she got to looking out
At the lights across the channel, and really felt sad,
Thinking of all the wine and enormous beds
And blandishments in French and the perfumes.
And then she got really angry. To have been brought
All the way down from London, and then be addressed
As a sort of mournful cosmic last resort
Is really tough on a girl, and she was pretty.
Anyway, she watched him pace the room
And finger his watch-chain and seem to sweat a bit,
And then she said one or two unprintable things.
But you mustn't judge her by that. What I mean to say is,
She's really all right. I still see her once in a while
And she always treats me right. We have a drink
And I give her a good time, and perhaps it's a year
Before I see her again, but there she is,
Running to fat, but dependable as they come.
And sometimes I bring her a bottle of *Nuit d'Amour*.

Anthony Hecht

The Man Who Married Magdalene

Variation on a Theme by Louis Simpson

Then said the Lord, dost thou well to be angry?

I have been in this bar
For close to seven days.
The dark girl over there,
For a modest dollar, lays.

And you can get a blow-job
Where other men have pissed
In the little room that's sacred
To the Evangelist –

If you're inclined that way.
For myself, I drink and sleep.
The floor is knotty cedar
But the beer is flat and cheap.

And you can bet your life
I'll be here another seven.
Stranger, here's to my wife,
Who died and went to Heaven.

She was a famous beauty,
But *our very breath is loaned.*
The rabbi's voice was fruity,
And since then I've been stoned –

A royal, nonstop bender.
But your money's no good here;
Put it away. Bartender,
Give my friend a beer.

I dreamed the other night
When the sky was full of stars
That I stood outside a gate
And looked in through the bars.

Two angels stood together.
A purple light was shed
From their every metal feather.
And then one of them said,

'It was pretty much the same
For years and years and years,
But since the Christians came
The place is full of queers.

Still, let them have their due.
Things here are far less solemn.
Instead of each beardy Jew
Muttering, "Shalom, Shalom,"

There's a down-to-earth, informal
Fleshiness to the scene;
It's healthier, more normal,
If you know what I mean.

Such as once went to Gehenna
Now dance among the blessed.
But Mary Magdalena,
She had it the best.'

And he nudged his feathered friend
And gave him a wicked leer,
And I woke up and fought back
The nausea with a beer.

What man shall understand
The Lord's mysterious way?
My tongue is thick with worship
And whiskey, and some day

I will come to in Bellevue
And make psalms unto the Lord.
But verily I tell you,
She hath her reward.

Samuel Sewall

Samuel Sewall, in a world of wigs,
Flouted opinion in his personal hair;
For foppery he gave not any figs,
But in his right and honor took the air.

Thus in his naked style, though well attired,
He went forth in the city, or paid court
To Madam Winthrop, whom he much admired,
Most godly, but yet liberal with the port.

And all the town admired for two full years
His excellent address, his gifts of fruit,
Her gracious ways and delicate white ears,
And held the course of nature absolute.

But yet she bade him suffer a peruke,
'That One be not distinguished from the All';
Delivered of herself this stern rebuke
Framed in the resonant language of St Paul.

'Madam,' he answered her, 'I have a Friend
Furnishes me with hair out of His strength,
And He requires only I attend
Unto His charity and to its length.'

And all the town was witness to his trust:
On Monday he walked out with the Widow Gibbs,
A pious lady of charm and notable bust,
Whose heart beat tolerably beneath her ribs.

On Saturday he wrote proposing marriage,
And closed, imploring that she be not cruel,
'Your favorable answer will oblige,
Madam, your humble servant, Samuel Sewall.'

LAURENCE LERNER

Arthur's Anthology of English Poetry[1]

To be or not to be, that is the question
To justify the ways of God to men
There was a time when meadow grove and stream
The dropping of the daylight in the west
Otters below and moorhens on the top
Had fallen in Lyonesse about their Lord.

There was a time when moorhens on the top
To justify the daylight in the west,
To be or not to be about their Lord
Had fallen in Lyonesse from God to men;
Otters below and meadow grove and stream,
The dropping of the day, that is the question.

A time when Lyonesse and grove and stream
To be the daylight in the west on top
When meadow otters fallen about their Lord
To justify the moorhens is the question
Or not to be the dropping God to men
There was below the ways that is a time.

[1] Arthur is a computer.

To be in Lyonesse, that is the question
To justify the otters, is the question
The dropping of the meadows, is the question

I do not know the answer to the question

There was a time when moorhens in the west
There was a time when daylight on the top
There was a time when God was not a question

There was a time when poets

Then I came

JAMES K. BAXTER

Obsequy for Dylan Thomas

A gallon of gin and a flitch of pork,
Thomas lies snug-a-bed in New York.
Flat on her back in the big whorehouse
The English Language mourns her spouse.
She weeps as she works and keeps the tally.
He won't bowl home from Dead Man's Alley.
He drinks with the Great Bear and the Plough.
    The short-stitch tailors,
    The coffin nailers
The bedlam jailors
        have her now.

From *Cressida*

1 In the Lecture Room

The lecturer's impartial prose
    Droned in the raftered room;

Through a mock-Gothic window rose
   The soft weir water's boom.

The blonde girl in the second bench
   Biting her pencil, sighed –
Thought 'If I lowered my frock an inch
   It would look well in that shade.'

The young man at the back, half-turning
   To see her profile, smiled;
Thought 'She has a scholar's learning
   And the innocence of a child.'

The clock in the college tower broke
   On sparrows' private lives:
The lecturer cleared his throat and spoke
   Of McDougall's instinctive drives;

Paused a moment in his talk,
   Massaged an itching wen,
Doodled a diagram in chalk
   And rubbed it off again.

2 Bar Room Conversation

A lorry made the windows shake
And noon light on the sour spilt beer
Quivered. 'A widow's an easy make,'

He said, 'you pedal and let her steer;
Or the next best is a girl inclined
To play, but her man's away for a year.

'And she's too shy or he's too blind.
None of your nattering flirts – they're hard –
But one of the Sunday school teacher kind

Ripe and ready behind her guard.'
Gently the other sipped his drink;
The barman wrote on a doubles card.

He said, 'I saw her first at the rink,
Danced and yarned and took it slow.
She's come to trust me now, I think.

'Ten weeks of bringing her home by moonglow
With a kiss and cuddle at the gate –
No more. Tonight we'll go to a show

'At Dan's – I bet you a dollar, mate,
With a drink or two she'll turn it up.'
In the yard a lorry unloaded a crate;
The barman polished a football cup.

The Private Conference of Harry Fat

Said Harry Fat to Holyoake,
'With fools outside the door,
Wise men within, I'll tell you straight
I hate the sulky boor
Who flaunts his dirty fingernails
And never owned a store.'

'Oh, yes indeed,' said Holyoake,
'We've met their kind before.'

Said Harry Fat, 'I've read about
A doll who liked to sing,
And when you tapped his wooden head
His little bell would ring.
I like the kind of country where
The little man is king.'

'I quite agree,' said Holyoake,
'It is a splendid thing.'

Said Harry Fat, 'I've heard it said
The Civil Service needs
Protection from the Communists
Who sow rebellious seeds.
The right man in the right place
Will pluck them out like weeds.'

'We must keep watch,' said Holyoake,
'On any man who reads.'

Said Harry Fat, 'If you will take
A business man's advice –
Tell me a voter's income
And I'll tell you his price;
Although it's wiser not to come
With the same promise twice.'

'Upon my word,' said Holyoake,
'The point is very nice.'

Said Harry Fat, 'I call the man
Who digs my garden, "Bert".
He has his place and I have mine,
His job's to shovel dirt.
But I'll have no truck with a Chinese ape
Who wears a peasant shirt.'

'Except with guns,' said Holyoake –
'The message then is curt.'

Said Harry Fat to Holyoake,
'To falter would be sin;
But oh I had a fearful dream
When the small hours begin;

I dreamt I was a mouse inside
   A mangy lion skin.'

'We are the truth,' said Holyoake,
'The truth will always win.'

(1956)

Harry Fat and Uncle Sam

Said Uncle Sam to Harry Fat,
   'Your folks are fine to know
And it's great the way your island
   Keeps afloat there Down Below,
But you need the global attitude
   To produce a first class show.'

'Just give me time,' said Harry Fat,
'And the tourist trade will grow.'

'It's not my place,' said Uncle Sam,
   'To give advice to you,
But you don't know how to break a strike
   Of monkeys in a zoo.
Our Company policemen could
   Teach yours a thing or two.'

'I'll change the Law,' said Harry Fat,
'It's an easy thing to do.'

'The dollar talks,' said Uncle Sam,
   'And you've a lot to learn.
How come you let your Varsity Reds
   Play possum in the fern
With no interrogations?
   Turn on the heat: they'll burn.'

'We'll start today,' said Harry Fat,
'And fry them each in turn.'

'Your folks don't know,' said Uncle Sam,
  'What entertainment means
For a trigger-happy tourist
  With a dollar in his jeans.
No whorehouse on the corner
  Was a grief to our Marines.'

'Try Mazengarb,' wrote Harry Fat,
'For some talent in the teens.'

'To tell you straight,' said Uncle Sam,
  'Your hotel service stinks.
Each dame should get an orchid
  At her table with the drinks;
And we're used to a Negro bellhop
  Who'll say sorry when he blinks.'

'Try Corbett next,' wrote Harry Fat,
'And find out what he thinks.'

'With a few things done,' said Uncle Sam,
  'I guess your country soon
Will make the grade – Jeepers! I'd like
  To hear a crooner croon
With an off-white broad beside me
  Under a Pig Island moon.'

'Bring dollars in,' said Harry Fat,
'And you can call the tune.'

(*1956*)

Spring Song of A Civil Servant

In corridor and cubicle
The vine is pulling bricks apart
Underneath my fishbone armour
Beats a wild Othello's heart
And between the cup and saucer

Many a savage dream is born
Of Desdemona's eyeballs popping
Fantasy ah fantasy
Above my dome the flies hedge-hopping
Come to a perfect three-point-landing

Nevertheless notwithstanding
Eighteen hundred memoranda
A girl with sand inside her socks
Would find me ready to philander
But my Sunday spouse awaits

Car-key door-key vacuum cleaner
And the lions [1] cannot win
Caged up in Athletic Park
Tonight I'll have a double gin
The outlook for the id is dark.

(*1956*)

CHRISTOPHER MIDDLETON

Adelaide's Dream

he came in she said he had come in
his mouth was over my nipple here
quietly behind me after we had driven
and I felt it to the bones all the way
in his truck beside him then down

[1] The British Lions, a Rugby Football team

my side a spring pleasure vague except
for his smile he was welling in my
stomach and he touched me black it was
beautiful then we were on between my
legs gently as his mouth the bed and
still it was vague taking down my body
and his body turned so my clothes off
and as he stripped his that before me
I saw his dark legs blackness shone
and you were here and I stroked them
with both hands as well sitting on
that chair but we lay and kissed them
and my mouth was open worried what you
would say for a moment over his phallus
he was holding my buttocks with both
hands his head was between my legs and
his tongue was working along my sex
which wanted inside of my legs and then
into me I wanted all of him to come in
as well touched his phallus with my
tongue first as this tongue working far
in and the tip with its small hole pink
flesh running my skin was off I mean it
was all from the top and down then the
veins my mouth moved up and down then
they stood out on it his shining phallus
sucking playing silk tendrils very warm
it was so hard heavy with little bites
his tongue was my mouth closed on the
top and I let it in me burning I began
to cry go into my mouth deep feeling
that cord with the pleasure of it with
my tongue against the insides of my legs
was the press of his head and then you
were standing naked near the skin of his
face he had turned now his cool black
body I wanted it all I knew that he was

over me and he sucked my breasts near
to coming as the head rosy mouth as he
lay on me now I felt his whole phallus
going in moist in spasms the bed he looked
up he was in me and his thrusts faster
enter me to the core I gripped and you
were over me his sides with my legs
bringing my knees pulsing in my mouth
as my tongue right up with you now
leaning into me then played with it
and I was and you and your phallus
coming too it was all at once was in
my mouth too I felt the warm stiff as
he came into me the huge hardness of it
there and sucked it and my hands warm
spurts rocking me held your legs
pressing so that I moaned and as I came
down over him you into me like spring
rains and your seeds spurted into my
mouth and we were all moving at once
in white jets I swallowed moaning I do
not know how long we lay there
afterwards I believe
we began again
with the Chinese girl
who must have come through the window
up to her thigh as she straddled
the sill I saw the black arm reach out
and hand take her down and was
running his hand under the knee
the dress pulled around her bottom
turned her over and I could not resist
giving a little suck pulled her dress
off her very black and as he held her
breasts from behind hair thrown out
across your phallus his black thighs

closed in on the rounds now so near
my mouth again of her buttocks and I
saw the whole length and I stood up
over her back offering his phallus slowly
drive into her she my sex to his mouth
his tongue was rocking back and forth
on him gently in me against my legs
holding his head under me I felt softness
her skin she had moved her head the
Chinese girl rocking and moaning sweetly
against the backs of my legs to take you
into her mouth then we changed places
you were in me between the Chinese girl's
thighs her warm and hard and he was over
me until I don't know how you were in
her his phallus in my mouth his head
so you could hold her knees and me
under him as I saw your mouth close
on her little left breast and his close
on the monkey came in the monkey came
in her right breast and planted on our
happy moaning mound and beat his chest
jumping his hairy feet and screaming
he was very hairy

EDWARD GOREY

Three Black Limericks

I

An incautious young woman named Venn
Was seen with the wrong sort of men;
    She vanished one day,
    But the following May
Her legs were retrieved from a fen.

2

The Dowager Duchess of Spout
Collapsed at the height of a rout;
    She found strength to say
    As they bore her away:
'I should never have taken the trout.'

3

As tourists inspected the apse
An ominous series of raps
    Came from under the altar,
    Which caused some to falter
And others to shriek and collapse.

GERDA MAYER

Drip Drip or Not Bloody Likely

I watch the grains of blood pour/ blood slides through his fingers/ somebody is killing me I think/ at my feet I see a river of blood/ blood is our birth rite/ my bridal gifts turn to blood/ an angel limping backwards in blood/ the moon will not stop bleeding/ my blood is running with the speed of ice/ a fungus in the bowels squeezing blood/out of a crowd comes blood/ he sliced the lean red bodies with the breadknife & dipped his fingers in the ooze and licked his fingers/ your fruits bleeding at knife point/ the breed is fed dim blood/ blood black over blackened skin/ the harvest field is black with blood/ hear my blood moving/ blood made cunning/ it bled with venom/ my pointed teeth always seek out flesh/ my head bleeds/ peck till the blood comes/ etc. etc.

Quotations (chapter and verse on request) from women's anthologies, women's poems etc.

Fashionable blood
is up
to no sort of good

It drips now & then
(after a lot of moonshine)
from the female pen

To show that woman isn't just ethereal
but womblike
deep and mysterial

Blood is a curse
I don't
let it slop over *my* verse

Echo and Narcissus

When sweet Echo met Narcissus
She desired to be his missus.
But Narcissus took a dekko
At himself and not at Echo.
Now forever must he shiver
As he hovers o'er the river.
Echo too is out of luck
All she wanted was a man to love and to cherish her.

Song

Does the policeman sleep with his boots on,
with his helmet on,
with his boots on?
Does the policeman sleep with his boots on
with his whistle at the ready on his pad?

PETER PORTER

The World of Simon Raven

Rooks are raging where great elms were felled,
Family silver's been lent for the Fête,
Nanny's facing Nigel with stained sheets,
Telegrams announce James is expelled,
Mrs Diamond from Sea View Estate
Tempts a team in training with boiled sweets.

Meanwhile sturgeon from Odessa packed
For Black's and Tan's, renowned St James's Clubs,
Laced with spanish fly, cause randy scenes
At Ascot, a Bishop's face is smacked;
Debs and guardsmen break up Chelsea pubs,
Blackmailers send snaps to dons at Queen's.

Unpaid Mess Bills get a Blue cashiered,
Boys from Balham pelt a First in Greats
With Latin Grammars, Israeli agents
Put pubic lice in Prince Muhammad's beard,
Doctor Boyce cuts off his cousin Kate's
Clitoris – the favourite fails the fence,

Bookies' reminders frighten Adjutants,
Crockford's man is found with a marked deck.
Somewhere beyond Maidenhead an old
Lady rings her bank for an advance
On her pension, sends her son a cheque,
Watches with the cat as it gets cold.

From *Nine Points of the Law*

Managed as they say about such men
To get his foot on the ladder; owed
His success to his first wife and his second
Wife to his success. Took that car
All the way to Smyrna, argued in Turkish,
Powers that helped him swing a boardroom.
Used nicknames in the pits and nobody
Winced, carved thin like a seaside
Landlady and everyone called it eccentric,
Mended his own fuses. Was seen once
Crying on a northern station, his book
On coarse fishing dropped and the tan boxer
Licking his hand with unforced love.
We do not mind if our city is known for him,
That the unnamed scavengers of fact
Catch him asleep, this ambitious planner
Who had no imagination and did well.
Call him suzerain of green – it will destroy him.

St Cecilia's Day Epigram

Annotators agree Composer X
Though always in love never had sex,

While a thousand motets and masses lie
To the credit of sex-mad Composer Y,

And that lover of life, Composer Z
In his operas wishes he were dead.

Each in his paradoxical way
Does a lot for the famous Critic K.

ANTHONY THWAITE

A Girdle Round the Earth

'King Rear was foorish man his girls make crazy'
Says something certainly about the play.
'Prutus fall on sord for bolitical reason'
Is unambiguous, though not the way
We native-speakers might have put it, who share
A language with the undoubted global poet.
In Tokyo or Benghazi, he abides
Our questioning syllabus still, will never stay
For an answer as the candidates all stare
Into the glossaried cryptograms he hides.

O Saku Seppiya, Shakhs Bey-er, O you
Who plague the schools and universities
From Patagonia to Pakistan,
From Thailand to Taiwan, how would it please
Your universal spirit to look down
And see the turbans and burnouses bent
Above your annotated texts, or see
Simplified Tales from Lamb by slow degrees
Asphyxiate the yellow and the brown?
To pick up the quotation, 'thou art free' –

But Matthew Arnold, schools inspector, who
Saw you 'self-school'd, self-scann'd', could not have known
How distantly from Stratford and the Globe
With British Council lecturers you've flown:
Midsummer Nights in Prague and Kathmandu,
Polonius stabbed dressed in a gallabiyah,
Shylock the Palestinian refugee,
And Hamlet's father's Serbo-Croat groan,
Dunsinane transported to Peru,
Kabuki for All's Well, Noh for King Lear.

'To be or not to be. Is that a question?'
The misquotations littering the page,
The prose translations fingermarked with sweat,
You prove again, world-wide, 'not of an age
But for all time', the English Ala' ad-Din,
'The Western Chikamatsu', more than both
And different from either, somehow worth
Those sun-baked hours in echoing lecture-halls,
On torn tatami or dune-drifted stage:
'Lady Macbeth is houswif full of sin',
'Prince Hel is drinkard tho of nobel berth'.

On Consulting 'Contemporary Poets of the English Language'

Dannie Abse, Douglas Dunn,
Andrew Waterman, Thom Gunn,
Peter Redgrove, Gavin Ewart,
Susan Fromberg Schaeffer, Stewart
Conn, Pete Brown, Elizabeth
Jennings, Jim Burns, George MacBeth,
Vernon Scannell, Edwin Brock,
Philip Hobsbaum, Fleur Adcock,
Brian Patten, Patricia Beer,
Colin Falck, David Rokeah,
Peter Dale and David Gill,
David Holbrook, Geoffrey Hill,
David Gascoyne and John Hewitt,
William Empson and Frank Prewett,
Norman Hidden, David Wright,
Philip Larkin, Ivan White,
Stephen Spender, Tom McGrath,
dom silvester houédard,
A. Alvarez, Herbert Lomas,
D.M., R.S., Donald Thomas,

Causley, Cunningham, Wes Magee,
Silkin, Simmons, Laurie Lee,
Peter Jay, Laurence Lerner,
David Day, W. Price Turner,
Peter Porter, Seamus Deane,
Hugo Williams, Seamus Heane-
y, Jonathan Green, Nina Steane,
C. Busby Smith and F. Pratt Green,
Fullers both and Joneses all,
Donald Davie, Donald Hall,
Muldoon, Middleton, Murphy, Miller,
Tomlinson, Tonks, Turnbull, Tiller,
Barker, Brownjohn, Blackburn, Bell,
Kirkup, Kavanagh, Kendrick, Kell,
McGough, Maclean, MacSweeney, Schmidt,
Hughes (of *Crow*) and (of *Millstone Grit*),
Sir John Waller Bt. and Major Rook,
Ginsberg, Corso, Stanley Cook,
Peter Scupham, John Heath-Stubbs,
Fenton, Feinstein, both the Grubbs,
Holloway G., Holloway J.,
Anselm Hollo and Peter Way,
Logue, O'Connor, Kevin Crossley-
Holland, Hollander, Keith Bosley,
Matthew Mead and Erica Jong,
Henry Reed and Patience Strong,
Kunitz, Kiser, Kops, Mark Strand,
Creeley, Merwin, Dickey and
The other Dickeys, Eberhart,
Bunting, Wantling, Pilling, Mart-
in Booth, a Dorn and then a Knight,
A Comfort following on a Blight,
Skelton (not the Rector of Diss –
The Poet's Calling Robin, this),
Alistair Elliot, Alastair Reid,
Michael Longley, Michael Fried,

Ian Hamilton (twice – the Scot
With 'Finlay' at the end, and the other not),
Adrians Henri, Mitchell, Stokes,
Lucie-Smith and Philip Oakes,
Father Levi of the Soc-
iety of Jesus, Alan Ross,
Betjeman, Nicholson, Grigson, Walker,
Pitter, Amis, Hilary Corke, a
Decad of Smiths, a Potts and a Black,
Roberts Conquest, Mezey, Graves and Pack,
Hugh MacDiarmid (C. M. Grieve's
His real name, of course), James Reeves,
Hamburger, Stallworthy, Dickinson, Prynne,
Jeremy Hooker, Bartholomew Quinn,
Durrell, Gershon, Harwood, Mahon,
Edmond Wright, Nathaniel Tarn,
Sergeant, Snodgrass, C. K. Stead,
William Shakespeare (no, he's dead),
Cole and Mole and Lowell and Bly,
Robert Nye and Atukwei Okai,
Christopher Fry and George Mackay
Brown, Wayne Brown, John Wain, K. Raine,
Jenny Joseph, Jeni Couzyn,
D. J. Enright, J. C. Hall,
C. H. Sisson and all and all . . .
What is it, you may ask, that Thwaite's
Up to in this epic? Yeats'
Remark in the Cheshire Cheese one night
With poets so thick they blocked the light:
'No one can tell who has talent, if any.
Only one thing is certain. We are too many'.

GREGORY CORSO

Marriage

Should I get married? Should I be good?
Astound the girl next door
with my velvet suit and faustus hood?
Don't take her to movies but to cemeteries
tell all about werewolf bathtubs and forked clarinets
then desire her and kiss her and all the preliminaries
and she going just so far and I understanding why
not getting angry saying You must feel! It's beautiful to feel!
Instead take her in my arms
lean against an old crooked tombstone
and woo her the entire night the constellations in the sky –

When she introduces me to her parents
back straightened, hair finally combed, strangled by a tie,
should I sit knees together on their 3rd degree sofa
and not ask Where's the bathroom?
How else to feel other than I am,
often thinking Flash Gordon soap –
O how terrible it must be for a young man
seated before a family and the family thinking
We never saw him before! He wants our Mary Lou!
After tea and homemade cookies they ask
What do you do for a living?
Should I tell them? Would they like me then?
Say All right get married, we're not losing a daughter
we're gaining a son –
And should I then ask Where's the bathroom?

O God, and the wedding! All her family and her friends
and only a handful of mine all scroungy and bearded
just waiting to get at the drinks and food –
And the priest! he looking at me as if I masturbated

asking me Do you take this woman
for your lawful wedded wife!
And I trembling what to say say Pie Glue!
I kiss the bride all those corny men slapping me on the back
She's all yours, boy! Ha-ha-ha!
And in their eyes you could see
some obscene honeymoon going on –
Then all that absurd rice and clanky cans and shoes
Niagara Falls! Hordes of us!
Husbands! Wives! Flowers! Chocolates!
All streaming into cosy hotels
All going to do the same thing tonight
The indifferent clerk he knowing what was going to happen
The lobby zombies they knowing what
The whistling elevator man he knowing
The winking bellboy knowing
Everybody knowing!
I'd be almost inclined not to do anything!
Stay up all night! Stare that hotel clerk in the eye!
Screaming: I deny honeymoon! I deny honeymoon!
running rampant into those almost climactic suites
yelling Radio belly! Cat shovel!
O I'd live in Niagara forever! in a dark cave beneath the Falls
I'd sit there the Mad Honeymooner
devising ways to break marriages, a source of bigamy
a saint of divorce –

But I should get married I should be good
How nice it'd be to come home to her
and sit by the fireplace and she in the kitchen
aproned young and lovely wanting my baby
and so happy about me she burns the roast beef
and comes crying to me and I get up from my big papa chair
saying Christmas teeth! Radiant brains! Apple deaf!
God what a husband I'd make! Yes, I should get married!
So much to do! like sneaking into Mr Jones' house late at night

and cover his golf clubs with 1920 Norwegian books
Like hanging a picture of Rimbaud on the lawnmower
Like pasting Tannu Tuva postage stamps
all over the picket fence
Like when Mrs Kindhead comes to collect
for the Community Chest
grab her and tell her There are unfavourable omens in the sky!
And when the mayor comes to get my vote tell him
When are you going to stop people killing whales!
And when the milkman comes leave him a note in the bottle
Penguin dust, bring me penguin dust, I want penguin dust –

Yet if I should get married and it's Connecticut and snow
and she gives birth to a child and I am sleepless, worn,
up for nights, head bowed against a quiet window
the past behind me,
finding myself in the most common of situations
a trembling man knowledged with responsibility
not twig-smear nor Roman coin soup –
O what would that be like!
Surely I'd give it for a nipple a rubber Tacitus
For a rattle a bag of broken Bach records
Tack Della Francesca all over its crib
Sew the Greek alphabet on its bib
And build for its playpen a roofless Parthenon
No, I doubt I'd be that kind of father
not rural not snow no quiet window
but hot smelly tight New York City
seven flights up, roaches and rats in the walls
a fat Reichian wife screeching over potatoes Get a job!
And five nose running brats in love with Batman
And the neighbours all toothless and dry haired
like those hag masses of the eighteenth century
all wanting to come in and watch TV
The landlord wants his rent
Grocery store Blue Cross Gas & Electric Knights of Columbus

Impossible to lie back and dream
Telephone snow, ghost parking –
No! I should not get married I should never get married!
But – imagine if I were married
to a beautiful sophisticated woman
tall and pale wearing an elegant black dress
and long black gloves
holding a cigarette holder in one hand
and a highball in the other
and we lived high up in a penthouse with a huge window
from which we could see all of New York
and even further on clearer days
No, can't imagine myself married to that pleasant prison dream –

O but what about love? I forget love
not that I am incapable of love
it's just that I see love as odd as wearing shoes –
I never wanted to marry a girl who was like my mother
And Ingrid Bergman was always impossible
And there's maybe a girl now but she's already married
And I don't like men and –
but there's got to be somebody!
Because what if I'm 60 years old and not married,
all alone in a furnished room with peestains on my underwear
and everybody else is married!
All the universe married but me!

Ah, yet well I know that were a woman possible as I am possible
then marriage would be possible –
Like SHE in her lonely alien gaud waiting her Egyptian lover
so I wait – bereft of 2,000 years and the bath of life.

ROY FISHER

Paraphrases

for Peter Ryan

Dear Mr Fisher I am writing
a thesis on your work.
But am unable to obtain
texts. I have articles by Davie, D.,
and Mottram, E.,
But not your Books since booksellers
I have approached refuse to
take my order saying they
can no longer afford to
handle 'this type of business'. It is
too late! for me to change
my subject to the work of a more
popular writer, so please Mr Fisher
you must help me since I face the alternatives
of failing my degree or repaying
the whole of my scholarship money . . .

Dear Mr Fisher although I have been unable
to read much of your work (to get it that is)
I am a great admirer of it and your landscapes
have become so real to me I am convinced I have, in fact,
become you. I have never, however,
seen any photograph of you, and am most curious
to have an idea of your appearance,
beyond what my mirror, of course, tells me.
The cover of your *Collected Poems*
(reproduced in the *Guardian*, November 1971)
shows upwards of fifty faces; but which is yours? Are you
the little boy at the front, and if so have you
changed much since then?

Dear Mr Fisher recently while studying
selections from a modern anthology with
one of my GCE groups I came across your interestingly titled
'Starting to Make a Tree'. After the discussion I felt strongly
you were definitely *holding something back* in this poem
though I can't quite reach it. Are you often in Rugby?
If you are, perhaps we could meet and I could
try at least to explain. Cordially, Avis Tree. PS. Should we
arrange a rendez-vous I'm afraid I wouldn't
know who to look out for as I've never unfortunately
seen your photograph. But I notice you were born in 1930
the same year as Ted Hughes. Would I be right
in expecting you to resemble *him*, more or less?

– Dear Ms Tree,
It's true I'm in Rugby quite often, but the train
goes through without stopping. Could you fancy standing
outside the UP Refreshment Room a few times so that
I could learn to recognize *you*? If you could
just get hold of my four books, and wave them,
then I'd know it was you. As for my own appearance
I suppose it inclines more to the
Philip Larkin side of Ted Hughes's looks . . .
See if you think so as I go by . . .

Dear Mr Fisher I have been commissioned
to write a short
critical book on your work
but find that although I have a full
dossier of reviews etcetera
I don't have access to your books. Libraries
over here seem just not to have bought them in.
Since the books are quite a few years old now
I imagine they'll all have been remaindered
some while back? Or worse, pulped? So can
you advise me on locating second-hand copies,

not too expensively I hope? Anyway,
yours, with apologies and respect . . .

Dear Mr Fisher I am now
so certain I am you that it is obvious to me
that the collection of poems I am currently working on must be
your own next book! Can you let me know –
who is to publish it and exactly when
it will be appearing? I shouldn't like there to
be any trouble over contracts, 'plagiarism'
etcetera; besides which it would be a pity
to think one of us was wasting time and effort.
How far have *you* got? Please help me. I
do think this is urgent . . .

ALAN BROWNJOHN

Negotiation

In the same post, the Old Fox receives
Word that he is in overdraft at the bank,
And a gas bill for £3.69

Ten days later, the Gas Board write again, in red, 'They would
Be grateful if . . .' The Old Fox waits.

Two weeks later, the Gas Board write, in red again, some
Phrases underlined, 'Regret, you do not tender payment within
Seven days, supply disconnected, charge for re-connection.'
The Accounts Officer's signature is stamped below.

Six days later, the Old Fox carefully writes a letter:
'Thank you for, apologies for any inconvenience,
Do not wish to cause difficulty, wonder if payment
Of sum outstanding *by instalments*, very grateful, Yours etc.'

A week having passed,
Drinking coffee made on his undisconnected cooker,
The Old Fox reads, 'Must regretfully state, not customary,
Payment by instalments when sum entailed so small,
No alternative but to ask, within five days,
Supply disconnected unless, Dictated by the Accounts Officer
And signed in his absence . . .'

Four days passing, the Old Fox writes, 'Thank you courteous
reply,
Recollect (which is untrue) kindly permitting me
Payment by instalments, previous occasion, some years ago,
Comparable sum, possibly consult your records, appreciate
Your looking into this, regret any delay caused,
Only anxious to settle account as soon as possible.'

The Gas Board writes after a week, ignoring this.
'Supply disconnected unless . . .' The Old Fox rejoins,
'May I direct your kind attention, my letter of,
Possibly held up in the post, possibly crossed with yours of,
Sorry to put you to this, Yours etc.'

'We have looked into our records,' the Gas Board two weeks
later,
'Can find no precedent in your case, not our custom with small
amounts,
Must insist on immediate settlement, otherwise steps
Will be taken, supply disconnected, recovery of sum
By legal action, Yours very truly. Accounts Officer'
– Personally signed.

Sadly, then, the Old Fox writes a cheque for £3.69,
Omits (on purpose) to sign it,
And posts it to the Board.

In eight days the cheque is returned, 'For your signature,
Yours truly.' The Old Fox waits.

A month later, 'We do not appear to have received cheque
On which your signature was requested, bring this
To your kind attention.'

It is winter by now, and the gas fire gleams.
The North Sea roars on the cooker to heat
The Old Fox his supper of Irish stew from a tin.
Lighting his gas water-heater, he runs a bath.
It mellows him. He writes his name at the bottom of the cheque
(Which will come back 'referred to drawer' in nine days' time.)

Returning from the pillar box, he picks up the next quarter's
invoice from the mat.

JOHN UPDIKE

Meditation on a News Item

Fidel Castro, who considers himself first in war and first in peace, was first in the Hemingway fishing tourney at Havana, Cuba. 'I am a novice at fishing,' said Fidel. 'You are a lucky novice,' replied Ernest.

'Life,' June, 1960

Yes, yes, and there is even a photograph,
of the two in profile, both bearded, both sharp-nosed,
both (though one is not wearing a cap
and the other is not carrying a cat)
magnificently recognizable (do
you think that much-photographed faces grow
larger, more deeply themselves, like flowers
in sunlight?). A great cup sits between their chests.

Life does not seem to think it very strange.
It runs the shot cropped to four inches,
and the explanation is given in full above.

But to me it seems immeasurably strange; as strange
to me as if there were found,
in a Jacobean archive, an unquestionably authentic
woodcut showing Shakespeare
presenting the blue ribbon for Best Cake Baked
to Queen Elizabeth.

And even the dialogue: so perfect –
'You are a lucky novice.' Succinct,
wry, ominous, innocent: Nick Adams talking.
How did it happen? Did he,
convulsively departing from the exhausting regimen –
the rising at 6 a.m. to sharpen twelve pencils
with which to cut, as he stands at his bookcase,
269 or 312 or 451 more words into the paper
that will compose one of those many rumored books
that somehow never appears – did he abruptly exclaim,
'I must have a fishing tourney!'
and have posters painted and posted
in cabañas, cigar stores, and bordellos,
ERNEST HEMINGWAY FISHING COMPETITION,
just like that?

And did he receive, on one of those soft Havana mornings,
while the smoky-green Caribbean laps the wharf legs,
and the *señoritas* yawn behind grillwork,
and the black mailmen walk in khaki shorts,
an application blank stating CASTRO, Fidel?
Occupation: Dictator. *Address:*
Top Floor, Habana-Hilton Hotel (commandeered).
Hobbies: Ranting, U.S.-Baiting, Fishing (novice).

And was it honest? I mean, did Castro
wade down off the beach in hip boots
in a long cursing line of other contestants, Cubans,
cabdrivers, pimps, restaurant waiters, small landowners,

and make his cast, the bobbin singing,
and the great fish leap, with a splash
leap from the smoky-green waves,
and he, tugging, writhing, bring it in
and stand there, mopping the brow
of his somehow fragile Apollonian profile
while the great man panted back and forth
plying his tape measure?

And at the award ceremony,
did their two so-different sorts of fame –
yet tangent on the point of beards and love of exploit –
create in the air one of those eccentric electronic disturbances
to which our younger physicists devote so much thought?
In the photograph, there is some sign of it:
they seem beatified, and resemble
two apostles by Dürer, possibly Peter and Paul.

My mind sinks down through the layers of strangeness:
I am as happy as if I had opened
a copy of 'Alice in Wonderland'
in which the heroine *does* win the croquet contest
administered by the Queen of Hearts.

Vow

(*On discovering oneself listed on the back of a concert programme as a 'Museum Friend of Early Music'*)

May I forever a Muse-
um Friend of Early Music be;
May I, no, never cease to thrill
When three-stringed rebecks thinly trill,
Or fail to have a lumpish throat
When crumhorns bleat their fuzzy note.

I'll often audit, with *ma femme*,
Duets of psaltery and shawm;
Cross-flutes of pre-Baroque design
Shall twit our eardrums as we dine,
And Slavic guslas will, forsooth,
In harsh conjunction with the crwth
(Which is a kind of Welsh vielle,
As all us Friends know very well),
Lull both of us to sleep. My love,
The keirnines (Irish harps) above
Tune diatonically, and lyres
Augment august celestial choirs
That plan to render, when we die,
'Lamento di Tristano' by
Anonymous. With holy din
Recorder angels will tune us in
When we have run our mortal race
From sopranino to contrabass.

Movie House

View it, by day, from the back,
from the parking lot in the rear,
for from this angle only
the beautiful brick blankness can be grasped.
Monumentality
wears one face in all ages.

No windows intrude real light
into this temple of shades,
and the size of it,
the size of the great rear wall measures
the breadth of the dreams we have had here.
It dwarfs the village bank,
outlooms the town hall, and even in its decline
makes the bright-ceilinged supermarket seem mean.

Stark closet of stealthy rapture,
vast introspective camera
wherein our most daring self-projections
were given familiar names:
stand, stand by your macadam lake
and tell the aeons of our extinction
that we too could house our gods,
could secrete a pyramid
to sight the stars by.

Upon Learning that a Bird Exists Called the Turnstone

A turnstone turned rover
And went through ten turnstiles,
Admiring the clover
And turnsole and fern styles.

The Turneresque landscape
She scanned for a lover;
She'd heard one good turnstone
Deserves another.

She took to the turnpike
And travelled to Dover,
Where turnips enjoy
A rapid turnover.

In vain did she hover
And earnestly burn
With yearning; above her
The terns cried, 'Return!'

ADRIAN MITCHELL

The Oxford Hysteria of English Poetry

Back in the caveman days business was fair.
Used to turn up at Wookey Hole,
Plenty of action down the Hole
Nights when it wasn't raided.
They'd see my bear-gut harp
And the mess at the back of my eyes
And 'Right,' they'd say, 'make poetry,'
So I'd slam away at the three basic chords
And go into the act –
A story about sabre-toothed tigers with a comic hero,
A sexy one with an anti-wife-clubbing twist –
Good progressive stuff mainly,
Get ready for the Bronze Age, all that,
And soon it would be 'Bring out the woad!'
Yeah, woad. We used to get high on woad.

The Vikings only wanted sagas
Full of gigantic deadheads cutting off each other's vitals
Or Beowulf versus the Bog People.
The Romans weren't much better,
Under all that armour you could tell they were soft
With their central heating
And poets with names like Horace.

Under the Normans the language began to clear,
Became a pleasure to write in,
Yes, write in, by now everyone was starting
To write down poems.
Well, it saved memorizing and improvising
And the peasants couldn't get hold of it.
Soon there were hundreds of us,
Most of us writing under the name
Of Geoffrey Chaucer.

Then suddenly we were knee-deep in sonnets.
Holinshed ran a headline:
BONANZA FOR BARDS.

It got fantastic –
Looning around from the bear-pit to the Globe,
All those freak-outs down the Mermaid,
Kit Marlowe coming on like Richard the Two,
A virgin Queen in a ginger wig
And English poetry in full whatsit –
Bloody fantastic, but I never found any time
To do any writing till Willy finally flipped –
Smoking too much of that special stuff
Sir Walter Raleigh was pushing.

Cromwell's time I spent on cultural committees.

Then Charles the Second swung down from the trees
And it was sexual medley time
And the only verses they wanted
Were epigrams on Chloe's breasts
But I only got published on the back of her left knee-cap.

Next came Pope and Dryden
So I went underground.
Don't mess with the Mafia.

Then suddenly – WOOMF –
It was the Ro-man-tic Re-viv-al
And it didn't matter how you wrote,
All the public wanted was a hairy great image.
Before they'd even print you
You had to smoke opium, die of consumption,
Fall in love with your sister
And drown in the Mediterranean (not at Brighton).

My publisher said: 'I'll have to remainder you
Unless you go and live in a lake or something
Like this bloke Wordsworth.'

After that there were about
A thousand years of Tennyson
Who got so bored with himself
That he changed his name
To Kipling at half time.
Strange that Tennyson should be
Remembered for his poems really,
We always thought of him
As a golfer.

There hasn't been much time
For poetry since the 'twenties
What with leaving the Communist Church
To join the Catholic Party
And explaining why in the C.I.A. Monthly.
Finally I was given the Chair of Comparative Ambiguity
At Armpit University, Java.
It didn't keep me busy,
But it kept me quiet.
It seemed like poetry had been safely tucked up for the
night.

ADRIAN HENRI

Adrian Henri's Talking after Christmas Blues

Well I woke up this mornin' it was Christmas Day
And the birds were singing the night away
I saw my stocking lying on the chair
Looked right to the bottom but you weren't there
there was
        apples
          oranges
            chocolates
              . . . aftershave
– but no you.

So I went downstairs and the dinner was fine
There was pudding and turkey and lots of wine
And I pulled those crackers with a laughing face
Till I saw there was no one in your place
there was
        mincepies
          brandy
            nuts and raisins
              . . . mashed potato
– but no you.

Now it's New Year and it's Auld Lang Syne
And it's 12 o'clock and I'm feeling fine
Should Auld Acquaintance be Forgot?
I don't know girl, but it hurts a lot
there was
        whisky
          Vodka
            dry Martini (stirred
              but not shaken)
. . . and 12 New Year resolutions
– all of them about you.

So it's all the best for the year ahead
As I stagger upstairs and into bed
Then I looked at the pillow by my side
. . . I tell you baby I almost cried
there'll be
                    Autumn
                        Summer
                            Spring
                                . . . and Winter
– all of them without you.

GEORGE MACBETH

The Orlando Commercial

1
EEK!
Her legs are caught in something.

        What appalling catastrophe
has trapped and is so
    atrociously torturing
this beautiful naked girl's
legs?

Why, ORLANDO, of course.

Elusive, exclusive Orlando
    the new seamless nylon
has stolen up in secret
    and caught her in his lure.

2
Orlando yawns.

He is tired of being a fabric.

He wants out.

Heh, you can't do that
you'll tear the screen!

The screen tears.

Just shows.

It can't have been made
of elusive, exclusive ORLANDO
the new seamless nylon.

The Five-Minute Orlando Macbeth

1
ACT I

Orlando hails
the weird sisters
and rides home like a maniac.

Eschewing the
rooky wood, he
gallops across four blasted heaths
towards his castle.

There, washing her hands

HERE'S YOUR TRAILER
Lady Orlando
stands
with harness on her back.

DUNC'S HERE
    she says

    HI, DUNC
    he calls

2

    Meanwhile, Lady O
screws his courage to the sticking-point
    and they have a stiff night together.

    Pretty probably.

    Next, Orlando dips
the bloody dagger
    in his wife's history book

and sets about gilding the faces of the grooms withal.

    UNFORTUNATELY

    it keeps cropping up
    at awkward times
                        like
in his dreams, during banquets, etc.

3

    MOREOVER

    Hired lads
got in to put the
    Macduff fry

out of their misery
    don't help much,

though admittedly going in the catalogue for men.

4
   Finally, it's

WITCH TIME AGAIN

   and Thane Orlando
runs his eye along the cauldrons

   BAD NEWS THERE, BUD
but
   he takes it like a man
   being, as he says,
so far advanced in gore
to return were as tedious as go o'er.

   SO

5
ACT V
   Drums. Trumpets. Marching trees

and the old woman with her bad scene
   about all the perfumes of Arabia
not being a spot-lifter

   RIGHT

   not of woman born
   untimely ripp'd

a hard choice, but
   we all know it has to go at last to the goodies

THANK YOU, MAC ORLANDO

and stick his bloody head on the battlements
on your way out, please.

ANNE STEVENSON

Larousse Gastronomique

I

How entrancing are the 124 ways
of eating the baby of a cow.
Amourettes, *en blanquette*, *paupiettes*, *escalopes*.
Raw, the white flesh has a green iridescence.
The fat's white, like satin
and smells like milk.

II

L is for lark, so gentle and savoury
bred in some countries for cage or aviary,
prized for its song.
To the French this is wrong.
So the *alouette*, *mauviette* (derived from 'mauvais'),
is esteemed for the preparation of a pâté.

III

Song thrushes make an excellent food.
They grow fat on grapes.
They are best roasted whole, served on bread,
but can be boned and stuffed, *gratin*, instead,
or braised in their original shapes.

IV

People who like eating woodcocks
insist that it should be cooked undrawn,
as should also the blackbird (with the gizzard gone)
and the garden warblers, and so on,
and so on . . .

EGBERT MOORE ('LORD BEGINNER')

Victory Calypso, Lord's 1950

Cricket, lovely cricket,
At Lord's where I saw it;
Cricket, lovely cricket,
At Lord's where I saw it;
Yardley tried his best
But Goddard won the Test.
They gave the crowd plenty fun;
Second Test and West Indies won.

Chorus: With those two little pals of mine
Ramadhin and Valentine.

The King was there well attired,
So they started with Rae and Stollmeyer;
Stolly was hitting balls around the boundary,
But Wardle stopped him at twenty.
Rae had confidence,
So he put up a strong defence;
He saw the King was waiting to see,
So he gave him a century.

Chorus: With those two little pals of mine
Ramadhin and Valentine.

West Indies first innings total was three-twenty-six
Just as usual.
When Bedser bowled Christiani
The whole thing collapsed quite easily,
England then went on,
And made one-hundred-fifty-one;
West Indies then had two-twenty lead,
And Goddard said, 'That's nice indeed.'

Chorus: With those two little pals of mine
Ramadhin and Valentine.

Yardley wasn't broken-hearted
When the second innings started;
Jenkins was like a target
Getting the first five into his basket.
But Gomez broke him down,
While Walcott licked them around;
He was not out for one-hundred and sixty-eight,
Leaving Yardley to contemplate.

Chorus: The bowling was super-fine
Ramadhin and Valentine.

West Indies was feeling homely,
Their audience had them happy.
When Washbrook's century had ended,
West Indies' voices all blended.
Hats went in the air.
They jumped and shouted without fear;
So at Lord's was the scenery
Bound to go down in history.

Chorus: After all was said and done,
Second Test and West Indies won!

ROGER McGOUGH

Let Me Die a Youngman's Death

Let me die a youngman's death
not a clean & inbetween
the sheets holywater death
not a famous-last-words
peaceful out of breath death

When I'm 73
& in constant good tumour
may I be mown down at dawn
by a bright red sports car
on my way home
from an allnight party

Or when I'm 91
with silver hair
& sitting in a barber's chair
may rival gangsters
with hamfisted tommyguns burst in
& give me a short back & insides

Or when I'm 104
& banned from the Cavern
may my mistress
catching me in bed with her daughter
& fearing for her son
cut me up into little pieces
& throw away every piece but one

Let me die a youngman's death
not a free from sin tiptoe in
candle wax and waning death
not a curtains drawn by angels borne
'what a nice way to go' death

JOHN FULLER

Linda

1

Linda, Linda, slender and pretty,
Biscuit girl in a biscuit city,
Packing the biscuits in paper boxes,
What do you dream of? How do you dream?
The cutters rise and fall and rise and cut
The chocolate, the coconut,
The Orange Princess and the Gypsy Cream.
The biscuits gather and the boxes shut,
But things are never what they seem.

In the school the bells are ringing,
In the playground girls are singing:
Lily, paper, hard-boiled eggs,
Mr Swain has bandy legs.
Linda, Linda, rude and sweet,
Skipping girl in a skipping street,
Singing and skipping all summer long:
Worms in the classroom, worms in the hall,
Mr Swain will eat them all.

The cutters fall and rise and fall
And biscuits are unending like a wall
And school is over and the summer's dream.

2

The day the sun invented flowers again
Her heart unfolded with the spring.
Paul had appeared and nothing was the same.

The railway's on its sleepers,
The river's in its bed,
All Berkshire is beneath us and
The sky is overhead.

Linda crossed the platform to the train.
Her warm little mouth reached up to his
And kissed and whispered his exciting name.

What was it like before we met?
What did we ever do?
Can't think of anything like it
Or anyone like you.

Weaving fingers find out that they fit
And all the secret pleasures they commit
Are like the touch of flowers in the rain.

3

A whistle from the primus:
The water's nice and hot.
I've got the milk and sugar
And teabags in the pot.
Sometimes there are sandwiches
And sometimes there are not,
But fishing is a fiddle
And Paul requires his tea.
He hasn't time to make it
So he leaves it all to me,
And there are always biscuits
(I bring along the tin.
I think it might be useful
To put the fishes in).
Fishing on the island, only me and him,
Fishing on the island all the afternoon,

The river flowing by us, full to the brim,
And the fishing is over all too soon.

  When I packed the basket
  Was there something I forgot?
  It says *Plum* on the label
  And Paul likes apricot.
  I usually forget things
  Though sometimes I do not,
  But fishing is a fiddle
  And Paul requires his tea.
  He hasn't time to make it
  So he leaves it all to me,
  And there are always biscuits
  (I bring along the tin.
  I think it might be useful
  To put the fishes in).
Fishing on the island, only me and him,
Fishing on the island all the afternoon,
The river flowing by us, full to the brim,
And the fishing is over all too soon.

  The river's full of fishes.
  You'd think he'd catch a lot.
  I'll call out: 'Have you got one?'
  And Paul will answer: 'What?'
  Sometimes he will land one
  And most times he will not,
  But fishing is a fiddle
  And Paul requires his tea.
  And when his basket's empty
  He holds it out to me
  And grins to say he's sorry
  (I love that silly grin
  And I find it very useful
  To put my kisses in).

Kissing on the island, only me and him,
Kissing on the island all the afternoon,
The river flowing by us, full to the brim,
And the kissing is over all too soon.

4

When we went down to Maidenhead
Paul had his clarinet.
I tried to do the steering and
We both got very wet.
But how he blew that liquorice stick!
The music on a thread
Rose like a nest of rooks above
His black and curly head.

There's a rookery at Dorney
But all the rooks have gone,
Flapping their wings like overcoats
They're struggling to put on.
I love their wild black music,
But all the rooks have gone.

We took a tent and Mum was mad.
Paul had his clarinet.
I had this spoon and china mug:
We made a fine duet.
But how he blew that wooden throat
Like a musical millionaire!
The black night-sound inside forced out
In squiggles on the air.

There's a rookery at Dorney
But all the rooks have gone,
And clouds blow over empty trees
Where once the summer shone,
And Paul and his black music,
And all his love, have gone.

5

Linda went out in her wedges.
The day was average,
And masses of water were moving
Under Caversham Bridge.

Paul had promised to meet her
And take her on the river.
She looked again at her wristwatch
And gave a little shiver.

Well, wasn't he worth forgiving?
The hour ticked slowly on,
And she threw her Wrigley paper
Down at a frowning swan.

Several boys passed by her
And all of them managed to stare.
But Linda looked right through them
As if she didn't care.

You believe him if he tells you.
You think he's ever so nice
And it's hard to find he can never
Say the same thing twice.

Promises break like biscuits.
Nothing keeps for ever.
But time runs on and on and on,
Deep as the lying river.

6

Linda, Linda, older and wiser,
Far from childhood in a biscuit town,
Making biscuits where the Thames winds down,
Under the eyes of the supervisor,

Under the hands of the factory clock:
  Tick, tick, tick, tick,
  Crisp and crumbly, thin and thick.
The cutters rise and fall and rise,
Cutting out (surprise, surprise)
The chocolate, the coconut,
The Orange Princess and the Gypsy Cream.

But things are never what they seem.
The trains pass clanking on the track,
Distinct and jewelled in the quiet night:
  Tick, tick, tick, tick,
  In life's absurd arithmetic.

And Linda in the tunnel of her dream
All night is restless, staring back
As wisps of the dragon drift into the wind
And, smaller and smaller, Paul is waving,
Smaller and smaller, Paul is standing there.
And Linda dreams and dreams and dreams
Under the hands of the bedside clock,
Till bacon smells are in the air
And combs tug sleepily through morning hair
And nothing is ever what it seems.

Two Songs from *Fox-Trot*

1 Polka

A fox don't make a faux pas!
  Oh no, sir!
We have our family pride.
We're very very proper
And it makes us warm inside.

We like to see some action
And we're nifty on our paws.
There's a glow of satisfaction
With a bird between your jaws.
But we're very very proper
We don't do it without cause.
We have to have our *breakfast*
For it makes us warm inside.

A fox don't make a faux pas!
  Oh no, sir!
We're gentlemen through and through.
No grasping interloper,
It's 'please!' and 'after you!'
We like our small adventures,
We like to come and go:
A duck between your dentures?
Well done! Oh damn' good show!
No grasping interloper
We'd have you jolly well know.
Our tastes are very *civilized*
(We're gentlemen through and through)
Our *tastes* are very civilized
And it's 'please!' and 'after you!'

2 Can-can

The hounds are breathing at my tail.
The hunt behind is in full cry,
  Grimly grim.
The Master knows he will not fail
To see his tiring quarry die,
  Horrible him!

Another fence won't keep them back.
They have the panic scent too strong,
  Grimly grim.

The Master close behind the pack
Knows that now he can't go wrong,
  Horrible him!

Now I am running for my life.
The Hunt's upon me in a rush,
  Grimly grim.
The Master holds a little knife
With which to amputate my brush,
  Horrible him!

God Bless America

When they confess that they have lost the penial bone and outer
  space is
Once again a numinous void, when they're kept out of Other
  Places,
And Dr Fieser falls asleep at last and dreams of unburnt faces,
When gold medals are won by the ton for forgetting about the
  different races,
God Bless America.

When in the Latin shanties the scented priesthood suffers
  metempsychosis
And with an organ entry *tutti copula* the dollar uncrosses
Itself and abdicates, when the Pax Americana cuts its losses
And a Pinkville memorial's built in furious shame by Saigon's
  puppet bosses,
God Bless America.

When they can be happy without noise, without knowing where
  on earth they've been,
When they cease to be intellectual tourists and stop wanting to
  be clean,

When they send their children to bed at the proper time and
say just what they mean,
And no longer trust the Quarterly Symposium and the Vicarious
Screen,
God Bless America.

When they feel thoroughly desolated by the short-haired
Christ they pray to,
When they weep over their plunder of Europe stone by stone,
releasing Plato
And other Freshman Great Books, when they switch off their
Hoover and unplug Nato,
Pulling the chain on the C.I.A. and awarding *Time* a rotten
potato,
God Bless America.

When qua-birds, quickhatches and quinnets agree at last to
admit the quail,
When Captain Queeg is seen descending from the bridge as
small and pale
As everyone else, and is helped with sympathetic murmurs to
the rail,
When the few true defenders of love and justice survive to tell
the tale,
Then, perhaps then, God Bless America.

Alex at the Barber's

He is having his hair cut. Towels are tucked
About his chin, his mop scalped jokingly.
The face in the mirror is his own face.

The barber moves and chats among the green
And methylated violet, snipper-snips,
Puts scissors down, plugs in a plaited flex,

And like a surgeon with his perfumed hands
Presses the waiting skull and shapes the base.
He likes having his hair cut, and the man

Likes cutting it. The radio drones on.
The eyes in the mirror are his own eyes.
While the next chair receives the Demon Blade,

A dog-leg razor nicks a sideburn here;
As from a sofa there a sheet is whisked
And silver pocketed. The doorbell pings.

The barber, frowning, grips the ragged fringe
And slowly cuts. Upon the speckled sheet
The bits fall down and now his hair is cut.

The neighing trams outside splash through the rain.
The barber tests the spray for heat and rubs
Lemon shampoo into his spiky hair.

Bent with his head above the running bowl,
Eyes squeezed shut, he does not see the water
Gurgle and sway like twisted sweetpaper

Above the waste, but, for a moment, tows
A sleigh of polished silver parrots through
Acres of snow, exclaiming soundlessly.

Then towel round head. Head swung gently up.
Eyes padded. As the barber briskly rubs,
The smile in the mirror is his own smile.

De Sade

There once was a Marquis de Sade
From whose novels we seem to be barred,
For he said that one's leisure
Should be given to pleasure,
A belief against which we must guard.

He said you must treat number one
As the one most entitled to fun,
But if you are weak
Then the outlook is bleak,
And not very much can be done.

It will work for a Count or a Monk
Who can cut up a corpse in a trunk
Or hire a spruce valet
With whom he can dally,
But if you're a peasant you're sunk.

It's the man with most power and craft
Who can see that his château's well-staffed
With housemaids and hordes
Of terrified wards:
But what if the victims just laughed?

If they chatted they'd lessen their trial.
Such behaviour would cripple his style,
For the sexual invention
Supplies the intention
But action's dismayed at a smile.

Yes, he almost convinced us but I'm
Afraid that it's certainly time
To cast final doubts
On the cruel ins and outs
Of his logical theory of crime.

The rich men are ruled by the poor,
And the way that they do it is Law,
And it's Law that comes after
That primitive laughter
That stifled the cave-man's roar.

De Sade went inside for a season
For his dubious sexual treason.
It was groaningly tame,
But he's known all the same
As the dark *ne plus ultra* of Reason.

JOHN FULLER and JAMES FENTON

Poem Against Catholics

The boring executors approach their locks,
Fumbling with keys and more than half-way dense:
Sylvia Plath is given to C. B. Cox,
Lawrence to Leavis, Pope to Joseph Spence,
Pound to *Agenda*, Eliot to his wife,
Hopkins to Bridges and Kafka to Max Brod –
But Jesus gave the *Church* eternal life!
God we hate Catholics and their Catholic God.

It isn't that we'd rather someone who
Instead of singing simply *says* you it.
The whole palaver simply isn't *true.*
We'd not *prefer* a Quaker to a Jesuit.
But in the Proselytizing Handicap
The odds are even where they ride roughshod
And drive their spurs into the suffering map.
God we hate Catholics and their Catholic God.

Graham Greene finds them everywhere he travels
With submachineguns underneath their cassocks.
You can be certain, as the plot unravels,
They're smuggling opium in knee-worn hassocks.
Police-chiefs quote Pascal. Priests hit the bottle.
Strong men repent in Nishni-Novgorod.
The whole *galère* one could with pleasure throttle.
God we hate Catholics and their Catholic God.

The object of their worship makes us *cross*,
Since their employment of it is so gainful.
They sold it off like bits of candy-floss.
(Surely the Romans meant it to be painful?)
Their tortured idols are so psychedelic
With gold and lapis artwork *à la mode*,
And nearly every thumbscrew is a relic.
God we hate Catholics and their Catholic goad.

They call their horrid children after saints
And educate them by such dubious means
They eagerly succumb to strange complaints
Or turn psychotic in their early teens.
'Ursula worries me,' exclaims her mother.
'Her manner recently has been so odd.
I've told her she must *not* cremate her brother.'
God we hate Catholics and their Catholic God.

See in the summerhouse where Father Flynn
Fingers his rosary and sets to work
Explaining why the church holds it a sin:
'You mustn't ever hold it. That's called jerk-
ing off. Six *mea culpas*, Benedict.'
He's coaching him for Ampleforth, poor sod.
He'll get some education, we predict.
God we hate Catholics and their Catholic God.

'Not now,' cries Mrs Nacnamara, '*later*!'
When leapt on by her husband (what a beast).
'It says so on my Catholic calculator.
It also says so on my Catholic priest.'
She'd do much better with a mortal coil
To spoil the child and spare the husband's rod.
Why don't they put a bill through in the Dáil?
God we hate Catholics and their Catholic God.

Their sheer resourcefulness one can't disparage.
External Combustion was their own invention,
So (indisputably) divorceless marriage
Which like a sardine key creates some tension.
But *only once*. What moral supermen!
Or else what Paul said must have been a cod
Since those who marry twice must burn again.
God we hate Catholics and their Catholic God.

Rich English Catholics, busy doing good work
For filthy mission schools in fascist states.
Oily confessors crawling from the woodwork
With first-class tickets to the pearly gates.
How nice that Lady Priesthole looks so well.
She's left her housemaid's knee behind in Lourdes.
But where's the housemaid? God alone can tell.
God we hate Catholics and their Catholic Gourdes.

High Anglo-Catholics are beneath contempt –
All intellectual and moral wrecks.
They love the frills but hold themselves exempt
From self-denial in the line of sex.
As press-ups are to health-fiends, genuflection
Is to the average Anglo-Catholic Prod.
What a good way to nourish one's erection.
God we hate Catholics and their Catholic God.

When Sister Flanagan from Houston Texas
Edited Baron Corvo for her Master's,
She changed the pronouns to reverse the sexes
As frills on chesterfields concealed their castors.
The text was passed unnoticed by the Syndics
And causes some confusion in the Bod.
Wait till she gets the Bible on the Index!
God we hate Catholics and their Catholic God.

A rugby-playing Catholic novelist,
Piers Paul Read, was lucky to be chosen
(Out of, we gather, a distinguished list)
To write about a new idea in frozen
Foods: when a rugby team crashed near Peru
On slopes the human toe had never trod
They ate each other. What a thing to do!
God – they ate Catholics and their Catholic God!

SIMON CURTIS

Satie, at the End of Term

The mind's eye aches from Henry James,
Like arms from heavy cases, lugged for miles.
Theme and structure, imagery and tone.

From Lawrence, too: how hard I dug
For insights sunk, yards deep, in turgid prose.
Theme and structure, imagery and tone.

Web of necessity in *Daniel Deronda*,
Gloom in *Dorrit*, gloom in Flaubert,
One more week to go, at
Theme and structure, imagery and tone.

So fitful-fresh as April sun,
You're welcome, clown;
Your good melodic dissonance
Will pierce low clouds of syllabus
With humour's grace,
Mercy of irreverence.

KIT WRIGHT

A New World Symphony

What plucky sperm invented Mrs Gale?
(All starless in her first degree lay she.)

What head-of-the-river victor
plunged for her sake
down to the makings of a whale
in the amniotic sea?

Fortune the germ.
(Luck likewise it took
to get to be a sperm.)

Oh
the little bit kept its head and it flashed its tail
and there on the leaking waters –
furious, mauve, harpooned to life –
was Mrs Gale, I'm glad to say,
a beautiful daughter to Mr and Mrs Elkins,
to Mr Gale: a bouncing wife.

Time out of mind so many minds
prized out of time to consider the light of day!
Let us rejoice in the work of the sperm
and that of the fortunate egg in Mrs Elkins
(the role of its life to play)

who made Mrs Gale for our Delight
as, happily, we
freely may.

Fortunes of War

I was thinking about her all the way from Troy
  (I slipped town when the Greek Horse showed)
Till at the pub at World's End called the World's End Arms
  I laid down my heavy load,
Then I called her from the pay-phone at the hamburger counter
  At the top of the New King's Road.

I said,
    'Darling Cassandra!
    How could they call you
    The Priestess with the Leastest,
    Deaf, blind, dumb,
    When the Greeks in the Horse
    Were making with the Morse
    And rat-tat-tapping
    On their wooden drum?
    Oh darling Cassandra,
    How could it be?
    Cassandra, Cassandra,
    Speak to me!'

Well, the line was as dodgy as Achilles' heel
  And I couldn't hear a word she said
So by Stamford Bridge I jumped a Number 14
  And I followed where the Fulham Road led
To a grey block of flats in Elm Park Gardens:
  I rang but the bell was dead.

I yelled,
'Darling Cassandra!
You've got a visitor!
Prophetess, scoff at us,
You've got a right:
When it comes to women it's
Quite indiscriminate,
Trojan taste,
But you're out of sight
In my view! Cassandra,
Throw me the key!
Cassandra, Cassandra,
Speak to me!'

That's what I said,
Then out of the window she poked her head,
Sighing,

'Slow down, boy.
Easy, feller.
You don't rob the cage till you've
Stuck up the teller. Take it
Easy, babe.
Gentle, child.
War game losers don't drive me wild.
You've got one chance
Or else you're dead.
Tell me, honey, did you bring any bread?

Well, I thought about that and I thought about a lot
And I stood in the road feeling dumb.
'Slow down, boy' when you've hitched in from Troy?'
Now that was a long way to come

To get this shit. Still the truth of it
  Was I'd won me a tidy sum
At Troy's Last Stand and a hundred grand
  Was riding against my bum.

So:

'Darling Cassandra!
I've got money!
Peeress of Seeresses,
Open the door!
That treasure chest of Priam's
Was flush as Harry Hyams –
Ripped it all off
And a good bit more.
So darling Cassandra,
Stick with me!
Cassandra, Cassandra,
Throw me the key!'

So I went straight up and Mama Cass and me,
  Now we've had our share of luck,
She prophesies the horses and I bet at all the courses
  And we've never yet come unstuck
So we own West London – well, it gives her an interest –
  But sometimes at night I'm struck
By the thought of Troy Town and the big blood apple
  And I think, well, what the fuck

Was *that* all about? That grey ghost Helen?
  Was she what they all died for?
Patroclus? Hector? Achilles? Priam?
  You can call it the luck of the draw,
I suppose. Well, you have to. I'll drink to that.
  Roll on, fortunes of war.

Red Boots On

Way down Geneva,
All along Vine,
Deeper than the snow drift
Love's eyes shine:

Mary Lou's walking
In the winter time.

She's got

Red boots on, she's got
Red boots on,
Kicking up the winter
Till the winter's gone.

So

Go by Ontario,
Look down Main,
If you can't find Mary Lou,
Come back again:

Sweet light burning
In winter's flame.

She's got

Snow in her eyes, got
A tingle in her toes
And new red boots on
Wherever she goes

So

All around Lake Street,
Up to St Paul,
Quicker than the white wind
Love takes all:

Mary Lou's walking
In the big snow fall.

She's got

Red boots on, she's got
Red boots on,
Kicking up the winter
Till the winter's gone.

PETER READING

Correspondence

Dear Martin,
Bumped into Arthur tonight
(after a concert of, can you guess?
Sibelius – do you remember how
you and I loved his 2nd and 7th?)
and we got talking somehow about you.
I'm back here now. I had to write to you.
My marriage turned out a bit of a mess.
How are you? Drop me a line,
Love,
Heather.

Dear Heather,
Just a note to thank you for
writing. My marriage has broken up. Karen
has gone to live in a caravan with
a Welsh self-taught painter who recently
got a grant from the Welsh Arts Council to make
a cartoon film. She took the child with her.
I'm living here at the house and would like
to see you if you could make it,
Love,
Martin.

Dear Clive,
Just a few lines to tell you the
score. My marriage has broken up. Karen
has gone to live in a caravan with
a Welsh self-taught painter who recently
got a grant from the Welsh Arts Council to make
a cartoon film. She took the child with her.
I'm living here at the house with a girl
called Heather,
Hope to see you soon,
Mart.

Dear Clive,
I came across Arthur the other
night. (I'd been to a concert of Symphonies
2 and 7 by Sibelius
– thought of those 78s you bought me!)
Somehow we started talking about you.
Marriage for Martin and me was a mess.
I went to live with an artist – but now . . . well,
never mind. Drop me a line,
Love,
Karen.

Dear Karen,
I'm on my own again now.
Me and Heather have parted company.
I feel sorry about it – lonely
and sad would be more accurate. But
I couldn't live with her any more
I'm afraid. I feel I've sort of betrayed her
– and now I think I prefer being hurt to
hurting someone else,
All the best,
Martin.

Dear Karen,
Just a short note to say thanks for
writing. I'd heard from Mart that you'd broken up.
Sorry to hear it – you know I was always
very very fond of you. I should've
liked to invite you over some time but, well,
it's a bit awkward to tell you the truth, I'm
sort of involved with someone called Heather – look,
why not come over and see us *both*?
Love,
Clive.

Ballad

I'll tell you a story
concerning John and Joan;
in student days each clung to each
as flesh will cling to bone,

as a fluke clings to a liver or
a lichen to a stone
Joan would cling to Jonathan
Jonathan to Joan,

as Eurydice and Orpheus
  as Leda and the Swan
as Hero and Leander
  so were Joan and John.

You would see them at a lecture
  on Les Fauves or Les Nabis
or Intimisme, sat at the back,
  his hand above her knee.

You would see them at a seminar
  discussing Form or Taste
or Aesthetics or Cybernetics
  with his arm round her waist.

You would see her in a life class
  cross-hatching aimlessly
gawping at not the model but
  John and his charcoal 6B.

You would hear them talk through lunchtime
  (of Puvis de Chavannes,
Erich Heckel, Karl Schmidt-Rottluff,
  Maurice Denis, Mondrian,

Matthew Smith, Odilon Redon,
  Edvard Munch, Chaim Soutine,
Emil Nolde) holding hands
  in the college canteen.

John had a one-room basement flat
  in Percy Street, where she
would dust or satisfy his lust
  (to a certain degree)

or tidy up or make a cup
   of lotus blossom tea
or iron or sew, but was prompt to go
   at midnight (usually).

And he would walk her to the stop
   to board the late night bus
and he'd kiss her glove then see his love
   borne to the terminus.

Now they would have liked to marry,
   or at least co-reside,
but the Calvinist prigs where she was in digs
   – aunts on her mother's side –

forbade her staying out all night,
   disliked him from the start,
and 'anything might happen at that
   permissive College of Art.'

You could see them growing separate
   yet could not interfere.
They were doing Dip. A.D.,
   their penultimate year.

You could see them quarrel more and more
   with each successive week.
In their final year of A.T.D.
   things had reached a peak.

One day John said to Joan 'Joan
   you're becoming a bore'.
Joan said to John 'John I don't want
   to go with you any more.'

And so they finished there and then.
   It's cliché but it's sound
– what they say about no good coming
   of love on the rebound.

For John got stuck, it was just his luck,
   (to cut a long story short)
with a girl he'd filled at a party
   who you'd never have thought

could fit Joan's niche, but he married the bitch,
   bought a place, settled down,
got a teaching job at a Secondary Mod.
   in the roughest end of town.

And Joan got wed to a bloke who was Head
   of Games at a school where she
found herself a post teaching Art to a host
   of snotty-nosed peasantry.

*

On a Spring day ten years later
   a small assembly
of teachers met to discuss and set
   papers for C.S.E.

and one of those teachers was John
   who now had a Scale 4 post
and the next to come in was Joan, drawn and thin,
   and you'd think she'd seen a ghost

the way she blanched when she saw him,
   said 'John, I didn't think . . .'
He said 'thank Christ I've seen you – let's slip off
   for a talk and a drink'.

In the snug of The Grapes she told him,
   through whisky laced with tears,
her marriage was bad and her husband hadn't
   slept with her for two years.

And John said, sucking his Guinness head
   creamily off the top,
'between me and you my marriage is through,
   it's been an almighty flop'.

And Joan said, watching the barmaid
   draw another pint of stout;
'it's funny ha ha ha ha ha ha
   funny how things turn out'.

from *Travelogue*

Camping Provençal. Notices: (1)
Tourists may only settle in the camp,
after if having checked in at the office
they know their places. (2) The campers' dresses
must be correct in camp. (3) Please no noise
between the 22 and seven-o-clock.
(4) In the camp, parents must watch across
their children. (5) Take care of the plantations,
don't set up nails nor pour dish-water on
the trees. (6) Fire-woods are forbidden. (7)
Linen must dry discretely. (8) Detritus,
put this into the dustbins. (9) Showers-bath,
wash-house and W.C. must be kept clean.
Water is quite uncommon in Provence.
(10) Management is NOT responsible
for thefts. (11) Speed don't exceed 5.
(12) *That* box is reserved alone for throw
sanitary-towels and periodicals.
(13) These rules must be respected under
penalty of your time expiring here.

ABIGAIL MOZLEY

The Summer I Taught English to the French

the summer I taught English to the French
it was hot and blue
the house was full of defeated flowers
abortion posters
and the plaster waltzers
Walt Disney dancers, curves of green and gold
chipped plaster
the perfect sadness of an odeon romance
and my head was a language tank
words under glass
like fishes

I got interested in jukeboxes and photography
demonstrated for abortion on demand
I carried on teaching English to the French
'Excuse me but I seem to have overwound your cuckoo clock.'
'Don't worry I never did like that cuckoo clock anyway.'
it was hot and blue
and dying flowers miscarried red petals
all over the dusty house
a rank smell of dead nasturtiums and geraniums
I studied the situational dialogues
and photographed the plaster statuette
from sixteen different angles
caught their Palais glide
against lace curtains, concrete, roses, long grass, lettuces
an obsessive succession of passionate swoons
quel trucage

the trouble with love is the language
such heavy duty Anglo-Saxon stuff
like those trees outside

heaving, restless as women
shifting their silks, their skirts,
too much
kitsch et charmant, c'est mon style
I like it danced on ice
to Wurlitzer or Mills or AMI
ami, cheri

ah me it was always hot and blue as a movie
and I was always teaching English to the French
'Excuse me but I seem to have damaged your plastic flowers.'
'Don't worry I never did like those plastic flowers anyway.'
so hot and blue the beach was stopped by it
laid out flat
even the people silenced by it, diminished by the heat
a real french navy hello sailor afternoon

I was thrown, I was blown
by his Billy Budd looks and his matelot top
by his thighs and his bleu de ciel eyes
and I thought I would blow it
sink toute la boutique
in his sailor blue, movie blue, navy blue thighs and his eyes
have a whale of a time
short as a postcard
I blew it
washed him down with soda water

he left at 8 a.m.
looking tired, a denim blue fatigue
I put on my glasses and my soft black dress
and went on teaching English to the French
'Excuse me but I seem to have broken your Skegness
souvenir ashtray, lost your Robin Hood hat, run over
that plastic gnome outside and also the cat.'
'Don't worry I never did' etcetera
we all laughed and the blackboard rattled

but then he started sending
indecipherable messages
morse code poems
to do with the sea and trees
and referring to some disaster I didn't recall
some accident
he felt he must redress
in verse
I was depressed

I like it danced on ice
I didn't reply
I carried on teaching English to the French
apologies, small ruptures, ballroom fractures
distressed the blackboard
the chalk dust settling like fall-out
on my soft black frock
I continued to admire the plaster waltzers
for their chipped and plastered style
the only injury I could uncover
was a soft bruise
gently bluing the skin, no blood
and it continued hot
the house full of red defeated flowers
abortion posters
plaster statuettes

DUNCAN FORBES

Politics of Envy

In the Jackdaw folder of 'Historical Genitalia',
The suitors of Elizabeth and reasons for their failure,
The Bonsai quality of Buonaparte's regalia,
What Hitler was missing in the region of Westphalia
Would all be investigated *inter* many *alia*.

Elizabeth I in a miniature by Hilliard
Scanned for masculinity by Hotson, Rowse and Tillyard,
The gusset of Napoleon expounded like 'The Iliad',
Hitler in his bunker playing pocket billiard,
Would all be reproduced by the chiliad or milliard.

But if the young princess's *pudenda* were like Alice's
And only redetermined by Elizabethan malices,
If Buonaparte's was small because he owned huge palaces
And Hitler lost a ball when he gave the globe paralysis,
Do malicious jealousies provide all phallic fallacies?

JAMES FENTON

South Parks Road

When they have completed its re-edification
And eradicated the tell-tale traces of its former
Yellow-bricked Gothic style, when the lease has run out for
  The Commonwealth Services Club, when the nuns
  From St Frideswide's Cherwell Edge

Gather like swallows whistling on the telegraph wires,
Why will I be bothering with my homunculus?
Already committees have been set up to decide
  On a more potent name, like Avogadro
  Avenue or Zeta Strip.

Summer has stumbled upon South Parks Road and found it
Both wilderness and formal garden, the sultry heat
Dancing the seven veils on the car-tops, blossom and
  Birdlime on windscreens and a drain spluttering
  Froth under the laburnums.

Though by the flowering cherry there is a location
For something of glamour to emerge from a lecture
Shaking its locks and swinging a satchel, while guitars
  Tell of green fields and the beau revs his M.G.,
  That is something I have yet

To observe. Things are unhappy. The fretful measures
Of a blackbird to secure its acid plot beneath
The Institute windows, the squirrels' precarious
  Flights down the avenue are suitable and
  Desperate appliances

At both levels. I hear a voice from a garden hut
Relating the case history of a chimpanzee
Which, faced with an elementary learning problem of
  Peanut-here or peanut-there, chose knowingly
  To administer itself

A lethal electric shock, in pique at being used
As a guinea-pig. Hunter, who was conducting the
Experiment, gives no credit to the story as
  Such. Why then, asks the voice, was the animal
  Refused Christian burial?

There is a taste associated with hot exhaust,
Of a carious tooth and nicotine on the gums
And there is a feeling as if a poisonous moth
  Has landed softly on the nape of my neck.
  The struggle is already

Over before I emerge into the street with its
Architecture of Goede Hoop. How can you expect
Me to rise to the eagle holding the rotunda
  Like a victim, if it watches the School of
  Inorganic Chemistry

Pure Cinema Inca? I deal in minutiae,
Not with the fungus growing on the low walls but its
Globose vesiculate hyaline conidia.
  On the context of the basidioscarp
  I am seldom mistaken,

Though baffled in sunlight by gardens as fertile as
Chlorine, where the process of the seasons is something
Unfortunate. Blossom is not enough, it swirls
  In the gutters and collects at the drain-mouths.
  And besides there are stronger

Attractions at hand, the bleached facing of new buildings
And the orange cranes lit up against the cobalt sky
At evening. There is not much I could not tell about
  This road, as it is now, were the subject not
  Frustration and ignorance.

Notes

For the context of the basidioscarp Singer states:
'. . . context yellow or white,
changing or unchanging,
often blue at the base of the stipe.
Otherwise not blue or bluing . . .
all hyphae without clamp connections . . .'

The genus Stephanoma
was established by Wallroth in 1833
on the basis of Stephanoma Strigosum,
the type of the genus. Wallroth
described the fungus as possessing
a pezizaform hairy sporochodium
with a flattened powdery surface layer
of globose, vesiculate, hyaline conidia.

from *Wild Life Studies*

1 The Wild Ones

Here come the capybaras on their bikes.
They swerve into the friendly, leafy square
Knocking the angwantibos off their trikes,
Giving the old-age coypus a bad scare.
They specialize in nasty, lightning strikes.
They leave the banks and grocers' shops quite bare,
Then swagger through the bardoors for a shot
Of anything the barman hasn't got.

They spoil the friendly rodent rodeos
By rustling the grazing flocks of mice.
They wear enormous jackboots on their toes.
Insulted by a comment, in a trice
They whip their switchblades out beneath your nose.
Their favourite food is elephant and rice.
Their personal appearance is revolting.
Their fur is never brushed and always moulting.

And in the evening when the sun goes down
They take the comely women on their backs
And ride for several furlongs out of town
Along the muddy roads and mountain tracks,
Wearing a grim and terrifying frown.
Months later, all the females have attacks
And call the coypu doctors to their beds.
What's born has dreadful capybara heads.

2 Of Bison Men

with apologies to Roy Fuller

A bison *in the bath, the image noted*
Reminds one that it's time to go to bed.
One's home from dinner, feeling rather bloated.
One's had to drive the baby sitter back.
Naturally one's resolve is fairly slack.

Next day, with some surprise, one finds it there
Soaping its fourfold armpits with a will
And whistling some infuriating air.
It's probably used up all one's shampoo,
And look, its soggy hooves have turned to glue.

Quite obviously it came up through the waste,
Emerging through the sponges and the loofahs,
And found the wire bathrack to its taste.
It's quite at home. The children are enthralled.
The dirty uncle has been badly mauled.

One jibs at murder, so one writes a letter
Begging a friend to take it for a week.
'It's bound to get on well with your red setter
And you can exercise it on Blackheath.
I find wire wool is splendid for its teeth.'

We certainly would like thus easily
To palm our troubles off on our acquaintance.
But just as one's prepared its flask of tea
The kids rush in to collar the grownups.
The airing cupboard's full of bison pups!

Lollipops of the Pomeranian Baroque

The skies remind one of one of those mounds of custard
Tylman de Gameren so loved to scoff,
With loads of capercaillies, fully-busted,
And soft asparaguses to suck off.

The richest, loving earth cow ever manked on
Is there, to burden down your dreadful shoes.
But where are all the men? they've turned to plankton,
Or are departing on a winter cruise.

Then are these nuisances really so pesky?
Even the poor mazurka in the snow.
Enough of that! If I was John Sobieskie,
I'd tell those rich Cachoubians where to go.

E. J. THRIBB

Lines on the Hundredth Anniversary of the Birth of W. Somerset Maugham

So. You were
Born A
Hundred Years
Ago, Great
Story Teller.

Somerset. That
Is a strange
Name and
Yet W. Workshire
Maugham would
Hardly sound right.

Personally, I have
Not found the
Time to get round
To reading the books
That have made you
A household name.

Keith's mum always
Watches your plays
On the television
And she says that usually
They have a Far
East setting and
A twist at the
End quite often.

25 January 1974

Erratum

In my last poem
'Lines on the
100th Anniversary
Of the Birth of
W. Somerset
Maugham'

The word 'Yorkshire'
Appeared as
'Workshire'.

Keith's mum
Spotted it
Immediately though

I confess I did
Not when I read
The proofs.

I regret the
Inconvenience this
May have caused to readers.

One mispelt word
Like this can
Completely destroy
A poem.

8 February 1974

In Memoriam The Master – Noel Coward (1900–1973)

So. The curtain has come
Down at last on
Your highly successful
Career as playwright,
Song-writer, performer,
What you will.

To my mind you
Epitomised the highly
Sophisticated night
Life of Theatre World.

Farewell then
Sir Noel:
With your long cigarette holder and
Silk Dressing Gown
You had style
That indefinable something
Which has gone forever
Out of our life.

Keith's mum apparently
Can remember seeing
You in the Vortex
But I believe
They've pulled
That pub down now.

8 April 1973

Lines on the Return to Britain of Billy Graham

Greetings, great evangelist!
So you have come
Back to London.
Once again your vibrant
Tones ring out
At Earls Court
And other venues.

Stand up and
Be counted is
Your cry.

You have a great
Influence on people
Especially the young.

Keith and I
Have terrific arguments
About Religion.

My view is
Far too complicated
To explain in a
Poem.

7 September 1973

Index of Titles and First Lines

Index of Authors